GUESTS BEHIND THE BARBED WIRE

German POWs in America: A True Story of Hope and Friendship

Ruth Beaumont Cook

CRANE HILL
PUBLISHERS

Published by Crane Hill Publishers

Cover design by Miles G. Parsons
Text design by Scott Fuller
Front cover photo *(top)* shows German and American flags hanging outside Jo Anne Young's State Farm Insurance office in Aliceville in 1943 (photo taken by Morris Hickman of Aliceville), and *(bottom)* prisoners arriving in 1943, #81 in the Aliceville Internment Camp Scrapbook, Aliceville Museum and the Alabama Department of Archives and History, Montgomery, Alabama. Back cover photos, Plate 14 *(top)* and Plate 18 *(bottom)*. See Sources on page 609.
Author photo by Barney Cook.

Library of Congress Cataloging-in-Publication Data

Cook, Ruth Beaumont.
Guests Behind the Barbed Wire: German POWs in America: A True Story of Hope and Friendship / Ruth Beaumont Cook.
p. cm.
ISBN-13: 978-1-57587-260-5
ISBN-10: 1-57587-260-9
1. Camp Aliceville (Aliceville, Ala.) 2. World War, 1939-1945—Prisoners and prisons, American. 3. Prisoners of war—Alabama—Aliceville—History—20th century. 4. Prisoners of war—Germany—History—20th century. 5. Aliceville (Ala.)—History—20th century. I. Cook, Ruth Beaumont.
D805.5.A43C66 2006
940.54'7276185—dc22

2006016032

For Mary Bess

The day a person gives up on the Geneva Convention is the day a person gives up on the human race.

Sarah Vowell
Assassination Vacation

For not with swords loud clashing, Nor roll of stirring drums; With deeds of love and mercy, The heav'nly kingdom comes.

Ernest Warburton Shurtleff
"Lead on, O King Eternal"

Table of Contents

Foreword

When the Aliceville Museum received Ruth Cook's first inquiry in 2002 about a book on Camp Aliceville, we doubted her determination. Many others had been interested in the camp, but none had shown any continued interest. Her follow-up visits to the museum and her close attention to the smallest of details confirmed that the Aliceville story had a voice.

Ruth's visits were exciting. The manuscript and archival materials that the museum had assembled were being used. The museum's goal of preserving the history of Camp Aliceville and educating the public to that history was in sight.

Since I had grown up in Aliceville, I knew that the story of Camp Aliceville and the German prisoners of war was an accepted part of the town's history. My father's family had had close connections with the camp. I was aware of the Aliceville stories about the camp and many of the stories about Aliceville's WWII veterans.

Not until 1993 when I chaired the 50th Anniversary Reunion of Camp Aliceville and met several POWs did I have a personal connection with the camp. In 1994, I was fortunate to be one of about forty-two people with ties to Camp Aliceville who visited Germany as the guest of former POWs. However, it was not until 1996, when I became executive director of the Aliceville Museum, that Camp Aliceville became one of the passions of my life.

From my years as a reference librarian, I knew the types of information historians would one day seek about Camp

Aliceville. During those early years, the museum began actively collecting personal narratives, letters, and diaries along with the artwork, photographs, and militariana collected for displays associated with Camp Aliceville reunions in 1989 and 1993. One of the museum's objectives was to document the Camp Aliceville experience of not only the POWs but also of the U.S. Army service people, the camp's civilian employees, and the town of Aliceville.

Slowly the museum began to assemble a glimpse of life in Aliceville and in Camp Aliceville. With major assistance from videographer Sam Love of Public Productions in Washington, D.C., the museum was able to offer visitors a fifteen-minute video of eyewitness accounts of Camp Aliceville. Sam had made the 1994 trip to Germany and filmed over thirty hours of interviews with POWs, military police escort guards, and civilian employees. A visitor to the museum could now see the faces and hear the voices of eyewitnesses. Later, the History Channel produced a forty-five-minute production, *Nazi Prisoners of War in America* centered on Camp Aliceville. But there was no in-depth study of Camp Aliceville.

By the time of the 60th Anniversary Reunion of Camp Aliceville in April 2003, Ruth had carefully studied Dr. Arnold Krammer's pivotal study on German POWs in America and had spent hours reading microfilmed issues of the *Pickens County Herald*, the *Aliceville Informer*, and *Der Zaungast*, the newspaper published by Camp Aliceville POWs. She knew more than most locals about what happened in Pickens County, Alabama, in the 1940s. As the visiting POWs and their families began to arrive, Ruth knew each of the participants without having personally met any of them. She knew exactly what she wanted to ask each one. The POWs immediately felt her sincere desire to tell the story of their Camp Aliceville experiences. Ruth spent four days attentively listening to everyone who wanted to share their accounts. Over the next few years, she continued her pursuit of Camp Aliceville through extensive reading on World War II and her pursuit of eyewitnesses and their families to further document Camp Aliceville.

Ruth graciously allowed me to read each completed chapter. How excited I was, knowing that the POWs would appreciate her sensitive interpretation of their experiences. Along with the excitement of her book taking shape came the sadness over the death of an increasing number of the eyewitnesses. Those individuals would have been thrilled to know how Ruth wove their experiences with that of their friends' to tell the Camp Aliceville story.

And so, I want to thank Ruth Cook on behalf of each of those POWs, military police, civilian employees, residents of Aliceville, and the American people to whom she has given voice. Ruth has captured a glimpse of small town American life in the midst of sending her sons and daughters to war. She has captured the spirit of reconciliation experienced by former enemies in that same town sixty years later. There is so much that America and the world in the twenty-first century can learn from the Camp Aliceville experience about the Golden Rule.

Mary Bess Paluzzi
Former director of the
Aliceville Museum

Preface

The story of the German prisoner of war camp in Aliceville, Alabama, interested me for a number of reasons. First, my life began during World War II. Anyone in my parents' generation could tell you exactly where they were and what they were doing on December 7, 1941.

My father worked for Western Union in Cleveland, Ohio, and was operating the teleprinter that Sunday morning, receiving messages for local delivery. In the middle of one message, a long dash came through and then the words, "Holy Smokes! Japan bombed Pearl Harbor!" My parents were engaged at the time, and my father immediately called his parents and then my mother because the news had not yet been announced on the radio. Six months later, when my parents returned from their honeymoon, my father's draft notice was waiting for him. It was followed by orders to report to Fort Bragg in North Carolina.

As a child, I often leafed through a tweed-bound album of black-and-white photographs from the war years. Held in place by black photo corners on black album pages were photos of my parents holding me outside Cross Creek Court and other makeshift rental properties in Fayetteville near Fort Bragg. That was before my mother and I returned to Cleveland when Dad shipped out for Hawaii and then the Philippines in the spring of 1944. Those apartments were not unlike several apartments occupied by Kay and Bob Fillingham in Aliceville, Alabama, when Bob became a guard at Camp Aliceville in 1944.

The "war years" album also contained photos of Dad and his infantry buddies clustered around a jeep named *Ruth Alice* (after me) in Okinawa, not long before the atomic bombs were dropped on Hiroshima and Nagasaki in August 1945. Those bombs voided the planned land invasion of Japan, in which my father was training to participate. The bombs also led to the liberation of American POWs L.D. Orr and James Scott Browning of Reform, Alabama, who'd been held by the Japanese under much worse circumstances than those at Camp Aliceville. The bombs ended the conflict begun only twenty-one years after the war that was supposed to end all wars—The Great War that, sadly, came to be called World War I.

In the summer of 1961, I went to Germany as an exchange student. Sending me off to live in the other country that had been America's archenemy must have been more difficult for my parents than I realized at the time, but from my generation's postwar perspective, I was more fascinated than afraid. I lived with the Ott family in Ravensberg who spoke no English but welcomed me into their home, their neighborhood, and their country.

We did not talk much about the war, but I knew that Frau Ott's first husband, a German soldier, had been killed in Paris. I remember visiting a war memorial near Innsbruck, Austria, with my German "sister" and friend Charlotte, where I stared at book after book containing handwritten lists of the dead from small Austrian villages and felt the irony of reading memorials to soldiers who had fought against my uncles and the fathers of my friends.

Once, when the subject of the Holocaust and the concentration camps came up, the Otts and their neighbors said quietly, "We didn't know. We didn't know." During my research for *Guests Behind the Barbed Wire,* former German POWs from Camp Aliceville often mentioned their shock at the *Knochenfilmen* ("bone films" showing piles of emaciated corpses in camps like Auschwitz) they'd been forced to watch after the war ended. Whenever former POWs insisted they hadn't known about the camps when they went to fight the British in North Africa, I remembered my conversation with the Otts.

I left West Germany for home on August 13, 1961—the day the barbed wire and then the wall went up between East and West Berlin. At the time, the news did not seem monstrously significant—in fact, I barely mentioned it in my youthful trip diary—not realizing that the wall would loom in the middle of Berlin for twenty-eight years. President Kennedy had not yet gone to Berlin to deliver his famous "*Ich bin ein Berliner*" speech (June 26, 1963), but German people already admired him. Often, during that 1961 summer when the Cold War was still very real, someone had said to me, as if I had a personal pipeline to the White House, "When you go back to America, tell your President Kennedy that the German people love him."

In the 1970s, as a young adult with a growing family, I believed the one benchmark moment in my own life would always be the afternoon of November 22, 1963, when I arrived for an American history class at Ohio State. A classmate sat down next to me and whispered that he'd just heard something he thought never to hear in his lifetime—twelve bells on the teletype—a signal of the highest priority news story about to come across. Moments later, our professor entered the room and announced in a solemn voice, "Ladies and gentlemen, it is my sad duty to inform you that the President of the United States is dead. Class dismissed."

I remember wandering through that weekend in shock and disillusionment—disillusionment that would permeate not only that year, but the next several years, and strike new dread each time the television screen went blank and an unseen voice rumbled, "We interrupt this program..." with coverage of riots in Watts and in Detroit, and then the deaths of Martin Luther King Jr. in April 1968, and Robert Kennedy in June 1968. In May 1970, not long after I moved to Alabama, another news bulletin etched into my memory the faces of four student war protesters shot to death by National Guard troops in a Kent State University parking lot not far from my Ohio hometown.

Once the Vietnam War ended and the Civil Rights Movement gave African Americans a threshold for justice, our generation preferred to believe peace would be ongoing for our children and our children's children. We hoped our country had learned the costly lessons of ignoring bigotry at home and of becoming entangled in "elsewhere" wars.

When I began researching and writing the story of Camp Aliceville in early 2001, these experiences were not foremost in my mind. The tale of German POWs in Alabama interested me because it reminded me of my first book, *North Across the River,* about Georgia cotton mill workers during the Civil War who were charged with treason and sent north across the Ohio River to keep them from making cloth for the Confederacy. The story of Camp Aliceville—its German prisoners captured in North Africa and later in France and its inexperienced MPEG guards recruited from all over America—was also a story of displaced people caught up in war.

I was intrigued to discover that most Alabamians had no idea there'd been as many as six thousand Germans right outside Aliceville in Pickens County during World War II. In fact, more than seventeen thousand German and Italian prisoners of war had been held in four base camps and twenty satellite camps in Alabama between 1943 and 1946. I also discovered how few Americans realized there'd been prisoner of war camps in many parts of the United States, housing a total of more than four hundred thousand mostly German POWs between May 1942 and June 1946.

Americans who did know about these stateside camps assumed, as German POWs did at the time, that when the war ended, the Germans simply went home and resumed their civilian lives, but this was not the case for many of them. Because the American government wanted to protect American soldiers like Selma native Wendell Parrish, who was captured by the Germans, our country treated German POWs in camps like Aliceville extremely well, strictly according to Geneva Convention dictates.

We did not remain dedicated to this "golden rule" approach, however. When German concentration camps and prisoner of war camps were liberated in 1945, shocking incidents of human cruelty came to light. As a result, and in retaliation once our own soldiers were safely rescued, POW rations in the United States were cut, privileges were revoked, and labor requirements were increased. Many POWs returned to Europe in 1945 and 1946 only to be turned over to France and England, where they labored under harsh conditions for several more years before returning to their homes.

The story of Camp Aliceville has classic elements—escape and death, loneliness and fear, disillusionment and despair, but also humor, hope, and romance, as well as incredible creativity flourishing in confinement. As I sifted through the correspondence, the artifacts, the biosketches, and the photographs carefully preserved by Mary Bess Paluzzi and others at the Aliceville Museum, my curiosity grew about why so many former POWs and former guards had returned to this isolated Alabama location again and again. The more I read and connected with people, the more I understood the strands of experience that had drawn so many back to Aliceville over the years. They came searching for landmarks and familiar faces to help them relive memories of that time in that place. Prisoners remembered having been treated well by an enemy. Guards and former camp employees remembered nurturing trust and trying to be fair.

In the months following September 11, 2001, when my life acquired a second benchmark moment, the story of Camp Aliceville took on more contemporary relevance, though I realized it only gradually. I was finishing breakfast that Tuesday morning when my husband, who had kissed me goodbye minutes earlier, returned to the kitchen and turned on the television. Like everyone else in America, we sat transfixed for the next several hours as the magnitude of the tragedy in New York, and then in Washington and Pennsylvania, unfolded.

Much later in the day, I went upstairs to my office and sat down at the computer, thinking it would be good to write for a while. I simply could not absorb any more television commentary. On that September afternoon, the only real connection in my mind between what I was writing and what I'd been watching on television was the surprise plane attacks on the World Trade Towers and the surprise plane attacks on Pearl Harbor.

In January 2002, with the hunt for Osama bin Laden in full swing in Afghanistan, President Bush announced that captured members of Al Qaeda and the Taliban would not be protected by the Geneva Convention. He based his decision partly on advice from White House Counsel Alberto Gonzalez, who had concluded that these terrorists were not affiliated with a legal government and, therefore, should not have rights or be considered military captives.

By that time, I'd read a great deal about the Geneva Convention standards followed with zeal by the United States during most of World War II. I knew the very positive effects those standards had had on captives held in Camp Aliceville—the respect generated by simple things like hot coffee after a long journey; abundant meat and vegetables; adequate clothing and shelter; recreational, educational, and spiritual opportunities—respect ongoing for a lifetime and now being shared with those captives' children and grandchildren. I thought about the ginkgo tree former German POWs had planted in front of the Aliceville Museum as an expression of their profound belief in world peace.

In August 2002, when the Iraq war drums began to boom, Aliceville Museum Director Mary Bess Paluzzi sent me an e-mail photograph she'd taken of that gingko tree with a bright yellow Monarch butterfly poised on one of its leaves. Attached was the comment, "Peace to you all." The "all" who received that e-mail included Aliceville residents, former German POWs and their family members, former MPEG guards, and personal friends with an interest in the legacy of the camp.

By the fall of 2002, Muslim captives were behind barbed wire in Guantanamo Bay, Cuba, amid persistent rumors of abuse. In April 2004, when incredible photographs of Abu Ghraib prison saturated the media, I could not help but contrast them in my mind with photos of Camp Aliceville—photos of Hitler's hated soldiers landscaping their prison barracks, digging drainage ditches and doing work details at the local sawmill, studying English and mathematics, peeling potatoes for their own supper and that of their American guards, staging plays and performing orchestral concerts—even being allowed to conduct a memorial service for their beloved Desert Fox, Field Marshal Erwin Rommel. Their punishment, when necessary, was bread and water for several days.

The story of Camp Aliceville is certainly not all kindness and light, but standards of humane treatment were followed without resorting to convoluted definitions of "humane." Efforts were made to teach by example the meaning of democracy. Abuse occurred, often under cover of darkness, but the abusers were primarily Nazi fanatics trying desperately to keep fellow captives from appreciating and learning from good treatment at the hands of their captors. The truth is that the memory of that good treatment fostered priceless good will now being shared with ongoing generations.

Spring 2006

Acknowledgements

I owe profound thanks to Mary Bess Paluzzi, former director of the Aliceville Museum and now city clerk/manager for the City of Aliceville, who welcomed me and made available the records of the Aliceville Museum on several occasions. She also put me in touch with local residents, former POWs, former guards, and other authors. Her generous heart and enthusiasm were inspiring. I am also indebted to her father, Robert Hugh Kirksey, who wrote the memoir *With Me*, which painted a vivid image of Aliceville in the 1940s and before. Mr. Kirksey also shared personal photographs and written accounts of local history. Thanks also to Ann Kirksey, who is now the director of the Aliceville Museum.

Many thanks, too, to my publisher, Ellen Sullivan, for once again believing in a story I wanted to tell, and to my wonderful editor, Linda J. Beam, who kept this work on track in such a fantastic way.

This book could not have been written without the shared memories of the people who lived this story. Many, many thanks to Aliceville residents Tom Parker, Stanley Pendrak, Will Peebles, Scarlett Shriver Parker, P. M. (Pep) Johnston, J. T. Junkins, Robbie Davis and others; to Reform residents Betty and Hubert Taylor and to long-time POW reunion hosts Jan and Chuck Gwin. Thanks also to all those who shared memories of coming to Aliceville during World War II—to former POWs Hermann Blumhardt, Walter Felholter, and Wilhelm Schlegel and their families, among many others; to POW descendants Ellen Wanders, Sarah Schiffling, and Gunther Wening; to Mary Lu Turner Keef for her generous memories of a rich childhood in a strange place; to Mary Lu's sister Joyce; to former MPEG guards George Bristow and Kenneth Eugene Dakan; and to Kay Fillingham, widow of former guard Bob Fillingham.

Some experiences profiled in this book were first described in the Aliceville Museum newsletter. Some were recorded in 1994 by documentary film maker Sam Love, a native of Aliceville, who generously shared audio tapes that, in many cases, contained memories and corroborating information no longer available from any other source. I am also grateful to historian John D. (Daniel) Hutchinson for his mutual interest in this subject and for his help in obtaining clear images of life in Camp Aliceville.

Thanks, too, to the Birmingham Public Library—Yvonne Crumpler in the Southern History Collection, Jim Baggett in the Archives Department, and Artramice Harrison in Government Documents for their generous assistance with clip files, microfilm, and other local records; to Abigail Leah Plumb, Librarian and Information Specialist at Lippincott Williams & Wilkins who tracked down an ancient issue of the *American Journal of Nursing;* to John Otte at the Society of Military Engineers in Alexandria, Virginia, publishers of *The Military Engineer;* to Roger Mansell with the Center for Research, Allied POWs under the Japanese; to Aileen Kilgore Henderson for writing in *Stateside Soldier* about Alabama military women during World War II; and to Randy Sowell, Archivist at the Harry S. Truman Library.

I wish to thank the Ott family of Ravensburg, Germany, and their daughter Charlotte, for opening their home to me as an American Field Service exchange student in 1961. My summer with them gave me a more global perspective on life, a second language, and an appreciation for German life and culture that transcended the dark years of the Nazi government.

Finally, I wish to thank my parents, Norma and Larry Beaumont, for sharing their wartime memories and photos, and Helen LaFlaur, Steve Coleman, and my brother Larry Beaumont and his wife Sue for reading early drafts. As always, I am grateful to my husband, Barney, for listening with his good, practical ear and for involving himself in Aliceville in so many helpful ways—from interviewing his childhood mentor Wendell Parrish to photographing town landmarks and reunion events, and yes, even vacuuming up the popcorn after the children's birthday party for Wilhelm Schlegel.

GUESTS BEHIND THE BARBED WIRE

Those who have said there would never be any prisoners stationed in the Aliceville Interment [sic] Camp won't have the pleasure of saying, 'I told you so.'

Approximately 1,000 arrived Wednesday, full three train loads, who were marched from the station to the camp about mid-afternoon...Others will arrive today (June 3) and from day to day until the camp is filled.

• Thursday, June 3, 1943 •
The Pickens County Herald and West Alabamian

CHAPTER ONE
Camp Aliceville Appears

In the summer of 1942, a rumor spread in west Alabama that a military complex was about to be built in Pickens County, probably near Aliceville. The rumor bubbled and brewed like the black coffee idling on the hotplate in Simon Jones's drugstore.

Anchoring one corner of Third Avenue and Broad Street in downtown Aliceville, the drugstore was a haven on muggy afternoons. Above its soda fountain, wooden paddle fans churned the heavy air. Some folks sipped steaming coffee from thick white mugs in spite of the heat, while others tipped up icy Coca-Colas in plumped out green bottles as they speculated till dinnertime about what might be coming.

Tiny Aliceville, with a population of about fifteen hundred, was not well known outside Pickens County. The drugstore locals thought their town an odd choice for any kind of military installation. However, the Army Corps of Engineers and the Provost Marshal General's office were surveying land in several sections of the country that summer for secure new facilities. They searched mainly in the Fourth, Seventh, and Eighth Service Commands—eighteen southern and southwestern states considered unlikely targets for enemy sabotage. Alabama belonged to the Fourth Service Command, and Aliceville in Pickens County fit the army criteria perfectly.

The town marked time in a rural, mostly isolated agricultural area nowhere near shipyards, munitions plants, or vital war effort industries. It was, as required by the army criteria, more than 170 miles from the east or west coast, and more than 150 miles from the Canadian or Mexican border. In addition, it enjoyed a climate suitable for heavy construction during any season of the year, a climate that would not run up high heat and maintenance costs because of extremely cold weather.

Some evidence suggests national agencies considered land near Aliceville for a government internment camp before 1942. As early as 1939, the United States worried about how to deal with troublesome foreign nationals (aliens) who might have to be arrested if the country went to war. In March 1941, the War Department promised to give the nine regional Service Commands estimates of how many such foreign nationals each might have to accept and detain. War Department directives called for three permanent Alien Program internment camps—two sites for three thousand people in the Eighth Service Command (Texas, Oklahoma, Colorado, New Mexico, and parts of Arizona), and one site for six thousand in the Fourth Service Command (North Carolina, South Carolina, Georgia, Florida, Alabama, Tennessee, Mississippi, and Louisiana). Since the properties purchased near Aliceville late in the summer of 1942 created a site large enough to handle six thousand detainees, it is likely the government had had its eye on this land as early as the 1941 directive.

Pickens is a sleepy cotton and pulpwood county nestled right up against the middle of Alabama's western border with Mississippi. Its first inhabitants were Choctaw and Chickasaw tribes believed to have been visited by Hernando DeSoto in 1540. Pickens became an official county in 1820, almost exactly a year after Alabama became a state. By the end of the 1830s, most of its Native American inhabitants had left. Reluctantly, they'd accepted the insistent dominance of European settlers and either headed west on their own or were forcibly relocated to reservations after their leaders ceded land to the United States in a series of treaties supported by President Andrew Jackson.

When the Army Corps of Engineers began combing areas like Pickens County, they were looking for properties of more than 350 acres with even terrain and a moderate slope for surface drainage. The Corps wanted land less than five miles from a railroad line (to facilitate the transfer of detainees and the delivery of food supplies), and more than five hundred feet from any public road (to protect private citizens in the event shots had to be fired).

Aliceville's good rail service most certainly attracted attention. John T. Cochrane had brought the Carrollton Short Line down between Bridgeville and Franconia in 1902. He'd put up a depot and named the town that grew up around it for his wife, Alyce Searcy Cochrane. By 1942, the AT&N (the old Carrollton Short Line) and the Frisco (the St. Louis and San Francisco Railroad) both served the town well.

The drugstore speculators thought Aliceville might be getting a massive training base. An internment camp, especially one for prisoners of war, was hard to imagine. Most folks in town kept their war images up to date with the MovieTone newsreels over at the Palace Theater. Sooner or later, in any given week, just about everybody took in a movie at the Palace—Nelson Eddy and Jeanette McDonald in *I Married an Angel* or *True to the Army* with Judy Canova and Allen Jones. Saturdays, kids enjoyed double features like *Hurricane Smith* and *Code of the Outlaws* and maybe a suspenseful new episode of *King of the Texas Rangers*.

Whatever the marquis announced, MovieTone added a newsreel with a dramatic, deep-voiced narrative, tinny-toned music, and flickering images of faraway horrors like the Japanese defeat of American troops on Bataan or the German seizure of British troops in the swirling sands of North Africa. Such news made it difficult to envision enough Allied victories to warrant prisoner of war camps popping up in places like Pickens County. In May 1942, only thirty-two enemy soldiers were imprisoned on American soil—thirty-one Germans and one Japanese. By July, that number had grown only to forty-nine—thirty-nine Germans and ten Japanese. As far as anyone in Aliceville knew, not one of these military captives was anywhere near Alabama.

Of course, there were all those civilian Japanese and Germans and Italians the government had rounded up and investigated once the Alien Program was put in place. Aliceville residents had read about Italian merchant ship sailors impounded in American ports and sent off to detention at Fort Missoula in Montana. There'd been photos in the newspaper of little German children peeking through barbed wire in Texas where they were held in captivity with parents suspected of sabotage, and there'd been newsreel footage of Japanese families being evacuated from neighborhoods in San Francisco and sent inland by the Wartime Civil Control Administration. Maybe Pickens County was getting a camp for people like these.

Throughout the summer, Aliceville residents pondered such rumors as they went about their regular business. Because of an abundance of rain, they worried about the cotton crop. Wet bolls could rot and fall off without blooming. Soggy cotton was next to impossible to pick, and fiendish weevils lurked in anticipation of just such weather as this. Farmers prayed for hot, dry days and scheduled eight boll weevil poisoning demonstrations around the county—one of them at Elmore Owen's farm near Aliceville and another at Johnny Bert Craft's farm in nearby Benevola.

Farmers also concerned themselves with planting and cultivating a curious crop called kudzu, a fact that amuses Alabama residents today. The kudzu vine is a native of Asia, but it was introduced to the American South through the Japanese pavilion at the New Orleans Exposition in 1884. Before the turn of the century, Southerners used it mainly as a shade vine for porches and arbors. Then, in the 1930s, the United States Department of Agriculture began to import kudzu cuttings as a means to control erosion on bare river banks and in vacant fields around the South. They actually paid farmers up to eight dollars an acre to plant the thick vines with their huge, three-lobed leaves.

An article in the *Pickens County Herald and West Alabamian* in November 1941 called kudzu the "magic vine of Alabama agriculture" and declared it would enchant farmers by enriching soil, stemming erosion, and providing good grazing for livestock. During World War II, the agricultural extension insert in the Pickens County newspaper carried frequent articles about the care and cultivation of kudzu. Because the vine was high in protein, some farmers believed it would make good fodder, but unfortunately, whenever cows and other animals grazed in a field of kudzu, they trampled the vines to death. Eventually, domestic cultivation was abandoned, but the vines continued to thrive in the timberland at the edges of pastures, often strangling a tall tree to death in one season by choking off any sunlight. Today, kudzu is considered a bothersome weed and has become a focal point for jokes throughout the South.

When not planting kudzu or cotton, folks in Aliceville kept their ears open for more rumblings about the possible camp in their midst while they supported the war effort in whatever ways they could. Sam Wise, who had a clothing store across the street from Simon Jones' drugstore on Aliceville's Busy Corner, put a stamp in one corner of his ads reminding local citizens to ensure victory by buying war bonds and stamps. George Downer worked so hard as war council chairman that Pickens County sold double its quota of bonds that summer. When the county held a huge scrap rubber campaign, D.B. Love got the Boy Scouts and the members of the Exchange Club to help his Gulf service station collect more scrap than any other establishment in the county—thirty-two thousand pounds of it.

In the middle of 1942, America was waging war on two fronts, but Pickens County residents seemed most clearly focused on the war with Japan. Half-page advertisements in the *Pickens County Herald and West Alabamian* continually reminded housewives to clean out their cellars. One cartoon featured teakettles, a cast iron stove, a well pump, a hot water bottle, an iron, and an old washtub battering a Jap soldier above a caption that read, "Bomb 'em with Junk." Another popular slogan was "Slap the Jap with All Your Scrap."

In August, when an appraiser from the Federal Land Bank showed up to set a value on Doc and Nannie Parker's pastureland two miles outside Aliceville, their son Tom was already milking cows on that land twice a day. He'd just put up a new barn and tenant houses, and he'd improved the broad pastures. He'd built a small house and was carving out a nice life with his wife and two small daughters.

"They were courteous, and I was courteous to them," Tom Parker has said of his several encounters with the government appraisers and surveyors. "For the same money, we could have sold that land to someone else, I suppose, but I don't think we could have got much more for it." Legally, the Parkers had two choices—accept the government offer or go to court, and with the country at war, they weren't likely to win in federal court.

They accepted the offer ($29,295) for three tracts totaling slightly more than four hundred acres, and Tom was given just ten days to move his family and his cows off his parents' land. Whenever he considered voicing a complaint, he reminded himself that there was a war on. Like his neighbors and other patriotic Americans, he believed supporting the war called for all-out cooperation.

"I was standing in the middle of a field with the appraiser when he let me know what was about to happen, what they were going to do…." All Tom found out for sure was that the army did indeed plan to build an internment camp of some sort, but neither he nor anyone else in Aliceville would discover the identity of the intended occupants until just before they were marched behind the barbed wire the following June.

Tom was proud of the initial success of Thomas R. Parker Dairy. He'd had cardboard disks printed in red and blue with the company name, and they fit neatly into the necks of the smooth glass bottles of raw milk he was already delivering to customers.

In August 1942, there was so much new hustle and bustle in Aliceville that the army didn't complain when it took Tom twenty extra days to vacate. Fortunately, when the federal government flexed its wartime muscle, he was able to sell his cows and move into cotton farming which, like five generations before him in that part of Alabama, he'd been doing some already. "Once the dairy land was sold, I didn't go back out there," he remembers. "They didn't want us out there."

Local citizens who did venture out to the construction site got no definitive answers. The men in army khakis who set up tripods and transits and then waved in bulldozers weren't talking, and neither were the civilian workers. "We don't know. We're just building," shrugged the employees of Algernon Blair, the Montgomery, Alabama, contracting firm charged with implementing the army blueprints.

The Parkers' four hundred acres, along with a combined four hundred acres belonging to six other sellers, was soon bulldozed completely in order to make the camp easier to guard. By the time the first barracks and security towers rose up on the facility, the flat, rust-colored fields had been shaved bare of every living thing—pine trees and hardwoods, shrubs, even tall grasses—as called for in the name of security by Army Corps of Engineers specifications.

Gone were Tom Parker's new barns and tenant houses. Only his small family home, with its striped awnings, flower-filled window boxes, and screened-in porch, remained. According to the memories of many local residents, it became the camp commander's residence and endured the remaining war years in the shadow of a wooden guard tower.

Funeral director Gerald Stabler's wife was out mowing her front lawn on an afternoon in early September when an official-looking military vehicle pulled into her driveway, and a handsome young soldier jumped out. He hurried over and asked with a grin, "What's a pretty girl like you doing mowing this lawn?" Mrs. Stabler discovered later that the soldier was none other than an outstanding young athlete named Ed "Foots" Bauer, who would star as an offensive guard at Auburn University in the late 1940s after the war. On that afternoon, Foots Bauer took the handle of the mower and gallantly finished the lawn for Mrs. Stabler.

"I wasn't exactly a girl," she wrote years later. "I had a six-year-old daughter by then." Still, she enjoyed the flattery, and it certainly made her more receptive when Major Karl H. Shriver stepped sedately out of the staff car and introduced himself. He explained that he'd already made the acquaintance of Mr. Stabler in town and had heard about the Stablers' recent remodeling project. The major wanted to know if Sue and Gerald would board several Army Corps of Engineers personnel for the duration of the construction project.

Sue Stabler was stunned at the request, but like Tom Parker, she considered it her duty to support the war effort. "We only have one bathroom, but it's heated," she told Major Shriver. Heating in the rest of the house was a problem. The Stablers had started their remodeling project and then been unable to buy new equipment because of military priorities. They'd installed a temporary coal-burning laundry heater in the kitchen, attaching a water heater to it and a pipe that stuck out through a kitchen window. Until further notice, the only other heat in the house was a huge fireplace in the newly enlarged living room.

None of these hardships deterred the major. Bag and baggage, four of his team moved into the funeral director's home as soon as the Stablers agreed. A fifth guest joined them a few days later. Foots Bauer, the muscular football player, snuggled into a ruffled canopy bed each night, and the men often kept forty-inch logs crackling in the Stabler fireplace all day and into the night.

Because war mobilization had created peculiar bedfellows in communities all across the country, the Stablers decided to make the best of their situation. "We gathered around the friendliness of that fireplace and became good companions in its warmth," Sue told the Pickens County Chapter of the DAR in October 1988.

On Thursday, September 24, the *Pickens County Herald and West Alabamian* referred specifically to the construction project outside Aliceville as an "alien concentration camp," but people in town weren't sure what all that implied. They wondered if they should assume "alien" more likely referred to sabotage-prone foreign nationals or captured enemy soldiers. One widespread rumor conjured up the tabloid image of six thousand Japanese soldiers grinning diabolically as American bayonets prodded them into the compound right outside town. That rumor prompted Mrs. Wallace S. Kirksey, an active member of the Aliceville Arts Club, to voice the concern that if such a thing turned out to be true, local citizens "would be sitting on a powder keg."

Townspeople soon began referring to the construction project as "The Jap Camp." Mrs. Gerald Stabler wasn't happy about the possibility of Japanese prisoners just outside Aliceville either. "Everybody was fearful about that," she told Alabama Public Television in 1989. "We certainly didn't want them."

No matter who the camp occupants would turn out to be, getting ready for them jolted the sleepy local economy. Farmers reported their fat calves and pigs fetching meat prices more typical of Texas, and eggs going for forty-five cents a dozen. "Every citizen of the county will prosper directly or indirectly by the construction of the camp," crowed the newspaper as retail cash registers began to ring in as much as $75,000 a week more than usual. Sam Wise's clothing store, D.E. Day City Grocery, the Summerville Service Station, and Minnie Merle Brandon's People's Cafe were among the businesses that opened wide their doors in anticipation of new customers.

"After the camp has been completed, there will be eight or nine hundred guards, and most of them will spend their money in Aliceville," declared the newspaper. Even before the guards arrived, however, boarding houses and private homes like the Stablers' began to bulge with construction firm employees and U.S. Army Corps of Engineers personnel paying good rent. Those who didn't already have paying guests began stepping back and contemplating ways to partition off a room or two to create rental apartments and tap into this welcome source of extra income.

By October 1, Mayor Holmes Sanders was urging the people of Carrollton, the Pickens County seat ten miles away, to come up with additional room and board for engineers, army officers, and construction workers. Mayor Sanders suggested that Carrollton citizens who happened to own old school buses could make a good profit hauling workers to and from Aliceville during the ninety-day construction period.

Army orders called for the Aliceville camp to be completed by December 10. Not only was the land to be cleared and drained by then, but four hundred housing units had to be built, a complete sewage system installed, and more than seven hundred acres fenced in completely.

These orders arrived like manna from heaven for the depressed farm economy of Pickens County. As in much of the country, but especially in the South, Pickens continued to struggle with the devastating aftermath of the Great Depression. The newspaper announced encouragingly, "There is work for every able-bodied man in the section, if he can use a saw, a trowel, a wrench, or a truck."

In the middle of October, Jack Pratt took Wednesday afternoon off from his editor's desk in Carrollton and drove over to Aliceville to gather information for his weekly "Here, There and Everywhere" newspaper column. He stared in amazement at the partially constructed barracks already lined up as far as his eye could see in the direction of the dark swamp beyond the Parker property. "Laborers and carpenters are busy as dirt daubers in May," he wrote, comparing construction workers to the wasp-like insects that build long, tubular nests of clay on every conceivable Alabama surface each summer. His choice of simile was ironic. Shiny black, long-legged dirt daubers capture prey with a type of paralysis and then deposit their prisoners in cellular compartments within their nests.

As Jack scuffed along dusty pathways between the rows of barracks, he was greeted on every side by Pickens County men elated to be making the best wages of their lives. Some were sawing, hammering, and cussing as many as ten housing units a day into existence, while others were preparing fencing to surround the entire camp and rolls of barbed wire to string atop the chain link enclosing the prison compounds themselves. To the newspaper editor, the sight of two thousand local country boys—both black and white—and busy with tools—was a thing of sheer economic beauty. A field of forty or fifty cotton choppers was about the biggest group of laborers Jack Pratt had ever seen in one place.

"If I were a Jap, I'd not want to escape," he wrote the next morning. "A single thread would hold me in; in fact it would take an army to make me leave. It wouldn't be healthy on the outside."

Aliceville folks had a distinct local connection to the war in the Pacific. Two young Pickens County boys who had volunteered for the Marine Corps before December 1941 had

had the misfortune to be captured by the Japanese shortly after the surprise attack at Pearl Harbor. Both young men were from Reform, a small former stagecoach relay station northeast of Aliceville and Carrollton. The town of Reform supposedly acquired its unusual name when Lorenzo Dow, a Methodist circuit rider and legendary backwoods missionary preacher, visited in the late nineteenth century. The preacher's bush arbor revival had not been successful in spite of his fiery sermons, and as he rode out of town, several roughnecks shouted after him to ask what they should name their town. "Reform!" he shouted back, and the name stuck.

Twenty-one-year-old Luther (L.D.) Orr, a popular county football hero, had been captured on Guam just four days after the Japanese bombed Pearl Harbor. He'd been held on Guam for a month and then sent to Japan, where he mailed home several oddly cheerful letters from the infamous Zentsuji prison camp on Shikoku Island. This camp was considered a "show camp," which allowed the Japanese to use it in propaganda releases suggesting they treated all prisoners humanely. Zentsuji contained mostly Allied officers, but there were also enlisted prisoners like L.D. who'd been captured on Guam and Wake Island.

"I'm…receiving very good treatment under the circumstances," he wrote (or more likely, was coerced to write) in a letter printed in the Pickens County newspaper on September 10, 1942. "The Japanese people are very nice to us and I hope the Americans treat the Japanese people in America likewise…. I see no reason why my health should get bad, because we eat three times a day and work in the open air. We take exercise each morning and get plenty of sleep...." Although L.D. does not say so in his letter, published reports from other Zentsuji prisoners would suggest his "open air" work was probably backbreaking slave labor at either the Sakaide Rail Yards or the Port of Takamatsu.

James Scott Browning, also from Reform, had been captured at Wake Island sometime between December 7 and December 23, 1941. He, too, was being held in a Japanese prison camp.

Jack Pratt probably thought about his own connections to the war as he drove back to Carrollton from his inspection of the internment camp. His son-in-law, Jimmy Mills, had just left for military glider training in Roswell, New Mexico, and his son, Jack Jr., was stationed at Camp Sutton in North Carolina as a member of the Field Artillery. Jack had written in his column at the end of July that his son's hefty weight (214 pounds) was coming in handy when firing the big guns. "He's big enough to stay on the ground," the father wrote.

The rumor in October was that the Aliceville camp would definitely house five to six thousand aliens—probably soldiers, and possibly Germans and Italians as well as Japanese. The British, who'd been in the war much longer than the Americans, already held one hundred thirty thousand Italian soldiers. On October 23, their forces under Lieutenant General Bernard Montgomery launched a major offensive against the Germans in North Africa. They defeated the *Afrikakorps* under Field Marshal Erwin Rommel at El Alamein and then pursued them out of Egypt, across Libya, and into East Tunisia. With the victory at El Alamein, the British acquired another thirty thousand prisoners—mostly Germans—and this made them eager for the

United States to agree to a housing arrangement on American soil for as many "British-owned" prisoners as possible.

This development added to the growing speculation that tiny Aliceville was well on its way to hosting one of the largest military internment camps in America. Townspeople also heard that another smaller camp, designed for about three thousand prisoners, was being constructed near the eastern Alabama town of Opelika and that eleven other base camps were planned or already under construction in other parts of the Southeast. In November, the United States reached agreements to accept seventy thousand Axis (primarily German and Italian) prisoners held by the British, but Aliceville residents received no specific reports that any of these prisoners would be coming to their town.

The county's leading citizens welcomed the construction project even as they dreaded its possible occupants. The Rotary Club invited Algernon Blair to address its Tuesday evening meeting in the Aliceville Hotel dining room on October 27. Mayor Sanders introduced Blair as one of the nation's leading contractors and speculated that if good weather continued, he would have the alien camp completed on schedule in December. Major Karl H. Shriver, United States Army Corps of Engineers supervisor for the project, attended the dinner as a guest, along with newspaper editor Jack Pratt.

During the ninety-day whirlwind construction of the camp, Major Shriver endeared himself not only to the funeral director and his wife—Gerald and Sue Stabler—but also to many other people in Aliceville with his pleasing combination of military professionalism and gentlemanliness. On pleasant afternoons, when the Major finished his supervisory work at the camp construction site, he often saddled up his horse, Cokey, and rode all over town, visiting with local folks. "He rode a really beautiful black horse," says one long-time Aliceville resident. "He kept it out at the camp in an old dairy barn that they later turned into a motor pool."

A civil engineering graduate of the University of Pittsburgh and an officer in the Army Corps of Engineers since World War I, Shriver knew a thing or two about building military facilities and bringing them to completion on time. Born into a northern family that included in its past Revolutionary War and Civil War veterans, French Huguenots, and the first woman dentist in Massachusetts, he understood how important heritage was in the lives of Aliceville's long-established families.

Although he would move on to even greater challenges as World War II progressed, Major Shriver found a niche for his heart during the months he spent in Aliceville in 1942. Much later in life, he looked back on this time and commented, "I found that the people here appealed to me more than in any other country or state I had ever lived in, on account of their friendly nature, their mode of living, and their inherent honesty."

In early November 1942, everyone involved was confident the camp would be completed ahead of its Army Corps of Engineers deadline in December. It was a massive undertaking. Most American internment camps going up that winter had three or four compounds designed for 500 to 750 men, but Aliceville's design dictated six compounds for one thousand men each, creating a total capacity of six thousand prisoners plus offices and quarters for nearly one thousand American military personnel. According to the county newspaper, Camp Aliceville would become the largest and the first of seventy-two all-new POW camps completed in the United States during the war.

After November 8, those who frequented the drugstore soda fountain found it less difficult to imagine the Allied need for huge prisoner of war camps in the United States. Newspaper front pages and radio broadcasts that day were full of headlines about American Expeditionary Forces landing in the French colonies of North Africa. These news stories proclaimed Africa the long-awaited second front of the war. Even Adolf Hitler recognized grudgingly that, if the Allies seized North Africa, they would have the perfect staging area for an invasion of southern Europe. "To give up Africa is to give up the Mediterranean," he said.

Great Britain's wartime Prime Minister, Winston Churchill, put it another way: "Now this is not the end. It is not even the beginning of the end. But it is, perhaps, the end of the beginning."

As the Aliceville camp neared completion, those who would administer it began to arrive. Construction crews were tacking up tarpaper to enclose barracks walls when Ward Turner showed up November 1. He'd been hired as chief clerk to Major Paul Dishner, head of post engineers. The small wooden check-in shack at the main gate was in place by this time, and the outlines of the six large compounds were taking shape between the headquarters buildings and the large black water swamp near the banks of the Tombigbee River.

Ward Turner was a civilian from Frankfort in central New York state, but in the years after the Depression and just prior to World War II, he'd moved his family from New York to Pennsylvania and Maryland, and finally to Georgia in pursuit of various jobs. His daughter and stepdaughter remember that he worked for Underwood Elliott Fisher Typewriter Company in Decatur, Georgia, until just before he came to Aliceville.

A photo from the time shows Major Dishner's chief clerk standing with a group of coworkers in bright sunshine outside the post engineer's office. He's wearing light-colored slacks and a collared shirt with the sleeves rolled up. A pipe is tucked jauntily into his mouth. In the background, short metal awnings shade the windows of the one-story office building. A stovepipe and a louvered air vent poke up through the roof.

Almost exactly a month later, Ward Turner's family joined him just as Aliceville was decorating for a second wartime Christmas. Eight-year-old Mary Lu arrived from Decatur, Georgia, with her mother and her stepsister, Joyce, on December 1. It was the family's fifth move in her lifetime, and Mary Lu had concluded that this was how all people lived—picking up every year or so and heading to a new place for new experiences.

Joyce remembers the family car creeping slowly along Main Street that day. When Ward Turner pulled up in front of the Aliceville Hotel and went inside to check in, Joyce scrutinized the town through the car window and remembers that it didn't look like much to her. "I was feeling very sorry for myself, a sixteen-year-old moving for the third time in three years," she has said. Joyce was already very much aware of the war, which had started the year before when she was in the tenth grade in

Baltimore. "Being a seaport, that city was big on civil defense. My stepfather became an air raid warden and patrolled our neighborhood during the frequent blackouts, and we had routine air raid drills at school."

Both girls are sure they spent their first night in Alabama at the Aliceville Hotel on the northeast corner of Third Avenue and First Street, right in the middle of town. The hotel, which burned in the early 1960s, was impressive then—two stories of white masonry with rows of slim dormers set into a mansard-style roof. There were shade trees out front. On the first floor, next to the alley that separated the hotel from the MS&C Hardware Store and the Palace Theater, was a beauty salon where a pretty young woman named Jeanne Holiday worked.

The next night, the Turners crowded into two rented rooms in a private home. They stayed there until they could find a house to rent. Mary Lu's mother, Mary Womer Turner, took a clerical job at Camp Aliceville almost immediately. She worked in the Post Hospital, which was much deeper inside the camp than her husband's office at the Post Engineering building. Each day, she checked in at the main gate, and then again at the barbed wire-topped inner perimeters surrounding the prison compounds. She worked for First Lieutenant Harold L. Smith and then was promoted from under clerk to junior clerk typist. Eventually she became clerk to First Lieutenant Henry Nat Aicklen, a dashingly handsome young officer from San Antonio who came to Camp Aliceville in December as Headquarters Administrator and soon caught the eye of a local girl named Bobbie Kirksey.

The camp had no prisoners at this point, but more and more American personnel—both military and civilian—began to assume their assigned roles in anticipation of a drama expected to unfold in the early weeks of 1943. The name of the place was still officially "Aliceville Internment Camp," and the county newspaper, which always misspelled the word as interment [*sic*], often referred to it as a concentration camp. Townspeople still called it the "the Jap camp."

A number of Pickens County residents accepted camp jobs in December. Among them was Ed Jones from Carrollton. He and his wife rented an apartment in the home of Mrs. Trudie Love in Aliceville so he could be closer to his job. Miss Harrice Moore, who'd been working for the health department for more than a year, began new secretarial duties "at the concentration camp below Aliceville," and Murray Clements became the warehouse keeper.

Sam McCaa took a job at the camp hospital just before his daughter Janie's sixteenth birthday, which she managed to celebrate with punch, cookies, candy, and birthday cake in spite of rationing. Among the guests who danced and played parlor games were Janie's sisters, Barbara and Sue; Bobbie Kirksey's sister, Mary Emily; and Nap Griffin, who had a brother already in the service and two sisters working at the camp.

Rationing played a big role in Aliceville that winter. People were warned in mid-December that if they ate more than fourteen meals a week at places like the People's Café or Cleo's, they'd have to turn over their sugar and coffee coupons to the restaurant owner. Young people couldn't use ration coupons to buy coffee unless they were fifteen years old, and if they bought a ration book at age fourteen, they couldn't use the coupons in that book to buy coffee when they turned fifteen.

True to predictions, the Aliceville camp was ready for prisoners ahead of schedule. Most sources give the official completion and activation date as December 12, a year and five days after the attack on Pearl Harbor. The smaller base camp over near Opelika in Lee County was also activated on this date.

At Camp Aliceville, approximately 400 one-story, wood frame, tar-paper-covered buildings now dotted what had once been Tom Parker's pastureland, along with several large mess halls and lavatories, a hospital, administration buildings, and sentry towers. The old Carrollton Short Line had become the AT&N (Alabama, Tennessee and Northern) Railroad, and it had run two spur tracks into the warehouse area. The Alabama Power Company had set up service for electricity.

By the time opening ceremonies were held on December 18, the town of Aliceville was gleefully close to 100 percent employment. Mayor Sanders addressed a grateful crowd of area citizens. The Aliceville High School Band played in celebration, and the mayor introduced Colonel Frederick A. Prince, who had come from Maxwell Field in Montgomery to assume command of the camp on opening day. Prince, a career officer set to begin retirement when the war broke out, brought two other officers with him—C.E. Lemiell, his executive officer, and Edwin Auerbach, who would serve as inspection officer for branch camps in Alabama.

One day later Captain Scott C. Strohecker arrived, coming to the position of Post Adjutant at Camp Aliceville from temporary duty as a police and prison officer at a military base in South Carolina. Captain Strohecker had a military education from The Citadel, one of the country's foremost military colleges, and had served in World War I. When he came to Aliceville, he'd just returned to active duty after almost twenty years as an insurance agent and an officer in the reserves.

Aliceville residents were familiar with The Citadel (The Military College of South Carolina). Robert Hugh Kirksey, a graduate of Aliceville High School and a cousin of Bobbie and Mary Emily Kirksey, had recently received two high honors as a cadet there. He'd been named editor-in-chief of the college's weekly newspaper, and he'd been elected to its most prestigious honorary—the Round Table. Robert Hugh's father, R.J. (Bob) Kirksey, a local cotton buyer, was a past president of the Rotary Club, was chairman of the local Red Cross, and served on the Salvation Army board of directors.

Down at the drugstore, discussion of the camp's opening ceremonies was overshadowed by reports about a local boy missing in action. The William H. Somerville family received terrible news that week. The bomber on which their son, Richard, was a gunner had failed to return to England from a raid over France. The boy had been in England only a few weeks; he'd written his parents while touring Ireland on his first leave. The parents received their son's letter from Ireland one day after delivery of a missing-in-action telegram from Washington. Everyone in town was praying that the twenty-one-year-old former Auburn University student was alive in a prison camp.

"Richard was one of the finest young men of the county, and had a promising future," the newspaper reported with chilling finality on December 17. "He was strong, courageous, ambitious and clean in his life...."

Another topic of discussion at the drugstore soda fountain was Minnie Merle Brandon's sister, Lillian. Minnie Merle ran the People's Café in Aliceville, but her two sisters, Sally and Lillian, had gone to work for the Alabama Power Company after high school. In November, Sally married an army lieutenant, but Lillian took off on an entirely different effort of war support. After five years in an excellent sales office position with the power company up in Birmingham, she'd suddenly applied for and had been accepted into the WAACs, the Women's Army Auxiliary Corps formed just a few months after Pearl Harbor. The big news was that Lillian was in Des Moines, Iowa, for six weeks of training as the very first WAAC from Pickens County. Imagine that.

Most Americans, and especially Southerners, weren't quite sure what to make of women serving in the military, even if they were not in combat positions. Alabama author Aileen Kilgore Henderson has written a book about her own experiences as a WAAC from Alabama and says that Southern women who applied for the military were often considered reckless and daring. Civilians who toured bases where they served sometimes shouted "Quacky Wacky" at them, and male soldiers had mixed reactions—some cheered their patriotism and others were skeptical about their abilities. Lillian Brandon's decision to join the WAACs probably generated both kinds of comments at the drugstore counter in Aliceville.

One of the businesses that prospered most with the arrival of the internment camp in Aliceville was the Coca-Cola bottling plant. James Murphy Summerville, Hugh S. Summerville, and E. J. Pierce had bought the operation in 1917. George M. Downer Sr. bought Pierce's share in 1922 and was still managing the plant when the war broke out. As more and more military and civilian personnel streamed into the area, Downer kept adding production hours and employees to meet the growing demand for the soft drink with "that extra something" and "a taste all its own." Aliceville residents, like most Alabamians, used the general term "Coke" for any carbonated beverage and were often both puzzled and amused by military personnel who came to town asking for "soda" and "pop." No matter how it was ordered, Coca-Cola was by far the most popular soft drink of the World War II era, in Aliceville and throughout the country.

Will Peebles went to work for George Downer in the fall of 1942 while he was still in high school. He delivered Cokes for Mr. Downer all morning, went to school all afternoon, and in spite of having been born with only one arm, played football all evening. "That's the reason I didn't go to service when all my buddies did," says Will, "but I never did have no handicap—I played football and baseball all through high school, and later when we had a semi-pro baseball team here, I played on that, so I didn't ever let it be a handicap."

Will graduated from high school in December and went to work full-time for the bottling plant. "Mr. Downer was mighty good to me," he says of the man who also served as the county's war council chairman. "He treated me just like a son, maybe better. He was on the city council, and he did a lot of things for this town. He was interested in the schools and later they named the airport for him. He was a community man, I tell you now. You don't find many like him."

A few lucky servicemen managed to make it home on leave during the Christmas holidays in 1942. Jack Pratt Jr., the Carrollton newspaper editor's son now stationed at Fort Sill, Oklahoma, was one of them. Another was recent Aliceville High School graduate Frank Murphy, who had enlisted in the Army Air Corps in July and completed aerial gunnery school at Wendover Field in Utah on November 28.

Back in July, Jack Pratt Sr. had printed a military profile of Aliceville resident Frank Chappell in the *Pickens County Herald and West Alabamian*. He reported to the community in December that Frank was now a squadron commander in the air corps and had recently married Miss Eloise Martin of Gordo and Auburn, Alabama. Frank had risen rapidly in the service, spending only sixty days as a First Lieutenant before being promoted to Captain.

The Chappell family was prominent in Aliceville. Frank's father, Robert, and his uncle James had founded the Aliceville Iron Works in a small blacksmith shop in 1905, shortly after the town became the southern terminus for the Carrollton Shortline railroad. Jack Pratt was a close friend of Robert Chappell, and he described his friend's son as a "clean, honest, sober, patriotic young man who is giving all he has for the defense of his country."

A year had passed since the captures of Pickens County residents James Scott Browning and L.D. Orr in the Pacific. James Scott's mother was facing Christmas with the knowledge that her son was half a world away in a Japanese prison camp as she directed a special Christmas program on Sunday evening, December 20, at the Reform Baptist Church. More than thirty young people took part.

The Orr family knew where their son was, but they had no knowledge of his struggle for survival or the beatings he endured and the lack of decent food, or how constantly he and others were reminded that if the Americans invaded Japan, prisoners like them would be the first ones killed.

Elma Henders was home from college for the Christmas holidays when she met Captain Arthur John Klippen, M.D. , who came to Aliceville in mid-December to organize the camp medical service. He took a room in the home of Miss Annie Mae Coleman over in Carrollton and immediately set about hiring hospital employees. "I don't remember how we got to talking, but we did," Elma told an interviewer. "He knew I was a home economics major."

When the captain asked Elma if she'd like to come work at the camp, she told him she wasn't a registered dietician. She hadn't fulfilled all the qualifications yet. "You've had some food training, haven't you?" he said. Elma nodded, and that seemed to be enough. She was hired on the spot, gave two weeks' notice at her college job, returned to Aliceville, and began checking in at the guard shack each morning. Elma Henders became the camp hospital dietician well before any prisoners arrived, but there was plenty to do. She set about planning menus and worked with the mess sergeant ordering kitchen equipment.

When the American government agreed to accept "British-owned" prisoners for camps on American soil that winter, it announced to the world that the United States would treat whatever prisoners came into its custody in strict compliance with the Geneva Convention of 1929 (The Geneva Convention Relative to the Treatment of Prisoners of War). That document's ninety-seven articles contained general provisions to regulate every facet of military captivity, including clothing and housing, sanitary conditions, quantity and quality of food, medical care, and work assignments.

The War Department and other government agencies emphasized that, as called for by the Geneva Convention, it would be absolutely necessary to build housing for war prisoners to the same standards as housing for American military personnel. The thinking was to implement a sort of golden rule that would encourage hostile governments to treat American prisoners humanely. The United States government was determined to convey this message to its enemies: Please do unto our prisoners as we are doing unto yours.

At least through the war years, the American government insisted on implementation of this policy. Barracks for the anticipated prisoners at Aliceville were constructed on top of concrete slabs just like the barracks for American military guard units. Prisoner barracks inside the barbed wire had wooden frames wrapped in tarpaper just like the guard unit barracks outside the barbed wire. Since an American base camp required a mess hall and a recreation hall for a certain number of soldiers, a prisoner of war camp had to have the same, along with a canteen and an infirmary in each compound. The only major difference was the tall, hexagonal guard towers with searchlights positioned at intervals along the perimeter fences of the prison compounds.

Camp Aliceville stood ready by the end of 1942. Town residents kept a wary, curious eye on the camp gates as they celebrated the holidays, still trying to guess what sort of prisoners would be locked up in the huge camp sprawling at their doorstep. Construction crews left town for other projects, but the local economy continued to thrive, thanks to the paychecks of civilian personnel like Ward Turner and newly arrived members of Headquarters Company like Nat Aicklen and Harold Smith.

Back in November, Winston Churchill had dubbed North Africa "the beginning of the end," but in December, victory was still far from within reach. Half a world away from Aliceville, a brutal Allied defeat in Tunisia tempered the optimism generated the previous month by American Expeditionary Forces landings in North Africa. Drenched by freezing rain, British and American troops struggled through rocky passes on Christmas Eve and Christmas Day but were repelled with terrible losses. Pleased with the victory for their side, the Germans celebrated by renaming Longstop Hill *Weihnachtshügel* (Christmas Hill).

[North Africa] is where Allied soldiers figured out, tactically, how to destroy Germans; where the fable of the Third Reich's invincibility dissolved; where, as one senior German general later acknowledged, many Axis soldiers lost confidence in their commanders and "were no longer willing to fight to the last man."

• Rick Atkinson •

An Army at Dawn: The War in North Africa, 1942-1943

CHAPTER TWO

North African Front

Wilhelm Schlegel set out in life to become a banker. He was born in Asslar, a small town about fifty miles north of Frankfurt, Germany, in March 1918, during the last year of the Great War. He considers it a sad irony that his father made it home successfully from the horrors of that war and then died in an accident two years later. Though his mother had great difficulty operating the family's small farm after her husband's death, she managed a good education for her son.

Wilhelm attended *Volkschule*, the German equivalent of elementary and junior high school, in Asslar. At age fourteen, he entered a two-year program of commercial studies at the business school in nearby Wetzlar and then returned to his hometown for a three-year training program in banking. When he completed this in 1937, the bank in Asslar hired him as a clerk, and Wilhelm was on his way to a solid career in the financial world.

Two years later, however, Adolf Hitler plunged Germany into another great and terrible war. At the beginning of 1939, Wilhelm was called to six months of mandatory service in RAD *(Reichsarbeitsdienst)*, the German National Work Service. RAD had evolved from a voluntary work service created in the early 1930s. In its original form, it resembled the New Deal Civilian Conservation Corps established in the United States in 1933. Both organizations sought to lessen the high unemployment rates of the Great Depression by hiring workers for various civic projects. In the first half of the 1930s, RAD volunteers in Germany reclaimed marshland for cultivation, built roads, felled trees, and, like CCC workers in America, completed other projects to improve the infrastructure of the country.

By 1939, RAD had become something else entirely—a tool of the Nazi (National Socialist) government to provide auxiliary services for an army about to be unleashed on most of Europe. All German young men between the ages of eighteen and twenty-five were required to serve six months in RAD and then join the military for two years. RAD supported the *Wehrmacht* (German army) when it occupied Austria and the Sudetenland in 1938, and RAD units helped build the *Westwall* (Siegfried Line) fortification along the western German border and the *Ostwall* line along the eastern German border.

While Wilhelm performed his mandatory six months of manual labor, he wore the RAD arm badge insignia—a downward pointing shovel—on his uniform and his great coat. Then, as required, he joined the *Wehrmacht* a few short months before Hitler launched his *Blitzkrieg* into Poland on September 1, 1939. Assigned to the 2nd *Panzer-Nachrichtenabteilung* (tank signal corps), Wilhelm received training in wireless communications and then participated in campaigns in France and Russia.

Almost exactly a year later, in August 1940, as his unit was crossing the Beresina River in the part of Russia just east of Poland, Wilhelm was wounded—his left thigh shot clear through and his right index finger grazed. He began a long convalescence, moving from the main first-aid station at the Russian front to a military hospital in Warsaw and then to another in Vienna. While in Warsaw, he received the *Verwundetenabzeichen in Schwarz* (wound stripe in black) emblem for his uniform and documentation recognizing his sacrifice for the German military. Following treatment, he served in a convalescence company in Magdeburg and then was assigned to the 4th *Panzer KNA 475* (the 475th signal corps in the 4th Panzer).

By this time, Wilhelm was a seasoned soldier who took pride in military service. He'd come to love the marching songs that declared the glories of his homeland:

Heute wollen wir marschiern,
einen neuen Marsch probiern,
in dem schönen Westerwald,
ja da pfeift der Wind so kalt.
(Today we want to march,
to try a new march,
in the beautiful Westerwald,
where the wind blows so cold.)

He was also a young man who was careful not to let his heart become involved in a long-term relationship. "I enjoyed friendships with young ladies, but I always let them know that, because it was war time, I had no idea whether I would be coming home or not."

Though he didn't realize it at the time, assignment to the 4th Panzer would dictate the circumstances of Wilhelm's life for the next nine years. It began with training in desert warfare at a base in the Rheinland Pfalz area of Germany. Then, in the spring of 1942, after being issued sand-colored tropical uniforms, he and his unit moved south to Naples, Italy, where ships waited in the harbor.

Wilhelm remembers watching as the ships loaded up with tanks and transport vehicles. Later the same day, he put on a life vest, hoisted his pack, and climbed into a Junkers 52 with sixteen other soldiers for a low flight over the waters of the Mediterranean. Their destination was the port of Tripoli, capital city of Libya, in northern Africa. Wilhelm was relieved to arrive safely, especially after hearing that one of the transport ships had been torpedoed during its crossing.

On May 20, 1942, he took his first steps on African soil, discovering quickly that his sand-colored tropical uniform matched just about everything in sight except the stark white buildings of Tripoli and the clustered greenery in places where water was plentiful. There was a sense of having been dropped into a land from which all color except that of the deep blue sky had been drained away. Sand dunes, buildings, tents and military vehicles, even mountains in the distance—everything was beige.

The 4th Panzer wireless unit was assigned for duty with the 15th Panzer Division, which had already participated in many tug-of-war battles with the British for possession of key cities in Libya. Wilhelm's radio training quickly became useful. At one point, his job was to keep communications open between an artillery group and the *Fieseler Storch,* a fabric-covered observation monoplane that guarded the low air space over their position. Later, his team of wireless operators handled communications for Commander-in-Chief Erwin Rommel's detachment. Keeping up with Rommel required efficient mobility because the commander moved so swiftly and so often from one location to another.

Americans in Aliceville, Alabama, would have recognized the name Rommel more readily than that of any other German military leader in North Africa. The charisma and elusiveness of Rommel—the Desert Fox, as he came to be called—fascinated the Allied media. Across the boundaries separating wartime enemies, American and British journalists as well as generals maintained a grudging respect for this brilliant tactician. Stories of his exploits peppered newsreels and newspaper articles in both Allied countries. Fascination with Rommel was especially prevalent in the South, where people enjoyed knowing that Rommel had once studied the military tactics of Confederate General Nathan Bedford Forrest. There is even a persistent legend that in 1937, during a period when he was teaching in Potsdam, the great general toured the United States as part of a German military delegation. He is supposed to have visited Civil War battlegrounds in the South and then used this knowledge in conducting the North Africa campaign. Gregg and Deborah Morse, proprietors of the Highland Inn in Monterey, Virginia, have no absolute proof that Rommel stayed at their inn, but they do keep a few Rommel-related items in Room 26 so guests can decide for themselves.

In June 1940, long before America entered the war, Rommel had headed the 7th Panzer Division, one of the German units that successfully chased Allied troops up through France to the coastal town of Dunkirk. More than three hundred thousand soldiers had had to be shuttled across the Strait of Dover from northern France to the safety of the English coast, with every English watercraft of any size mobilized for the effort.

The year after this rout, Rommel received a promotion to lieutenant general and assumed command of the dreaded *Afrikakorps*. He launched a highly successful campaign across the coastal regions of North Africa in the spring and summer of 1942. By the time Wilhelm Schlegel's unit arrived, the Desert Fox was busy pushing Allied forces east towards Egypt, with the goal of forcing them out of Libya completely.

Wilhelm was with the German *Afrikakorps* when it retook the Libyan port city of Tobruk on June 21, 1942. In fact, one of the wireless operators in his unit received the communication from Hitler the next morning rewarding Rommel for this victory by giving him the grand title of *Generalfeldmarschall.*

Afrikakorps troops took a great deal of plunder when they captured Tobruk. Wilhelm considered it a sign of good leadership when his immediate commander, Colonel Bayerlein, honored the signal group with a large box of apricots after the battle. He remembers how wonderfully refreshing the fruit was and what a welcome addition to their regular provisions.

For a time after Tobruk, life in the *Afrikakorps* remained a satisfying challenge for those under Rommel's command. As the signal unit moved from place to place, Wilhelm learned much about leadership from the quick decisions he watched commanders make, and he knew this kind of learning would serve him well in civilian life just as it did in the military.

He received the *Verwundetenabzeichen in Silber* (the wound stripe in silver) on July 3 from Lieutenant Colonel Baron von Behr, and the Iron Cross, second class, on July 12, with documentation signed by Walther K. Nehring, Commanding General of all Panzer troops in Libya, Egypt, and Tunisia. Later in the year, he also received the *Sturmabzeichen*, a front line attack emblem awarded to soldiers with infantry or tank units who met specific battlefield criteria.

In October, however, the British Eighth Army, under the leadership of Lieutenant General Bernard Montgomery, dealt Rommel a shocking defeat at El Alamein. Most historians agree that El Alamein, and the landing of American troops under General Dwight Eisenhower the following month, combined to create the turning point of the war in North Africa.

When characterizing the discouraging months that followed, Wilhelm speaks of the steady retreat of the *Afrikakorps*. The causes, he says wistfully, are sufficiently documented in history books and don't need his elaboration—primarily, lack of reinforcements and dwindling stores of supplies. For him, personally, combat ended on May 11, 1943. His unit was among those captured by the British on Cape Bon in Tunisia as they carried out delaying tactics against French troops fighting in cooperation with the Allies.

Karl Silberreis was also a member of the famed *Afrikakorps*. He volunteered for this service because he didn't want to go to Russia. In the fall of 1942, his unit was sent to Italy, then flown to Athens, to Crete, and finally to Derna in Libya. Karl remembers that the *Afrikakorps* forged ahead towards Cairo and Alexandria until the crushing defeat at El Alamein. He remembers that things began to change when the American troops landed in Algiers. "All of a sudden we had two fronts, one coming from Egypt and the other at our back from Algiers. This was the beginning of the retreat—from El Alamein all the way through, and a lot of people got killed or captured."

When Walter Felholter arrived in North Africa with the Hermann Göring Division at the end of February 1943, German troops were experiencing the last of their major victories in that part of the world. They had humiliated the Allies at Kasserine Pass, but then German officers had wasted precious strategic days bickering over what to do next. They did not push forward soon enough and lost momentum. Meanwhile, naive American troops and their leaders were gaining valuable battle experience. In a series of particularly brutal encounters, they learned to loathe their German enemies enough to become a formidable fighting force alongside the British.

Walter Felholter was a member of the reorganized Hermann Göring Division that arrived in Tunisia on February 28 as reinforcements for German troops struggling to hold North Africa. Five of the division's battalions were teamed with the 10th Panzer division against British and American troops determined to drive the Germans and the Italians out of Africa and back across the Mediterranean. If the Allies succeeded in this venture, they would turn their attention to Sicily, the triangular island just west of the booted toe of Italy and only a short distance northeast across the Mediterranean from the Gulf of Tunis.

The British and the Americans had not always agreed that North Africa should be the launching pad for their eventual invasion of Nazi-occupied Europe. Early on, Eisenhower favored building up American troops in Great Britain during the summer of 1942, then crossing the English Channel and going at Hitler through France—a plan referred to as Operation Sledgehammer. The British, however, remembered too well their humiliating retreat and daring rescue from Dunkirk in June 1940. As Rick Atkinson points out in *An Army at Dawn,* British Prime Minister Winston Churchill did not wish to see another Dunkirk and believed an invasion of France in the fall of 1942 was "the only way in which we [the Allies] could possibly lose this war." The British preferred a less direct approach—surrounding and squeezing Hitler's various armies instead of heading straight for Berlin—and they preferred that this surrounding and squeezing begin in Morocco, Algeria, and Tunisia rather than in France.

Tunisia, the smallest country in northern Africa, has always been strategic. From its long Mediterranean coastline, it points south like a skinny finger between much larger neighbors—Algeria to the west and Libya to the southeast. The ancient city of Carthage once faced the Mediterranean on the northern coast of Tunisia, not far from where Walter Felholter and his unit of the Hermann Göring Division were assigned to connect telephone cable.

By April, weapons were scarce in German units. Official gunners had them, but men who did what Walter did carried only the tools to perform their communications assignment. If shot at, Walter and others like him could not shoot back.

Walter's orders were to keep the telephone cables connected between the command position of the Hermann Göring Division and its front lines. Taking one or two others with him, he would creep forward under cover of cool darkness, dragging cable through sand and rocks that still held the heat of the day in the craggy terrain above Tunisia's fertile Medjerda Valley. The men would make their connections, and then, if English artillery cut the wires during battle, creep forward again at the next darkness-shrouded opportunity to splice them back together.

During the day, Walter helped keep the switchboard up and running inside a dun-colored command bunker gouged from a rocky Tunisian hillside. Each afternoon he managed short naps but no sound sleep.

By April, the most basic foods and potable water were becoming scarce among German troops. The American forces that had landed the previous November had fumbled their way into battle but were now a serious threat. Recently, their raids by sea and by air had taken a huge toll on the German supply line from Sicily. Provisions as well as weapons had fallen far below the minimum needed to support an effective fighting force.

On the afternoon of April 20, Adolf Hitler's fifty-fourth birthday, Walter curled up in the dust outside the command bunker, hungry and thirsty and unable to sleep. He'd been handed a coarse biscuit and some tepid water that morning, but nothing since. How very different his life was from what he'd imagined three years earlier when he began studying engineering at a technical school in the German city of Friedberg. Then, his life had been on track. His apprenticeship as a mechanic was complete. He had a year of work experience and was studying for a career he knew he would enjoy. And then, to complete the picture, while browsing in the Catholic bookstore soon after arriving in Friedberg, he'd met Lieselotte Custor and fallen in love.

Despite growing tensions in Germany and throughout Europe, Walter's life stayed on track until February 1941, when he was forced to put his education and his romance with Lieselotte on hold. He was drafted into RAD for his mandatory stint of manual labor and spent six months in Lorraine, France, using a spade to help dismantle the Maginot Line built by the French in the 1930s. The French had considered the Maginot Line an impregnable defense, but they designed it only to repulse a frontal assault, so the Germans simply went around it and invaded France easily in May 1940.

On October 1, 1941, having completed his RAD service, Walter was drafted into the Hermann Göring Division and sent to Utrecht in the Netherlands for training. He served in Berlin and then in occupied France before being sent to Italy during the Christmas holidays in 1942 and then to Tunisia in February.

Walter Felholter was twenty-three years old as he lay in the dust and thought about the assault planned for that evening (April 20). A birthday gift—that's what *Feldmarschall* Kesselring was calling it. Officially, it was code-named *Fliederblüte* (Lilac Blossom) to fit the time of year, but it was really a not-so-well-thought-out tribute to the *Führer*'s birthday. What an optimist the field marshal was—urging his men onward no matter the odds, and especially tonight. Walter sensed that the English enemies were much closer and dug in much more obstinately than Kesselring and his officers either realized or were willing to admit. He wished the German leaders had come up with another birthday present for Hitler like the one they'd unveiled the previous April—the deadly Mk VI Tiger tank that had helped the 10th Panzer division devastate Allied positions back in December. The Germans needed more tanks like that, not hastily planned, poorly armed assaults.

Field Marshal Kesselring miscalculated when he ordered the *Führer's* birthday assault. It was an overly ambitious maneuver for troops armed with little more than machine guns. The attack began after dark, and within only a few hours, the British had pushed Kesselring's troops back with relentless artillery fire. German telephone lines to the front went dead before dawn, and the order came down from *Generalmajor* Schmidt for Walter to take his men and scuttle forward to repair the wires. Cross over that hill, he was told, and reconnect.

Thirst and hunger crept with the men as they dragged the precious communication cables forward and upward inch by inch. They'd received no more biscuits or tepid water the entire day, and they had not slept, but the booming skies had quieted somewhat by the time Walter pulled himself to the crest and looked down. A campfire flickered, and his stomach growled in anticipation of sharing food and water once the cables were reconnected. Then he looked again and felt a discouraging chill as he realized that the sentry silhouette directly below him in the dim orange glow wore the basin-shaped helmet of the English.

"Lie down," he whispered to the men behind him. "Don't make a sound." Without taking his eyes from the shadowed figure by the campfire, Walter pulled a field phone from his pocket and twisted its connecting wires to the cable he'd been dragging forward. Immediately, a crackle sounded close to his ear. "There are English troops up here," he whispered, thinking he was offering new information.

"Yes, we know," came the reply. "We're waiting here for you to come back. Do it quickly."

Walter led his men back down the pebbled hillside and wondered what would happen if they did not return to the command position quickly enough. If left behind, they could be captured and taken God knew where. Walter had heard rumors about the barbed wire prisoner pens the English had set up along the coast—huge enclosures with terrible treatment and no cover from the desert sun.

The transport truck was already loaded when the men staggered back to the bunker. Walter's tongue was thick, and he wanted to lie down, but that was not a possibility. He and his men were ordered to keep moving. For the rest of that night, they plodded slowly behind the transport truck, saying nothing, and backtracking through terrain they'd held confidently a few days earlier.

For two more days, their pattern was the same—plod slowly back through the darkness, and then lie in hiding during the heat of the day. They shared what little liquid they had, and no one mentioned food. It was too painful a subject to discuss.

As dawn swabbed an orange glow across the wasted horizon between Bou Arada and Pont du Fahs on the third day, the bedraggled caravan struggled up one last hill to the shores of a small lake that offered no refreshment in spite of its appearance. The whole thing was salt water.

"Everyone has to dig a hole," ordered an officer. "Be quiet and wait."

Walter pulled the entrenching tool from its canvas carrier on his hip and unfolded the handle. He tried to dig, but his legs ached from walking all night, and his tongue had swollen to the point where it would soon stick out of his mouth. He poked at the rock-hard soil that had baked in the sun after hard winter rains, but he made little progress. He was too weak to dig down more than a few inches, and so were the others around him. Satisfied with the pitiful ruts they'd scooped from the colorless shore of the salt lake, the men lay down in a cactus patch and waited.

How awful to be incapable of helping yourself, Walter thought. Their division had fought so hard and gained so much ground, and now it had come to this. He thought of Lieselotte and wondered what she was doing on this April morning. It was Holy Week—Good Friday, he realized. Perhaps Lieselotte had gone to church and prayed for him. He would remember the exact date distinctly for years to come.

Walter felt a tap on his shoulder and turned towards the man curled like a fetus in a shallow depression next to him. "Here is something at least," said the man, pointing to the outstretched hands of a *Feldwebel* on his other side. The sergeant was holding up a canister of wine. Walter sidled on his belly and held his meal tin under the canister until it was full. He would have preferred water, but wine was better than nothing. He sidled back to his small rut, gulped the vinegary liquid, and soon felt a welcome drift of sleep that fogged his hunger and thirst.

Walter woke an hour later to a rumbling sound in the valley below. He scrambled to his feet for enough seconds to determine that their hill was surrounded and that enemy tanks were lumbering towards them from every direction.

Then the artillery fire began, and Walter hunched back down. The tanks below could not yet reach their position with the big shells. The men around Walter who had guns held their fire, knowing their bullets would only glance off the tank armor.

Walter checked his pocket watch. It was three o'clock in the afternoon. Could they hold out until dark and then break through at some point after the sun had set? The pocket watch brought thoughts of home, of saying goodbye to his mother in Osnabrück on his last day of leave before coming to Africa. He'd taken off his good wristwatch that day and left it with her, choosing to bring along the cheap metal pocket watch instead.

It was soon evident there was no possibility of holding out until dark. The men huddled amid the cactus, with little cover and no more wine. Within minutes, the snouts of the first English tanks poked above the crest of the hill. Like alien beasts, several of them crunched along on their metal haunches and surrounded the cactus patch. Their big guns belched and spit, and Walter was not sure then, or in later years, whether the tanks were actually shooting at them or just shooting around them for intimidating effect. If they were trying to shoot directly into the hollows where the Germans were, they were not very good in their aim.

Walter heard the collective gasp, including his own, when the tin can lid of one of the tanks flew open and an English Tommy popped up for a look around. Walter expected his German sergeant to shoot, but he did not. What would have been the point?

Soon the other tanks opened, and more English soldiers clambered out. "C'mon, c'mon," they growled, motioning with jerks of their arms. "Hands up!" they said. Walter recognized these two English words, and he knew how to respond. His commandant had told them, if a Tommy says, "Hands up!" then you do like this.

One of the captors approached and began going through Walter's pockets as he stood with his hands in the air. The man found nothing but the cheap pocket watch, which he held up in the sunlight. "Hmmph!" he said and shook his head that it wasn't worth keeping. He stuffed it back in Walter's pocket and moved on to the next man.

Once they'd completed the body searches, the English offered their canteens. They seemed to recognize how thirsty the Germans were and smiled with satisfaction as they watched them gulp their first cool drinks of water in more than two days.

Hans Kopera was also captured on Good Friday, and capture was certainly the most fortunate scenario he could have experienced on that day. A native of Austria, Hans had spent his teenage years under Nazi rule.

Through an agreement between its Chancellor and Adolf Hitler, Austria had stepped into its role as "a German state" as early as 1936. In 1938, when the Chancellor had second thoughts and called for a vote on Austrian independence, Hitler demanded and received his resignation, then ordered German troops into the neighboring country. A Nazi government was formed, and Austria became known as the *Ostmark*, a seven-district region under the central authority of the Third Reich.

Like many of his high school classmates, Hans enlisted in the German army at age seventeen and was assigned to the Second *Kradschützen* (motorcycle) Battalion of the 10th Panzer Division in the spring of 1942. He first saw action in northern France, arriving there with German occupation forces at about the same time as Walter Felholter and the Hermann Göring Division.

The motorcycle battalion transferred to Tunisia in late November 1942—part of a massive troop buildup. One of Hans Kopera's first major battles was near Tebourba the last week of November, when the 10th Panzer was ordered to destroy enemy troops in the vicinity. The Division's most effective new weapon was the Mk VI Tiger panzer—the huge armored tank developed as a birthday present for Hitler the previous spring, but the motorcycle battalion attached to the Division was also effective. Each motorcycle carried two infantrymen—one to drive, and the other to ride in the sidecar with a weapon. Because of their maneuverability and speed, *Kradschützen* units often surprised and outflanked the enemy far ahead of the heavier tank units. They were also useful for quick missions in the narrow mountain passes.

With his *Kradschützen* battalion, Hans participated in a number of battles in Tunisia in late 1942 and early 1943. He was promoted to sergeant and received the Iron Cross for bravery. He faced the enemy at Kasserine Pass, Tebourba, Tebessa, and Medenine. At times, the weather above the valleys was so cold, and the competition for each individual hill so intense, that both sides measured their advances in yards. Often, the same hills and valleys were taken back and forth over and over again.

By mid-April, however, British and American troops had doggedly won control in North Africa. They had pushed the Germans and Italians into the northeast corner of Tunisia with their backs to the Mediterranean.

Generalfeldmarschal Erwin Rommel, the infamous Desert Fox, had flown secretly to Rome on March 9, taking a medical leave he'd postponed for many months. Hitler had become preoccupied with outlasting the Russians at Stalingrad and was ignoring pleas from his North African commanders for more food, fuel, and other supplies for their segment of the war. While undergoing medical treatment in Europe, Rommel urged Hitler to change strategies in North Africa, but the *Führer* refused and declared, "If the German people are incapable of winning the war, then they can rot."

On Good Friday morning, Hans Kopera's motorcycle unit was attempting to defend access to the capital city of Tunis when they surprised the command group of a Scottish battalion in an open field somewhere in the hills above the Medjerda Valley. Their barrage of artillery fire killed the battalion staff and its bagpipe major, and midday heat caused many more in the battalion to collapse in the open field. When a captured German prisoner pulled a concealed weapon and shot even more Scots before being shot and killed himself, the enraged remaining Scots won the intense battle that followed. Hans Kopera was fortunate to be captured rather than killed because, as the day wore on, the Highlanders were in no mood to spare the lives or dignity of German soldiers, and they took few prisoners.

One of the German soldiers the enraged Scottish Highlanders chose to kill rather than take prisoner was probably Walter F. Meier's younger brother, a machine gun operator. The two were serving in the same unit, and Walter grieved deeply at the loss. After his own capture, as he was moved from transfer camp to transfer camp in Tunisia and then, eventually, across the

Atlantic to the United States, he rarely sought relationships with other prisoners and preferred to spend his time contemplating his misfortunes and considering what the future might hold.

Walter F. Meier was several years older than many of his fellow soldiers. Born in Bremen on August 4, 1915, he'd learned the trades of typesetting and printing and had been a labor service leader in the RAD work service before reporting for military duty in 1937 at the age of twenty-two.

Early in 1940, he'd become a member of an elite force of 424 men specially chosen to train in great secrecy under the leadership of Captain Walther Koch for the German assault on France and Belgium. On May 10, 1940, Walter Meier and seventy-eight other men from that unit boarded several wood and canvas gliders that were towed before dawn to a spot above Belgium's supposedly impregnable Fort Eben Emael. There, they parachuted down silently to the flat top of the fort and completely surprised its defenders. For his participation in this successful assault, Walter received the Iron Cross and became the sergeant-major of the 10th Company of the Stormtrooper Regiment Koch.

He could have remained at this rank, but he gave it up in order to jump with a paratrooper unit into Crete almost exactly a year later on May 20, 1941. Unfortunately, this operation was not as smooth or as wildly successful as the one at the Belgian fort. Although the German airborne invasion of Crete was ultimately successful—driving more than forty thousand Allied troops from the island over a ten-day period—the cost in human life was huge. Again, the German gliders came in low, but this time they became easy targets for the Australian, British, and

New Zealand troops who joined the local troops in what one defender compared to the opening of duck hunting season.

Walter Meier was shot in the elbow before he ever reached the ground, and his wounded arm dangled painfully as he struggled to free himself from his parachute and seek cover. He spent a miserable day hiding in thick bushes, hearing what sounded to him like every New Zealander from the entire world thrashing about hunting for him. Finally, he was rescued by some of his paratrooper companions and transported to Greece for hospital treatment.

After more treatment at a military hospital at Hildesheim, back in Germany, Walter rejoined his unit, proud to be serving this time in the company of his younger brother. Although Walter's arm was never fully mobile again, he was again appointed sergeant-major and flown to North Africa, where he participated in the battle against the Scottish Highlanders that killed his brother.

Leopold Dolfuss was captured in the same general area of Tunisia on April 25. Like Hans Kopera, Leopold was Austrian but had joined the German army at age twenty and trained in Poland. He fought on the front lines in the Ukraine until long marches in military shoes caused an infection in his foot that landed him in a recovery hospital in Czechoslovakia.

Leopold was one of many German foot soldiers relieved to learn he would not be returned to the Russian front. His company traveled by train to southern Italy and then by ship to Tunis in December 1942. He remembers feeling relief when capture came—relief that he would no longer need to fight.

Hermann Blumhardt was fifteen years old in 1936 when he graduated from *Volkschule* and went looking for an apprenticeship in printing. This was hard to come by, partly because his hometown of Stuttgart already had too many printers and partly because members of the *Hitler Jugend* (Hitler Youth) received preference for all apprenticeships.

When the Nazi Party seized power in 1933, the Hitler Youth absorbed all other independent youth groups in Germany. By the time Hermann finished *Volkschule*, more than 60 percent of the country's young people between the ages of ten and eighteen were members of this group that introduced them to Nazi ideology, including anti-Semitism, and prepared them for full membership in the party at age eighteen.

Hermann was not a member of the Hitler Youth, but after a lengthy search, he secured a four-year printing apprenticeship in a small newspaper office outside Stuttgart. One experience from this time in his life stands out in his memory—the newspaper manager's departure in 1937. Nazi authorities ordered the man to divorce his Jewish wife, but he refused, resigned his position, and left the country with her. During this same period, Hermann developed great admiration for the parish priest who led his Catholic Pathfinders youth group and courageously refused to support Nazi doctrines. On several occasions, the priest narrowly escaped a concentration camp sentence. "I was an altar boy," Hermann said later, "but I have to admit that, as an ignorant teenager, I was often torn between loyalty to the priest and home on the one hand and the glory and sky-is-the-limit promises of the Hitler regime on the other."

The Versailles Treaty that ended the Great War (World War I) in 1919 imposed such heavy war reparation payments on Germany that many in the country believed their economy would never recover. When Germany failed to make payments on that war debt, her currency collapsed, and French and Belgian troops occupied the Ruhr Valley, Germany's largest industrial area. By 1923 severe inflation had almost destroyed Germany's middle class, leaving farmers and shopkeepers, small business owners, and disillusioned civil servants ripe for the radical political ideas of Adolf Hitler and the Nazi party.

Economic conditions improved somewhat in the middle 1920s with the Dawes Plan, which eased the reparation payment schedule and returned the Ruhr Valley industries to Germany. A new currency and numerous foreign loans, primarily from the United States, triggered an impressive economic recovery, but it was short-lived. Beginning in 1929, the Great Depression drained all foreign support, including that of the United States. The weakened Weimar Republic could not cope. Industry slowed, unemployment rose again, and agricultural prices fell to new lows.

Hermann Blumhardt remembers the astounding promises Adolf Hitler made when he campaigned to become chancellor—he would eliminate unemployment and tear up the stranglehold provisions of the Versailles Treaty. When President Paul von Hindenburg reluctantly appointed Hitler chancellor in 1933, Hitler succeeded in reducing unemployment by 40 percent during his first year in office. He brought about a tolerable standard of living for most Germans and did indeed tear up the provisions of the so-called Versailles "treaty of shame" with no reprisals at all from the Allies.

Hitler soon abolished the office of President held by von Hindenburg. He terminated the Weimar Republic by declaring himself *Führer* of a new Third Reich in Germany. "He promised and did unify the German people, but he did it by smashing all political parties and the free press, and building a 'folk community.'" Hermann remembers that the fulfillment of those breathtaking promises suggested almost supernatural skill and turned Hitler into a revered demi-god among the people. "The few voices of mostly older, wiser people who could see the handwriting on the wall were drowned out by the enthusiasm of the young and the working class of the big cities."

On the morning of September 1, 1939—the day Germany invaded Poland—Hermann and other employees gathered around the radio in the newspaper office to hear the two-hour speech in which Hitler effectively convinced the majority of the German people that war was necessary for the good of the country. He boasted that he'd solved the problems of German society and that the Third Reich would remain in power for a thousand years. "The radio kept the people stirred up, and newsreels at every movie house. [The newsreels] showed the heroism on the front lines and caught many a youngster with his mouth open in awe."

Hermann was not anxious to go to war, but when his draft notice came on October 4, 1940, he resigned himself to the duty of marching off to serve his country. At age eighteen, he was learning to play the accordion and much preferred music to battle, but duty claimed a long heritage in his family. His grandfather had fought in the Franco-Prussian War in the 1870s, and his father had served as a chauffeur for German officers during the Great War. Hermann never knew for certain what his father experienced in war because he would not talk about it, except to say that after the Germans surrendered in November 1918, he'd walked all the way home to resume his civilian life.

Hermann was drafted into the RAD labor service earlier than many of his friends because newspaper work was not considered essential to the war effort. Like Walter Felholter and Wilhelm Schlegel, he was given a spade and put to work at manual labor. In Hermann's case, this meant dismantling barbed wire along the Siegfried Line or *Westwall,* which Germany had put up in the 1930s as a fortification against France. After Germany conquered France in 1940, this wall was no longer needed, so Hermann's work unit was given the tedious task of removing the barbed wire from a section of it, in freezing December weather.

After discharge from the labor service in January 1941, Hermann spent a short time at home but soon received orders to serve in the Germany army. By June 22, he was with troops that stormed into Russian-occupied eastern Poland. In October, he found himself headed for Moscow, chasing retreating Russians. He has characterized these battles as easy *Blitzkrieg* against an inferior enemy still fighting with weapons from previous wars. The more sophisticated German units captured at least a hundred thousand Russian soldiers that summer.

"Have no fear," Hermann kept repeating in his mind. He convinced himself he would come out of this adventure alive, and that that was all it would be—a grand adventure!

Hermann gained a reprieve from combat, along with a rude awakening from his adventure delusions, when a German plane mistook his unit for Russians and opened fire, killing several of his comrades and wounding him in the upper thigh. Slowly and painfully, he made his way back to Germany through several primitive aid stations and makeshift hospitals.

Near the small village of Bargau about thirty-five miles east of Stuttgart, he was cared for at a Catholic convent converted to a hospital for wounded soldiers. Hermann remembers that the nuns there outdid the "brown nurses" (as German army nurses were called) in their devotion and treatment of the wounded.

Meanwhile, the others in his unit remained in Russia through a severe winter that took heavy tolls on both sides in late 1941 and early 1942. At times, it was so cold that Russian and German soldiers stared at each other across battle lines so frozen that neither could make a move. In the spring of 1942, while Hermann was still recuperating, the 10th Panzer Division was pulled from the Russian front and sent to northern France to regroup.

One Sunday afternoon, the village of Bargau invited the walking wounded from the convent to attend a dinner and entertainment. While seated at a long table, Hermann took notice of a pretty young woman who served him bratwurst and beer. "Please, come sit down here and tell me about yourself," he said, motioning to an empty chair next to him.

The young woman blushed and shook her head. "No, I have to work," she said. Hermann persisted. Each time she walked by, carrying trays of food and beer, he again invited her to sit down. Although she continued to refuse, Hermann knew from her shy smile that it would not take much to persuade her. He called to one of the older women working in the hall. "Are you so busy now? Can't you spare that young woman for a little conversation?"

"Oh, we don't need her," the woman called back with a laugh. "She can sit down and visit with you."

So Kaethe (Katie) Emberger sat down and visited with Hermann Blumhardt. A while later, when she stood to return to her serving chores, she caught her white apron on the back of Hermann's chair. "We weren't using money," Katie remembers, "but the soldiers had been given tokens for us to collect, and when the apron caught, my tokens fell out of the pocket, all over the floor. Hermann jumped up and helped me gather up all the tokens, and that was it."

Hermann remained at the convent near Bargau and then with a convalescent military company near Stuttgart for nearly a year, falling in love with Katie and feeling good about his future. On October 4, 1942, just before his departure to rejoin the 10th Tank Division under Field Marshal von Rundstedt, Hermann asked Katie to become his wife. He'd been promised a furlough in May 1943, and he thought perhaps they could be married then.

"My wounds healed all too soon," Hermann wrote later. "Never in my life had I been so despondent as when I was discharged from the convent hospital and sent to the convalescent company near Stuttgart. This was when I realized for the first time what a mess I had fallen into." He knew then he'd be returned to combat, and he knew also that he was not the same soldier he'd been before. He guessed that being in love had something to do with that.

Hermann was back with the 10th Panzer Division in northern France by November 8 when General Eisenhower launched his invasion of North Africa—Operation TORCH, the landing of British and American troops in Algeria and Morocco. Despite tremendous loss of life and supplies, this initial assault was a success for the Allies, with American air-borne shock troops parachuting into Vichy French North African territories while Marines stormed ashore from barges.

The Vichy government of France was a puppet government that collaborated with the Germans. Until the time of Operation TORCH, it exercised some independent control in French colonial territories and in southern France, which Germany had not yet occupied. After Eisenhower's landings in North Africa, however, Germany rushed fresh troops to occupy southern France in retaliation. The newly reorganized 10th Panzer Division (Hermann's unit) and the Hermann Göring Division (Walter Felholter's unit) were among those troops.

Hermann remembers standing near the harbor at Toulon and watching French crew members scuttle much of their war fleet so the Germans could not commandeer their ships. Then he boarded a train for Naples, feeling poignant regret at his situation as he traveled along the French and Italian Rivieras through some of Europe's most beautiful scenery.

In his mind, Hermann can still picture the half-starved Italian children who seemed to know exactly when meals were served in the German military camp at Naples. They stood back timidly, watching as he and others ate, then ventured closer and closer until they were handed the mess kits so they could devour the leftovers.

Hermann knew the German high command was considering the 10th Panzer for one of two extremely shaky battlefronts that needed immediate reinforcement—Stalingrad and North Africa. When he discovered that his unit was being ordered to Tunisia, he was, like Leopold Dolfuss, greatly relieved not to be returning to the cold, disheartening Russian front.

On December 14, 1942, twenty soldiers, including Hermann, boarded a Junkers 52 German cargo plane, just as Wilhelm Schlegel had six months earlier. They flew almost low enough to touch the waves, across the Mediterranean to the airport at Tunis. As the plane prepared to land, British fighter planes approached, and the men had to jump from the plane and make a run for the meager borders of brambles in order to hide from a strafing of the landing strip. Fortunately for them, because of fuel limitations, the Allied planes could not loiter more than ten minutes over the German airfield before returning to their own crude airfield more than one hundred miles away.

The march from Tunis to the battlefield was slow and tiring. At one rest stop, officers handed out cans of sand-colored vehicle paint and told the men to camouflage their field-grey continental helmets so they would blend with the desert around them. The 10th Panzer's vehicles had not yet arrived from Italy, so the men had to walk, each carrying sixty pounds of equipment. Tunisia gets about sixteen inches of rain a year, and almost all of that falls between November and March. Hermann was certain the sky had dumped all sixteen inches just before his group began their slow, slogging march.

In January, the 10th Panzer coordinated with other units in support of General von Arnim's drive to push French forces out of the Eastern Dorsal of Tunisia. In spite of considerable losses, German forces secured the vital mountain passes by the end of the month. Control of these passes protected the corridor along the Mediterranean coast that could link von Arnim's troops with those of Field Marshal Rommel who was moving into Tunisia from Libya. It also helped protect the water supply for the German-controlled city of Tunis.

Mid-February brought *Unternehmen Frühlingswind* (Operation Spring Breeze), and the 10th Panzer was ordered to attack along the Faid-Sbetla Road. In a cold drizzle, the men moved more than one hundred tanks south towards Faid Pass without being detected by Allied pilots. Over a twelve-hour period, the 10th Panzer cooperated with the 21st Panzer to create a double envelopment around Sidi bou Zid, forcing an Allied retreat and abandonment of key positions. The Allies lost more than a thousand men, nearly one hundred tanks, and numerous smaller artillery pieces in what the Germans labeled a stunning success against their enemy. The victory could have been a rallying point for future German operations, but the three major commanders—von Arnim, Kesselring, and Rommel—spent two days arguing about what to do next.

Rommel had been poised for a thrust from the south that now seemed unnecessary to Arnim. Kesselring was in Germany conferring with Hitler, and Rommel sent a message asking to have both the 10th Panzer and the 21st Panzer put under his command for an immediate operation to force the Allies to pull most of their forces back into Algeria. Arnim disagreed, and the battle of wills continued. Eventually, Rommel was given the two Panzer divisions, but he was ordered to shorten the reach of his plan, which he did reluctantly.

Although German forces were stunningly successful in these battles of Kasserine Pass, they were not able to maintain a unified high command in North Africa beyond this point. The British intelligence discovery of Rommel's final assault plans led to his defeat at Medenine, and it was after this battle that Rommel took his medical leave in the Austrian Alps and tried to change Hitler's attitude about strategy in North Africa.

Hermann Blumhardt has described the early months of 1943 as a period of ironic reversal, a period when the hunters who had waged *Blitzkrieg* in Poland and Russia gradually became the hunted in North Africa as German supplies of heavy armor dwindled and the Allies began to gain the upper hand. Early in March, he heard the rumors that Field Marshal Rommel had returned to Germany and wondered for the first time if defeat might be a possibility.

March 13 began as a cold and rainy, generally miserable day. The temperature did not dip below forty degrees, but with the wind off the sea and the dampness in the air, it seemed a good twenty degrees colder in the open. Below in the valleys, the almond trees had bloomed, but up in the mountain crevices, it was hard to picture blossoms. Hermann remembers that his clothes were wet and that, although he would have preferred to walk around to keep warm, he was ordered to stay in his foxhole to avoid detection by the enemy.

About noon, the sun finally came out, and Hermann felt the clothes begin to dry on his shivering body. Then a messenger sneaked through the scrub shrubbery and announced that the English were about to attack. Hermann and two others were ordered to man a machine-gun about twenty feet away. As they scuttled towards the gun, an observation sergeant from a heavy mortar platoon scrambled into Hermann's foxhole to use it as an observation post.

Five minutes later, a mortar shell buzzed loudly and then exploded nearby, temporarily deafening the three men manning the machine gun. Hermann turned just in time to see the observation sergeant's torn body fly out of his foxhole. For a long time, he sat frozen next to the machine gun, realizing how close he'd come to being that body himself. Though he and the others waited all day, mostly in horrified silence, the rest of the announced attack did not materialize.

By March 23, the 10th Panzer Division was down to fifty-seven tanks and fared badly in an encounter with American forces. The Americans suffered heavy casualties and loss of supplies, but the 10th Panzer lost thirty-seven of its remaining tanks and was forced to retreat and regroup. When the dust settled, they were no longer a panzer division, except in name. It was a significant victory for the Allies against a German division that had seen victories on battlefields in Poland, Russia, and France as well as Tunisia.

Hermann has written that confusion and despair began to invade the ranks. The Allied forces now had three times more men and ammunition, and they were shelling the German positions from eight o'clock in the morning until five o'clock at night. "Some of the German soldiers, most of them older and married, showed extreme emotional stress. Friends tried to cheer them up, but others teased them." The situation became one of learning to cope with one's own problems or perishing.

After a promotion to corporal on April 1, Hermann clung to the hope that he would be able to take his scheduled furlough on May 5 and go home to marry Katie. He knew in his heart and in his soul that this hope was unrealistic, but holding onto it helped him keep his sanity.

Early in April, the 10th Panzer regrouped and had some success in defensive encounters against American troops less used to desert warfare, but this success was short lived. The balance was clearly shifting. More than two hundred thousand German and Italian troops were now contained in an area of roughly fifty by eighty miles right on the edge of the Mediterranean in Tunisia, and nearly a thousand Axis prisoners per day were being marched into the hastily erected open-air cages that Walter Felholter had heard about.

By April 24, Hermann was so exhausted and discouraged he no longer cared what happened to him. He was desperate for sleep, but the unit's tanks and other vehicles had been destroyed, so there was no transportation or cover. Day and night, the men walked along in retreat or dug into the hard, rocky soil to hide. Sometimes they had a hand-drawn wagon for their equipment and ammunition. Whenever he had a choice, Hermann preferred getting behind the wagon so he could close his eyes and nap a little as he walked and pushed.

Hermann's tour of duty in North Africa ended in a Tunisian cemetery on the day before Easter in 1943, the day after the capture of Walter Felholter and Hans Kopera. Shortly before ten o'clock that morning, Hermann dug only a shallow foxhole, assuming from experience that his unit would be moving on again in an hour or so. He lay down in a sort of sleep-deprived daze, aware that his neck hurt as he tried to relax with the heavy steel helmet pushing his head down.

A short while later, he woke to a rumbling noise, squinted his eyes, and caught sight of a large number of enemy tanks moving directly towards his unit. The men still had their heavy machine gun, but he doubted it would do any good against tank armor. As the tanks lumbered closer and closer, Hermann and the others were too tired to think what they should do next. They looked to their sergeant for leadership, but he was staring ahead just as numbly as they were.

Hermann knew no English at this time, but when the English soldiers began shouting, "C'mon, boys!" he understood instinctively what they wanted. When one of them moved in his direction, Hermann held his arms up in surrender, but then quickly saw that none of his comrades had raised their arms.

Realizing he could not surrender alone, Hermann hunkered down as well as he could in his shallow foxhole. Within seconds, bursts of automatic pistol fire whizzed above his head, and the big guns on the enemy tanks swiveled in his direction. This time, when the English shouted, "C'mon, boys!" all the Germans raised their arms.

"It is indeed an awful moment when you have to surrender," Hermann has written. "Nothing but uncertainty lies ahead of you. You are in enemy hands—a terrible, frightening thought—and you are cut off from your homeland, completely at the mercy of your captors."

Erwin Schulz was born in Berlin in 1912, the son of a union laborer who never joined an organized political party. Like Hermann Blumhardt, Erwin had difficulty finding an apprenticeship position when he turned fourteen. Eventually, he became a salesman and a member of a labor youth union. As he reached adulthood, the German economy worsened and jobs became impossible to find. Erwin soothed his feelings of hopelessness by attending lectures on social theory.

After Hitler came to power in 1933, Erwin often helped distribute pamphlets arguing against German rearmament, and he participated in political demonstrations against the Nazi government. In 1935, Erwin was arrested and sentenced to five years in Luckau prison on a charge of treason. He spent two miserable years in Luckau, located in eastern Germany near Brandenburg, and three more in various other concentration camps before being released in 1940.

After his release, the local police kept Erwin under strict surveillance. He was often interrogated by the Gestapo, the internal security police force of the Nazi government, fearing each time when they hauled him from his home that he might not make it back.

In December 1942, after the Allied landings in North Africa, Erwin was drafted into the *999 Afrika Brigade* or *Strafbataillon* (punishment battalion) as it was sometimes called. This newly formed unit of German forces consisted primarily of court-martialed German soldiers assigned to combat duty as a means of rehabilitation. The unit also drafted petty criminals, social "misfits," and political prisoners like Erwin, in an effort to offset growing manpower shortages in the military. The men were carefully supervised by handpicked regular army officers and non-commissioned officers. Although many of those drafted had served or were serving long prison sentences, none of them was considered a hardened criminal.

In March 1943, the *999 Afrika Brigade* was renamed the *999 leichte Afrika-Division*. Two of its regiments arrived in Tunis in late March, and Erwin Schulz was a member of one of them. By this time, he did not trust anything connected with the military. He knew it was the job of certain officers to spy on the "999ers." Within his own heavy mortars unit, one sergeant had attended an elite Ordensburg training school for Nazi students, and Erwin knew this sergeant's primary assignment was to report anyone who did not express support for the proper beliefs.

Erwin freely admits he deserted the *999 leichte Afrika-Division* on May 1, 1943. Desertion was not an agonizing issue of conscience for him. He had not had his heart in fighting for Adolf Hitler's goals in the first place. On May 1, Erwin's heavy mortar unit was perched in plain sight atop a bare hill, and artillery shells were exploding in among the men. Death for all of them was the probability if they remained where they were.

As he watched German and Italian troops begin to retreat in the valley below, Erwin realized the confusion would make it difficult for officers to figure out who was missing and who had deserted. He thought again about the evening a few weeks earlier when he'd been forced to stand at attention and watch a firing squad mow down seven good and fit German soldiers who'd been court-martialed because they muttered that they hoped to be captured by some Canadians. He decided then that he'd seen too much death and that he didn't want his life to end as the target of a mortar shell on a hilltop in Tunisia.

When the unit began to move down the hill, he and another artilleryman hid in a cluster of bushes and eventually turned themselves over to a group of Moroccans who were more than happy to commandeer their weapons. The Moroccans turned Erwin and his friend over to French troops, who put them in a cramped temporary prison compound in their rear lines. The two were just settling into a tent when a chaplain poked his head inside and suggested Erwin and the others huddled there be very careful. He warned that Nazi prisoners were stalking the camp and that they'd already murdered one anti-Nazi. Erwin did not realize it at that moment, but the warning about stalkings and murders was one he would hear frequently during the next three years of his life.

The number of German and Italian prisoners captured by the Allies in North Africa climbed steadily through April and into May. By the middle of May, their numbers reached two hundred fifty thousand, according to most accounts.

Karl Silberreis and Georg Casper, members of the *Afrikakorps*, were captured May 4 and 5 on the outskirts ofTunis, just before a massive Allied bombing raid along the line from Medjz-el-Bab to Tunis. Horst Uhse became a prisoner at about the same time.

Among others captured in early May was a twenty-four-year-old sergeant in the *Luftwaffe* (the German air force) named Werner Meier who'd flown a Stuka Junkers 87 bomber in France and Russia before being sent to serve with ground forces in North Africa. Another was Fritz Hagmann, a sergeant in an engineer reserve company. The German military situation had become so desperate that officers were ordering medics into battle with rifles as British and American troops advanced on the white walls of the capital city.

The battered remnants of the 10th Panzer, in which Hermann Blumhardt had served, laid down their weapons on May 9, and what was left of the 999 "punishment battalion," from which Erwin Schulz had deserted, began their march into captivity with the rest of the *Afrikakorps* at about the same time. One of the last few Divisions to yield to the Allies was the Hermann Göring, Walter Felholter's division, after a few of its officers escaped by air to Sicily.

Former banking clerk Wilhelm Schlegel and a fellow soldier who considered himself an amateur poet were captured when German resistance dwindled and the British occupied Cape Bon, the fertile Tunisian peninsula across the Mediterranean from Sicily. On May 11, the banking clerk and the poet and many others were marched through a small village on their way to a prison enclosure. French de Gaullists lined the narrow streets and jeered as they marched. The poet later wrote that, from his perspective, the French behaved more like pigs than soldiers but that the Tommies who took the Germans prisoner treated them with respect, as he would have expected of a worthy opponent.

The official surrender took place on May 12. Crowds of Tunisians and French nationals lined the streets of Tunis to cheer the Allied victory as twenty thousand dejected remnants of Rommel's *Afrikakorps* and other German units marched into a flat, open compound at Mateur, near the foot of the mountains west of the capital city.

Aliceville Internment Camp, as it was then called, didn't have very much to offer. The compound was as bare as, well, it was bare. The roads were dirt, and this dirt became knee-deep mud after a good rain, and we had lots of that.

• November 15, 1943 •
Camptown Crier, Volume I, Issue I

CHAPTER THREE
Preparing for Whom?

At the beginning of 1943, the stage was set in Aliceville, yet weeks went by, and the key players—expected Japanese or German civilian detainees or war prisoners of some sort—did not appear. The drugstore crowd began to suggest that the big government camp outside town might never fill up.

No one was complaining, however, about the town's booming economy. Headquarters company officers, enlisted men, and civilian office personnel settled in and began to spend their weekly paychecks with local establishments. They enjoyed lunch and dinner at the People's Café and Cleo's, bought groceries at D.E. Day's, and set up leagues at Mack's Bowling Alley. They mingled with local residents at the Palace Theater for newsreel updates of the war and for movies like *Stardust on the Sage*, starring Gene Autry and Smiley Barnett or *Pardon My Stripes* with Bill Henry and Shelia Ryan. Soldiers bought army caps and other military accessories with labels that read, "Be Wise and Patronize Sam Wise—Aliceville, Alabama."

Elma Henders served nutritious meals to enlisted men who arrived to staff the camp medical service Captain Klippen was setting up. She planned her menus carefully. If American soldiers at Camp Aliceville were having roast pork, corn on the cob, potato salad, and carrots for lunch, she knew she would soon have to provide the same menu—or at least one with equal calories and nutrition—when prisoners arrived. That's what the

Geneva Convention dictated, and she'd been charged with following that convention exactly.

In early 1943, the pendulum of war swung between the Allies and their Axis enemies in Europe and in the Pacific. The United States Air Force began bombing Germany during daylight hours in January, and American and Australian troops made headway in New Guinea. The last German troops in Stalingrad surrendered in February, and the Japanese evacuated Guadalcanal, but German U-boats sank twenty-one Allied merchant ships in the Atlantic in March and retook several other Russian cities. The British Eighth Army met fierce opposition from German troops in Tunisia in April, and the Japanese conducted major air raids on American shipping and airfields in the Solomon Islands.

Prime Minister Winston Churchill and President Franklin Roosevelt agreed to invade Sicily once they achieved victory in North Africa. They also agreed to delay an invasion of France until 1944. The Allies were making steady progress, but neither leader considered victory a sure thing.

During the early months of 1943, Pickens County boys continued to train in faraway states and ship out for foreign battles. Henry "Boots" McCaa was an army sergeant out in Oregon. Dr. T.R. McLellan's son Beverly had received his silver wings at the Harlingen Army Gunnery School in Texas after five weeks of intensive training and would soon join the crew of a bomber as an expert aerial triggerman. "If he's in the service, send his Valentine now," the county newspaper urged on January 14.

Beverly McLellan was a graduate of Aliceville High School who'd become a radio man gunner on a B-42 after entering the service in April 1942 at the age of thirty. While he was stationed at Lowry Field in Colorado in the spring of 1943, one of his Aliceville friends made the comment, "Beverly will give 'em hell when he gets over there, for he has what it takes." He wrote home that he was quite ready to drop one of the "big capsules" on Berlin or Tokyo.

Mary Lu and Joyce Turner were delighted when their parents moved them out of cramped, rented rooms and into the much bigger green shingled bungalow their father rented up on Red Hill. Townspeople called it "the old Harkins place" after one of its previous owners. Joyce remembers that the living room was heated by a potbellied stove and that the linoleum floor was patched and worn. Each bedroom had a fireplace, and on cold mornings, Ward Turner shuffled from room to room to stoke the fires.

Red Hill was a quiet, tree-shaded extension of Broad Street. The Harkins' place was three doors up from the stately home of Dr. W. W. Duncan, which had been built by Charlie Horton in 1909 with white pillars out front and upper and lower sleeping porches on the right side to catch night breezes in the summertime. Decades after the war, Mary Lu Turner Keef would return to Aliceville and once again enjoy the hospitality of Red Hill. By then, Dr. Duncan's home would have become Myrtlewood, an elegant bed and breakfast serving full plantation breakfasts within a setting of Victorian furnishings and stained glass windows.

Mary Lu has vivid memories of living in the Harkins' place for several months before government housing was built for civilian employees of Camp Aliceville. She often stood on a chair and filled the big kitchen sink with soapsuds so she could pretend to create frothy sodas just like the ones at Simon Jones' drugstore. She still has the rubber doll that was once her constant and patient playmate, allowing her to glue strips of newspaper to its head and then roll them up with bobby pins to make curls the way Jeanne Holiday did in the beauty shop down at the Aliceville Hotel.

Mary Lu entered the third grade at Aliceville Elementary School when the school term resumed after the Christmas holidays. Like third grade girls everywhere, she adored her teacher, Miss Daisy Earl Day. Mary Lu was conscious of being an outsider in a small, southern town, yet she was soon at home among her teachers and among fellow students like Mary Stapp, Billy Summerville, and J. T. Junkins' younger brother, Earl Dean. Sometimes she heard the transplanted grownups joking about being called Yankees, but she felt welcome.

The one-story school had been built in 1913. It had wide, murky hallways with high ceilings and dark-grained hardwood floors. When the janitor wanted to clean the floors, he threw down oily sawdust, left it down for the day, and then swept it up along with dust and litter. Sixty years later, Mary Lu can still close her eyes and breathe in the pungent aroma of that oily sawdust.

The school was not in good repair—post-Depression times had been difficult in the rural counties of Alabama, and with the war on, fixtures and supplies were hard to come by. Using the little girls' room was something to avoid if possible, and if a person did have to go in there, the likelihood of finding a working toilet was slim to none. The school buses weren't much better. They held together, but on the way to school, children could look down from their seats through jagged gashes in the rusted out flooring and watch the country roads whiz beneath them.

On Saturday afternoons, the Turners, like other civilian families who had moved to town to support the new military operation, did their grocery shopping at the grocery and general merchandise store owned by Miss Day's father, Mr. D.E. Day. Mary Lu learned to love the simple country foods of west Alabama—thick white grits with a pat of butter melting in the middle the way it did on mashed potatoes up in New York state, tangy turnip greens simmered all day on the back of the stove, black-eyed peas boiled with a ham hock or two, and chunks of fresh okra dipped in cornmeal and fried to a crispy golden brown.

One weekend, Mary Stapp and her mother invited Mary Lu to spend the weekend with them at their family farm outside Aliceville, just off the road to Mississippi. Mary Lu loved roaming the endless woods and farm fields with her friend. She remembers how good grits with fresh butter tasted for supper as the three of them sat at a table lit only by an oil lamp.

While Ward Turner clerked for Major Dishner at the Post Engineer's Office, his wife, Mary, worked full-time at the post hospital, typing morning reports and maintaining ledgers and cost questionnaires for the army. Lulabelle Farmer walked up

Red Hill each afternoon to take care of Mary Lu because Joyce did not get out of school as early as her younger sister. Lulabelle's mother, Lillie, worked for Mrs. James Murphy Summerville in the big white house where Major Dishner and his wife rented rooms on the first floor. Lulabelle's family lived in one of several servant houses behind the big house, and Lulabelle's sister worked for Mary Turner's new friend Barbara Ann Gordon, a nurse at the camp. James Murphy Summerville operated a store, a cotton gin, and a lumberyard about a quarter mile from the big white house.

"Lulabelle was so much fun to be around," Mary Lu says of the young black woman who was nineteen or twenty and already had children of her own. Lulabelle would push Mary Lu in the big swing on the shady front porch and fill her head with Alabama ghost stories. "If we were having chicken that night, I'd follow her down the steep steps from the kitchen into the backyard where she'd wring the necks of live chickens to kill them. I can't imagine now, but I remember wanting to try it, and she'd give one to me, but I could never do it."

Mary Lu remembers visiting Lulabelle's house once and being surprised at the obvious poverty. "It was just a shack, really, by the railroad tracks, as I recall."

In 1943, white superiority, black poverty, and separate public facilities pervaded life in Aliceville and throughout the South. Racial discrimination existed in other parts of the country, but it was usually more subtle. In Alabama, segregation was the law—prisons and churches, hospitals and cemeteries, train cars and elevators, hotels and restaurants, schools, swimming pools, and drinking fountains were all completely separate. Segregation had the full support of the state government, the local legal system, and the police. Though some challenges were made in the courts—even the United States Supreme Court—court decisions against segregation rarely occurred before or during World War II.

Mary Lu's sister Joyce experienced Deep South segregation for the first time one spring afternoon when she was walking towards a store on Third Avenue after school. "I'd gone to get something for my mother, and as I walked along the sidewalk, every time a Negro came towards me—male or female—they'd step down into the street as I passed by. This was totally new to me and difficult."

It was an era when minstrel shows were popular, poking fun at black culture. The county newspaper announced one such show—"the hit presentation of the year"—to be presented by the Carrollton PTA in April 1943. "This great show has in the background old Southern hymns brought to you by the best singers in Carrollton [appearing in black face]. It brings back all the laughter of the Southern Negroes, their days, their jokes, and their fundamental reaction to musical melodies."

Mary Lu, eight years younger than Joyce, was not as aware of racial issues as her sister was. "It affected her much more than it did me," Mary Lu has said. "I saw it, and I accepted it. We had moved around so much and met so many people, and to me, it was just life." Mary Lu knew she loved Lulabelle, and she didn't think beyond that.

Because public facilities remained separate in Alabama in the 1940s, the county newspaper often used headlines that made clear distinctions of color when reporting the news. An occasional column appeared with the title, "What Pickens County Negroes Are Doing." It mentioned sports activities or Red Cross drive participation among black residents and the considerable amounts raised for war bonds by students and faculty at black schools in the county.

One 1943 issue of *The Pickens County Herald and West Alabamian* honored a Carrollton area man named Newte Temple Sr. with the headline, "Temple Negroes Are Good Service Men." The article announced that Newte's son Alva was completing basic flight training at the army flying school in Tuskegee, Alabama, and that two other sons were also in service—Andrew, a sergeant in the quartermaster corps and Abraham, a private first class in the medical corps. Newte Temple Sr. was well-known around Carrollton and had the reputation of producing "the kind of stuff that will blow your head off"—in other words, really good home-brewed spirits. The article concluded with the comment that these three young black men had good reputations at home. They were making good soldiers in the service of their country.

Alva Temple was born near Carrollton in 1918 and received his early education at the Pickens County Industrial School, a school for black students. He studied agricultural education at Alabama A&M University before becoming an aviation cadet. Alva was twenty-five years old when he became one of 992 black pilots who graduated from the experimental flight-training program at Tuskegee that led to the creation of the 99th Fighter Squadron. He would go on to become one of the famed

Tuskegee Airmen, a member of the "Red Tails," named for the color painted on the rear section of their planes. Before the war ended, he would complete 120 missions over Italy, France, and the Balkans with the 99th Pursuit Squadron and choose to continue a two-decade career in the United States Air Force after the war.

Lillian Brandon's friends were predicting an exciting military career for her as well. She'd just completed her WAAC training out in Iowa—including infantry drill and special aircraft warning service instruction—and was awaiting assignment to duty.

But not all the war news in Aliceville was about achievement. Early in March, the J. M. Davidson family received the ominous news that their son Newton had been missing in action in North Africa since February 22. No further information about the twenty-three-year-old young man was available, but the family hoped he'd been captured rather than killed.

Long before there were any prisoners to guard at Camp Aliceville, military duty and social activities for camp personnel were fully operational. Jack Pratt noted in his newspaper column that Aliceville and Carrollton were gaining a fine group of "distinguished gentlemen and attractive women" in the officers and their wives at the Aliceville Internment Camp. He commented that they came from every station in life and were interesting to know. He also noted that Colonel Prince, the camp commandant, was making a real effort to get to know the people of Pickens County, stating that his officers and men were "just folks, and they like to meet and mingle with their neighbors, hear the gossip and swap yarns." Jack also wrote that the colonel enjoyed inviting groups of local citizens to experience the hospitality of the camp, and he suggested that anyone who received such an invitation should accept it and expect to have a delightful time.

The Officers' Club opened with great fanfare on the evening of February 11. On the outside, the finished club building looked pretty much like all the other camp buildings—a squat, rectangular structure with six or so wooden steps leading up to doors on the front and side, and ventilation louvers on the roof. It had a metal awning over the front door and a wooden sign declaring it to be the Officers' Club. Inside was a smooth wood dance floor, along with a bar and seating areas.

Colonel Prince, the camp commandant, invited members of the community to join in the opening festivities that evening. A written invitation to Mr. Harvey M. Stapp, dated February 4, 1943, expressed Colonel Prince's hope that "the cordial relations which we believe already exist between the officers of this post and the citizens of Aliceville and adjoining communities be cemented so that military and civilian populations may become better acquainted. We hope you will honor us with your presence."

Harvey Stapp had gone to work at Camp Aliceville soon after it opened. A civilian employee of the Aliceville Fire Department, he is listed in various employment capacities at the camp, including "senior operations engineer," between early

1943 and the end of its existence. Long after the war, those who returned to relive their memories often sought him out at his small farm or at his maintenance position with the Aliceville Water Board. He was always happy to point out whatever landmarks still existed.

Perhaps Mr. Harvey, as most Aliceville residents called him, escorted his sweetheart Miss Nettie Marlowe, to the Officers' Club opening that February evening. Their presence is not recorded, but Mr. Harvey did receive an invitation, and it is likely that he and Nettie, along with other local residents, enjoyed the many dance contests that evening and also the free flow of alcoholic beverages, something non-existent in the rest of Aliceville because Pickens was a dry county.

Most certainly, that first Officers' Club event included a Grand March with captains and lieutenants in best dress uniforms escorting their ladies in evening gowns. Eugene Schillinger, editor-in-chief of the Camp Aliceville newspaper for enlisted personnel, once wrote a humorous article about an Officers' Club Grand March. "Personally," he wrote, "I like to forget about marching when I'm at a dance.... In the Grand March, everybody lines up in a column of twos, and they march. It's fun as far as the officers are concerned, but to you and I, it's just close order drill. They call it fun. Then the lights are turned lower, the music comes up slowly, softly, romantically, and they dance. At the enlisted man's dances, when the lights are dim and the music is soft, nobody has time for dancing. Other maneuvers are taking place."

Sometime in early March, nineteen-year-old Margie Archibald drove along Broad Street in Aliceville with a decided frown on her pretty face. Margie was a stunning brunette with gently waving hair and large, bright eyes beneath softly penciled brows.

Aliceville was not the place she wanted to be, even though she knew it well. Her father had grown up here, but Margie had been born in Camden. When Margie was a baby, her father had taken a job way over in Union Springs. Each summer, Margie's mother packed up her six children and drove back to Aliceville for a month-long family visit, and then Margie's aunt, who lived in Aliceville, packed up her five children and drove the 180 miles east and south to spend a month in Union Springs to return the visit.

Now Mr. Archibald's health was failing and with the war on, he decided to move his wife and children back into the house he'd built in Aliceville when he married. This decision shocked Margie. All her friends were in Union Springs, and everything she wanted to do was in Union Springs, so she vowed she wasn't leaving *her* home just so her father could return to his. Such a move would ruin her social life.

When her parents and her five brothers and sisters moved to Aliceville, Margie stayed behind with friends. This plan worked well for a few winter months, but then towards spring, her mother insisted she join the family.

Spring usually begins about the end of February in west Alabama. Forsythia and daffodils bloom first, brightening the borders between yards and creating golden sentinels at driveways. About the same time, redbud trees, with blooms more lavender than red, beckon from stands of timber out beyond the pastures. Most years, from late February on through March to early April, spring continues to wash over the countryside with wave after wave of brilliant color.

The forsythia and redbud would not yet have faded when Margie made her fretful return drive to the hometown of her father. Their blossoms would have blended with long, drooping clusters of wisteria winding even more lavender through the high, still leaf-barren branches of roadside hardwoods.

In spite of the familiar array of spring blossoms, Margie sensed something different about Aliceville the moment she drove into town. "That was the first thing," she has said, "the soldiers just leaning around on the sidewalk where the two drugstores were, and the bank on the corner."

It didn't take long for Margie to change her grudging attitude about returning to her father's hometown. Within hours, she discovered that her two first cousins and her very own sister Emmie were having the time of their lives dating the handsome young officers from Headquarters Company out at the Aliceville Internment Camp. Emmie couldn't talk fast enough to fill her sister in on all the fun. Here were these perfectly delightful young men, all plunked down just outside tiny Aliceville. What were they supposed to do with their time when they weren't busy guarding prisoners? The girls considered it their patriotic duty—and a pleasant one at that—to plan as many social activities as they could.

As March flew by, Margie decided the camp officers were the cutest bunch of young men she'd ever seen. Mary Turner's handsome boss, Captain Henry Nat Aicklen Jr. from Texas, was the headquarters administrator, and Lieutenant Walter Rosskopf was there from Oakland, California. Margie met both of them, along with Captain Lawrence (Larry) Persons, Lieutenant J.E. Daugherty, Lieutenant Lester Lombardi, First Lieutenant Robert A. Barnes, and Second Lieutenant Albert F. Setzer. The fact that these officers had come to west Alabama from all over the United States made them even more intriguing. "We hadn't seen very many Yankees at that time, really," she has said. "Just this one family from up north that lived in Union Springs."

Margie soon joined Emmie and her friends in inviting the officers to church and to their homes for fancy dinners. "We'd serve them a beautiful meal—use the china and the silver and everything, and they just loved it." In return, the handsome young officers escorted the pretty young ladies to the Officers' Club, where they entered the dance contests, and the young ladies swished their knee-length skirts to the swing tunes of Glenn Miller, Benny Goodman, and the Dorsey Brothers. According to Margie's memories, "We could go out every night with who we wanted. It was sort of like a dream. They had the officers' club, the noncommissioned officers' club, and the enlisted men's club. We dated [them all]...some of the best-looking Yankee boys you ever saw."

As pale white dogwood blossoms and pastel azaleas opened to full glory, the young people enjoyed picnics down by Lubbub Creek. Sometimes they drove the thirty-five miles or so over to the nightclubs in Columbus, Mississippi. "We'd pile up in one or two cars because we didn't have any gas. You had to have the ration coupons to buy gas, so everybody would get those all together, and then we'd have enough to go over to Columbus...."

Margie took a job at Aliceville Bank and Trust. "James Verner Park wasn't president of the bank during the war, but his uncle was, and he thinks I'm correct in saying the economy of our little town was up two hundred percent or more from what it was before that camp came here. Why, we just thought Aliceville was going to be a big city from then on."

Captain Persons was camp finance officer that spring. Whenever he called into town to order the denominations of bills he needed to pay the enlisted men in cash, the bank would order the bills and then send someone to the railroad depot to pick them up. "Here Larry would come with his armored car," Margie remembers. "He'd have the MPs with their guns and station two of them on each side of our small bank, and then he and his men would come in with their guns—shotguns, or whatever they used back then. They'd get that money, and we were all so bemused because it was unusual to see something like that in Aliceville."

Looking like the feds from a James Cagney movie, Captain Persons and his men would climb back in their armored car—MPs hanging on the outside—and roar off to the camp to make payroll, which, for most enlisted personnel, was about twenty dollars a month.

American servicemen who came to Aliceville at least as reluctantly as Margie Archibald found the springtime pageantry of the town's residential streets a glorious contrast to the scraped bare terrain of the developing internment camp. Out at the camp, spring rains had turned the unpaved roads and grounds to slippery clay the color of flowerpots. The clay exuded a metallic smell, like clotting blood.

A few servicemen found the lacy spring beauty, along with the beauty and charm of certain Aliceville young ladies, so appealing that they surprised themselves and their northern and western families by returning to the tiny cotton town after the war and taking up permanent residence. Their affection for Aliceville grew steadily during military duty in spite of their discovery that, no matter what part of the country they came from, town residents would forever refer to them as Yankees.

On March 6, 1943, the 305th MPEG (Military Police Escort Guard) Company arrived in Aliceville long after midnight. Activated at Fort Oglethorpe, Georgia, on January 15, this unit included 2 officers and 135 enlisted men from Georgia, Alabama, and Tennessee. They'd had only four weeks of military training (instead of the usual nine weeks) when orders came to ship out to what was still being called the "Aliceville Internment Camp." Among them was Sergeant Hubert R. Jordan of Dallas, Georgia, a thirty-eight-year-old recalled to military service in January 1942.

As the first guard unit to arrive, the 305th quickly grabbed their choice of barracks sites in the American sector of the camp. Even in the dead of night, these men could sense it would be wise to choose the highest ground. Oozy red clay sucked at their combat boots and testified to the one major flaw in the Army Corps of Engineers' design for the camp. Poor drainage would plague its occupants for months to come, along with mosquitoes nurtured to mythical size in the stagnant waters of the nearby swamp. Irritable displaced snakes slithered in every time it rained.

At dawn on March 7, the men of the 305th set about making their chosen barracks site fit for habitation. They dragged in lumber for duckboards to walk on and filled mud holes with dry dirt. Because their orders referred to Aliceville as a "permanent station," they did their best to improve their surroundings for the long haul.

On the morning of March 8, the 305th took over guard duty from the Station Complement and instituted a three-week rotation schedule. One week they practiced interior guard duty, policing installations at ground level—headquarters, the PX, the motor pool, warehouses, and other buildings—along with challenging strange creatures and noises all night long. The second week two groups of three men each drew tower duty—working and sleeping two hours per shift—in each of the high-rise hexagonal guard towers situated at strategic sites around the camp perimeter. Finally, the third week they went through additional basic training and "recreation," which 305th member Joseph Samper remembers was not literally a time for fun and relaxation. "You know, close order drill, clean up those guns, polish your shoes, and get everything ready before you had to go back up in the towers." Occasionally, they got the opportunity to leave the base for the athletic field in town to play some baseball.

When they could, the soldiers also enjoyed mingling with local residents for movies at The Palace Theater. Movies were shown primarily on Wednesday and Friday evenings and on Saturday afternoon and evening. Shortly after the 305th arrived in Aliceville, an election was held to decide if the Palace Theater should begin showing movies on Sunday afternoons between one o'clock and six o'clock—at least for the duration of the war. "We promise to secure only desirable and elevating pictures and maintain a high standard for all Sunday movies," promised a full-page ad in the *Pickens County Herald and West Alabamian* on March 18. The ad carried comments from the mayors of Fayette, Vernon, Eutaw, and Livingston, assuring Aliceville residents that Sunday movies in their towns had been beneficial and had never been allowed to conflict with local church activities. Colonel Prince was quoted as stating that Sunday movies would help keep up the morale of his men and that he would favorably recommend Sunday motion pictures as an advantage to his command.

Apparently, the good citizens of Aliceville rejected this proposal. Subsequent issues of the county newspaper carry ads for movies only on Wednesdays, Fridays, and Saturdays as before.

In late April and early May, the 305th received twenty-one additional recruits, mostly from Fort Sheridan in Illinois. Among them were Bob Siddall and Chet Eisenhauer. Eighteen-year-old Chet Eisenhauer had volunteered for a special assignment, somehow getting the impression he'd be trained to do motorcycle repair. Next thing he knew, he was stepping down from a Frisco railroad car at the Aliceville depot in the middle of a rainy night and being assigned to guard duty with the 305th.

Byron Kauffman arrived as a 305th replacement from Camp Sutton in North Carolina and distinctly remembers his first impressions. "It was still pretty much a swamp when I got down there. No streets laid or duckboards, just buildings. We was walking around in mud up to our ankles. The mess hall was across the street from our barracks, and out behind was the latrine—a little old six-holer. When it rained, you better have your shoes on because there'd be two or three inches of water on the doggone floor all the time." Gradually, he says, army engineers got the place cleaned up, but it took six or seven months.

The 324th MPEG reached Aliceville from Fort Devens, Massachusetts, on March 26 with 2 officers and 135 enlisted men. They were followed in late April by the 389th (3 officers and 146 enlisted men), which had been activated the day after Christmas at Camp McCain near Elliott, Mississippi.

Twenty-year-old Stanley Pendrak, a native of New York state, was a member of the 389th. "I had never left the town I was born in," he once told a newspaper reporter from Mobile. "This was going into manhood in a short while. No two ways about it, it was an exciting, adventurous time."

One mid-afternoon in early May, Stanley and two other transfers from Camp McCain pulled into Carrollton in an army transport truck on their way to Aliceville. Their monotonous 150-mile drive from central Mississippi had taken most of the day, on bumpy, winding roads between endless stands of scrub pine and pastureland. "We've been around this thing three times," Stanley complained to the driver as they circled the Pickens County courthouse in Carrollton, trying to figure out which offshoot road would take them to Aliceville.

The courthouse in Carrollton is the stuff of Alabama's most famous ghost story—the "face in the window legend." One version, which Lulabelle Farmer had certainly already told to little Mary Lu Turner, describes a young black man named Henry Wells who was arrested for robbery and arson during a rainy night in January 1878. Many around Carrollton believed he was responsible for the fire that had destroyed the previous courthouse and all its probate records two years earlier. After his arrest, town officials hid him in the attic of the courthouse to protect him from an angry mob.

When an electrical storm erupted, a bolt of lightning struck across the street from the courthouse, and the flash forever etched the image of Wells' frightened face into the bottom right pane of glass as he peered at the mob from an attic window on the north side of the courthouse. According to writer Kathryn Tucker Windham, Alabama's premier ghost story collector, the various versions of the story differ about whether Wells was killed by the lightning bolt or by the mob, but "everyone agrees that this was the last night of Henry Wells' life."

Robert Hugh Kirksey remembers hearing one version of the story during his childhood and staring up in wonderment at the image in the window. Many, many years later, after the war, Robert Hugh would practice law on Courthouse Square in Carrollton with John Hardy Curry. Later still, he would climb the steep steps inside the Courthouse and sit as Probate Judge in the building's massive courtroom. The frightened face in the pane of glass is still visible today, marked now by an arrow that points to the correct pane. There is even a coin-operated telescope aimed at the window from across the street.

The face would have been visible when Stanley Pendrak and the other Camp McCain transfers arrived in Carrollton on that

May afternoon in 1943. Stanley doesn't remember specifically, but it is possible that they heard the story and stared at the window before someone pointed out the correct road to Aliceville.

Ten miles farther, when they checked in at the camp, the men discovered they had no immediate orders. "So," Stanley remembers, "we loaded up again in the troop carrier and went into town [Aliceville]. The driver let us off down by the People's Café and the Palace Theater. They had an old street light with a circular reflector on it right in the middle of town. I don't remember there being a stop light."

The first place Stanley stepped inside was Simon Jones's drugstore, which, he remembers, had a light bulb hanging on a cord in the window. He was amazed, even in 1943, at how old fashioned the drugstore was with its dark wood shelves, black and white checkered linoleum floor, and tiny soda fountain tables surrounded by chairs with twisted wire, heart-shaped backs. He remembers Simon Jones's daughter Peggy standing there when he stepped inside, and how friendly she and the others in the drugstore were. They spoke to him first, almost as if they'd been expecting him, and that just didn't happen up in New York state.

Stanley was a sergeant. Back home in New York, he'd been cutting meat since he was fourteen or fifteen years old, so at the Aliceville camp, he became "first cook" and worked in the mess hall, cooking for American service personnel. Breakfast was often cereal, but some mornings he'd fix French toast and boil up a syrup with sugar and water and a little coloring. Dinner was always some sort of meat with mashed potatoes and corn and one other vegetable. Sometimes the "meat" was a stew that could be stretched thin enough to serve everyone. Other times it was cream chipped "beef" on toast, which could also be stretched.

Later in May, on another trip into town, Stanley spotted an attractive young woman stepping out of the Aliceville Hotel beauty shop for a break. He followed her into the coffee shop and mustered the courage to start a conversation. Before he knew it, he'd invited Jeanne Holliday to an evening of bowling over at Mack's, and she'd accepted.

Two other large MPEG companies became involved in the life of Camp Aliceville in the first half of 1943. The 425th sent an advance detachment of fourteen escort guards from Fort Custer in Michigan on May 9. They would be followed in September by the rest of their company. The 436th, activated at Fort Custer in February, escorted a trainload of German POWs from the pier in Boston to Camp McAlester in Oklahoma in May. They returned to Michigan for additional training and arrived in Aliceville in early July.

Local high school students like Dorothy (Dot) Latham were delighted by the arrival of the MPEG units and the opening of a noncommissioned officers' club at the camp. Dot had a sweet smile and a rounded face framed by lots of curls. She loved to dance more than just about anything. Before the internment camp came to town, the only opportunity she and her friends had for dancing was after football games on Friday nights when the town blocked off Broad and Third Streets and the whole community gathered for a bit of toe tapping under the stars.

"That was the only dancing unless you were lucky enough and old enough to go to an out-of-town club," Dot remembers. "When we found out there was a dance hall and all those soldiers, it wasn't long until the senior class was going down there all the time. No one had a date or anything, we just all went down there. It was a magnet. The jukebox was fixed to keep playing one song right after the other. There was no putting in a quarter or fifty cents. It just played music all the time. We had men here from Ohio and Pennsylvania, and I even learned to polka. We loved it. We'd go around and around the room, dancing to all kinds of music."

During the "dark, muddy days of April," as the camp newspaper described them, Special Service Officer Jerome Diamond decided the NCO club needed a live dance band to replace the jukebox. Drawing from several of the newly arrived MPEG units, Jerome pulled together a five-man combo that included Frankie Mulligan as leader and trumpet player, Bill Day on trombone in "the Tommy Dorsey manner," Georgie Osborne on the alto sax, Harry Thompson "beating the hides," and Don Quimby "picking on the ivories." They called themselves the Stardusters. The band played only eight tunes during its first gig, including appropriately, "I've Heard That Song Before."

It was soon decided that the group needed a singer, and someone suggested Dot Latham. Dot sang in the high school glee club and also shared her voice as a soloist at the Methodist church. Everybody knew her. She was the oldest of Henry and Edith Latham's ten children, and her father had opened the first ever service station and repair shop over in Gordo when Dot was a youngster.

In the spring of 1943, Dot was a cheerleader at Aliceville High School and worked afternoons at Johnson's Drugstore. She auditioned for the position of singer with the Stardusters, and, after interviews and fingerprinting, was soon leaving the drugstore each evening for a few hours in the spotlight. "I even had security guards. They'd pick me up in a Jeep and take me right to the door of the NCO club. We did all the music of the forties. Tommy Dorsey was number one, and all the polkas and the romantic songs—'I'll Never Smile Again' and 'Always.'" She continued to sing with the band for several months before joining the United States Navy WAVES program. Assigned to the Heart of Dixie Unit 22, Dot headed off to Washington, D.C., where she worked in Naval Intelligence until the end of the war.

Earline Lewis finished her senior year at Carrollton High School in May. The army was encouraging young women who weren't going right to college to take a civil service test. Earline expected her mother to be upset when she announced she wanted to take the test and go to work at Camp Aliceville. To her surprise, her mother didn't say no. "I had two brothers in the military, and she was suffering through that, so I guess she knew that what I could do for my country was the right thing."

Earline was a little intimidated by the two-day civil service test, which was designed to qualify applicants for a wide range of government positions, not just secretarial jobs. She went as far as she could with the math and foreign language and knew she excelled in the sections on typing and shorthand. "That's what the military was looking for, a good secretary," she has said.

Earline scored high, and within two weeks was employed full-time at Camp Aliceville. She describes herself as coming from a very sheltered family. When she went to work taking dictation and typing for a lieutenant in the Quartermaster's office, she didn't know a soul at the camp, but she remembers being pleasantly surprised when she fit in just fine. "We were all about the same age, and we all had family or loved ones or sweethearts in service."

J.T. Junkins was the older brother of Mary Lu Turner's third grade friend, Earl Dean Junkins. J.T. was a wide-eyed thirteen-year-old when the various MPEG units began to bring a touch of the war's excitement right into his own home and neighborhood. "Most all of those MPs were real young," he says. "There were some older career soldiers, but they were in positions that we didn't get to associate with them too much. The guards, though—they'd been drafted into the service in their late teens or early twenties."

J.T. and his buddies became friends with the young guards. "I don't think it was according to regulations, but they enjoyed having someone to talk to at night. They were from all over the country, and they were lonely, I guess. I don't think they were supposed to do it, but they'd let some of us sit in the back of the jeep and ride around with them. "

Weeks before any prisoners arrived, the MPEG guards were busy patrolling the camp and the town, keeping the various military personnel in line. That task included chasing after soldiers who visited the "bawdy" houses over in Shacktown and tracking down soldiers who went AWOL. Shacktown, as it was called then, was the hilltop neighborhood where most of Aliceville's black community lived. "Those MPs would drive up out front of a place, and the guys would run out the back door and take off down the hill."

J.T. lived in a house next to a vacant lot full of high weeds. Across the street was a house occupied by a young woman who had married one of the soldiers from the camp. When the soldier husband went AWOL, J.T. remembers watching with fascination as the MPs hid in the tall weeds day after day waiting for him to come home so they could catch him. "To us, at that age, combat couldn't have been any better than getting to watch that."

J.T. and his friends loved to go to the Palace Theater on Saturdays, as much for the battlefield updates in the MovieTone newsreels as for the movies and serials. "Being that age, we wanted to be in the battle and fight. Of course, we weren't old enough, but I remember that most all my friends and I would have loved to go into the service."

In April 1943, the flickering, boomingly dramatic newsreels carried footage of Japanese planes bombing American airfields in the Solomon Islands and of the fierce fighting in the Warsaw Ghetto. The boys would have cheered film clips of American naval ships shelling Attu Island in the Aleutians and musically enhanced scenes of the British Royal Air Force sending waves of planes over German industrial complexes in Stuttgart and Pilsen.

J.T. had older friends and family friends who did go to war, and he remembers how traumatic it was when someone didn't come back. "I knew Samuel Windle," he says with quiet respect as he scans a list of Aliceville servicemen killed in World War II.

"And Johnny Driver and Dawson Hall. And oh yes, Thomas Napoleon Griffin. We called him Nap. Most of them were students that got drafted."

J.T.'s parents worked at the cotton mill, and like many local families, they decided to supplement their income by renting a room to a married couple associated with the camp. J.T. and Earl Dean slept out on the screened porch, even when winter came, so their room could be rented out. "Most everyone in town did this. At the start, there were no quarters at the camp for married people, and even later, there weren't enough. Over a period of years, we rented to several couples."

Years later, a friend of the Junkins family flew to New York City to meet her husband's ship when he came in from a tour of peacetime duty with the Merchant Marine. During the ride from the airport to her hotel, the taxi driver picked up on the woman's southern accent and asked where she was from. "Oh well," said the driver. "I've been to Alabama. I was stationed in Aliceville, and my wife and I lived with Mr. and Mrs. Junkins while we were there."

Now a slim, soft-spoken gentleman in his early seventies, J.T. smiles at this memory. "It's just a small world. We were good friends of that woman's family. You never know where you're going to run up on some of these people."

Earlier in the year, Mayor Holmes Sanders had heard from Alabama Senator Lister Hill that the federal government had approved new housing for Camp Aliceville—one-story concrete block apartment units that could be rented to civilian employees like Ward Turner at reasonable rates. Now, Algernon Blair had received the $8,000 contract to construct forty-eight units during the next sixty days, and local sawmill owner B. F. (Johnny) Johnston had seized the opportunity to create a new business—a concrete block plant—so he could supply the block to Algernon Blair. The new units would offer every modern convenience and greatly ease the wartime housing shortage in Pickens County—maybe even to the point that kids like J.T. and Earl Dean Junkins could move back into their bedrooms.

Life in Aliceville and Camp Aliceville ticked along through April and May as local residents padded their bank accounts with extra rent and retail sales. Newly recruited soldiers practiced close order drills and wondered among themselves exactly what would be expected of them in the months to come.

On May 19, the Johnson Drug Company set up tables in its lobby and hosted a luncheon of chicken salad and strawberry shortcake to honor the 1943 graduating class of Aliceville High School. Dr. J. A. Johnson had opened his drugstore in Aliceville on May 19, fifteen years earlier, and wanted to celebrate the anniversary by honoring the twenty-two seniors. His guest list reflected the toll the war was taking, even at the high school level. Only five of the seniors were young men.

During the final week of May, heavy rains continued to saturate the county. A violent hailstorm struck between Carrollton and Pickensville, shredding corn stalks and cutting off cotton plants at ground level. In Sue Stabler's memory, it was also during that last week of May that the normally quiet and uneventful atmosphere of Aliceville began to rumble again with rumors about what kind of prisoners would occupy the internment camp—even more than it had rumbled when

Colonel Shriver and the construction crews arrived almost a year earlier.

On the very last day of May, the people of Aliceville discovered exactly which prisoners would be marched behind the barbed wire outside their town. The Germans were coming in on the Frisco—and not just any Germans.

Ammunition shot off. Arms and equipment destroyed. In accordance with orders received, the D. A. K. has fought itself to the condition where it can fight no more. The Deutsche Afrikakorps must rise again. Heia Safari.

• Lieutenant General Hans Cramer •
Afrikakorps Commander
May 13, 1943

CHAPTER FOUR
Atlantic Crossing

For Walter Felholter, captivity began with the same plodding drudgery he experienced in the last days of battle leading up to Good Friday. He was grateful that the English Tommies shared their canteens of cool water with him and his men before forcing them to move on. Walter's tongue returned to normal size, but his belly remained nearly empty. One or two hard crackers—that was all he received to eat during the first days of captivity.

He was handed a tag with information about his capture and told in halting German to wear it at all times. Then he was marched, with his hands up and clasped behind his visored field cap, from one small collecting point to another in northern Tunisia, often to the accompaniment of catcalls from passing columns of British soldiers. After several days, he arrived in a large encampment near Bone (now called Annaba), the principal harbor on the Mediterranean coast of eastern Algeria.

Food was as scarce here as it had been before capture. The British took pains to explain that they were not trying to starve their prisoners. Their own food rations were meager, too. The German U-boats had been too successful against their supply convoys, they said.

Walter learned quickly that the large tag fluttering from a cord pinned to his uniform was, in a sense, his meal ticket when food was available. Though he did not read English, another captive translated the words on the back of the tag: "No tag—no food. Do not lose or mutilate."

Nights were cold and so was the ground inside the various barbed wire enclosures. He was not given a blanket, and there were no tents. When rain came, he had no choice but to let it soak him and then endure the chafing dampness until the desert sun reappeared.

Eventually Walter arrived at a huge processing camp set up by American troops near the Algerian port city of Oran, far to the west of Algiers. Leopold Dolfuss and Karl Silberreis ended up in the same camp after the Americans captured them. They came by truck from Algiers. Others arrived by train, some in freight cars under the control of bitter French guards who allowed them to eat the food placed in the cars but gave them no opportunity to relieve themselves with dignity.

Both Walter and Leopold received superficial medical examinations and went through the unpleasant but necessary procedure of being deloused, probably with DDT, which the American military had recently discovered to be an effective killer of lice. With the huge numbers of soldiers and civilians crowded together in the war-torn regions of North Africa, lice had become proficient at transmitting typhus as they fed on human blood. The pyrethrum-based powders most often used to kill lice had not proved practical in battlefield areas because the powder had to be applied in a systematic manner and on a weekly basis. By May 1943, the United States was shipping millions of pounds of the more effective, less complicated DDT to war zones every month. They puffed it into the clothing and personal effects of prisoners from small, hand-pumped insecticide sprayers.

German prisoners arriving in Oran thought it a good sign that the seriously wounded among them were immediately transported to Allied military hospitals for treatment. As the able-bodied prisoners stood in line before makeshift reception tables in the open air, they watched in amusement as some of their fellow Germans took advantage of obvious language barriers and playfully ignored commands from their captors or gave misleading information about themselves. They were surprised to see American soldiers, in full view of their commanding officers, snatch Iron Cross medals and other decorations from the uniforms of Germans and pocket them as war souvenirs.

Every German soldier, regardless of rank or branch of service, carried a *Soldbuch,* a small fifteen-page booklet that functioned as a condensed personnel file in the field. It contained the soldier's height and weight, birth date and birthplace, parental and medical information, and information about types of training and duty. The inside cover carried a photo of the owner and his signature. These booklets were helpful in processing prisoners and sometimes provided useful intelligence information when combined with the information on the "meal ticket" tags issued at the time of capture. Unfortunately, overzealous souvenir hunters among the American guards often confiscated them to show off as souvenirs and, in doing so, made prisoner identification more difficult.

By the time of the final surrender in North Africa on May 12, three weeks after Walter Felholter's capture, more than two hundred-fifty thousand German and Italian soldiers were crammed into stark holding camps along the Mediterranean while the British and the Americans struggled to work out a good plan for dispersing and managing them.

According to an agreement between Great Britain and the United States at the beginning of the campaign, all prisoners captured in northwest Africa were to be held in American custody. For security reasons, both countries decided to send most of their German captives to the United States. Those held by American troops went first, and the numbers crossing the Atlantic quickly swelled to twenty thousand per month from May through October. The two countries evaluated Italian captives on the basis of security—low risk Italian prisoners would remain in North Africa to fill labor details, and high risk ones would join the Germans headed for places like Camp Aliceville in America.

Hermann Blumhardt's first days of captivity were similar to those of Walter Felholter and Leopold Dolfuss. Immediately after Hermann's small, exhausted unit surrendered on Saturday, April 24, German artillery in the area began firing in their direction. Four British guards hustled the captives eight miles back to an open stockade in the rear of the British line of attack. The stockade was makeshift, with barbed wire nailed at five-inch intervals up the sides of skinny, crooked sapling trunks pounded into the ground every few feet.

Hermann remembers that as they neared the stockade, a British soldier leaped out from a mess hall line and waved a pistol angrily in front of their faces. The guards were not ruffled by this behavior. They simply nudged the man back in line and directed their prisoners into the barbed wire stockade.

Here, Hermann, too, had only the ground for a bed, but he was grateful for the opportunity to stop marching. He fell asleep as soon as he was allowed to lie down and was soon oblivious to everything and everyone around him. He woke the next morning, feeling much better after his first good night's sleep in as many weeks as he could remember.

That afternoon, a British officer stepped into the stockade and ordered the prisoners to line up. He then counted them off in groups of ten and ordered those to whom he'd given the numbers 10, 20, 30, and 40 to step forward. Hermann was Number 20 and stepped forward with the other three. The officer motioned for these four to remain standing and ordered all the other prisoners to climb into several trucks that pulled up outside the stockade. Hermann remembers how devastated he was as he huddled with the other three and shared whispered speculations about what would happen to them.

The afternoon wore on, with the four men standing on the bare, fenced-in ground and the rest of the prisoners marking time in the beds of several trucks outside the stockade gate. When darkness fell, a sense of doom overpowered the four. They were certain they would soon be shot or hanged as some sort of example.

Then, suddenly, the British officer returned and ordered the prisoners in the trucks to climb down and step back inside the barbed wire. He offered no explanation, and Hermann has no idea what the purpose of this maneuver was. "It is an incident I will never forget," he has said. "To this day, I ponder what evil they had in mind."

Arnold Krammer, a professor of history at Texas A&M University who has written about the German POW experience in camps throughout the United States, suggests a more benign possible explanation: "Roads to the front lines were perpetually choked with military traffic, as convoys of trucks moved endlessly, bringing fresh troops and ammunition to the battle zone. Since the trucks generally returned empty after unloading their supplies, theater commanders decided to utilize them to take prisoners back to the processing stations. Squabbles over the use of such vehicles for POW evacuation were not uncommon,..." It is possible that such a squabble over truck use created the incident Hermann remembers.

Within a few days, Hermann and a crowd of others were "packed like sardines" into a freight car and transported by rail to another stockade, and then in a few days to another. Eventually, they, too, reached Oran on the coast. The aroma of fresh coffee is the detail Hermann remembers most clearly about climbing out of a freight car inside the stockade at Oran.

While inside this stockade, one of Hermann's fellow prisoners decided he would try to escape by posing as an Arab. The man took off his soldier's uniform, put on a long-sleeved white robe and scarf-like head cover he had somehow acquired, and slipped out of the compound. His pink skin and lack of awareness of local culture soon betrayed him, and he was brought back. By wearing Arab civilian clothing, the soldier had voided his status as a soldier and thus also voided his right to protection under the Geneva Convention. What impressed Hermann about this incident was the fact that the soldier had studied English for six years and was able to understand when the British officers who recaptured him talked about shooting him on the spot as a spy. "He immediately pleaded for his life and told them he wasn't a spy," says Hermann. "It took a lot of convincing, but they finally let him rejoin us in the stockade." Hermann made up his mind then that when he arrived at a prison camp in the United States, his first priority would be to learn English, the language of his captors.

The city of Oran, on the Mediterranean coast in northwest Algeria, came under Allied control in November 1942. By May 1943, it had evolved into a huge supply depot used to disperse troops and supplies throughout the regions of the North Africa campaign. When that campaign ended successfully, it became not only a supply depot for the planned assault on Sicily but also one of three primary holding sites for prisoners of war soon to be shipped to the United States. The other two POW holding sites were in western Morocco—Marrakesh, a railroad and caravan center at the foot of the High Atlas Mountains, and Casablanca, a seaport on the Atlantic Ocean and the site of the January 1943 meeting between Roosevelt and Churchill at which both men pledged their countries to fight the German Axis until it surrendered unconditionally.

When Lieutenant General Hans Cramer, commander of the *Afrikakorps*, sent his last message to the German High Command on May 13, he ended with the defiant declaration "*Heia Safari,*" a Swahili war cry the *Afrikakorps* had adopted as its own. Later in the day, General Kenneth Alexander, commander of the British

First Army in Tunisia, signaled to Winston Churchill that the Tunisian Campaign had ended. "All enemy resistance has ceased. We are the masters of the North African shores."

Even before the surrender on May 12, however, German prisoners were on their way from the Mediterranean and Atlantic coasts of North Africa to the United States. At least one large convoy of more than sixty ships weighed anchor in Oran on May 10 and spent the next three weeks zigzagging its way to New York City.

Prisoners were transported in all kinds of vessels, but the vast majority crossed the Atlantic in Liberty ships. These welded freight haulers had been built to carry jeeps, tanks, and ammunition—not human cargo—from American ports to the battlefields of Europe and North Africa. They were part of the Emergency Shipbuilding Program authorized by the U.S. Maritime Commission in 1941. Originally, there were to be no more than sixty Liberty ships, contracted under a lend-lease program to the British. After Pearl Harbor and America's entry into the war, however, sixteen American shipyards eventually produced more than twenty-five hundred of them.

Each ship was 441 feet long and 56 feet wide. Its five holds could carry more than nine thousand tons of cargo. In addition, airplanes, tanks, and locomotives were sometimes lashed to the deck. Each ship carried a crew of more than forty and anywhere from twelve to twenty-five Navy guards who could operate a stern gun, two bow guns, and six machine guns if the ship came under attack.

The Liberty ships, with their broad bows and wide beams, were anything but sleek. President Roosevelt nicknamed them "ugly ducklings," but they got the job done, and once the theater commanders decided to fill them up with prisoners for the return voyage to America, the Liberty ships did double duty for the rest of the war.

Walter Felholter did not know where he was going when an American military escort guard checked his name off a list as he boarded one of the Liberty ships in the harbor at Oran on May 10. Another guard went through his pockets, looking for metal objects like mirrors or spoons that might be used to signal German submarines. His cheap pocket watch had already disappeared into the hands of a less discriminating American souvenir hunter than the one who first searched his pockets in the desert.

Walter was directed down a narrow passageway into the ship's hold. For twenty-one days, he endured most hours of the day and night sitting or lying with his one blanket on the iron planks of a freight compartment well below deck. One of his strongest memories is of the smell. There was no water to wash with and one toilet for far too many men. Added to that, on most days, was the sour stench of the seasickness that plagued many of the POWs during the rough ocean crossing.

Walter remembers feeling safe from attack while aboard ship, even though he knew German submarines were patrolling the Atlantic. "We were going zigzag," he has said, "and we were on the inside with destroyers on the outside so that a U-boat could not penetrate the outer ring."

Ultimate authority over the prisoners on board the Liberty ships and other troop transports rested with American military police escort guard (MPEG) units like those already assigned to Camp Aliceville in the spring of 1943. Prisoners received information from them about abandon-ship emergency drills, blackout regulations, meal provisions, and debarkation procedures. On most ships, prisoners were fingerprinted and had their processing forms completed while at sea. They also received a message, through translators, that eased the fears of some about what would happen to them in America: "You are now under the control of the Army of the United States. The United States is a party to the Geneva Convention of 1929…and has clearly indicated that it intends to abide by its provisions. You will be humanely treated and protected according to international law."

It was the German NCOs among the captives, however, who enforced day-to-day discipline just as they had on the battlefield. Yvonne E. Humphrey, a second lieutenant in the Army Nurse Corps, considered the discipline of the German NCOs extreme. She made a return trip to the United States aboard one of the ships carrying German prisoners from North Africa as well as wounded American soldiers. "If a [German] soldier failed to salute a superior with sufficient snap," she wrote in the *American Journal of Nursing* in September 1943, "he would be severely reprimanded or perhaps confined to quarters." She told of one young German enlisted man who tossed some apples and peelings overboard—a serious offense in wartime. His German superior locked him in solitary confinement on bread and water for three days.

Most days the prisoners went on deck in shifts for an hour or two of fresh air. This was a relief, but not much of one. With two thousand men crammed onto one small ship, several hundred were on deck at one time, making it almost impossible to walk around freely. They edged up and down the deck, stretching their limbs as much as they could, most still wearing the dank, sodden uniforms they'd been captured in. Their American guards, in clean coats and caps, stood on the bulkhead with guns at the ready, serving as constant reminders to the proud Germans of their humiliating status as captives.

Hermann Blumhardt probably made the Atlantic crossing in the same large convoy, but like Walter, he does not remember the name of his ship. He remembers that it was a converted cargo ship and that the cots he and his comrades slept on were stacked three high in the freight compartments.

At boarding, Hermann received a meal card, which he was to present for punching at nine in the morning and again at three in the afternoon. "The child-size portions we received only whetted our appetites," he remembers. "There was absolutely no way of getting seconds or cheating with that punched card." The men watched each other carefully for signs of seasickness, hoping to gain an extra portion from someone who had lost his appetite.

Hermann stared with envy at the American sailors who heaped their trays with plentiful food. One day as he returned his empty tray after devouring his own small meal, Hermann passed the garbage can and spotted two slices of white bread that had just been tossed in. "I looked cautiously around me, then reached in and was so happy with those two slices of bread, but a guard poked my shoulder. He pointed at the bread and then at the garbage can. I knew what he meant, and sad as I was, I tossed the bread back into the garbage can."

Although the danger of attack was always present, no ships carrying German prisoners of war were sunk in the Atlantic during World War II. Heino Erichsen was nineteen years old when he surrendered in Tunisia and was put aboard a Liberty ship headed for the United States. "I was scared stiff," he told an interviewer many years later. "I was glad it was over. I figured if I made it to America, I would be all right, but until I got there, it was very much a toss-up."

Heino's biggest fear was that the ship would be torpedoed while he was locked below in a freight compartment. That fear almost played out about the time his ship reached the mid-Atlantic, on its way to Norfolk, Virginia, the headquarters of the Atlantic Fleet. Heino remembers that the ship's commander ordered all prisoners to put on their life vests because U-boats were in the vicinity. The commander then sent a cable to the International Red Cross asking that the German Navy high command notify its U-boats to leave their convoy alone because four of the ships were carrying German prisoners. The order came back that the four ships with prisoners should pull out of the convoy, leave all of their lights on both day and night to signal who they were, and change course for a different port. Eventually the ship made its way safely to Boston, and Heino Erichsen traveled on to a POW camp in Texas.

Horst Uhse was captured near the end of the North Africa campaign and sat for several days on the barren ground of the

POW enclosure at Mateur in Tunisia. From there, he was sent west to Constanten for interrogation and then to Marrakesh in Morocco. His journey to Marrakesh was, in his own words, "a horrible ordeal." The men were loaded into small French boxcars that became unbearably hot once the sliding doors slammed shut. The French left American rations and polluted water in the cars, but the men had only empty ration cans in which to relieve themselves. Long before they reached Morocco, most of them were miserably sick with diarrhea.

Before being sent to Casablanca for shipment across the Atlantic, Horst endured bouts of jaundice and malaria that left him weak and emaciated. At Casablanca, he boarded the troop transport *West Point* along with several hundred other wounded and sick prisoners of war and learned he was headed for Boston in the United States.

Erwin Schulz, the 999 "punishment battalion" soldier from Berlin who had deserted and then surrendered to a group of Moroccans, also left Casablanca on an American hospital ship, but he was bound for New York City. This ship, like the one Army Nurse Yvonne Humphrey wrote about, was transporting not only prisoners but also a large number of wounded American soldiers. Erwin says many of the pro-Nazi German prisoners on board harbored the hope that a German U-boat would suddenly appear, attack the ship, and liberate them. According to Erwin, these prisoners would stuff themselves with the good food in the mess hall and then boast that the Germans would "*machen die Amerikaner kaput!*" (destroy the Americans).

Yvonne Humphrey, the American army nurse, wrote of the good food and good treatment received by prisoners aboard these combination ships (carrying American wounded as well as German prisoners). She speculated that the prisoners' first meal on board—meat and potatoes—was probably the best they'd had since before the African campaign. Each prisoner also received an ample supply of cigarettes.

Yvonne viewed the boyish-looking German enlistees and draftees as complete contradictions to the fanatical Nazi political philosophy on which they'd been raised. Most were between nineteen and twenty-two with round pink cheeks and fair hair. Communicating with her meager German and their "smattering of English," she learned that most had been in the army for two to five years. She developed the impression they were willing to cooperate with American officers and respect military authority. They liked the good food and cigarettes they'd received and also the "dignity and respect—if not…warmth and enthusiasm" with which they'd been treated.

Yvonne drew a clear distinction between the cheerful and cooperative German enlisted personnel and their more arrogant officers. When she commented to one of the officers that she was impressed at what good workers the German soldiers were, he answered her by saying, "But of course, *Fräulein*. Everyone in Germany works. We are trained to work and fight. There is no time for pleasures. And so we shall win this war!"

During the course of their Atlantic voyage, Yvonne Humphrey administered anesthesia for an emergency appendectomy on one German prisoner and provided special nursing care to another with second degree burns. She also helped treat prisoners whose feet were covered with sores and blisters from walking in poorly made footwear—hobnailed boots with cloth uppers that gave the foot no support.

She noted in her article that several of the German prisoners were quite musical. "From somewhere or other we dug up a few instruments for them and every night they gave us a concert," she wrote. "They were quite good and it was pleasant to hear some of their fine old drinking songs and waltzes out in the middle of a war-infested ocean. It took our minds off the blackout, the threat of subs, and the general uncertainty of our trip home."

After twenty-one days, the convoy that had left Oran on May 10 arrived in New York harbor, where the German POWs were astonished at what they saw when they crowded on deck for their first view of the United States. It was foggy that morning, but as the sun rose and the skyline of the city came into view, the Germans muttered among themselves in surprise that the huge skyscrapers and the Statue of Liberty were still standing. Propaganda in Germany and at the front had led them to believe that German air raids had leveled many major American cities. Early that evening, they were also surprised to see the lights of the city blink on while motorcars with bright headlights progressed steadily along the roadways. All of Europe had been blacked out at night since 1939, yet here in America, life appeared to be continuing as if the world were perfectly normal.

For most of the German POWs from North Africa, the first stop on American soil was Camp Shanks in Rockland County, just up the Hudson River from the piers of New York City. Residents of Orangeburg in Rockland County, New York, had something in common with Tom Parker, the young Alabama dairy farmer whose land had been appropriated for the bulk of Camp Aliceville. In September 1942, 130 Orangeburg families learned that their homes, yards, and farms—2,040 acres of them—were to be seized for the immediate construction of Camp Shanks. This new camp would expand the army's facilities near the Atlantic and streamline the transportation of troops and equipment to Europe. During the course of the war, 1.3 million American soldiers would be processed here before being shipped overseas.

Just after Camp Shanks opened in May 1943, the government decided to use it for a second task—processing North Africa prisoners arriving in New York City. When the first convoys arrived from Oran, procedures were still being developed for disembarking prisoners and transporting them to their destination camps. The head of transportation for the army was given the task of arranging for the right number of railroad cars, figuring a timetable of stops on each journey, and guaranteeing security along the way.

During the summer of 1943, seventy-two POW camps opened in the United States. The majority were located in the South and the Southwest where they could help alleviate agriculture labor shortages and where they would not constitute a sabotage threat to the country's war industries. The number of camps would grow steadily as the war continued. By June 1944, there would be 300 camps on American soil, and by April 1945, the number would jump to 150 base camps with 340 branch camps.

It was the responsibility of the commanding general at the Port of Embarkation (Camp Shanks in this case) to transfer POW responsibility to the commanding general of the service command where a camp was located (for example, Camp Aliceville in the Fourth Service Command). It was the responsibility of the Intelligence Division to compile POW reports that included a breakdown of the number of officers, litter cases, protected personnel, and enlisted men. These reports also listed the place of capture, the age of the prisoner, and any other useful intelligence information (for example, which prisoners might merit special attention as informers).

Just after these procedures were set up, thousands of German POWs like Walter Felholter, Leopold Dolfuss, Hermann Blumhardt, Bruno Schneider, Theo Klein, and Erwin Schulz began to arrive in New York on ships that docked at the long piers on the west side of Manhattan. Most likely, these men were ferried across the Hudson River and then marched the four miles up to Camp Shanks—a reverse version of the journey experienced by American soldiers leaving for the battlefields of Europe.

At Camp Shanks, the main activity for the POWs was another thorough delousing procedure with DDT puffed into their clothing and belongings. Those designated to be sent to Alabama—more than a thousand men in the first contingent—remained at Camp Shanks for less than forty-eight hours before boarding three special trains for their long journey south.

The railroad cars used for the transfer of prisoners were specially prepared for security, and few escapes were made or even attempted. Some prisoners who traveled more than one hundred hours by train from Boston to Camp Trinidad in

Colorado or other western state destinations concluded that the Americans had taken them in circles in order to mislead them about the size of the country. They couldn't believe America was so big.

Government records contain complaints from some early POWs who traveled by train from New York and Norfolk to camps around the country. They didn't like having to sleep sitting up or being confined to their seats for hours and hours at a time. The War Department answered these charges by acknowledging that it had an obvious lack of experience in these types of transports. It pointed out the huge numbers—ten thousand prisoners on twenty-six separate trains on one particular day in June, for example. By September 1943, the department reported that it had made provisions for exercise and for better riding conditions.

Hermann Blumhardt had never heard of Aliceville, Alabama, when guards prodded him along between two rows of slim green fence pickets in the railroad yard in New York City, but he was pleasantly surprised to discover that the train car designated to take him to this strange place was for passengers. It was certainly a vast improvement over the boxcar that had transported him to Oran in North Africa. "Frisco," it said on the side, in gold letters. A huge black steam engine belched and pawed at the head of the train, champing to get on down the tracks. Hermann climbed the three metal steps, gazing up at another guard on top of the car who stood with his Tommy gun stiffly in front of his chest and stared straight ahead.

Hermann was amazed at the comfort when he moved down the aisle, removed his field cap, and folded it with his blanket on the shelf above his upholstered seat. He dropped into the cushioned seat, exhausted and longing for some fragment of stability in his life. All he really cared about at that moment was somewhere to sleep, even sitting up, and somewhere to eat a decent meal.

The journey took two full days. As the cars swayed down the tracks in a lulling rhythm, the men began to relax. The routines of their captivity were finally slowing to a manageable pace, and that felt good.

Walter Felholter was aboard the same train. He stared out the windows at the lush, green countryside, surprised, as he had been in New York City, at how calm and untouched by war the landscape seemed. When the train passed through cities, the POWs were amazed at the abundance of automobiles. Some speculated that the Americans were taking them on a special route so they wouldn't see any devastation.

As the train traveled south through Virginia and Tennessee and into Alabama, the prisoners discussed what they thought might happen next. There were rumors that they would become slave labor in the fields and factories of America, that they would be beaten and go hungry.

Three more months would pass before Wilhelm Schlegel and his poet friend made the train trip down to Alabama. On the morning of May 13, 1943, three days after the convoy carrying Walter Felholter and Hermann Blumhardt left Oran, Wilhelm and his friend blended with the sun-scorched panorama of twenty thousand German captives inside the massive, flat prison compound near Mateur, west of Tunis. Endless clusters of dejected men sat idly on the baked beige ground, bitter about their state of affairs and trying to imagine their fate.

Wilhelm was grateful to discover that there was plenty of clear water to drink, but food was another matter. He continued to experience the same wrenching hunger cramps he had in the final weeks of the military campaign on Cape Bon. Like Walter Felholter, Wilhelm was warned to take good care of the information tag tied to his uniform if he wanted to eat when food was available.

Over the next three weeks, Wilhelm puzzled about why he was constantly being marched from one camp to another. Each new camp was similar to the previous one—a flat, dusty expanse surrounded by a crude barbed wire enclosure. In no place that the prisoners stopped was there any kind of shelter from the glaring heat of the day or from the sometimes bone-deep cold of the night.

Wilhelm and his friend spent the night of May 23 in a transfer camp at Souk-el-Khamis and then moved the next morning to a place called Souk-el-Arras, which the poet described as being "steep as a mountainside." The ground was so uneven that the men joked they would have to sleep standing up so they wouldn't roll into each other.

By now, they were filthy. The grit of sand had invaded not only their clothing but also their eyes and ears and every sweaty fold of skin. There was water to drink, but never enough to squander on washing.

Three miserable days passed, with the men sitting and sulking. The one welcome diversion was a few rain showers one afternoon that soothed their skin and broke the merciless glare of the sun.

Wilhelm became increasingly depressed and bitter. This miserable existence was very different from the enthusiastic marches into battle a few months ago. Sometimes he closed his eyes and tried to hear again in his mind the strains of the militant melodies he and his comrades had sung in praise of the *Vaterland* as they marched along:

Wenn wir marschieren, Ziehen wir zum Deutschen Tor hinaus; Schwarzbraunes Mädel, du bleibst zu Haus... (When we march, we set out through the German gate. My dark maiden, you remain at home.)

Their weapons were gone, but sometimes Wilhelm imagined, as he sat, how impressively the men could have presented themselves if they had had weapons. Even now, under these conditions, he was determined to remain a proud German soldier dedicated to serving his country.

After darkness fell on May 26, the men moved on again, marching in a guarded line through the town of Souk-el-Arras to the train station. They marched proudly, singing since no one told them not to:

Der Wirt muss borgen, er soll nicht rappelköpfig sein, sonst kehrn wir morgen beim andern sein. (The innkeeper better give us credit. He should not be stubborn, or tomorrow we will take our drinking business somewhere else.)

At the train station, the men were prodded into boxcars for the uncomfortable transfer to Bone—the processing camp that had been Walter Felholter's first stop on his journey towards Alabama. If the open-air stockades in Tunisia and the boxcars that transported the men to Bone had been unpleasant, they were nothing compared to the misery of the next leg of Wilhelm's journey—a four-day ship's passage from Bone to Oran. According to the poem composed by Wilhelm's friend, it would be best to remember this ordeal only briefly in the overall scheme of one's life. French deGaullists, soldiers who harbored a bitter, two-war hatred of all things German, guarded the prisoners. "We lay like herrings in a barrel," wrote the poet. "A heat, a sweat, a smelly atmosphere, it was a mess."

The Germans were hauled on deck in groups once a day for fifteen minutes, just long enough to grab a breath of fresh air and relieve themselves. In the evening, at seven, the hatches slammed shut from above, and the men were left to cope as best they could until morning with their stench and thirst and hunger, and also with the sicknesses these conditions allowed to fester.

When the ship finally docked in Oran, the prisoners were turned over to the Americans and processed at an open-air reception center. Wilhelm found the behavior of these new captors amusing. The Yankees (Americans), as he thought of all of them, were hesitant. Perhaps, he decided, they were awed by the opportunity to be in charge of real-life Nazi prisoners. He spent the next week in yet another open-air holding camp, grateful for its wide-open spaces, after the cramped and putrid ship that had brought him to Oran.

Each day the men watched the harbor where American ships were taking on long lines of prisoners and wondered how soon they themselves would board. Wilhelm hoped the ordeal at sea, though longer, would not be as bad as the passage from Bone. Perhaps they would be sent to England or Scotland. Some were saying they might go all the way across the Atlantic to the United States.

On June 9, Wilhelm and those with him were surprised to be ordered back into a land transport truck. Puzzled, they stood with their feet braced in the truck bed, gripped its side panels as they lurched back out into the desert, and squinted for a last glimpse of the blue Mediterranean as it disappeared beyond the northern horizon. On and on they traveled, a full 118 miles south to another temporary camp in the desert.

Here, the men were divided into two groups for searching and delousing, and then assigned, four at a time, to tents designed for two. The poet declared his certainty that there must be nicer places out in the middle of the desert but added that at least here the men had shelter, even if it was crowded.

Wilhelm soon discovered an unwelcome trade-off. He now had shelter, but as if in cruel exchange, he was plagued by thirst. The water facilities were inadequate, and the Americans magnified this problem by shutting down what trickle there was whenever they felt like it. A pipe has burst, they would say, and then laugh. Or, the pump has broken down. According to the poet, the cooks played similar games with the food.

One morning the prisoners were ordered to clasp their hands behind their heads and march outside the camp. While they stood in the blazing sun under one set of guards, another set searched through every tent. "Oh, what a horror!" wrote the poet. "They found all sorts of terrible things—little knives, scissors, mirrors."

The prisoners sought ways to keep their spirits up in spite of what they viewed as unfair treatment and in spite of the constant dirt and dust, compounded frequently by fierce sandstorms. When the air cleared, they staged boxing matches and organized soccer games on fields marked out with sticks in the African sand. Friendly rivalries cropped up among the various camps within the compound. Camp Five housed Italians—"war brothers" of the Germans. The Italians also knew how to "handle the leather" (play soccer), and a sports rivalry developed between the two countries.

On July 13, after more than a month, Wilhelm's group received orders to vacate the camp. The poet painted the scene from his perspective, referring to himself and the other prisoners. In spite of the taunting tricks played on them, these German soldiers could not be broken in their morale. The French and American guards marveled, he wrote, that these were still true men and that they still looked impressive as they marched and sang their way to the train station:

Des Wirtes Tochter, die trägt ein blaukariertes Kleid. (The innkeeper's daughter wears a blue-checked dress.)

Provisions were short on the train journey north, and Transfer Camp 127, just outside Oran, was not a pleasant place. It had deteriorated considerably since their last visit.

This time, Wilhelm, the poet, and the others boarded a troop ship in port just as they had watched thousands of others do more than a month earlier. Wilhelm wondered if there was significance to the name of the ship—the *Wilhelmina de Alegonde*—because it was close to his own name. It was a Dutch ship with a Dutch captain—the ship's name perhaps referring to Marnix van St. Aldegonde who wrote the Dutch national anthem about William of Orange in the 1500s. Thirty ships sailed together, surrounded by several destroyers.

Although the Dutch captain served with the Allies, the German prisoners identified more easily with him than with the English colonel who controlled their lives aboard ship. The prisoners were not told their destination, and for most of the journey they were locked below the hatches so they would not have the opportunity to signal U-boats. The poet wrote of their frustration at this. "That which is forbidden tears at one the most," he explained. It was not that they wanted to contact U-boats, he said, but rather that they were curious to see where they were and where they were going.

Smoking was strictly forbidden aboard ship, but some of the prisoners apparently found a way—blue smoke could often be sniffed and seen as it curled around the corner from the shower room. The food was poor and sparse, but it was palatable and better than what they'd had in the desert. There were rumors that some of the prisoners were eating better, along with speculation about what information they might be trading for that luxury. Every morning at eleven o'clock, a signal announced inspection, and the English colonel came along with his monocle and his assistant, nodding at the prisoners' complaints and concerns and moving on.

Wilhelm's stomach was still growling when the *Wilhelmina de Alegonde* docked in Glasgow, Scotland, on July 26. "Il Duce [Mussolini] has been captured," the guards announced to their prisoners in nonchalant but triumphant tones. "Italy has capitulated."

The Germans pondered this news as they settled in for a train journey into the interior of Scotland, enjoying richly upholstered and comfortable passenger cars like those Walter Felholter and Hermann Blumhardt had occupied on their journey from New York to Aliceville, Alabama, a few weeks earlier. Most concluded that the report about Mussolini was probably English propaganda designed to deflate German egos.

In fact, the situation in Italy was not so simple. Benito Mussolini had been the Fascist dictator of Italy for twenty-one years and had entered World War II as an Axis partner of Hitler in June 1940 after Germany conquered France. He sent his troops to fight the British in North Africa, invaded neighboring Greece, and joined Germany in attacking the Soviet Union and declaring war on the United States. His downfall began when American, Canadian, and British forces invaded Sicily from North Africa early in July 1943 and then bombed Rome.

On July 25, King Victor Emmanuel of Italy politely dismissed Mussolini after the Fascist Grand Council gave him a vote of no confidence. He ordered military police to place the deposed dictator in an ambulance and hustle him off in disgrace to a jail in Rome. The king then worked to help strip Mussolini of his power, form a new government without Fascist members, and begin negotiations with the Allies.

The news conveyed to the German POWs when they arrived in Scotland the next day was partially correct. Mussolini had been deposed and was in custody, but Italy did not surrender officially and unconditionally to the Allies until September. Even then, Hitler sent *Luftwaffe* paratroopers to perform a daring rescue from a mountaintop ski hotel so he could set Mussolini up as puppet ruler of the Italian Social Republic in northern Italy. This brutal regime, which lasted until April 1945, was recognized only by Germany, its various other satellite puppets, and Japan.

At the end of their train journey in Scotland, the German POWs spilled out of their comfortable passenger cars and enjoyed a good stretch. Since it had not been forbidden, they broke into song once more:

Weg mit den Sorgen, weg mit der Widerwärtigkeit! Schwarzbraunes Mädel, du wirst mein Weib. (Away with care, away with unpleasantness. My dark maiden, you'll become my woman.)

The Teutonic words and melody reverberated through the trees as the Germans made their way through a dense Scottish forest in Lanarkshire County. Here, the weather was a stark contrast to the desert heat of little more than a week earlier. It was cold and damp in the daytime, even in July, and no sunshine slanted down between the thick stands of trees. The poet, who often chose historical context for his verses, considered the possibility that the fathers of these German POWs might have marched into this same forest as captives during the Great War earlier in the century.

Still singing, the Germans entered a clearing and were ordered to count off into small groups. As always, when they acquired a new set of guards, the men were searched thoroughly. By now, there was little left to be confiscated, but the Germans noted that these new guards had obviously been searching prisoners for some time. Their "sticky fingers" missed nothing worth taking, no matter how well concealed, and they were quite skilled at ripping remaining insignia from German uniforms to relish as souvenirs.

After the searches and the usual disinfecting procedures, the Germans moved into a cluster of Quonset huts known as Camp Douglas, where they finally received more nourishing food. The best of it was eating potatoes again. No one could remember the last time he'd tasted a simple boiled potato.

On July 29, an Allied interrogation process began. Groups of Germans were moved to a separate building lined with tiny cells—an environment they quickly concluded was designed to frighten them into divulging information. The English had assembled a German-speaking interrogation team—Polish military officers, German emigrants, anyone they could find who could conduct the questioning in German.

The questions began in a friendly tone, but when none of the captured Germans confessed to having been anything but kitchen help, baggage handlers, or water truck drivers during their service in the German army, the questioners began to scold and yell. They placed their pistols on their chests while they waited for answers. They issued the truly ominous threat—"We'll pack you off to Russia and let the Soviets deal with you."

Sometimes the interrogators stuck Hitler postage stamps to the interrogation chair seat. "Do you know what you are sitting on with your Nazi ass?" they asked, with their sneering faces up close. When the German sitting on the chair answered no, they laughed and told him, "You're sitting on your Nazi *Führer*, that's what, you pig."

The questioning lasted only a few days. The Germans endured the long hours in groups of ten, waiting in cells designed for two—so narrow that one or two at a time had to stand up so others could sit or lie down. They were served a bucket of thin, watery soup and told to make it last for two days. And all the while, men were pulled out one or two at a time and dragged away for more questioning.

The poet has left no record of what information might have been sought or revealed during this process, but the interrogators finished their work with the group by August 2. Then they sorted the men alphabetically and marched them back to Glasgow, where they boarded the troopship *Pasteur* for the voyage across the Atlantic to America.

The *Pasteur* had a short, but interesting history. Built in France in 1939, the luxury ocean liner was designed to carry well-heeled passengers from French ports to South America. With the outbreak of war, however, her maiden voyage from Bordeaux to Buenos Aires was cancelled. Instead, the ship sailed from Brest to Halifax, Nova Scotia, on June 2, 1940—taking part with several other civilian and military ships in a mission to rescue and preserve French gold reserves in Canada.

When France fell to the Germans later in June, the Allies quickly seized the *Pasteur* as a war prize, painted her war-time gray, and converted her to a troopship. The *Pasteur* flew the British flag and continued operation with the Cunard-White Star Line, which also put the *Queen Mary* and later the *Queen Elizabeth* into service as troop transports. Considered the third fastest ship afloat at the time, the *Pasteur* could steam fast enough to make most of her troop crossings alone—without a warship escort and without the slower pace of a convoy. Because she could change course every six or seven minutes, the *Pasteur* was not considered vulnerable to submarines which required ten minutes to track the straight line of a ship and then launch a torpedo.

Once on board the *Pasteur*, Wilhelm Schlegel and those with him followed their guards through narrow passageways and down steep flights of metal stairs to a large open area furnished with nothing but picnic-style tables and hammocks. Having endured two other recent voyages as a prisoner, Wilhelm stared up at the low ceiling and wondered how long it would be before he would be allowed to move back up those passageways and breathe fresh air again.

The ship sailed the same day. Once out on the open sea, she began to pitch and roll among the huge waves. Those not used to sea travel soon fouled the space below deck with their vomit, and the first business of the voyage became organizing mop crews to clean up the mess. The latrine consisted of a long room with a trough of running water extending the length of it. There were boards on each side for seating, and at any given moment during the first few days, it was not surprising to find twenty or thirty white-faced men sitting on these boards and retching into the trough.

That evening, there was much laughter among the non-seasick men as they went through all kinds of clumsy moves, trying to figure out the best way to climb in and out of the hammocks that would be their sleeping quarters for the next seven or eight nights. Once they finally fell into them, sleep was quick and easy, swinging with the roll of the ship.

By day, they were allowed short stints on deck, where they were surprised to discover that there were no other ships in sight—no destroyers and no other transports—just an occasional school of flying fish and dappled waves stretching off in the distance. Someone with knowledge of navigation explained that the ship sat shallow in the water, which made her fast enough to outrun U-boat threats. The shallowness in the water also accounted for the strong pitch and roll, even in calm seas.

When the *Pasteur* reached New York at the end of the first week of August, the German POWs were taken by ferry up to Camp Shanks. There, like those who'd arrived in June, Wilhelm Schlegel and his poet friend were deloused and disinfected in a huge metal building and then marched under heavy guard to a Frisco passenger train that would transport them south to Alabama.

Wilhelm remembers how luxurious that final leg of the journey seemed to him, after all he'd been through. To his surprise, he traveled to Alabama in a passenger car made by the Pullman Company of Chicago, a car he later described as being "like the Mercedes of trains" by European standards.

In just a short while, we heard the train whistle off to the North and in a minute or so the steam engine pulled the long passenger train into the yard. It stopped right at the highway crossing, about thirty yards from where we were standing. A hush fell over the crowd as the train doors opened and out walked about 300 German veterans of Rommel's Afrika Korps. They lined up in an orderly formation in the street, ready for a command to move out.

• Robert Hugh Kirksey •
With Me

CHAPTER FIVE
Germans on the Frisco!

On Tuesday morning, June 1, 1943, the Aliceville Arts Club held its last meeting before a summer break. Members gathered at the home of Mrs. T. H. Sanders for an old-fashioned country breakfast of tomato juice cocktail, broiled country ham, rice, egg omelets, flour muffins, strawberry jam, and coffee. The serving table was centered with a bouquet of sweet peas, and Mrs. Wallace S. Kirksey presided over a brief business meeting. Twice within the coming year, Mrs. Kirksey would take on the traditional duties of mother-of-the-bride as two of her daughters, Bobbie and Edwina, married United States army officers who'd come to Aliceville as part of Headquarters Company.

The summer visiting season had begun. Carolyn Ray came down for a few days from the tiny college town of Montevallo to visit her cousin. Sue Stabler and Sam McCaa and his wife went up to Birmingham to visit some of their relatives.

Military personnel were snapping up living quarters offered by local residents. Captain David J. Klapman, a staff member at the prison camp hospital, moved his wife and daughter from rented rooms over in Carrollton into an apartment in the George Downer Jr. home in Aliceville.

The first week of June, Aliceville residents used Ration Stamp No. 24 to purchase one pound of coffee or No. 17 to purchase a pair of shoes. In keeping with the national effort to conserve fuel for the war effort, the newspaper warned local drivers not to be caught driving more than 35 miles per hour if they wanted to keep their gas supply and tire replacement privileges and avoid having their names published. "It's a pity that a civilian on a business trip can't make over 35, while an army officer can make 80 going to and from his work," the newspaper editorialized. "But such is the case. A uniform gives a fellow lots of privileges."

The *Pickens County Herald and West Alabamian* makes no mention, but the ladies attending the Arts Club breakfast meeting must have discussed the pending arrival of the first prisoners of war. Rumors were all over town that week about the blond "supermen" who would soon occupy the camp. Sue Stabler was a member of the Arts Club, and she remembers hearing that the soon-to-arrive POWs were the pride of the German army, members of the feared and famous *Afrikakorps*—well educated, superbly fit, and fiercely loyal to the Nazi party. Most likely, Mrs. Kirksey and the other ladies expressed relief that the prisoners soon to be locked up outside their town would be German rather than Japanese. The "powder keg" Jap camp they'd feared earlier in the year would not come to be. German enemies at least looked more like Americans, and some Aliceville families, like the Stablers, actually had German ancestors. Although Hitler and his fanatical Nazism had taken over their country, German families had a European cultural heritage much more familiar than Asian cultural heritage.

E.B. Walker was a teenager up in Birmingham. He'd just landed a summer job with a company located right next to the Frisco railroad tracks (near where the Birmingham-Jefferson Civic Center is now). Those tracks ran through Birmingham, then down through Tuscaloosa to Aliceville, on to York, Alabama, and finally to Mobile on the Gulf Coast.

E.B. loved the wail of train whistles and the rhythmic chug and hiss of steam engines as trains passed by each day while he worked. On Wednesday morning, June 2, he was surprised to glance up and see armed military guards posted rigidly on the platforms between the passenger cars of one train. "What's going on?" he asked a coworker.

"That's the train carrying the Nazis down to Aliceville," he was told. E.B. was fascinated, and the memory of that day stayed with him the rest of his life.

Down in Pickens County, the skies turned gunmetal gray and threatened rain—as if there hadn't been enough downpours already that spring. Throughout the morning, subtle rumblings of thunder rolled among the clouds to the west. Behind the clouds, the sun climbed towards noon, but the rain did not come down. The temperature and the humidity climbed, too, so that the air became almost too thick to breathe.

As word spread that a special Frisco passenger train would arrive late that very day, shopkeepers shut their doors early. Telephones wires hummed all over the county, and a steady stream of humanity began to make its way in the direction of the train depot over by Highway 17.

Sue Stabler received a telephone call from her husband, Gerald, at the funeral home in town. He told her the first contingent of prisoners would come in on the Frisco around five o'clock. Sue was with her sister, Louise Griffith, and her friend, Anne Meek Cunningham, when Gerald called. She immediately got in her car and drove herself, Louise, and Anne Meek towards the depot. She took the back way and turned into a lot shaded by a large grove of pecan trees, parking just thirty feet or so from the highway near the railroad crossing. The serene pecan grove was a perfect retreat where the women could gather and wait on a sultry summer afternoon. Pecan trees grow tall and stately, and their thickly leafed branches spread out as wide as sixty feet, offering plenty of cooling shade.

As the women left the car, they spotted dust-covered army trucks parked by the side of the road, and the Red Cross ambulance with them. Crowds of townspeople clustered in whatever shade they could find all along the route to the camp, waiting for their first glimpse of the hated Nazis.

Johnny Johnston parked his car across the street from the railroad crossing, too. Because he owned a local sawmill and was planning to contract with the army for labor from some of the prisoners, he was eager to see what they would be like. Johnny had his wife, son, and daughter with him, and they all got out, spread a quilt on the hood of the car, and sat there to watch the arrival. P. M. (Pep) Johnston, the boy who sat on the car hood with his parents and sister that afternoon, remembers that nobody seemed seriously uneasy. Everybody was just curious, mostly.

Robert Hugh Kirksey's father, Robert (R.J.) Kirksey, was chairman of the local Red Cross chapter, and he got the word about the POWs through them. Robert Hugh had just completed his junior year at The Citadel. Because of the war, the entire Class of 1944 had recently been called to active duty. In March, they'd gone up to Fort Jackson in South Carolina for induction into the United States Army. Then they'd returned to The Citadel to complete the college year. For these young men, there would be no senior year filled with the rewards of their hard-earned status—no leave privileges or barracks privileges, no superior rank in the corps of cadets. Just active combat duty as soon as they were fully trained.

At the beginning of June, the army granted Robert Hugh ten days' leave before requiring him to report for basic training at Fort McClellan over near Anniston in northeast Alabama. On the afternoon of June 2, he was chatting with his father in the office at his uncle's general store when the call came from the Red Cross about the arrival of the POWs.

"We jumped in Daddy's car and headed over to the area of the depot," Robert Hugh remembers. "We left the car and walked out into a vacant field just west of the tracks and south of the state highway which ran west toward the camp."

By this time, army officials had issued an order for civilians to stay inside their homes during the transfer of prisoners from the train to the camp, but Robert Hugh and his father could see that this order was being ignored. Everybody in town was milling about. Even those who'd obeyed orders and stayed home were out in their yards, standing on tiptoe for frequent peeks at the highway from behind neatly trimmed front hedges. There was also an order not to take pictures, but judging from the many dramatic photographs that have survived, this order was also ignored.

Men in rolled-up shirtsleeves and well-worn fedoras, and some in overalls, stood on front porches or sat on the railings with their wives and children. MPEG guards moved up and down the road, keeping order and insisting, at the very least, that no civilians set foot out in the street.

Robert Hugh remembers how folks felt about the spectacle that day. "People wanted to see for themselves. Are they the kind of soldiers we've been seeing on newsreels and in *Life* magazine and places like that? With boots up to their knees and goose-stepping?"

Dot Latham, the teenager who served as the lead singer with the Stardusters dance band out at the NCO club, was with three of her girlfriends when news reached them that the first trainload of prisoners would arrive that afternoon. One of the girls said, "Let's go," and they all set out walking towards the train depot.

"I don't know who had the idea of crossing the road and climbing that lumber pile, but we all did it," Dot recalled in an interview. "We had a good view." The girls perched daintily on top of a lumber pile next to the railroad tracks, their hands in their laps and their ankles crossed demurely. With her puffy-sleeved pastel cotton dress and her curly hair pulled into two unbraided pigtails, Dot looked a lot like Judy Garland off to see the wizard as she and her friends speculated among themselves about what the Nazi super soldiers would look like when they got off the train. "We were Aliceville people that had never had an experience like that before. It was very exciting."

Ward Turner's older daughter, Joyce, was with her friend Mary Frances Killingsworth. She doesn't remember exactly where they stood to watch the train come in, but she knows they were together and looking down from some kind of vantage point on one of the main streets.

Mary Lu Turner didn't see the prisoners arrive. She was only eight at the time, and she stayed up on Red Hill to cool off with her friends. It was extremely hot and humid on June 2, and the highlight of such a summer day for many Aliceville children was the filling of the water tower each afternoon. The wooden tower, rising from its moss-covered cement slab, stood on a lot two doors up from the house the Turners were renting. On summer afternoons, Mary Lu pulled on her bathing suit and ran with her friends to stand in the knee-high grass under the tower. "Every afternoon they'd fill it up, and it would overflow. I can't imagine now—there must have been snakes all around—but we'd stand there, and the water tower would overflow with cool water, and it was just wonderful."

Back down in town, newspaper reporters wandered among the crowds that lined the highway eight to ten deep as the afternoon wore on. They jotted down comments and jockeyed for the best viewing positions along the highway. Emory Peebles Hildreth was one of them.

Mary Emory Peebles was a Pickens County girl, but she'd been trained in writing at Columbia University in New York City before returning home to become the second wife of Emmett Franklin Hildreth in 1927. When Emory tried to drive her car right up to the depot so she could write a special feature for the *Birmingham Age-Herald*, a uniformed soldier ordered her off the street. Because she had her eighty-year-old mother with her, Emory tried parking in a vacant lot directly across from the railroad tracks but was ordered to move her car another thirty feet away. Finally, she found an acceptable parking place, helped her mother out of the car, and hurried on foot towards the depot, a typical southern small-town depot built in the first half of the twentieth century—wooden, one-story, high-gabled, and painted a light color with darker trim.

"Four highway patrolmen were standing at the railroad crossing with commanding officers from the internment camp looking important and prepared," Emory wrote in her article.

"Companies of soldiers lined either side of the street between the Frisco tracks and the internment camp, a double row of them near the train tracks armed with rifles, shotguns, short machine guns, pistols, and bayonets."

Jack House had driven down to cover the arrival of the prisoners officially for the front page of *The Birmingham News*. "Germans comin' in on the Frisco!" was the phrase he quoted as passing from mouth to mouth in Aliceville that day. He wrote that it drew the entire town—men, women, and children—to offer a "curious, tense welcome to the first Germans most of them had ever seen."

The train was scheduled to arrive at 4:45 p.m. "It was unlike any other train time in Aliceville history," Jack House wrote with drama. He, too, described the double row of "husky, khaki-clad Americans bristling with rifles, short machine guns, pistols, bayonets, shotguns." Both Emory Hildreth and Jack House wrote that Aliceville hadn't been front-page news in Alabama since six years earlier when a cyclone struck the small town and killed fourteen people.

Chester (Chet) Eisenhauer was one of the guards from the 305th MPEG Company assigned to meet the train and escort the POWs out to the camp. It was only a month since the eighteen-year-old from Illinois had stepped off a Frisco train in Aliceville himself, surprised to find that he'd be guarding prisoners instead of studying motorcycle repair. Among others on duty with the 305th that afternoon were Joey Futchko, Joe Samper, Bob Siddall, Oscar Rich, Clayton Sadberry, and Fred Warnick. Byron Kauffman was there, too, wondering to himself what kind of evil demons would get off the train when it pulled in.

The whistle blew, far off up the tracks, and a hush fell over the crowds. Chet Eisenhauer watched the train approach. All he could think about was how silly he and his MPEG buddies must look, standing at attention in their chin-strap secured pith helmets with their khaki uniform pants bunched into the tops of laced up boots. "We were kind of a ragtag bunch," he has said. "Amateurs."

When the whistle blew, it also caught the attention of the German POWs inside the train. They were now nearing the end of their second day of rail travel from New York. Hermann Blumhardt remembers commenting to his seatmate, "The civilians will be curious. They'll want to get a good look at us."

Others on board that day included Heinrich "Heinz" Most, Bruno Schneider, and Theo Klein. Also, *Obergefreiter* (lance corporal) Otto Ulrich and *Unteroffizier* (sergeant) Rolf Schneider who would both come to sad fates by the end of the summer. Rolf Schneider had become acquainted with a German soldier of Austrian descent named Robert Mitterwallner on a Liberty ship as they crossed the Atlantic. When Rolf and Robert looked out the train window and saw the rows of guards armed with rifles and machine pistols, they wondered if the treatment here would be as rough as it had been in the transfer camps in North Africa. They were tired and thirsty and had been deep down hungry for longer than they could remember.

As the train slowed and pulled into town, the prisoners stood up in the aisles and gathered their few belongings. Steam sputtered and metal screeched on metal as the huge black engine wheezed to a full stop and then backed the train up slowly until the passenger cars stopped right in the middle of the Highway 17 crossing.

The order came to file off the train in an orderly fashion and line up, five across, for the march. Walter Felholter grabbed his folded, worn blanket and bent down for a last look through the window before descending the two metal steps out of the car. Scores of American soldiers stood at attention with their weapons ready. Walter could see one guard with a tropical helmet strapped tight beneath his chin writing on a clipboard while several civilians in suits and ties and fedoras stood by staring with their hands thrust deep in their pockets.

It was very quiet when Walter stepped down into the street. He remembers seeing a white frame house with a tree-shaded porch and front yard across from the train, and he remembers the big-eyed stares of the townspeople—stares he thought clearly communicated the American expectation that these Germans represented the Devil himself. "They are looking for our horns," he whispered to the prisoner next to him.

Hermann Blumhardt was embarrassed to appear so unkempt in front of his captors. "We were a mess," he said later. "Probably smelled a hundred yards, smelled worse than cattle." He was not intimidated by the guards with their loaded guns. By now he was used to that aspect of captivity. When he stepped down, he was much more interested in gauging the reaction of the civilians lining the streets. People were craning their necks, trying to get a good view. "Looking into their faces, I could detect one thing," he told Alabama Public Television years later. "They were disappointed in us. They expected us to be more arrogant."

Sue Stabler says you could hear a pin drop when the first Germans appeared. The only sound was people catching their breath. "I remember how I felt," she said in 1989. "I was expecting somebody real fierce, somebody to hate, but when I saw them, they were just young, just young boys, tired, weary, ragged. Your heart went out to them. I think everybody here had the same feeling."

Robert Hugh Kirksey also remembers how quiet it became when the doors opened and the first Germans appeared. "They lined up in an orderly fashion, ready for a command to move out. Their appearances ranged over a wide spectrum—some still appeared to be arrogant, but others looked dejected and tired."

One woman in the crowd wondered aloud how these prisoners, these menacing Nazis, could be so well behaved. "You would be, too," she was told, "if you were staring down that many gun barrels."

Perhaps Emory Hildreth was the person Hermann Blumhardt saw first when he stepped down. She wrote in her article that she was disappointed after all she'd heard about the "super race." She counted only six prisoners she would have classified as above average. "They all came through the same train door walking briskly, almost trotting to where they were halted to march in formation.... Some trotted in groups of four, six, or singly. Some glanced around curiously at the crowd, others showed no interest. Some were smiling broadly, others looked dejected, sad or humiliated. They were mostly young about 22, but some looked about 17. A few older ones, officers maybe, looked hardened and serious."

Emory described their uniforms as "nondescript and varied." Some wore faded moss green, and some blue, she said. There were also prisoners in khaki shorts, and one was wearing an overcoat in spite of the heat. Emory imagined that under the overcoat the prisoner might be wearing a uniform like that of

Gungha Din, the native water carrier for the British regiment in Rudyard Kipling's poem. She wrote that the POWs wore heavy shoes and that most carried either a knapsack or a makeshift bundle. One had a checkerboard and another, a briefcase. One was barefoot and was given a ride in the Red Cross ambulance.

According to Emory, most of the prisoners were blond and appeared to be in good condition. However, she didn't think they compared favorably with the "handsome, neat, clean-faced American soldiers guarding them."

Jack House noted in his article the recent announcement from Washington, D.C. that there were now 36,688 Axis prisoners in the United States—22,210 Germans, 14,516 Italians, and 62 Japanese. "For these men," he wrote, "the war is pleasantly over. Made up, for the most part, of young Germans, the prisoners have found something in defeat that they could not have found in an Axis victory—peace. They have found their 'Aliceville in Wonderland,' a world they did not know existed."

Jack reported seeing smiles on the faces of many prisoners. He speculated that, if these prisoners had escaped the trap set for them by Allied troops in Tunisia, they might have been forced to fight and die for Hitler and Mussolini in some other Mediterranean outpost. "As it is, though, these men will enjoy comparatively comfortable living conditions amidst peaceful surroundings for the duration."

Many Aliceville residents remember the prisoners being more sad than happy. Freckle-faced Jack Brookes was seven years old when he tagged along with his father to watch Hitler's men arrive in Aliceville. "I just remember that they all were very sad.

Their clothing was dirty, and they were sort of a tragic-looking group. At that age, I think I took up for them."

Joyce Turner had a similar thought as she stood with her friend Mary Frances. "They lined up, some with what appeared to be heavy uniforms. Some were just in army shorts and short-sleeve shirts. They all had haunting and frightened expressions on their faces.... They were the enemy, but to an impressionable teenager, they were someone's son, husband, or brother."

Jake McBride, who'd come back home to Aliceville from Fayette in February to chauffeur staff cars for the military, thought the prisoners looked worn out. "A lot of them were right off the battlefield," he told a newspaper reporter from Mobile. "They were so glad to get here they didn't know what to do."

Chet Eisenhauer stood at attention as the prisoners prepared for their march, but his eyes took in the whole scene. Despite their dirty and disheveled condition, he thought the Germans had a certain military bearing about them. "We looked like soldiers, but they acted more like soldiers. They had hobnailed boots on. They got lined up quick, and they had a leader."

MPEG Guard Joe Samper was impressed, too. "They were soldiers. They were one unit in unison. Not one German stepped out of line. Not one lost his step."

Corporal Byron Kauffmann did not see the demons he'd expected to. "They was [*sic*] nothing but a bunch of old men and young kids, haggard-looking and washed out and meek," he remembered. "You had to feel sorry for them because a lot of them, we found out later, did not want to be in the army any more than we did. They were pressed into service. The only ones that was real hard core was the SS troopers, and there was about 150 of them."

One guard went up and down the line, asking if anyone among the Germans spoke English. A thin prisoner wearing spectacles and a torn blue coat raised his hand, and he was brought forward to interpret the American orders.

The 389th, including Stanley Pendrak who usually worked in the mess hall for American servicemen, was also on escort duty that afternoon. "We were awed by them," Stanley has said. "They were combat veterans, and none of us, that I remember, had seen any combat up till that time. They had on hobnailed shoes, and when they started marching, it was all in unison. No skipping or nothing like that. The sound on the pavement just kinda put a chill up your back."

Stanley says most of the arriving POWs appeared to be in their twenties. "Very few were older. They were well-trained soldiers. That's what they were brought up to be."

By the time members of the various MPEG companies had the first trainload of prisoners lined up for their two-mile march to the camp, it was almost sundown. The state troopers were out in front, and they did their best to look important, striding up and down in their high leather boots and jodhpur-like pants. They wore dark, long-sleeved shirts in spite of the heat, and khaki ties. Their eyes were hidden by sunglasses, and they wore broad-brimmed hats that smacked of Canadian mounted police adventures.

Many Aliceville residents remember, as the march began, that the prisoners were singing their militant marching songs. *Wenn wir marschieren,* they sang, and *Heute wollen wir marschieren, einen neuen Marsch probieren, in dem schönen Westerwald, ja da pfeift der Wind so kalt.* How strange it seemed for these foreign soldiers to be singing these strange songs right here on Highway 17 within shouting distance of Aliceville homes and businesses.

Robert Hugh Kirksey watched as the prisoners, though tired and dejected, gathered their pride and set off goose-stepping and singing. "So *this* is what we have to fight," he thought to himself as he tried to imagine his own future in the army.

When the lines of men set off towards the camp, Emory Peebles turned to her elderly mother and asked what she thought of the prisoners. "They look like mere boys," said Mrs. Peebles. "They have mothers somewhere who are missing them. I feel sorry for the boys and their mothers."

The second train chugged onto the crossing before the first group of prisoners had finished their march, and a second group of five hundred prisoners detrained quickly and lined up. The scene was basically the same, except that some of the townspeople abandoned their posts along the highway as twilight settled in. A dogfight broke out, and when several small boys began pelting the animals with stones to make them separate, some of the Germans laughed out loud and smiled right along with the townspeople.

Over the next several days—at all hours of the day and night—the Frisco trains kept arriving and unloading. By the end of the week, more than three thousand Germans had marched behind the barbed wire and taken up residence at the Aliceville Internment Camp. Another of those new arrivals was Sergeant-Major Walter F. Meier, the melancholy paratrooper who had lost his brother near Medjez el Bab in Tunisia.

When Axis prisoners were far away, Americans regarded their treatment as mostly an academic question. We were content to let the matter be handled by officials in conformity with international conventions and practices. But when prisoners are brought to America and placed in prison camps close at hand, more interest is taken. The matter becomes personal, and touches the emotions.

• June 18, 1943 •
Editorial, *The Birmingham News*

CHAPTER SIX
Filling Up Compounds

As darkness settled over Aliceville Wednesday evening, June 2, long processions of prisoners marched out Highway 17, five abreast—some singing lustily in spite of their fatigue and some simply staring at their surroundings as their hobnailed boots clicked the pavement. The volunteer interpreter in the torn blue coat translated the American command "column left," and the men filed off, row by row, to cross the tracks of the Alabama, Tennessee & Northern Railroad—the tracks that would bring supply trains loaded with toilet paper, soap, shaving cream, and fresh foods to the camp. Then they marched through the main gate of the Aliceville Internment Camp and past the quarters of the American officers, the enlisted men, and the nurses.

Heeding the volunteer interpreter's shout again, the prisoners halted at the second gate, this one in a double inner fence. They peered beyond a tall wooden guard tower with double searchlights on its roof. To their left was a cluster of buildings they would soon identify as the main infirmary, a dental clinic, hospital wards, and a detention ward—even a morgue. Beyond that were the large barracks compounds, each within its own single perimeter fence constructed of hog wire with a barbed wire flange on top. A large water tower and several smokestacks punctuated the far horizon, and shorter hexagonal guard towers stood sentinel at the corners of the compounds.

The long lines of men backed up at this second gate as processing and assignment to barracks began. The Germans let their eyes wander as they waited, trying to imagine life in this place. Even as the sun set, the summer heat was oppressive, and mosquitoes—eager for their evening buffet—whined and zinged as they zeroed in on the menu of bare ears and arms. The paperwork went slowly, taking much longer than Colonel Frederick A. Prince, the camp commander, had anticipated. Forms had to be filled out and medical evaluations recorded. As late as two o'clock in the morning, temporary cooks in the mess halls continued to hand out food and hot coffee as group after group of prisoners stepped inside the perimeters, located their barracks, deposited their few belongings near their cots, and then headed for the lavatories and mess halls.

Title III of the Geneva Convention of 1929 required, among other conditions, healthful and hygienic housing with adequate heat, lighting, and fire protection. It also required forty square feet of living space per man and other conditions that would make the facilities equal to those provided for base camp troops of the detaining power—in this case, the United States. In order to meet this provision of the Convention, each of the six separately fenced compounds (labeled A, B, C, D, E, and F) consisted of thirty-seven tarpaper-covered buildings set on low stilts. Within each compound, ten barracks buildings stood on each side of a rutted roadway with two lavatory buildings out behind each barracks row. Each compound also contained mess halls, administrative and storage facilities, a small infirmary, a post exchange, a recreational building, and a maintenance shop. When filled to capacity, each self-contained space was intended to house 1,000 prisoners divided into four companies of 250 men. When the first prisoners arrived, the gates between these compounds were kept locked and guarded. Prisoners could move freely among the buildings within their own compound, but they could not "go visiting" in another compound.

Compounds A, B, and C were the first to be occupied and locked down. Sometime Wednesday evening, Heinrich Most, age twenty-five, was assigned to the barracks designated as Compound C, Company #11, and Theo Klein, age nineteen, was assigned to Compound B, Company #6. Robert Mitterwallner, age twenty-four, moved into Compound A, Company #2, and Hermann Blumhardt, age twenty-two, into Company #9 in Compound C.

Though all of these prisoners had spent weeks in a series of temporary enclosures, each felt a sense of what they could only describe as temporary finality as they stepped inside the compound gate and heard it creak closed behind them. Interpreters pointed out the "deadline," a row of warning stakes pounded into the ground ten feet from the inner perimeter fence of each compound. You are not permitted to step beyond those stakes, the prisoners were told. If you do, the guards in the towers will mow you down.

Hermann Blumhardt was surprised to discover how neat and clean his barracks building was. The sight of it muted his fears of mistreatment, starvation, and slave labor—at least for the time being. Inside, fifty sturdy canvas cots were lined up neatly—twenty-five on each side. A tube of toothpaste and a jar of shaving cream had been laid out on each cot, along with other toiletry items. How bad could this confinement be, Hermann thought, if the captors had bothered with things like these?

The flooring was wood and tightly constructed. Neatly framed light fixtures were bolted to the ceiling. Though it was hard to imagine ever needing it, a potbellied stove stood in the center of the room with a tall, fat pipe venting it through the roof. There were enough windows on each side, as well as on each end beside the doors, to create cross breezes if a good puff of cool air visited this steamy place during the night.

Walter Felholter, age twenty-one, was also assigned to Company #9 in Compound C. Taking stock of his surroundings, he was happy to see clean cots and to discover a lavatory with decent toilets, hot water, and showers. When he entered the mess hall, he was given a cup of steaming coffee and soft white "American" bread spread with a substance he did not recognize. "We didn't know peanut butter," he has said. "I didn't know what peanuts were, but we put peanut butter on the bread and ate it quickly. It tasted wonderful. And we had coffee that night—quite a lot of coffee. I had never tasted coffee like that before. It tasted so good. I will never forget that night. The peanut butter sticks to the roof of your mouth, and you have to drink and drink and drink—the coffee was good for that. When I think of good times at Aliceville, I remember the peanut butter."

Some of the Germans at the tables in the mess halls were less enthusiastic about the good food and coffee. Propaganda, they suggested. The Americans just want to fatten us up and get us feeling good. Then the real punishment will begin.

The need to eat was the first priority for most of these men. It shoved everything else into the shadows until they had eaten their fill and drunk all the coffee they could hold. Then they returned to their barracks and reveled in the opportunity to wash and shower, wash and shower again, and then prepare gratefully for a good night's sleep.

Sometime that evening, or perhaps the next day, Hermann Blumhardt and Walter Felholter shared stories of their experiences up to that time. They had not known each other before coming to Camp Aliceville.

Hermann was the more talkative of the two. He told Walter about being drafted in January 1941 after his RAD labor service and about thinking that combat might be an adventure. He told about chasing retreating Russians towards Moscow until the rude awakening when a German warplane accidentally killed half a dozen soldiers in his unit and wounded him in the thigh. He told about meeting Katie Emberger while recuperating and being shipped out again to Italy and then to North Africa, about the sergeant blown up in his foxhole just after he'd crawled out of it, and about raising his hands in surrender and then realizing that no one else around him had raised theirs. He and Walter compared notes on their similar captures by the British and on the long journey that had brought them to this place in Alabama in the United States of America.

The headline in the *Pickens County Herald and West Alabamian* on Thursday, June 3, read "Prisoners Are Arriving Now at Aliceville; Three Trainloads Arrived Wednesday, on Frisco, Others Today." Jack Pratt declared on the front page that most of the rumors and predictions of the past year had come true—and that those in Aliceville who'd been convinced no prisoners would ever occupy the Aliceville camp would not have the pleasure of saying "I told you so."

Captain Arthur John Klippen had had the Station Hospital open and ready for patients since mid-April. This was a War Department requirement because the camp was too distant for quick transportation by highway or railroad if a prisoner needed hospitalization. The Station Hospital was a 250-bed facility designed to meet the medical needs of American military personnel as well as German prisoners. It could serve civilian employees of the camp and, in emergencies, local residents. Prisoners would also receive medical care through dispensaries located in each of the compounds. A medical staff physician would conduct sick call each day and make referrals to the hospital as needed.

Elma Henders had the kitchen in the main camp hospital fully equipped before any prisoners arrived. Her crew was already serving meals to enlisted men in the medical service, but when the prisoners began to arrive in June, her daily routine changed drastically. "After the date that the prisoners arrived, I went home with twenty-five patients in the hospital, and the next morning I had five hundred," she has said. "That was just a little bit more than I had anticipated."

She served the prisoners the exact same food she served healthy American soldiers, but it had to be prepared a little differently, depending on the condition of the patient. "The interesting thing about it was that these men had been without food and especially without condiments like sugar. Some of them who could walk from their hospital beds to the dining room, would just pick up the bowls of sugar and eat from them—just like that—because they were so hungry for carbohydrates."

Prisoners came to the hospital for various reasons. Some had colds. Some had minor injuries or were suffering from malnourishment. Some had painful trench mouth or boils. Others, like Horst Uhse, had battled jaundice and malaria in the North Africa transfer camps and were in bad enough shape to be given beds in the hospital, outside their regular compounds. Horst remembers with gratitude the professionalism of Captain Klippen and the staff who nursed him back to health before transferring him to Compound B.

The Provost Marshal General's office had directed that prisoners brought to the United States be sent to different camps, based on whether they were German or Italian, whether they were army and air force or navy, and whether they were Nazi or anti-Nazi. Each area service command could transfer prisoners from camp to camp within its service command as long as it reported the transfers and did not mix the categories.

The prisoners who arrived at Aliceville during the first week of June came under the second category—"all other German army prisoners," but "all other" was an extremely general definition. It did not necessarily imply that prisoners who were not anti-Nazi were, by definition, pro-Nazi. Some prisoners, especially NCOs and higher ranking officers, held long established attachments to Nazism while others had less absolute beliefs about Hitler's ideology. Some had joined the Nazi party simply to avoid punishment or harassment in their personal lives, yet many admired the Nazis for carrying forward the traditional

German military values of rigid discipline and unquestioning obedience to commanders.

During initial processing in the port cities, most prisoners who were openly pro-Nazi were sent to Alva, Oklahoma, and most prisoners who were openly anti-Nazi were sent to Fort Devens, Massachusetts, or Camp Campbell, Kentucky. Robert D. Billinger Jr. has written about this confusing process in his book, *Hitler's Soldiers in the Sunshine State* about POW camps in Florida: "Germans and Americans soon discovered—at Camp Blanding's naval stockade and elsewhere at POW camps throughout the United States—that American-selected designations like 'Nazi' and 'anti-Nazi' were neither accurate nor very useful."

Those arriving at Camp Aliceville in the summer of 1943 were not supposed to fit either of these categories, but because America's initial methods of prisoner processing were basic and superficial, Aliceville, like many other early camps, detained prisoners who fit both categories as well as every persuasion in between.

Two other camps opened in Alabama in the summer of 1943. Like Aliceville, Camp Opelika had been constructed in the fall of 1942 and activated in December. It was located a little south and far to the east of Aliceville, near Auburn and the Georgia border. This camp was greeted by residents of its adjoining community with a mix of awe and curiosity similar to that in Aliceville. "At the first trainload, Opelika turned out like it thought the president or Jesus was coming," said one resident.

"I don't know what we expected—two-headed monsters!" Camp Opelika opened the same week as Camp Aliceville and received prisoners from North Africa who entered the United States at Boston Harbor.

The third camp opened on July 3 at Fort McClellan, a permanent army installation northeast of Aliceville near the city of Anniston in Calhoun County. The Opelika and Fort McClellan camps were half the size of Aliceville, each designed for approximately three thousand prisoners.

On June 8, the Palace Theater in Aliceville began showing *Hitler's Children*, with Tim Holt, Otto Kruger, Hans Conreid, Gavin Muir, and Nancy Gates. This movie certainly did nothing to promote feelings of security and good will among Aliceville citizens regarding the enemy prisoners nearby. Newspaper promotions promised it would reveal to the American public "the truth about the Nazi from the cradle to the battlefront." Based on Gregor Ziemer's book *Education for Death,* it was said to feature "Hitler's secret chamber of horrors unmasked in the one motion picture that dares tell all—all about how babies are bred for war, how kids are trained to kill, how 'romance' is regimented, how the 'Master Race' hates you and you and YOU!"

Later in the month, the Palace scheduled lighter fare, including *Lost Canyon* starring Hopalong Cassidy. It also offered Hal Roach's *The Devil with Hitler*—a war-time comedy that spoofed the Axis Powers with Three-Stooges-like characters named Adolf, Benito, and Suki Saki who put the devil on notice that they intended to replace him with Adolph Hitler unless the devil could convince the dictator to commit a good deed.

Although many Aliceville citizens expressed empathy for the prisoners and concern for their families back in Germany, not everyone harbored such feelings. Frances Edwards took a job at the Camp Aliceville hospital canteen and could observe the prisoners as they went about their activities during the day. Her feelings were "as close to hatred as you can get—because of the war." Frances didn't think the Germans deserved being treated that well. "They were playing soccer, and you watched that, and you'd think about our boys over there getting killed and in their POW camps, and we knew they weren't being treated like these were. I don't know. It just got under your skin. Some days really bad."

Another Aliceville resident says the community still harbors the long-term memory of prisoners being fed fresh meat, good coffee, and plenty of basic staples while townspeople scraped by on war ration coupons and what they could grow at home. Robert Hugh Kirksey's father set up a rabbit hutch in his backyard so he could provide healthful protein for his family. Because the internment camp was on federal government property and because it followed the Geneva Convention dictate to feed prisoners exactly as it fed American soldiers, the prison compound mess halls, like those of the American officers and enlisted men, were not subject to rationing. There were tight restrictions about food leaving the camp and some local residents—especially those out of work and living in poverty—resented this fact.

Earline Lewis, the shy young secretary from Carrollton who worked in the Quartermaster's office, was in charge of calculating food supply orders for the mess halls in the three prison compounds that opened in June. "The mess sergeants would bring me their menus two weeks before they were to be used, and it was my job to calculate how many pounds of potatoes, cans of tomatoes, loaves of bread, and so forth, would be needed. The prisoners ate well. They had a bakery and the materials to make desserts—any specialty they'd had in Germany, and special cooks to cook them. On the weekends, they had good cold cuts."

In her job, Earline did not go "behind the wires" where she would have had direct contact with prisoners, but she did see them out working around the grounds when she went to lunch and when she walked to the Headquarters building to work on menus. "We would go up the street as young ladies, and the Germans would stop their work and look at us, but no whistles, no talking. They were very quiet. If anything, they would smile. I was kind of shy in those days, but I was never, never afraid." She remembers that the prisoners did not do the maintenance or cleaning work in her office. The American enlisted men did that.

Among the food items Earline ordered in the early weeks of camp life was plenty of fresh corn in the shuck. It was issued to the prison mess halls for a vegetable with their evening meal. What Earline did not know was that corn—especially corn on the cob—was as strange to the Germans as peanut butter. They knew what corn was, but back in their country, it was fed only to livestock like pigs and certainly not to human beings. The German cooks had no idea how to prepare the corn and weren't at all sure they wanted to, but they also feared telling American officers they didn't want to eat it. Walter Felholter remembers his company leader in Compound C saying, "We must do something with this corn to make it go away. We don't want to give it back to the Americans because then they may think we have too much to eat." Most of these prisoners were enjoying their first decent meals in months, and they did not want their rations cut.

As the summer harvests began, more and more corn showed up on the mess hall menus. Walter's company leader came up with an idea—let's bury it, he said. When he asked for volunteers, Walter and two or three others went out and began digging. "We dug very deep, and then we packed in the corn," Walter remembers. "We filled up the hole, and no one noticed—at least for a while."

On Friday, June 11, the *Birmingham Age-Herald* printed an editorial commenting that the German prisoners in Aliceville were not supermen and never had been supermen. "But they were trained for war, and they were well commanded, and they made a telling showing before they threw up the sponge." The editorial went on to say, "These prisoners are happy, because they are no longer subjected to the terror in which they had their being for a long period. Only to live is for them a precious thing. And to live, even under the strictest discipline, is a tremendous gift, when they know that they will be decently treated. By now, they are sure of that much, whatever they may have thought in other days."

America and England were proud of the quality of life in their prisoner of war camps. Both countries publicized this quality as often as possible, in the sincere hope that such publicity would encourage the Germans to treat American and British captives more humanely than they otherwise might have. On the same day this editorial appeared up in Birmingham, a twenty year old Aliceville High School graduate named Frank Murphy was reported missing, and the people of Aliceville prayed that, if he'd been captured, he'd be treated as well as the German captives being held just outside his hometown.

At about the same time, Mr. and Mrs. Monroe Davidson of Aliceville, whose son had been reported missing several months earlier, received a letter from a stranger somewhere "up East" who wrote that he'd heard a foreign radio broadcast in which Newton Davidson had stated that he wanted his parents to know he was alive and safe. On July 1, Newton Davidson's parents would learn for certain that their son was a German captive when the United States War Department released a list of 922 American soldiers held by the Germans. They, too, prayed that the treatment of German POWs in camps like Aliceville would favorably affect the treatment of their son in Germany.

Among the German prisoners held at Camp Aliceville, the biggest fear was that once the fighting ended in Europe, they would experience the full wrath of their American and British captors. Many of them, including Hermann Blumhardt, concluded correctly that the umbrella of the Geneva Convention would probably protect them only as long as both sides continued to fight.

When they first arrived at Camp Aliceville, the German prisoners were not required to work outside their own compounds. The guard units were not large enough or trained and experienced enough to provide security for work details, and the American officers in charge had not yet determined which prisoners could be required to work and which could not. Although clearly recognizable POW clothing (loose denim pants and shirts with "PW" painted on in five-inch-high white letters) had been issued, the denim hats that had been requisitioned had not arrived. Colonel Prince would not allow bareheaded prisoners out on work details in the blazing Alabama sunshine.

Within certain guidelines, the Geneva Convention allowed a host government to require POWs to work, but it established three basic rules: Officers did not work unless they chose to, noncommissioned officers did not work except in supervisory positions, and enlisted prisoners only worked if they were physically fit.

According to Major C.E. Lemiell, Executive Officer at Camp Aliceville, there were definite plans to put the POWs to work outside the compounds as soon as possible. "There will be home raised but German-grown Irish potatoes, peas, and corn on Alabama tables in a few months," he told the *Birmingham Post* on June 10. "The Germans will be put to work on farms as soon as the necessary number of guards to supervise them is available."

Walter Felholter has said that even though they were not required to work when they first arrived, most prisoners welcomed something to do. "Some of us couldn't live without work. If they couldn't work, they wouldn't be happy." This is why so many busied themselves planting flowers, cleaning barracks, creating roads, and digging ditches.

Men in captivity react in different ways. Wilhelm Westhoff, an NCO who'd been a teacher in Germany before the war, wrote later in the camp newspaper that many prisoners were deeply depressed in their early days at Camp Aliceville. "Many only raised themselves from their beds to contemplate their comrades with envious eyes and ill will, passing on their distrust to others, disparaging the work of their neighbors, and maintaining that all of these actions were useless." Men like these, he wrote, would wake up, mutter their negative comments, and then, if not called to the mess hall for a meal, "yield again to Orpheus" or go back to dreaming and sleep.

Hermann Blumhardt agrees that boredom and depression were problems in the early days at Camp Aliceville. With thousands of men looking for something to do with their time, the chores of preparing food and cleaning up were quickly spoken for. He says some became depressed, but others fought the boredom by finding ways to turn their confinement into something of a home. They took on creative projects like forming soccer teams and theater groups and constructing handmade musical instruments.

Walter Felholter found a different use for his time. During his first week in Camp Aliceville, he went around to the other barracks within Compound C to see who was there and where they were from. "We were mixed up everywhere," he has said. "We were transported from [where we were captured] and put together with other guys, and we got new friends then....We went to the different barracks and looked to see who was there and talked to them to see if we were from the same army." Through this process, Walter located Carl Lohmann, a soldier he'd been captured with, who was in Company #12. "We had dinner together then, and he told me that in my barracks there is a man who speaks very good English. He wants to teach, but he wants to have no more than ten guys, and they must be intelligent because he doesn't want to teach stupid guys because it will take a long time and because, well, he doesn't like it."

Walter thought it would be good to spend his time learning English. From that morning on, he attended the English lessons in his barracks from eight to nine o'clock. "We started the lessons every day with ten words. We wrote the words on pieces of paper we got from the toilet or somewhere and were to learn those ten words for the next day."

Hermann Blumhardt was also determined to learn English. He remembered making that a priority for himself while still in North Africa, when he watched a fellow prisoner evade a death sentence by begging for mercy in English. He may have been in the same English class with Walter in Company #9 the first few weeks. He remembers that his class wrote words on empty cement sacks as well as toilet paper. He also remembers being pleasantly surprised that the camp administration not only permitted the POWs to study English but eventually ordered supplies for them.

It came as a shock to Hermann when his first instructor lost patience and told him he would never learn English. "I was devastated. I never before had been a complete failure, like this sounded to me, and I surely did not intend to take this lying down. I found another instructor, and he was satisfied with my progress."

In the early months at Camp Aliceville, American commanders arranged for some educational supplies requested by the POWs, but they did not offer courses or become involved in academic instruction inside the camp. There was good reason for this. The American Army was edgy about the subject of education in the POW camps. They didn't want to give the impression they were forcing democratic propaganda on their captives—something that could have a negative effect on the treatment of American POWs in German camps if it was construed as violating the Geneva Convention. The Army definitely didn't want to do anything that would encourage the German military to retaliate by forcing National Socialist propaganda on American prisoners.

The idea of trying to educate German POWs about democratic ideals had certainly been considered, even before Camp Aliceville opened. In March 1943, General Frederick Osborn received a proposal for a plan to introduce German POWs to American history and the workings of democracy. When he passed this plan on to Brigadier General S.L.A. Marshall, Marshall added the idea of screening prisoners as they were processed—"separating the bad eggs from the amenable ones, ignoring the former and starting education courses for the latter with emphasis on democratic theory and practice." The Provost Marshal General—Major General Allen Gullion at the time—did not consider an education program of this type a good idea, however. He objected to it for several reasons—the wording of the Geneva Convention, the high cost of setup and manpower for such a program, the possible loss of POW labor hours to the classroom, and the danger that Germany might launch a counter effort with American POWs. Although the screening process for prisoners was implemented to some extent in the spring of 1943, the re-education plan was placed on someone's shelf on June 24 and gathered dust for more than a year.

Birmingham newspaper reporter Jack House toured Camp Aliceville during its first week of operation, as the prisoners were settling in. He depicted himself as surrounded on all sides by "battle-scarred, desert-toughened German soldiers—more than 3,000 ruthless Nazi killers." However, he concluded that the German prisoners were now "calm as a kitten and as obedient as the most humble servant. [They] realize they have been soberly subdued by a superior foe [and] they now are willing and anxious to help make this a better world in which to live."

House acknowledged that some prisoners were sullen and stubborn in their allegiance to Nazism but suggested this might be because they were "mad at the world" rather than at their American captors. Some prisoners had told American officers they hadn't expected there to be a place in America suitable for a POW camp. Many were under the impression America had been leveled by bombs and that they would be starved to death if they were captured and sent across the Atlantic. Jack speculated that, when word got back to Germany that such propaganda was not true, perhaps the Nazis would begin to surrender in increasing numbers. He suggested that "fair treatment, good food and clean clothes have served to 'make Christians' of these one-time supermen."

Like many who wrote about the first German prisoners in this country, Jack House lumped together all those at Aliceville as "3,000 former members of the once-proud Afrika Korps." In truth, as historian E.B. Walker and others have pointed out, not all those captured in North Africa belonged to the *Afrikakorps* or fought under Field Marshal Erwin Rommel. Walter Felholter, for example, served in the Hermann Göring Division and Hermann Blumhardt in the 10th Panzer Division. Heinrich Most was a member of the 1st Afrika March Battalion, and Werner Meier, formerly a pilot in the German air force, served in ground forces other than the *Afrikakorps* before his capture.

Jack characterized all German prisoners with the stereotypical terminology of the time—a "Germanic" look and appearance. "The Nazis are exactly like one would expect them to be," he wrote, "just like those seen in newspapers and the newsreels. They are easy to identify. Most of them are blonds, medium, short or squat build, with a slouch way of walking that suddenly bursts into an upright, braced position at the mere sound of 'tenshun!'" He stated that even those who were not Nazis had that "Germanic" look about them. He noted several other nationalities represented, including Romanians, Bulgars, Hungarians, and a few Italians.

The reporter toured the camp with Colonel Prince and Major Lemiell and was surprised to observe prisoners using the Nazi salute when addressing American officers. Unflustered by this, the American officers returned the salute American style.

Jack entered one of the compounds with Captain Strohecker of South Carolina, the Stockade Officer and a veteran of World War I who'd captured Germans himself in that war. "This time I'm watching after them," he remarked and then pointed out how well disciplined the prisoners were even though they'd been in the camp only a few days. "The German prisoner, it must be admitted, could show the American soldier a thing or two when it comes to being perfectly drilled."

Colonel Prince agreed. "They are damn good soldiers," he said.

As they toured the various compounds, Jack observed prisoners digging and hauling dirt, painting guard towers, or just lying about in the sun. Most wore the loose blue denim pants and shirts that would be their prison uniform for the duration, with the letters P and W painted on the back.

Already during the first week, prisoners were peeling potatoes, making pastries, and cooking their own meals in the compound mess halls, but Hermann Blumhardt remembers that the early meals were not all that great. "When we arrived at Camp Aliceville…," he wrote later, "an American sergeant asked through an interpreter if any of us were cooks, butchers, or bakers." Thinking such an admission would lead to a good position in the camp, many men raised their hands. Hermann says the meals improved a great deal when things sorted out and only the real cooks were working in the mess halls.

Menus were adjusted frequently during the early weeks of the camp. Earline Jones received a request to order more potatoes and vegetables and less meat. She was also informed that the German prisoners were not fond of American white bread, and she was asked to order whole grain flours, molasses, and other ingredients so the POWs could bake their own coarse, dark breads in the compound kitchens. The prisoners kept their kitchens and mess halls spotless, and the United States Army provided specially constructed racks for all chinaware and tableware so that bacteria counts could be kept low by letting the utensils air dry.

Prisoners could be seen sitting here and there around the camp writing letters home (two letters and one card per week permitted), playing cards on their cots with fellow prisoners, or creating designs in the dirt for landscaping. Later, with funds provided by the camp, they would plant shrubbery and Bermuda grass, but in the early weeks, they gathered rocks and bits of brick and even pieces of coal to create circular mosaics to make each barracks yard unique. Jack House wrote that prisoners were allowed to create any design they wished except the hated swastika. He watched a group of young men in their twenties lay out a German eagle with pebbles and spell out "Frankfurt-M" (for *Frankfurt-am-Main)* in pebbles above it. Other yard mosaics honored German cities like Hamburg and Munich or created images of sailing ships or lighthouses. Some had familiar German slogans like the rather ironic one that translated, "Through German character, the world will be healed!"

"Give them two weeks and you won't recognize the place," said Colonel Prince.

Jack House concluded his article with the comment that the camp appeared solidly built, suggesting it would be in use for some time. "The Germans themselves expect a long war," he wrote. "They are spending much of their time dressing up their living quarters, planting shrubbery and grass, which doesn't grow overnight."

After reading House's feature story in the Sunday paper up in Birmingham, Mrs. Lucile Umbenhauer wrote a letter to the editor expressing her amazement and indignation at the description of POW life down at Camp Aliceville:

> Are we, the American people, to discount all information heretofore published in your and other papers, periodicals, radios, and every source possible, about the education of the Nazi youth—how he has been steeped in the doctrines of Nazism? Do you think a man taught to disregard all the precepts of Christianity; who has burned in glee the very books that carried these teachings; who has been taught from babyhood everything diametrically opposite of the teachings of Christ, and who has not the first conception of what a Christian should be, can be made into a Christian in two weeks time simply by giving him good food, clothing and fair treatment? How soon do you think this newly acquired Christianity would wear off if this same man had a gun and an opportunity to escape his prison?

Mrs. Umbenhauer concluded her letter with concern about Colonel Prince's reassurance that Camp Aliceville was not "coddling prisoners." "Is it customary to coddle war prisoners?" she asked. "And they may still give the Nazi salute but not allowed to 'say it with flowers.' How they must laugh up their sleeves. No wonder they call us 'stupid Americans.'"

The Birmingham News published an editorial on the same page with this and several similar letters from readers:

> *The News* is further convinced, and deeply, that the United Nations must scrupulously obey all international conventions and agreements regarding treatment of prisoners. It doesn't matter that we may have reasons for suspecting or believing that the Axis nations are not

> carrying out their obligations toward war prisoners. Our pledge in the matter runs deeper than a pledge merely to other nations. It is a pledge to the future conduct of the world. By adhering, even unilaterally, to the conventions regarding war prisoners, we will contribute to the making of a better postwar world. We cannot hope to build a world of good-will if we deliberately create ill-will among prisoners.

Many Americans during World War II had the same impression as the woman from Birmingham—that all Germans were atheists who'd never been exposed to Christianity. Understandably, such Americans found it difficult to understand how a German soldier could reconcile Christian doctrine with Nazi dictates, yet the large majority of prisoners who arrived in Alabama in 1943 considered themselves Christians, in spite of Hitler's efforts to override the influence of the church in everyday German life. Colonel G. Cronander, commandant of the camp at Opelika, stated in an interview that many of his prisoners had arrived with their rosaries and prayer books and appeared to be "one of the most religious groups of men he ever saw." Cronander also noted that the prisoners sang grace before meals and attended religious services offered to them.

In early August, Henry C. Flynn reported in Birmingham's *The Catholic Week* newspaper that he had toured Camp Aliceville and lunched with Chaplain Speer Strahan, a priest from the Diocese of Richmond and a former faculty member at the Catholic University of America who was now a member of the

United States Army Chaplain Corps. Strahan told Flynn that half the prisoners at Camp Aliceville had listed themselves as Catholics and were participating in Mass outdoors on Sunday morning and at evening Masses in their recreation and mess halls during the week. "There is no shortage of servers and the Chaplain was impressed with their knowledge of the Latin of the Mass," wrote Henry Flynn. Clearly, these men were not simply fabricating religious background in order to impress and appease their captors.

At Fort McClellan, there was a similar religious ratio. "Most of the prisoners are definitely religious," wrote John B. McCloskey. "Forty-two percent signed themselves as Catholics, 57 per cent as Lutheran or Evangelical. A few said they believed in God but had no religious affiliation. Not more than ten out of the entire group gave National Socialism as their religion, and about three said they had no religion."

While the prisoners were settling in, religious life in the town outside the barbed wire continued as usual during the summer of 1943. Each week brought Sunday morning services and Wednesday evening prayer meetings at a variety of Aliceville churches. On Saturdays, Jewish merchants like Sam Wise drove over to observe their Sabbath at a temple in Columbus, Mississippi. On Monday, June 14, Daily Vacation Bible School began at the First Baptist Church, with classes for ages four through fifteen. The Methodist and Presbyterian churches cooperated in this effort.

July would be a revival month. The Fellowship Church scheduled their week of spiritual services to begin on Sunday, July 11, and invited the entire community. The Methodists scheduled theirs to begin July 18 and continue through the end of the month. Later in the summer, young Aliceville women like Barbara Ann McCaa and Alma Shaw attended the Pioneer Camp for Presbyterian Young People at Judson College in the town of Marion. Others spent a week or two at Camp Cherry Austin near Tuscaloosa.

Camp Aliceville had a basic chapel for American servicemen who did not take the opportunity to attend services at local churches with pretty young women like Margie and Emmie Archibald and Bobbie and Edwina Kirksey. Mary Lu Turner remembers attending base chapel services with her parents on Sunday mornings. Sometimes more than one hundred people attended, and other times only a few. She remembers hearing Jack Sisty, the chaplain's assistant, sing beautiful solos during these services.

Jack had been a professional singer in New York City before the war. After the Pearl Harbor attack, he was surprised and pleased when the military accepted his enlistment application at Grand Central Station. He thought maybe he wouldn't be able to serve because he was a victim of polio. One of his legs was shorter than the other, but the army took him anyway and assigned him to the post of chaplain's assistant at Camp Aliceville. His duties involved visiting guards from one end of the camp to the other, and he soon became the only soldier at the camp in possession of a government-issue bicycle for his rounds.

Most American soldiers sent to POW camps to guard prisoners were young recruits like Chet Eisenhauer and Stanley Pendrak. Watch out if a prisoner tries to get too friendly, they were warned during training. Remember that that good-looking

German kid who exudes charm has probably blown American soldiers to bits or brutalized helpless peasants in his service to Hitler.

An article in the *New York Herald Tribune* quoted some of the advice given to new guards: "You don't have to be cruel to these guys, but you have to show them they're not going to get away with anything. If you start feeling sorry for them and soften up, they take advantage of you right away. We won't have to be mean, but we're going to have to be plenty hard-boiled."

Guards in the MPEG units at Camp Aliceville gained confidence as they settled into their four-week duty rotation. Bob Siddall, who entered the camp with a fresh group of 305th recruits in May, added tower duty to his scheduled rotation after the first prisoners arrived. He'd spend a week in basic training—marching, weapons drills, obstacle courses, more marching—and then a week on interior guard duty at ground level. Often, this meant patrolling the outer perimeter fence or the supply depot. Then came a week of guarding prisoners on work details—prisoner chasing, as it was called—and then a week of tower duty.

Like most of the guards, Bob was not fond of tower duty. It was boring. At the beginning of their week of Rapunzel-like existence, he and five others would signal the guards they were relieving to crank the hand winch and let down the retractable ladder that had been added as an extra safety precaution. Then they'd climb up through the trap door and spend the next seven days and nights scanning the prisoner barracks and the yards for signs of mischief or escape attempts. At night they were aided by searchlights mounted at fence-top level and focused on the ten feet of "dead zone" just inside the fence. Colonel Prince had had these extra searchlights installed so that any prisoner who tried to escape would cast a long shadow on the ground before he could get near the fence.

Each guard took a turn manning one of two thirty-caliber machine guns that could swivel left or right to cover its section of fence. Each guard wondered, as he stood behind the machine gun, if he would ever really have to fire the thing.

A somewhat amusing safety precaution resulted from Colonel Prince's awareness that most of these guards were new recruits and had very little experience. The colonel ordered the range of the tower machine guns restricted to one portion of the fence in order to safeguard American personnel on the ground.

If an alarm sounded, those guards not operating the machine guns would grab their Tommy guns and slide down the firehouse-type pole next to the retractable ladder. They would take up positions at intervals along the fence to the right of their tower. The idea was that, in a matter of seconds, after each tower had responded, a cordon of armed guards would completely surround the compound enclosure.

Except for trips down for meals and showers—one man at a time—Bob and his detail remained in the tower for the entire week. They rotated duty time and sleeping time in the three double-decked bunks—two hours on and four hours off or four hours on and eight hours off.

Harold Cover, who arrived with the 436th MPEG in early July, says three men from his unit would be on duty in the tower while three slept—a corporal and two privates. The privates manned the machine guns, and the corporal was supposed to alert the one who'd gone for a shower or a meal if there was an emergency.

During his week of interior guard duty, Harold often worked in the guard shack at the entrance to the prison compounds with another man named Max Cochran. He checked the credentials of military personnel and also of civilians like Mary Lu Turner's mother who worked at the post hospital. Sometimes Harold drew guard duty in the main tower opposite the post headquarters building. Because this tower was located right in the center of post activities, it had no machine guns. Colonel Prince had also decided this gun placement might be too dangerous if an inexperienced guard became overzealous in his efforts to protect the camp.

If Harold got a furlough or a pass, it came during his week of down time. Otherwise, he spent that week doing laundry, polishing his shoes and his weapons, catching up on letters home, or, as he once suggested to an interviewer, occasionally sneaking out of camp and then sneaking back in time for reveille the next morning.

Later that summer, the "prisoner chasing" week evolved into escorting prisoners on work details outside the camp grounds. In the early weeks, however, prisoner chasing occurred inside the camp itself. There were not enough trained guards in residence at Aliceville to supervise the work details planned for the local sawmill, the surrounding timberlands, and the cotton fields, and the denim hats that would protect them from long hours in the hot sun had still not arrived. Instead, the prisoners busied themselves cleaning up their barracks and the grounds or helping with the monumental task of improving drainage.

The digging and hauling of dirt Jack House observed during his first-week visit was connected to this project. Jake McBride, the civilian who came home from Fayette to work in the camp motor pool, remembers helping organize prisoners to dig a channel all the way across the back of the camp. Five hundred prisoners spread out with picks and shovels to dig the channel—ten feet wide at the bottom, thirty to forty feet wide at the top, and running from the back of the compound area all the way down to the Tombigbee River. Another group of prisoners set up a brick-making operation in one of the general purpose shop buildings and began producing bricks made with local clay to line the drainage ditches.

Although the channel and its tributaries kept the barracks areas and the roads among them somewhat drier when the rains arrived again, they certainly did nothing to alleviate the mosquito population. It so plagued the prisoners that one of them created a poetic lament. Two lines of it translate roughly as follows:

Aliceville in Alabama, where the ants and chiggers play,
And a hundred fresh mosquitoes replace each one you slay,...

Throughout the summer, prisoners worked continually to deepen the drainage ditches. Hermann Blumhardt has said another early task was building sidewalks in an attempt to control the amount of rusty red mud tracked into the barracks.

Robert Mitterwallner remembers a sudden thunderstorm that came up during his early weeks at Aliceville. "We heard a gentle drumming which got noisier. Within five minutes, Camp A was flooded and wet like a dog." To make matters worse, the flooding washed in unwelcome visitors—huge black spiders and irritated rattlesnakes.

Aliceville residents warned camp guards, and the guards warned prisoners that Aliceville sometimes found itself in the path of serious tornadoes both in the spring and in the fall. Everyone in town remembered the one Emory Hildreth and Jack House had mentioned when they wrote about the arrival of the POWs. About lunchtime on April 7, 1938, the sky above Aliceville had darkened like nighttime, and a powerful twister had roared randomly through town. Robert Hugh Kirksey was fifteen at the time. He grabbed his new Kodak camera and was awestruck when he looked through the viewfinder and saw that the swirling black cloud filled up his entire lens. "The suction power of the twister was so great that it pulled toward its center a giant oak tree which stood right in front of us about one block away," he wrote later. "I saw it literally pick up whole houses and suck them up into its powerful vacuum. All up inside the tornado, we could see large timbers, roofs of houses, and hundreds of unidentified objects flying around in the vortex, gradually rising higher and higher."

Robert Hugh counted five slow seconds, and the time exposure photograph he took was so good *The Birmingham Post* ran it with the headline, "Boy Braves Tornado To Snap This Picture." A precocious entrepreneur, Robert Hugh had dozens of prints made and sold them to people all over town for fifty cents apiece.

When the 1938 tornado had finished its run, thirteen Aliceville residents were dead, and the remarkable scenes of damage would be talked about for years to come—among them the mule pierced through by a two-by-four and the house blown away except for a kitchen table with a basket of unbroken eggs still on top. Robert Hugh wrote that Aliceville residents were as likely to ask each other, "Where were you when the tornado struck?" as they were to ask, "Where were you when you heard about Pearl Harbor?"

In spite of the heavy rainstorms in the spring of 1943—even an occasional frog strangler, as the worst ones were called—no serious tornadoes developed, and the cotton crop in Pickens County began displaying white blooms on schedule in mid-June. The newspaper held a contest each year to publicize the very first blossom of the season and reported on June 17 that Lester White, "a colored tenant on the F.B. Carpenter place near Aliceville," had delivered the first bloom of 1943 to the editor's office that week. The newspaper stated that Lester was a good worker who deserved a great deal of the credit for the fine cotton crop expected on the Carpenter place later in the summer.

Because the war had called so many local young men to military service, cotton farmers in Pickens County were short-handed. As they looked ahead to the harvest, they hoped the prisoners arriving each week by the trainload would prove to be good at picking cotton.

By treating German and Jap prisoners humanely, we shall at least not incite the Germans or the Japs to treat American prisoners any worse. We may even inspire them to do better by our boys—especially as our fighting men bore closer to the hearts of German and Jap power.

• August 12, 1944 •
Editorial, *Colliers Magazine*

CHAPTER SEVEN
Settling In

On an afternoon near the end of June, Walter Felholter noticed bright green seedlings poking up from the covered up trench behind the barracks in Compound C. He realized almost immediately what they were. Several times, he and others got down on their knees and pulled up the small sprouts, but so many ears of corn had been buried that it was impossible to stay ahead of the job. What had been buried in darkness was now clearly visible in broad daylight. Walter got a shovel and tried turning under the soil on top of the trench, but that didn't work either. The corn stalks were persistent and would not be ignored.

Before long, guards who walked ground patrol noticed the corn plants and puzzled among themselves. Were the Germans afraid the Americans wouldn't feed them enough? Were they growing extra food to hoard in their barracks? Surely that couldn't be the case. They'd been eating well for nearly a month.

Eventually, one of the guards reported the mysterious planting to Captain Strohecker, who took his interpreter and went to the mess hall to check with the cooks. "We don't know anything," they said, but after a good bit of questioning, one of them mumbled that the company leader had had the corn buried in order to solve a dilemma. He didn't want to insult the Americans by not eating the food issued, and he'd been afraid to explain. The cooks hoped the stockade officer would understand.

Captain Strohecker shook his head at this explanation, but the next morning he directed Earline Lewis to issue corn only to the American personnel mess halls and to order more potatoes for the POW kitchens.

One steamy evening during the same week, Camp Aliceville took in a group of wounded German prisoners from North Africa who did not march jauntily from the Frisco depot. Some were able to walk, but most were carried off the train on stretchers and taken immediately to the post hospital. These 160 men had received good medical treatment during their Atlantic crossing, but with no medical personnel on the train, their wounds had not been dressed since they left New York. It took the small medical staff at Aliceville several days to stabilize many of them. Several required surgery, and one died of a respiratory infection the day after he arrived.

Camp Aliceville had one permanently assigned Army nurse and two civilian graduate nurses in residence to assist three Medical Corps officers. Fortunately, eight other Army nurses were at the camp on temporary duty when the wounded prisoners came in. They were able to help but expected to be transferred overseas at any time.

More help materialized a few days later with the assignment of six new prisoners who were medical officers—a major, a captain, a first lieutenant, and three second lieutenants. They were well trained and went to work immediately to help the American medical personnel.

Appropriate housing for officer prisoners had not yet been constructed at Aliceville, so Colonel Prince directed the six German doctors to move into temporary quarters in what was designed to be the post hospital's psychopathic ward. These officer prisoners received treatment considered appropriate to their rank. Unlike enlisted prisoners in the compound barracks, they slept on steel beds with mattresses and mattress covers, sheets, blankets, pillows, and pillowcases. They were not required to wear clothing painted with the large P and W letters.

Something of a stir erupted one evening when the German medical officers showed up at the post theater to watch a movie. Enlisted prisoners were not allowed outside their compounds except for hospital treatment authorized by the medical staff. They did not watch movies until much later. When the German officers showed up for the movie and seated themselves quietly on the wooden benches farthest from the screen, an undercurrent of protest rumbled among Americans seated with their families. Why should any prisoners, no matter what their rank, be allowed to enjoy entertainment provided for camp personnel and their families? It didn't seem fair, but after a while, the Americans got used to seeing the German doctors slip in to enjoy such productions as John Ford's *The Grapes of Wrath.* They also got used to seeing the doctors enjoying afternoon strolls around town, outside the camp perimeters—something perfectly legal for captured medical officers, according to the Geneva Convention.

Captain Stephen Fleck joined the Camp Aliceville medical staff in early July and was also a great help with the influx of wounded prisoners. Captain Fleck had an unusual background. He was Jewish and had studied medicine at Goethe University in Frankfurt until one of his professors warned him he'd been targeted for arrest by the Nazis. Fortunately, he was able to flee Germany in 1933 while it was still possible for people of Jewish heritage to do so. Bringing family money with him, he came to America and completed his studies at Harvard Medical School.

By 1943, he was an American citizen and had been assigned as a doctor with the United States Medical Corps. Stephen spoke fluent German but kept this fact hidden from the prisoners he treated when he first arrived at Camp Aliceville.

On July 2, the 436th MPEG unit arrived in Aliceville from Fort Custer in southwest Michigan. This unit consisted primarily of married men already established in peacetime careers. Most were from Ohio, including an investment banker, two accountants, a lawyer, a schoolteacher, a farmer, several shop foremen, and a restaurant owner. The 436th also had eight young men from West Virginia—six from the Moundsville area along the Ohio River, including twenty-year-old Kenneth Eugene Dakan who was living at home with his parents when he was drafted in March 1943. Gene was the third youngest person in the company, which also included one nineteen-year-old and one eighteen-year-old.

Back in the spring, after the 436th was assembled at Fort Custer, First Lieutenant Joseph A. Dionne took on the task of turning this odd assortment into an effective unit of military police. From April through June, the fifteen-year veteran of regular army service put Gordon Forbes, Harold Cover, Gene Dakan, and 133 others through rigorous training and created an MPEG unit the regimental commander could be proud of.

Gordon Forbes remembers the troop train pulling in at the depot in Aliceville. After marching out to the camp, he watched prisoners tacking tarpaper to additional barracks that were just being completed. "No local gentry lined the streets when we came in," he has said.

At Fort Custer, Gordon had been trained for prisoner chasing on work details, with one guard for every three prisoners. He'd been warned not to let the POWs maneuver around him or get behind him. On one of his first work details within the camp, his three POW charges were thirsty and kept asking him for *Wasser.* Gordon marched them over to the latrine where the drinking fountain was, but they shook their heads. *"Nichts! Nichts! Eise Wasser!"* they said. They didn't plan to work unless Gordon marched them over to the officers' club where they could get ice water, which he did. Since German people do not generally drink ice water at home, it is likely that this "work slowdown" tactic by the German prisoners had a lot to do with the extreme summer heat in Aliceville.

When not on duty, Gordon enjoyed playing volleyball or pool and listening to the radio in the day room. There were dances periodically, and these were well attended by the servicemen, but whenever he had the opportunity, Gordon would get a pass and go up to Tuscaloosa or even Birmingham for a weekend.

He was not overjoyed about being in the service. "I guess my general feelings were that if it wasn't for those Germans, I wouldn't have to be there. We wouldn't have been in the war at all."

Harold Cover had no desire to be in the service either. "I was pulled away from my home and my friends, and my thought was—get in, get it over as quickly as possible." He never dreamed at the time that his years of military service would lead to friendships that would last through the years. He remembers marching through the main gate of the camp that hot July morning and seeing the guard shack to the left of the road and the nurses' barracks to the right with the dispensary and the Post

Exchange beyond. He remembers the contraption that was used to cool Colonel Prince's home—a huge fan with burlap hanging in front of it and water dripping down.

And he remembers the flagpole where the bugler stood to blow retreat and other signals. Once, the regular bugler was heading home on furlough, and another recruit really wanted his job. "They told him if he practiced, he could be bugler while the other fella was on furlough. Well, he practiced and practiced till his lips got sore, and then that evening, when it come time for him to blow retreat, he locked it up but good. Our commanding officer, whose name was Woods, was shaking with laughter. 'For God's sake, just hang that bugle up and let the wind blow it!' he said."

Harold thought Aliceville was the smallest place he'd ever seen. Occasionally, he went into town for a restaurant meal or for a movie at the Palace Theater, but mostly he stayed back at the barracks and wrote letters home when he wasn't on duty.

Gene Dakan had grown up in a town even smaller than Aliceville—Rosby's Rock, West Virginia (population 125), which claimed its only mention in history when the final spike of the B&O Railroad was driven there on Christmas Eve 1852, connecting Baltimore to Wheeling, West Virginia, and the Ohio River area by rail. Gene spent his youth enjoying regular sports like football and baseball. He also spent time hunting and trapping and, in winter, sledding with his friends down mile-long hills.

After graduation from Moundsville High School in 1940, Gene studied bookkeeping and typing and was recommended for a clerk typist position at the E.I. DuPont war plant seventeen miles south of Moundsville. He worked there until Uncle Sam sent him to Fort Custer.

In May 1943, the almost fully trained 436th was called to Fort Devens in Massachusetts and ordered to escort a trainload of German prisoners from the pier in Boston to Camp McAlester in Oklahoma. The trip was uneventful, but Gene remembers being warned not to trust the POWs. "You had to be on the alert, but after I guarded them for a while, I realized they were just soldiers more or less fighting for their country the same as we were. They were very disciplined, and they were very athletic."

On one of Gene's first ventures off base and into town, he visited Sam Wise's clothing store and bought himself a new army cap. He chuckled at the "Lost and Found" advertising card Sam tucked inside. It read, "SAY! You Damn Fool this Ain't Your Hat!" and included blank lines for the purchaser's name and address. Beneath that was Sam's slogan, "BE WISE and PATRONIZE SAM WISE, Aliceville, Ala."

Gene and his buddies assumed regular guard duty rotations along with the other MPEG companies already in camp. During the year and a half before they were shipped overseas, many of them continued to be called out occasionally to escort POWs to other camps like Fort Blanding near Jacksonville, Florida, and Fort Dix in New Jersey.

Gene helped escort prisoners from Aliceville to Camp Blanding and all the way out to the Papago Park POW camp in Tempe, Arizona. He says regular passenger trains were used for these transfer trips. "The Germans would be in several coaches. The guards would be on the platforms between coaches and in the coaches at each end of the train." The POWs were treated with discipline, but it wasn't difficult to guard them because they knew what was expected. Many told Gene they were relieved to be in American hands instead of in another enemy country like Russia.

One of these transfers took place on July 4 when 160 communists were sent out of Camp Aliceville, possibly to Florida's Camp Blanding. The incident is recorded in a calendar/diary book printed the following year after the camp acquired its own printing press. No other mention is made of this transfer, so the exact destination is not known, but it suggests the far-reaching political issues that complicated America's efforts to police its captives during World War II.

It is not surprising that some German POWs embraced communism. Although Karl Marx had been banished from Germany—and then from France and Belgium—nearly one hundred years earlier, he and Friedrich Engels were both German by birth and had developed their communist ideals while reading earlier German philosophers.

The American government shifted German prisoners from camp to camp frequently as it struggled to develop the best methods for handling the huge numbers being brought across the Atlantic each month. At the end of April 1943, only slightly more than two thousand German POWs were in the United States. By the end of July, that number had grown to more than fifty-four thousand and would almost double to more than ninety-four thousand by the end of August. The primary purpose of this shifting from camp to camp seemed to be distinguishing between extreme pro-Nazis and extreme anti-Nazis. (Both groups were considered troublemakers.) There were also efforts to identify men who accepted captivity and wanted to work and study to improve their lives within the POW system—whether Nazis or not. Later in the war, there would also be efforts to identify those who might be reeducated and encouraged to become model democratic citizens when they returned to a defeated postwar Germany.

One thorn that plagued this process was the fact that American commanders and guards had great admiration for German military discipline. Like American army nurse Yvonne Humphrey who had crossed the Atlantic with a group of POWs, they noticed how well the German non-commissioned officers maintained order and discipline among their enlisted soldiers, even though that discipline seemed overly harsh at times. Many American commanders, including Colonel Prince, concluded that the German NCOs could keep things running smoothly if they remained in charge inside the compounds.

However, most of these NCOs were loyal Nazis, which meant that, as the camps settled into their routines in 1943, these leaders remained faithful to Nazi ideals of leadership and ran the compounds accordingly.

This was a frustrating reality for passionate anti-Nazi prisoners like Erwin Schulz, the "999 punishment battalion" draftee who'd deserted in March in North Africa and turned himself over to a group of Moroccans who turned him over to the French. While still in North Africa, Erwin had been warned by his French guards that Nazi prisoners were murdering anti-Nazis in the transfer camps, and he was soon to discover that Nazi mistreatment of POWs with different political and social views would continue in the permanent camps in America.

Erwin had participated in anti-Nazi and communist demonstrations in Germany in the 1930s, though he had not joined the Communist Party. He'd served time in prison for these activities, and that was how he'd ended up in the punishment battalion.

When Erwin arrived at Camp Aliceville in the summer of 1943, he was just as surprised as newspaper reporter Jack House to see Nazi NCOs slicing their arms forward in a crisp "Heil Hitler" salute whenever they encountered American officers. At first, Erwin and other 999ers talked openly about their opposition to such Nazi behavior. After what they'd seen in North Africa and what they'd heard of Hitler's difficulties in Russia, they were convinced Germany would eventually lose the war and felt no obligation to continue behaving like members of the German army. They assumed their American guards would look out for them and become their friends.

To Erwin's amazement, when he and others refused to salute Nazi NCOs, the Americans labeled *them* "troublemakers." He has written that the 999ers in Camp Aliceville took turns standing their own guard watch each night because they feared persecution from the "*Gestapo* elements" in the camp and could not count on their captors for protection. The German NCOs "threatened us just to prove how powerful they were," he wrote of the *Lagergestapo* (prison camp secret police) who intimidated anti-Nazi prisoners with late night beatings and promises to sneak reports back to Germany so the official Gestapo could persecute their families.

Sometime in July, the 999ers asked Camp Aliceville authorities to protect them by isolating these "*Gestapo* elements." They suggested to Colonel Prince through a newly elected camp spokesman that the Nazi NCOs were exerting a "bad" influence on young prisoners. The Colonel's reaction stunned them. "Instead of the Nazis," Erwin wrote, "we were isolated into a rather primitive compound for a couple months and then sent to Camp McCain, Mississippi, which was an anti-Nazi camp."

This is probably when the first of the back three compounds (D, E, and F) opened at Camp Aliceville. An entry in the calendar/diary book printed later suggests the 999ers may have been housed temporarily in Compound D. Compounds D, E, and F bordered the black water swamp with all its creatures—especially mosquitoes—and would have been much more unpleasant than the front three compounds—at least until the drainage issue was resolved.

The early prisoners at Camp Aliceville represented a microcosm of the political views swirling through Europe just before the middle of the twentieth century—democracy and monarchy, but also national socialism (Nazism), fascism, communism, and many offshoots of these. Prisoner Wilhelm Westhoff, a former teacher from Düsseldorf who would later act as POW director of the prisoner education program within Camp Aliceville, wrote in the POW newspaper in 1944 that agitators and would-be politicians saw the camp as a "rich field to plow." Here, behind barbed wire, they dreamed of playing at politics and experimenting with the capabilities of their various ideologies. It didn't seem to matter that some of these ideologies had brought disagreeable circumstances in recent years.

Only a small segment of the prisoner population in Camp Aliceville obsessed over political and social issues, however. Most recognized that this time behind barbed wire was not a wise time for political and ideological arguments. In spite of their desire to resist regimentation, they accepted the disciplinary order of the camp and learned to function within it.

Most took an attitude close to that of Hermann Blumhardt. "Politics and religion got you into trouble in Camp Aliceville," Hermann told Alabama Public Television in 1989. "You didn't feel real easy in Camp Aliceville sometimes. You didn't know who to trust and who not to trust." Hermann assessed his situation when he first arrived, sensing that he would be a prisoner for quite some time, and set priorities for himself that did not involve politics. The first of those was learning English, and he focused on that. The second was avoiding political discussions at all costs.

It was prisoners like Hermann that Will Peebles came to know in the summer of 1943 as he moved in and out of the prison camp working for George Downer. At first, Will had a pass so he could deliver Coca-Colas and Big Chief orange sodas to the PX and the officers' and enlisted men's clubs inside the camp. He also delivered to the canteens inside the compounds where the prisoners were. "The soldiers and all knew who I was, so they just waved me on in, and I never did stop at the guard thing after the first two months. I had some colored boys on the truck with me, and we'd just go in there, and the prisoners would talk to us. A lot of them could speak English. They were smart, but they were just kids, nineteen- and twenty-year-olds, a lot of them."

George Downer also owned a farm, and Will sometimes went by the camp with a truck and picked up ten or twelve POWs to help chop or pick cotton or do other chores. "I'd be the only one over there with them," he says. "I didn't have a weapon or anything. The guards told me, if one of them leaves, just remember which direction he went, and we'll go find him."

Most of the prisoners Will talked to were not Nazis. "They'd tell us, 'Y'all are a little different than we are. Y'all can be conscientious objectors and you don't have to go fight, but when they told us we got to go, we had one choice—either go or get killed.' The majority of them hated Hitler worse than we did. You'd be surprised how much they enjoyed being here. They'd had it hard over there."

The German NCOs considered it their duty to establish a soldierly order within the compounds—a soldierly order that, like the Nazi party at home, did not tolerate dissenting views. With this in mind, they worked to discourage old cliques among the prisoners and to establish new associations that conformed to their political views. Under the watchful eye of the American authorities, they organized the prisoners into companies and set up a strict regimen for sports and the arts, for education and entertainment, and for maintenance of the facilities. In subtle ways, they made it clear that allegiance to Hitler was still expected.

One former prisoner notes that this discipline created a real danger even for POWs who were not fanatical in their anti-Nazi beliefs. "Remember that there were fifty guys in a barracks," he has said. "If you made one remark that rubbed the Nazis the wrong way, they could kill you before the Americans could even begin to help you."

Because the different compounds were locked off from each other in the beginning, there were often great differences in how the German NCOs interpreted their responsibilities. Some were more brutal than others in their attempts to maintain order. Their only opportunity to interact and to learn from each other's experiences was during regularly scheduled short discussion meetings with the American commanders.

One of these discussion meetings occurred on the morning of July 14. The Americans wanted the German NCOs to remind prisoners that mail would be collected only on Mondays and Thursdays and to announce that two concrete washtubs had been ordered for each latrine. The German NCOs wanted to submit a variety of requests: more musical instruments for the orchestra being formed in Compound B and more tools for clearing trees and brush from the areas in each compound that were to be used for recreation. They also presented requests from individual prisoners—one in Compound D wanted to contact a cousin in Compound C, and one in Compound A wanted permission to arrange a marriage by proxy with his fiancée back in Germany.

In the middle of the meeting, a courier arrived with a package from the YMCA War Prisoners Aid Program. What was in the package is not recorded, but it would have been items such as books or paper and pencils, perhaps used sports or music equipment, to help relieve boredom among the prisoners.

The YMCA's tradition of wartime service to soldiers and prisoners originated during the Civil War when its United States Christian Commission ministered to Confederate soldiers in northern prisons and sent supplies to Union soldiers in Confederate prisons. It continued during World War I when President Wilson gladly accepted the YMCA's program of morale and welfare services for the military.

After Germany invaded Poland in 1939, the YMCA again moved to coordinate its services with the military. It joined several other social service organizations to create the USO (United Service Organizations for National Defense) and also initiated the War Prisoners Aid Program, which lasted for seven years and served POW camps in thirty-three countries. Members of the YMCA War Prisoner Aid staff visited POW camps regularly, including Camp Aliceville. They made evaluations and ordered supplies. They also shipped supplies to twenty countries where personal visits were not possible because of battle conditions.

When the courier explained that an official representative or spokesman for the POWs had to sign for the YMCA package that arrived on July 14, the group realized that no such representative existed. Both the American commanders and the German NCOs agreed it would be a good idea to appoint a spokesman who could function as an official representative of the prisoners—not only to sign for packages from the YMCA and the Red Cross, but also as someone who could be trusted by both prisoners and guards and have the freedom to move from compound to compound as needed to coordinate actions, gather grievances, and disseminate information.

The courier wanted his receipt signed that day, so the German NCOs in the discussion group agreed to go back to their compounds, nominate candidates, agree on an appointee, and report back with their choice that very afternoon. Among those involved in the discussion that morning, the sergeant-major in charge of Company 13 in Compound D stood out as the most likely candidate. He was quiet and contemplative—perhaps still grieving over the loss of his brother on a Tunisian battlefield—but he had asked clever questions and, when asked if he would serve, objected less than the others to taking on the responsibility of spokesman.

By late afternoon, in mutual agreement among all the compounds, the Germans had elected as their spokesman twenty-eight-year-old Sergeant-Major Walter F. Meier—the former Koch detachment Storm trooper with one bad arm who had lost his brother near Medjez el Bab. Walter's first official act was to sign the receipt for the YMCA package.

From that day forward, Walter Meier became, as one fellow prisoner wrote of him later, "the crystallization point of our community life, the dumping ground for everyone's problems and for anything unpleasant." Other prisoners, including other NCOs, were often suspicious of the frequent contact with Americans required by Walter's new position. Still, they admired him and brought him every imaginable complaint and frustration, hoping his liaison with the camp authorities would bring resolution.

July 14 was also the starting date of the first inspection of Camp Aliceville by someone other than newspaper reporters. Captain Maxwell S. McKnight and his inspection team from the Prisoner of War Division of the PMGO (Provost Marshal General's Office) found their way to Aliceville that morning and spent the next two days evaluating every aspect of life in the camp. Their official report states that the camp held 3,416 prisoners in residence (including the six medical officers). All of the prisoners were German.

Captain McKnight was a graduate of Yale Law School. He was a member of a prominent New York City family with connections to the Roosevelts and had received part of his education in France. By the following year, he would be promoted to Major and become part of the PMGO's massive and controversial reeducation program to teach German POWs the principles of democracy.

McKnight noted in his report that the processing of records for the POWs in Camp Aliceville was not yet complete when he arrived. The first and second platoons of the 443rd POW Processing Company had arrived on July 12, but their equipment for photographing and fingerprinting each prisoner was still en route. The captain reminded Colonel Prince that each American officer was to read the Geneva Convention and certify in writing that he had read it and was familiar with its provisions.

Approximately two hundred prisoners reported for sick call each day, but the number was going down gradually as minor skin diseases and ailments resulting from battle conditions were treated. There were 172 prisoners in the hospital, with about 20 of these being considered for repatriation to Germany because of the severity of their condition.

No mental or neurotic cases were being treated, which was why the psychiatric ward was available as temporary quarters for the six German medical officers. Prisoners were providing orderly service in the hospital, and one prisoner with some dental training was able to clean teeth and handle minor fillings. Three or four prisoners were staffing the dispensary in each compound.

The inspection team met with Walter Meier, the newly appointed POW spokesman, who told them the morale of the prisoners was generally good. When Walter asked if money could be sent to the POWs from Germany, Captain McKnight gave him the address of the International Red Cross Committee, which handled such requests. When Walter asked if the prisoners could receive old magazines, the captain gave him the address of the YMCA War Prisoners' Aid office for this request.

McKnight's report mentioned the fourteen hundred denim hats that had not yet arrived and suggested more picks, shovels, and mallets were needed for general maintenance around the camp. He noted that three contracts had already been negotiated for the use of POW labor in the surrounding area and that these had been submitted to the Fourth Service Command for approval. Two of these contracts were for farm labor. Colonel Prince told the inspectors he expected that several hundred prisoners would soon be picking cotton in Pickens County.

The third contract was for a pulpwood project. Colonel Prince was disappointed when Captain McKnight explained the Judge Advocate General's ruling that the Geneva Convention would not allow prisoners to be involved in the harvesting of pulpwood because the work was considered too dangerous.

Later in the summer, reports were submitted to the War Department showing that pulpwood work was not the same as heavy logging—that the growths to be harvested were only six to eight inches in diameter and that the work would be supervised closely by trained representatives of the United States Forest Service. On September 1, the War Department would reverse itself and authorize the use of POWs in this industry. Over the next three years, nearly 20 percent of the pulpwood in the area of the Fourth Service Command would be harvested by POWs.

This War Department decision was of great importance in Pickens County. Close to 80 percent of the land in the county is covered with loblolly and shortleaf pine, oak, hickory, and gum trees. The coming of the railroad had caused a lumber industry boom in Alabama early in the twentieth century, and it was still a vital part of the county's economy during World War II. With more and more young men being drafted for military service, the prospect of POW help with the work was very welcome.

Once the War Department gave its approval, Camp Aliceville's NCO prisoners received instruction from representatives of the United States Forest Service Timber Production War Project, and these NCOs then supervised the enlisted POWs when they were sent into the woods to cut timber for Johnny Johnston's sawmill.

Captain McKnight's report outlined the many recreation projects already underway at Camp Aliceville. Jumping pits for broad and high jumping had been constructed and were in use, and a track for running events was being built. Amazingly, in only five weeks, the German POWs had organized an orchestra in Compound B and presented a concert on July 10, using musical instruments borrowed locally and even a few hand-built instruments innovatively fashioned from such things as empty sauerkraut cans. Stages were being constructed in the compound recreation buildings, and the workshops were busy turning out stage props and costumes created from scrap lumber, cardboard, burlap bags, and just about anything else available for planned productions of classic German plays.

The inspection report contained a number of additional recommendations from Colonel Prince, who told Captain McKnight that, even though Pickens was a dry county, he'd tried to obtain beer for the prisoners. The local retailers had been unable to supply it because of a recent Office of Price Administration ruling about not accommodating new customers. In typical military fashion, the colonel suggested the PMGO seek a new ruling exempting POW camps from the previous ruling. Eventually, beer became available in the compound canteens.

McKnight concluded his report with a generally favorable statement: "The roads throughout the reservation are well surfaced and the grounds attractively landscaped. Although all trees have been removed from the camp area proper, the camp is bordered by trees and farm lands. Numerous trees are in the recreation area. The camp presents a neat and attractive appearance."

Outside the POW camp gates, Aliceville residents were encouraged in July by news of the war in Europe. Newspapers and newsreels carried reports of the Allied invasion of Sicily on July 9 and 10, followed by accounts of the heavy bombing of Rome ten days later. By the end of the month, Mussolini had been overthrown, and a new government had been formed in Italy. The battle maps of Europe suggested hope, with Allied forces edging towards Hitler's strongholds.

Robert W. Adams, a captain in the United States army, was captured by the Germans in France on June 29. He wrote to his wife, Elizabeth (Kilpatrick) Adams, on July 11 from a German POW camp ninety-three miles from Berlin, assuring her that he was well fed, with friends, and "almost" his own boss. Though Robert was from Decatur in northern Alabama and "not very well known in Pickens," his wife was the daughter of Pickens County residents Mr. and Mrs. Howard Kirkpatrick. She was living in Carrollton and working in the office of the county school superintendent, James R. Swedenburg, while her husband was overseas.

It is clear from Robert's first letter that American POWs in Germany felt the need to supplement what their captors were providing. He told his wife she could send him up to ten pounds of supplies every sixty days and suggested she send, in whatever order she thought best, a toothbrush, three tubes of toothpaste, a razor with twelve blades, two good pipes with tobacco and matches, flannel pajamas, a heavy turtleneck sweater, summer and winter underwear, heavy socks, four handkerchiefs, a leather jacket, gloves, two pencils, and a mirror. She could fill in the packages with cigarettes and chocolate. Robert also asked his wife to donate liberally to the Red Cross because they were doing an excellent job of supplying food and books.

On July 21, Robert wrote again, telling Elizabeth it seemed as if all he did was eat and sleep. "Breakfast at 9, lunch about 1, dinner at 6 and cocoa about 9. Lights out at mid-night. In between I read, play cards, wander around talking (not to myself, yet), exercise and make little gadgets for our kitchen." He'd signed up to begin classes in French, German, math, and physics the following week and had also enrolled in a correspondence course from the University of London. "Perhaps," he wrote, echoing the sentiments of Aliceville German POWs like Walter Felholter and Hermann Blumhardt, "the time I am a prisoner will not be entirely wasted."

Jack Pratt announced in his "Here, There, and Everywhere" column on July 22 that Aliceville resident Vera Mae Cooper had enlisted in the United States Marines at the end of June. In his typical chauvinistic "snicker style," Jack cautioned people not to refer to Vera Mae as a leatherneck or a rubber neck but suggested they could assume that lady marines would probably do some necking while in the service. He also commented that the American armed services had nicknames for other women's branches—WAACS, WAVES, SPARS—but no nickname for lady marines.

The following week, Jack reported that Sergeant Lillian Brandon, Pickens County's first WAAC, was home on leave for a week with her parents, Mr. and Mrs. J.E. Brandon. She'd completed her training out in Iowa and was now stationed at Orlando, Florida.

Jack wrote that sawmill owner Johnny Johnston and his friend Ralph Pratt had caught a fine mess of bass recently—the largest seven weighing a total of twenty pounds. Determined not to have their bonanza fishing hole set upon by others, neither man would reveal where they'd caught the fish or at what time of the day or night. They wouldn't even say what kind of bait they'd used.

With July usually observed as spiritual revival month all over the South, large canvas tents went up on several vacant lots in Aliceville in spite of the heavy humidity, even in the night air. The degree of spiritual dignity or emotional frenzy involved in these nightly services depended to some extent on the denomination, but all of them evoked an Elmer Gantry flavor for both believers and the curious who crowded the wooden benches arranged on scattered straw beneath the canvas flaps. Under the dull glare of bare electric bulbs hung from tent supports, visiting preachers (some less ethical than others) threatened eternal damnation and issued altar calls for repentance while their audiences battled both heat and flies with colorful cardboard funeral home fans mounted on popsicle-type sticks.

Folks raised their voices in familiar gospel tunes like "Bringing in the Sheaves" and "Rock of Ages." They passed the hat for contributions. Bewildered adolescents tried sincerely to decide if they should line up on the right side of the tent—for those who were sure they were already headed to heaven—or on the left side of the tent—for those who thought they might be headed to hell. Eager church elders and their assistants waited in the tent corners to pray with those on both sides.

The Fellowship Church invited everyone in town to attend their evening services of preaching and testifying beginning Sunday evening, July 11. Aliceville Methodists, joining with sixty other Methodist churches in the Tuscaloosa District, scheduled their services beginning July 18 and continuing through the last week of the month. They, too, invited the entire community. The Presbyterians waited until August, holding services twice a day for a week, beginning Sunday, August 15.

One interdenominational series of services on the outskirts of Aliceville attracted folks from miles around, including a number of out-of-state soldier boys from Camp Aliceville who listened with fascination to the ranting messages of a visiting holiness preacher who quickly stirred the crowd to a frenzy. Women in flowered dresses waved handkerchiefs and spoke in tongues, and men in sweat-stained white shirts and suspenders let loose with fervent shouts of "Hallelujah!" When one "sister" rose up in response to the preacher's message and shouted "Praise the Lord!" a soldier at the rear of the tent immediately added, "And pass the ammunition!"

This less-than-reverent response caused many a gasp among the faithful, and some of them marched right over the next morning to express their indignation to Colonel Prince. The offending soldier was confined to post for several weeks as discipline for his outburst.

Mary Lu Turner remembers a religious experience from that summer of 1943 that has stayed vivid throughout her life. Through his work with the Army Corps of Engineers, her father met a Negro minister who invited the Turners to visit his church. On the Sunday morning that the Turners accepted the minister's invitation, they were surprised to be treated as special guests—seated together on the very front row and introduced at the beginning of the service.

Mary Lu's mother was the more adventurous of her two parents, always eager to experience new aspects of life wherever they were living. It was she who accepted the same minister's invitation for the family to observe a river baptism later in the month. Ward Turner took a movie camera with him and made a film of the event—a film his daughter still has. Mary Lu doesn't remember how far the family traveled by car or exactly which stream was used, but she remembers being fascinated by all the people gathered on the riverbank. "The minister stood waist deep in the water, and I watched several women dressed in white, gauze-type garments being led down to the water by men from the church. It was very subdued as each woman waded out to the preacher who would repeat holy words and then carefully place one large hand in the small of her back and the other on her forehead. Then he would submerge the woman three full times. Each one would come up flailing, just totally taken over by God, and as she was led back up out of the water, she would keep repeating, over and over, 'So glad, Lord! So glad, Lord!'" Mary Lu had never seen anything like this. "I was just really in awe," she has said, "—how something could affect an individual so profoundly. I can picture it as if I saw it yesterday."

Sometime that summer, the Turners made the difficult decision to send their older daughter, Joyce, back to Baltimore for her senior year of high school. Joyce had lost many credits in language and science when she transferred to Aliceville High School the previous December, and during the second half of the school year, it became clear that she could not get the same level of education she'd been used to back at Western High School. Mary Lu and her mother saw Joyce off on the train from Tuscaloosa, and Joyce returned to Baltimore to live with an aunt while she finished high school.

At about the same time, in early August, the Turners left the old Harkins place on Red Hill and moved into one of the cement block units in the newly completed civilian employee housing across the highway from Camp Aliceville. W.O. Kirk, manager of the camp commissary, moved in, too, with his wife and his son, Buddie.

Mary Lu remembers that this was a different experience from living in town because everyone in the complex had come there from somewhere else. She made friends quickly with children in other units and enjoyed playing with them in the yards and at the community center. Her favorite summertime memories are of the ice cold Coca-Colas and the box of chilled Hershey's chocolate bars her parents brought home from the base PX and kept on hand in the refrigerator. Chocolate was scarce during the war, and having a whole box of it was quite a privilege.

There was a big cotton field not far from the housing complex. One day Mary Lu and some of the other children decided they'd go over and pick some cotton. "They give you these enormous bags that you drag alongside you, and of course, us little kids, we didn't last long. I still have some of the cotton I picked, though."

Mary Lu also has a calendar from Sam Wise's store. "I remember going there with my folks," she says. "I can still remember the smell of that store—the smell of new clothes."

Sometimes, Mary Lu and her family drove to Tuscaloosa with Major Dishner and his wife to shop at a department store there. "My father would drive his old '39 Chevy, and I would sit up front between him and Major Dishner, and my mother and Mrs. Dishner would sit in back. We'd go and come back in the same day." On one of these shopping trips, Mary Lu fell in love with an outfit on a mannequin in the little girls' department. "It was a blue skirt with braid around it, maybe two inches up from the hem, and a white peasant-style blouse. I didn't ever get new clothes at that time—usually my mother made things for me or she had a seamstress in Aliceville make things, but the Dishners bought that skirt and blouse for me, and I loved it so much. For me to have a store-bought outfit was a real treat."

On Saturday afternoons, Ward Turner would drive his daughter into town to the Palace Theater where she could meet her school friends and watch a Fred Astaire dance musical or a Captain Midnight movie as a weekly treat. From the building she lived in, Mary Lu could look across and see the building where her father worked for the Army Corps of Engineers. She had a pass, and sometimes she'd cross the highway and go through the guard gate, take a right hand turn, and visit her father. "My mother worked at the hospital, and that was behind the barbed wire, so I couldn't just go in and see her, but sometimes she made special arrangements, and I did go in." Mary Lu remembers seeing the prisoners in their denim outfits working on the landscaping and the young soldiers standing guard with their rifles. She wasn't afraid. "It was just there. This is what my life was, and I didn't think anything of it at the time.

During the summer of 1943, Americans across the country were constantly reminded to "use it up, wear it out, make it do, or do without" as more and more ration limits were imposed—three pairs of shoes per year, twenty-eight ounces of meat per week, and no sliced bread. In mid-July, Governor Sparks was quoted on the front page of the county newspaper with the message, "Every home in Alabama can become a war factory in a very real sense by salvaging the small quantities of tin, grease, and other material which, amassed from thousands of sources, will mean a difference in our total munitions output."

Throughout July and August, the Home Demonstration Club offered tips on getting by with rationed clothing and food in its "Victory Notes" column in the *Pickens County Herald and West Alabamian*. In the July 15 issue, the column praised a woman who attended the Antioch Club's summer luncheon wearing a lovely dress that appeared to be made of fine handkerchief linen. The Home Demonstration Club reporter announced with great satisfaction that the dress had actually been fashioned from chicken feed sacks.

At Camp Aliceville, the guards as well as the prisoners were eager for more recreational facilities. American officers and NCOs had their own clubs, and now, finally, a recreation building with dance pavilion was under construction for Camp Aliceville's enlisted men, but there was little money for furnishings. The Citizens Committee of Aliceville, headed by Coca-Cola bottler George Downer, decided to make an effort to change that. Working with a number of local businessmen, including Sam Wise, R.J. Kirksey, Gerald Stabler, W.E. Barrett, J.W. Cox, W.C. Martin, and C.S. Stirling, the Citizens Committee sold tickets and staged a "gala boxing show" at the Aliceville Ball Park on an August Friday evening.

Since most of the tent revival preachers had moved on and football season was still a few weeks away, Aliceville welcomed a big event to end the summer. Some guards from the camp used their free time to build the boxing ring, and others trained hard for the tryouts Citizens Committee members held to select thirty "handpicked warriors of the United States Army" to compete in fifteen separate matches in categories from feather weight to welter weight to heavy weight. When the big night came, local residents as well as army personnel packed the ballpark to watch the matches while enjoying sandwiches, popcorn, and soft drinks. Proceeds from the event were used for book shelves, writing desks, tables and chairs, a record player, and other items to furnish the enlisted men's recreation building.

George Downer also made headlines in connection with his efforts earlier in the summer to spearhead a highly successful war bond drive. Under his leadership, Pickens County over-subscribed its quota for war bonds. The county newspaper carried an article on July 8 praising the "colored community" of Aliceville for the success of its War Bond Rally as part of that campaign.

A number of Aliceville businesses took out ads in support of this effort. "We Extend Congratulations to the Colored People on their patriotic movement for July 6th and wish them success in their efforts," said the ad from MS&C Hardware Company. "We hope your War Bond Rally will be a great success," said the Aliceville Drug Company.

Sanders Mercantile Company printed the following: "We are always proud to see our colored people promote a program that will benefit their race, and help build up the community. We hope your War Bond Rally will be a great success."

Although the black and white communities of Aliceville were strictly segregated socially, both communities worked hard to support the war with contributions, and both communities sent their sons to fight.

On August 12, the announcement came that the army's newest B-25 Mitchel Bomber would be named The Spirit of Pickens County in honor of the effort. "When this plane lands on foreign fields where Pickens County boys are in action, they will want to kiss her wings and bid her God's speed in her activities," the newspaper declared. "Some Pickens County flyer may have the privilege of driving her into the very heart of the enemy's camp. What a joy it would give him. And boys from Alabama everywhere, who have the good fortune to see her, will glow with pride because of her name." The article went on to point out that Major Jimmy Doolittle had flown the same type of bomber over Tokyo in April 1942 and that ten of the Mitchel B-25s had made an historic four thousand mile mission from Australia to the Philippines and back.

The public can't understand why they want to escape from quarters and food better than they were ever used to during the long years of fighting, and try to find a way out of the country and back to the homeland. Only the foolish-mad will attempt this again, for it usually means death or serious injury.

• August 26, 1943 •
The Pickens County Herald and West Alabamian

CHAPTER EIGHT
Escape and Death

Late one night in early August inside the POW camp, Wilhelm Stüdl came across camp spokesman Walter Meier working by the light of a small, handmade lamp in the library in Compound D. The library was sparsely furnished and had no books because the first Red Cross shipment had not yet arrived. Walter was poring over his "General Communications" report for the camp when Wilhelm came in, but he set the pages aside and began to talk eagerly about his plans to improve the camp in any way he could. On that dark and quiet evening, Wilhelm considered Walter's plans presumptuous, but he would look back a year later and realize that the plans had not been as farfetched as he'd originally thought.

Walter chatted to him about the large craft workshops he wanted to see built, the orchestra he wanted to assemble, and his dreams for a fine theater in Compound D. There were more sports fields to build, and beyond all that, Walter had set himself the goal of founding a great camp school with day and evening classes. He even wanted to obtain a printing press somehow and set up a German newspaper within the camp. Wilhelm scoffed to himself about these lofty ambitions—all to be accomplished with the money allotted for such things from canteen profits, but he said nothing to dampen Walter's enthusiasm. "To get that for the men," Walter said of the school and the newspaper, "that is my mission, the single true duty—from that even the red tape cannot dissuade me."

Towards the end of summer, guard details and POWs were well organized enough to begin work details outside the boundaries of Camp Aliceville. Now that the Geneva Convention legality question regarding use of POWs in pulpwood harvests had been resolved, sawmill owner B.F. "Johnny" Johnston was one of the first to contract for regular POW labor details. Johnny took his twelve-year-old son, Pep, with him the first day the POWs were trucked out to work on a tract of timber about a mile from Camp Aliceville. Pep had been fascinated by the German prisoner of war camp residents ever since that June afternoon when he'd sat on the hood of his father's car and watched them march out from the train station.

The logging foreman had an interpreter with him who explained to the prisoners how to notch trees and fell them in such a way that no one would be in danger of being pinned underneath. "We didn't have chain saws or power saws back then," Pep remembers. "All crosscut saws. They gave everybody an axe and a wedge and then a crosscut saw for every two or three prisoners—kinda dangerous weapons, if you think about it, even though there were a few guards there."

Within minutes, the POWs were cutting trees, delimbing them, and cutting them into logs. Johnny had several mules, each dragging something that looked like a set of ice tongs. When a mule came around, the Germans would fix the tongs to the end of a log, and then the mule would drag it back to a truck. Another piece of equipment called a "logger's dream" had an engine and a cable and was used to load the logs onto the truck.

One POW has said that the Germans were taught to yell "Timber! Timber!" to signal guards and other prisoners to stay out of the way when a tree was coming down. The timber-cutting work was exhausting, especially in the summer heat, but the prisoners soon realized they could snatch a short break in the shade if they yelled "Timber!" once in a while when it wasn't absolutely necessary. The guards would stay back when they did this.

The guards, many of whom were very green recruits with the 305th and the 436th, were impressed by and came to trust the POWs more than camp officials might have preferred. Gene Dakan kept one memory to himself until 1993 because he knew it was against army regulations. "One time myself and another guard were with a group of prisoners out in the forest, cutting down pine trees," he told Sam Love. "We had an empty rifle, and we knew the Germans were very good at doing the manual of arms and standing at attention, so we let one of them show us the manual of arms the German way. They were great, much more disciplined than what the American soldier was because they'd had so much more training. Of course, it was done with an empty rifle, and the other guard stood back and was still guarding. After fifty years, I don't mind telling that we did that."

Joey Futchko remembers being given a shotgun and two shotgun shells when he was sent out to guard POWs working in the woods. "Once we were out there, I'd take the shells out of the gun, put them in my pocket, put the gun and the stock under a tree, and go to sleep. When it was time to go back to camp, the Germans would wake me up and say, 'C'mon, I'm gettin' hungry. Let's go home.'"

Harold Cover remembers a similar experience. A guard (perhaps Joey Futchko) was asleep beside a tree one day when the commander of the company headed in their direction. A POW saw the commander coming and shook the guard awake so he wouldn't get into trouble. After the company commander left, the guard put his gun back up against the tree and went back to sleep.

Harold says the guards knew they weren't supposed to fraternize with the prisoners. Officials were afraid the POWs might develop contacts that could be used against the United States in the war, but he doesn't believe that was the case. In his view, the POWs were glad to be out of the war, and he remembers that they made the first friendly advances. He thinks it's probably something that goes on in all wars.

Will Peebles remembers hearing townsfolk joke about the time guards miscounted during their head count before they returned a work detail to the prison camp. One prisoner was left behind in the woods, and the guards didn't realize it until they returned to camp. When they hurried back, there was the prisoner, sitting on a tree stump, waiting to be picked up.

Gordon Forbes started out guarding just three POWs at a time, but gradually the numbers increased to where most details had three guards for every twenty-five prisoners. Byron Kauffman remembers when Verdy Claire was guarding twenty-five POWs with a Thompson submachine gun early one morning. They had to walk across a creek on a log to get to the work area. There was dew on the log, and Verdy slipped and fell into the creek with his gun. "The prisoners got across all right, and then they plucked Verdy out of the creek, disassembled his

Thompson, built a fire, dried it off, and handed it back to him all cleaned up."

Once, a guard accidentally shot himself in the foot while out in the woods on a work detail. One POW picked up the guard's gun and raised it above his head—a signal to indicate non-hostility—and held it there while the others helped the guard. They removed the man's boot, grabbed a mule to serve as packhorse, and carried him out to the highway where he could be put into an ambulance.

Young Pep Johnston was impressed with how smart the Germans were. After a short time, they looked as if they'd been doing log work for a long time. Most of the prisoners worked on crews in the woods, but a few spent time at the sawmill itself, loading up lumber for one purpose or another.

Pep's father was comfortable with the prisoners. He often took his daughter as well as Pep and his younger son, Ben, with him to the sawmill, and none of the three remembers feeling threatened. Johnny spoke to those who knew a little English and learned what he could about them. He became rather good friends with one of the prisoners—a POW named Werner Stein from the northeastern German area of Mecklenburg, near Poland. One day Johnny invited another POW named Hummel into his office because Werner Stein told him the young man was a talented artist. Within half an hour, Hummel had created a lifelike pencil sketch of the mill owner and was "hired" to draw portraits of the older two Johnston children. His pay was a carton of cigarettes for each portrait.

Once, while several POWs were stacking lumber at the sawmill, a black farmer drove by with a wagonload of watermelons. Johnny knew the Germans loved watermelon, so he told them to hurry out to the man's wagon and get all the watermelons they could carry. He'd pay for them.

The Germans loved this idea. They jumped down from the lumber stack and ran after the wagon, hollering in their own language. This scared the wagon driver so much that he jumped down from his wagon and started to run away. Johnny knew the man. He called him back, explained, and asked how much he wanted for the melons. "Just let me go. Just let me go," the man insisted, but Johnny paid him anyway, and each of the Germans was able to take two or three watermelons back to the barracks that evening.

On another occasion, Johnny brought all the prisoners on his work details to the sawmill for a barbecue and beer to show his appreciation for their hard work. Although he got into some trouble with camp authorities because such an event was strictly forbidden, the prisoners enjoyed it immensely and remembered it fondly long after the war. "Dad couldn't imagine there being any kind of rule where you couldn't have a party," Pep remembers. "It was beyond him, but anyhow, they worked through that, and the prisoners continued to work for him until the camp closed."

Such friendly relationships did not keep all prisoners from considering ways to escape. Just after ten o'clock on Sunday night, August 1, during a rainstorm, the wail of sirens infused the rainy night air at Camp Aliceville. The whining alarm startled prisoners and guards alike, as well as civilian adults and children all over town.

There'd been plenty of drills, but not this late. The sound proclaimed that something was out of the ordinary, and even those not close enough to hear the gunshots that preceded the sirens stirred in their beds and wondered sleepily if they should fear for their safety. It was loud enough to waken little Mary Lu Turner from a deep sleep in the civilian housing complex across the highway. She remembers hearing it but not understanding until the next morning what she'd heard.

Unteroffizier Rolf Schneider was trying to do what he thought a prisoner of war should do—escape. The twenty-four-year-old sergeant, who'd befriended Robert Mitterwallner during their Liberty ship crossing from North Africa, had somehow come into possession of a wire cutter. There is no record of any other preparation Rolf made—whether others in his barracks helped him, whether he acquired civilian clothes or money, whether he had any plan about where he would go if he were successful. Like many German prisoners, he may have dreamed of making his way to Argentina, one of two South American countries (Chile was the other) that refused to sever relations with the Axis Powers after the Japanese attack on Pearl Harbor. Argentina offered safe harbor to German nationals and continued to do so until just before the end of the war.

Under cover of darkness and rain, Rolf slipped from his barracks and made his way to the inner perimeter fence of his compound. Quickly, he snipped a hole wide enough and slipped through. Then he scrambled on his belly across the ten feet of bare clay separating this fence from the outer one, but just as he began snipping the wires of the outer fence, the searchlight mounted on the guard tower caught him in its glare.

A guard with the 389th then did what he'd been trained to do and what he knew he had to do, no matter how reluctantly—he swiveled the thirty-caliber tower machine gun and fired. As if in slow frames of arrested time, he listened to the repetitive sound of the bullets and then winced as they slammed into the wet, shadowy figure cowering by the fence.

Within seconds, other guards in the tower activated the siren and slid down the pole to take up positions along the fence to the right of their tower. Gordon Forbes, who'd just returned from a weekend furlough in Tuscaloosa, heard the siren and ran to the supply room to draw his weapon and be ready. Within minutes, a full line of armed guards circled the entire compound enclosure just as they had practiced numerous times, but no further action was needed. Rolf Schneider, mortally wounded by a shot through his jaw, was carried through the mud to the post hospital where he died a week later.

The guard who fired the shots, a young MPEG from a northern state, returned to his barracks with the 389th. "The guy was just trying to get out," he would tell his bunkmate over and over. "He was doing what he had to do, and…and so was I." Years after the war, the personal horror of that night continued to work in the MPEG's brain, and he continued to feel in his heart the heavy burden of many a soldier, knowing that both he and the prisoner had acted as they were expected to.

Through the years since, 305th guard Chet Eisenhauer has wondered about this escape attempt and others. "I could never understand why anyone would choose to try to go out of the camp at night when it should have been easier to slip away from a work detail during the day."

Byron Kauffman has wondered the same thing. "When they were out on work details, they could've walked away at any time." In fact, says Kauffman, a few did walk away, but they were soon brought back by farmers when they got confused after discovering that nearby Columbus was in Mississippi rather than Ohio.

For Joseph Samper, a member of the 305th, the work details changed his impression of the prisoners. "That's when you found out what kind of people they were—human beings, soldiers drafted and doing their duty just as we were doing." When he heard about the shooting the morning after it happened, he was surprised to realize he felt genuine sadness about it.

Less than three weeks after Rolf Schneider was shot, a second POW was killed during an escape attempt that made more sense to Chet Eisenhauer and Byron Kauffman. Accounts of the shooting of nineteen-year-old Friedrich Rauschenberg vary greatly and illustrate the fascinating way incidents spawn rumors with different details. Most versions agree that Rauschenberg was shot by a guard on the afternoon of Tuesday, August 17, while trying to escape from a group of twenty prisoners finishing a work detail at Johnny Johnston's sawmill. When a quitting time head count showed only nineteen prisoners lined up, guards searched the area and discovered Friedrich crawling through weeds along the bank of a drainage ditch. The county newspaper noted that this was the second prisoner killed while attempting to escape. "The first one [Rolf Schneider] lingered several days before dying, but the second [Friedrich Rauschenberg] died within 24 hours after he was shot."

Historian E.B. Walker described a slightly different version of this second escape. He stated that Friedrich came out of the latrine at the sawmill on his hands and knees, giving the impression he was trying to avoid being seen. "When confronted by a guard, he came up off the ground with a handful of dirt or gravel and threw it in the guard's face. The guard then fired a round from a 12-gauge shotgun, killing the prisoner."

A third version quotes Sergeant Jack Sisty, the polio victim and former singer from New York City who rode a bicycle around camp for his chaplain's assistant duties. Jack said the guard who shot Rauschenberg claimed the prisoner had picked up a stone to throw at him and that that was why he was shot. "In this part of the state, you can't find a stone larger than a pebble.... that was really a murder. He [the prisoner] was on a detail, and there was a guard... whose brother was killed in the war, and he vowed he'd 'get a German.' He was in charge of the detail."

This incident is also referred to in Robert D. Billinger Jr.'s book, *Hitler's Soldiers in the Sunshine State.* Billinger quotes one of four wounded German soldiers who'd been transferred to Camp Blanding from Aliceville and were repatriated to Germany in March 1944. When they returned to Germany, they were required to answer a German government questionnaire about their treatment in British or American prisoner of war camps.

A forty-four-year-old private from the 665th *Pionier* (combat engineer) regiment told the German government in 1944 that he'd been in the camp hospital at Aliceville when a POW was brought in with severe wounds from a shotgun blast to his face and chest. The man died several days later. This private stated that the POW had been shot by a Jewish guard who bragged to his fellows that he would kill a Nazi. He also stated that the POWs staged a work stoppage and demanded that the Jewish guards be removed. When this did not happen, the entire combat engineer company was transferred—some to Camp Blanding in Florida and some to Camp Alva in Oklahoma. No other reports refer to Jewish guards in connection with this incident or a work stoppage.

Gordon Forbes was also at the sawmill when shots were fired. "I think one of our men got a little jumpy," he has said. "He thought one of the prisoners was coming at him, and he actually shot him right in the face with double-ought buck. As far as I know, that prisoner lived."

In its report, the county newspaper noted that the public was genuinely puzzled about why any prisoners would want to escape from Camp Aliceville. It suggested that only the "foolish-mad" would try to get away from the place.

Colonel Prince withheld the names of the dead prisoners from the press but told *The Birmingham Age-Herald* on August 27 that both were given military funerals. "No prisoner has been shot at so long as he obeyed the regulations as fixed by the Geneva Convention," he said. "Our men simply were doing their duty in preventing escapes."

A series of black-and-white slides tucked away in the basement archives of the main library in Birmingham offers a possible record of the burial of one of these men or perhaps a prisoner who died later at Camp Aliceville. Though the slides are not captioned or dated, they show a group of tanned and shirtless POWs digging in an area surrounded by a white picket fence. In the background is a "swingset-type" pulley structure like those often seen in cemeteries and a flatbed truck with a wooden box. One of the POWs on the work detail wears a wide-brimmed sun hat, and the others wear the denim slouch caps finally issued by the camp. A civilian in dress slacks and a white shirt with rolled up sleeves stands with them. This is probably funeral director Gerald Stabler who worked with the prisoners whenever funerals and burials were necessary at the camp.

Harold Cover, a member of the 436th, remembers the respect with which Rolf Schneider was buried. Harold's company was assigned to provide an honor guard for the POW, complete with twenty-one gun salute. The company also supervised an honor guard of German soldiers (without weapons). "It was rather impressive to see a military funeral of that nature," Harold has said. "It was my first experience along those lines."

During the course of the war, eight prisoners, including Rolf Schneider and Friedrich Rauschenberg, were first buried on site at Camp Aliceville and later moved to the German-Italian cemetery at Fort McClellan in northeast Alabama. The other six died of disease or injury-related causes.

After these escape attempts, Camp Aliceville officials worked with civilian defense leaders to develop a plan for recapture and for protection of the public in the event of escape attempts. First Lieutenant Joseph E. Vincent, Post Intelligence Officer at Camp Aliceville, wrote to the Executive Secretary of the Alabama State Defense Council to describe his plan of action. He noted in his letter that he had also contacted Mr. R.J. Kirksey of Aliceville (Robert Hugh's father), the county chairman for civilian defense.

Lieutenant Vincent outlined his plan as follows: First, a cordon of Military Police would fan out for approximately six miles along major roads leading away from the camp. The assumption was that if an escaped prisoner were traveling on foot, he would not get through this cordon. Second, local railroad agents would be notified in case the prisoner tried to board a train. Third, roadblocks would be established on all major roads radiating from Aliceville in case the prisoner stole a car. It was thought that if major roadblocks could be set up within ten minutes of an escape, a prisoner driving as fast as sixty miles an hour could be apprehended before he left the area.

Because so few small towns and crossroads in that part of Alabama had full-time police, deputy sheriffs, or marshals to implement roadblock plans, Lieutenant Vincent requested help from civilian defense organizations in planning for roadblocks. He was concerned about approximately two dozen small country roads that ran like spokes out to paved highways and could be helpful to an escaped prisoner if he were able to get hold of a road map. The lieutenant suggested that secondary roadblocks would be effective if they could be set up within half an hour of an escape.

In his letter to the state defense council, Vincent gave the example of the tiny town of Pickensville to the northwest of Aliceville where the only telephone was located in the Frisco railroad depot a quarter mile from the crossroads relevant to the prison camp. Mr. Newton, the railroad agent, had agreed that, if he received a telephone call about a prisoner escape, he would round up several of the mill workers in Pickensville and go to the crossroads to set up a roadblock. Lieutenant Vincent pointed out that the men who would help Agent Newton had only shotguns as weapons and that because of war rationing, they were unable to get shells for their shotguns. He suggested that if these men could be taken into the defense council, it would "give them a little more prestige than being a mere civilian, with no authority, and even perhaps assist them in buying shells."

Attached to this letter was a list of general instructions to police and civilian defense officers for how to set up effective roadblocks. These instructions were incredibly detailed and basic. A two-car roadblock was one suggested method: Two cars could be parked diagonally so that a vehicle approaching from either direction would have to slow almost to a dead stop to get between them. If this method was chosen, the cars were to be parked with their engines pointing in the direction of the expected approach. There were two reasons for this—one, so that if the escapee slammed his vehicle into one of the cars, it would hit the engine end first (the heavier end) and prevent the car from turning over; and two, so that if the approaching escapee spotted the roadblock and turned around, the cars would be pointing in the right direction to engage in immediate pursuit. The instructions suggested that if those setting up the roadblock didn't know the direction of approach, they might point one car in each direction, and that if the road was extremely narrow, they might decide to block it with only one car.

There was also the suggestion to string a chain or rope across the road in such a manner that it could be drawn tight quickly and snapped if a car approached. Wooden fence posts were also suggested as temporary roadblocks, but the instructions noted that this was probably the least effective method.

Overall, there were surprisingly few escape attempts from Camp Aliceville. Dr. Erich Moretti, a former Aliceville POW, suggested to historian E.B. Walker that escape attempts were rare because most of those considering escape lacked three essentials for success—they had no money, they didn't speak English, and they had no trustworthy contacts in the United States to help them once they were outside the barbed wire.

Just as the Provost Marshal General's office had intended, Aliceville was isolated enough that most of those who did manage to escape did not get far and often returned on their own. "The few who tried were headed for York, Alabama, a small town about forty miles south," Jake McBride told a newspaper reporter. "They had it confused with New York, where they thought they could hide easily. They thought if they got to York, they would be free."

By the fall of 1943, Pickens County had become the temporary residence of more than three thousand German prisoners of war being treated strictly according to Geneva Convention guidelines in the hope of guaranteeing similar treatment for American prisoners in German camps. Pickens County was also home to the families of a number of American servicemen who'd become prisoners of America's enemies, and these families hoped and prayed their loved ones would also be treated humanely.

Elizabeth Adams received word from Washington that her husband, Robert, had been promoted to captain after his capture in Germany. While she lived at home with her parents in

Carrollton, Captain Adams began studying French and German, math and physics at a German POW camp ninety-three miles from Berlin. He was an officer, and his few letters suggested he was being treated well.

The parents of Newton Davidson of Carrollton, who'd learned of their son's capture when a stranger contacted them after listening to a foreign radio broadcast, used the county newspaper to ask readers to send Newton letters from home. He could only send out two letters a month, but he could receive everything sent to him at *Stalag 3B*, Internment Camp 110889, in Germany. Newton had been captured by the Germans in North Africa, marched to Tunis, flown to Italy, and then crowded into a railroad boxcar for a journey from Naples to Munich and finally to *Stalag 3B* on the Oder Canal in eastern Germany near the Polish border. Judging from reports of other Americans who spent time in this *Stalag*, Newton would have slept on a straw mattress crawling with lice and dined on ground bean soup and bread spread with grease. He would have had access to a library but not much else to relieve boredom. When German guards allowed the prisoners in *Stalag 3B* access to Red Cross food packages, they opened the boxes and insisted the food be eaten in front of them so it couldn't be saved to take along on an escape attempt.

The families of American servicemen captured by the Japanese had added concerns because Japan (and the USSR) had not signed the Geneva Convention agreements of 1929. Although Japan gave a "qualified promise" in 1942 to abide by the Geneva rules, few in America trusted them to guarantee humane treatment.

The August 26 issue of the county newspaper printed a letter received by Mr. and Mrs. F. M. Browning of Reform whose son Scott was still a prisoner of the Japanese after almost two years. Scott was being held in a POW camp in Shanghai, China, a city Japan had seized and occupied in 1937. He wrote that he'd received a batch of letters from his parents on May 19. He'd also received letters from "Lorene, Clarence, Clarise, Frances, and Aunt Susan" along with several packages from the American and the Canadian Red Cross. Scott asked his parents to encourage friends and relatives to continue writing to him even though he could not answer everyone. "There is nothing quite so good as getting letters here," he wrote. He also said he would truly enjoy getting a package with a pipe and lots of tobacco and cigarettes.

Scott Browning remained in Shanghai until July 1945, when he was transferred to Japan for slave labor in the Mitsubishi mines—specifically, Hakodate Mine #3 in Utashinai on Hokkaido, the northernmost and second largest of the islands of Japan.

L.D. Orr, also from Reform and captured at about the same time as Scott Browning, sent a card to his parents from Hirohata, a labor branch camp of a POW camp near Osaka on the southern island of Honshu in Japan. The card was dated April 9 but not received by the Orrs until September 10. It was only the third message they'd had from their son since his capture almost two years earlier. L.D. wrote that he was "well, strong, and working for pay." He also wrote that he'd received four letters from them and also letters from "Laudice and Mary Joe." He said he was working hard and feeling "pretty good." He joked that his mother should tell his friends not to forget him and not to get married—that they'd all be together again at some point. He suggested his parents send him anything good to eat and keep their chins up.

Frank Nichols Jr., an American soldier who was also interned in this camp, has described experiences that would have been similar to those of L.D. Orr. Nichols says that, after capture on Guam, he and others were marched to the Piti navy yard and put aboard barges which ferried them out into the harbor to board the *Argentine Maru* for transport to Japan. They made the journey crammed into the forward hold of the ship, with barely enough room for anyone to lie down. It was extremely cold when they arrived somewhere in Japan in only their summer clothes. They spent six to seven months at Zentsuji prison camp and then were taken by ship to Osaka, where they lived under the seats of an athletic stadium and worked in Japanese industry. From there, they were sent to the Hirohata camp and worked the docks of the Seitetsu Steel Mill.

The International Red Cross reported in March 1943 that Hirohata was a small labor camp of six barracks and a kitchen with six cauldrons where a Navy cook and three assistants prepared meals. It had decent ventilation and heating available for two hours every evening. The Red Cross report noted that the canteen in this camp was well supplied and that food for prisoners was more abundant than in other Japanese camps. The prisoners were allowed to hike in the countryside on Sundays, and there had been two slight work accidents, but no deaths.

More and more Pickens County boys in the United States military had "gone across" now that they'd completed their basic training. Newspaper editor Jack Pratt's son had left for overseas service with the Field Artillery, while his brother George was stationed at St. Petersburg, Florida, with the Merchant Marine. Robert and Ada Chappell's son, Major Frank Chappell, had been deployed in Europe, and the social column of the *Pickens County Herald and West Alabamian* suggested there would soon be "news of more German planes hitting the dust" because Frank was an excellent pilot and would certainly be heard from when he got into action.

Newte Temple's son, Alva, was flying, too. In August, he was commissioned a second lieutenant in the army air corps and left Tuskegee Institute for further training out west. Newte Temple told the county newspaper he was very proud of his son and did not resent his "months of trouble" because they'd helped make his son a success. He was referring to the fact that he'd had to supplement the income from his small farm by making a little home brew along the way in order to educate his sons. He said he'd been caught a few times and served some time for the state but would be willing to serve more time if he could see his son doing something for his country.

Many new recruits were leaving Aliceville for military training, too. Bubber Craft's mother hosted a dinner for three of her son's friends—Jack Hildreth, Harry Nethery, and John Wade—before they reported for duty. She served them a four-course dinner and set the table with red, white, and blue candles and flag place cards.

The denim caps finally arrived to protect Camp Aliceville prisoners from Alabama's brutal late summer sunshine, and local farmers were eager to get the Germans out into the fields because J.T. Belue, the cotton specialist over at Auburn University, was urging that cotton be picked soon after the bolls opened to prevent exposure to weather. Belue explained that "middling quality or better" cotton was needed for the manufacture of war goods. That meant farmers had to be careful about excess moisture. To get the better grades, and therefore better income, farmers needed to pick as much as possible under dry conditions and be sure they sun-dried any cotton that was damp from rain or dew before taking it to be ginned.

Aliceville supported three cotton gins at the time—Independent Gin & Warehouse Company, Farmers Gin & Warehouse Company, and J.D. and J.R. Sanders. All of them ran ads during August urging farmers to pick their cotton dry so it could be used for the eleven hundred different military items that required high quality cotton.

The Reform Gin Company ran an ad reminding farmers, "With flyers' lives at stake, parachutes and other equipment must be made of uniform high grade cotton. The farmer's job is to see that cotton is properly harvested." It then suggested three rules: "Pick it dry. Pick it clean. Keep poor grade from your good grade," and asked farmers to let Reform gin their cotton, where the job would be done right with the best service.

Camp officials cautioned that there weren't enough guards to police labor teams for every farmer. When the county agricultural agent urged those who wanted POW help to sign up early, Elmo Owens was one of the first to take advantage of this arrangement. He contracted for twenty-five POW pickers and transported them and their guards by truck out to his fields for the first time on Tuesday, August 24.

The Germans had never seen cotton in the field before. When Elmo explained through an interpreter what they were to do, several reached out and pulled off clumps of the fluffy, lumpy white stuff with obvious curiosity. They felt it, smelled it, and rubbed it on their faces. They pulled at it to test its strength.

Elmo was to pay the camp authorities $1.00 per hundred pounds for what the prisoners picked. He was to provide them with water and was cautioned that regulations prohibited him from giving them anything else—cigarettes, extra food, whatever. The camp would send along their noonday meal. Elmo was to deliver the prisoners and their guards to the fields at seven each morning and return fifteen minutes before four in the afternoon to weigh what they had picked and then return them to the camp.

Elmo reported on Thursday that he was pleased with the quality of the POW work—the Germans picked the cotton "clean from the bur" and picked out all the trash, but he was concerned about how much they could pick. They'd have to manage 125 pounds a day to be useful.

Since those who picked cotton would be paid at the government-approved rate of eighty cents a day, many POWs initially welcomed the work. Elmo told Camp Aliceville authorities and the county agricultural agent that if the Germans picked well and picked enough, he'd double his quota of prisoners so he could get his cotton in dry and clean before the fall rains began.

It took only a week or so for both the Pickens County farmers and the Germans to lose their enthusiasm for the cotton-picking project. Although the Germans picked the cotton neatly, they weren't used to the heat or the picking process and couldn't pick enough to be worth the trouble of getting them out to the fields. In spite of regulations, one farmer offered an incentive—a pack of cigarettes—to any prisoner who could pick a hundred pounds or more of cotton a day.

Concluding quickly that this was impossible, the prisoners decided to outwit the farmer. Each of them periodically contributed several handfuls to one picker who was then able to turn in a total of one hundred pounds, get the cigarettes, and share them with the others. The farmer realized what was happening and cut out the awards program after the first day.

Elmo Owens experienced a near disaster with one group of POWs who were picking for him. One day, after they loaded two bales onto a truck, ready to go to the gin, one of them sat down on the back of the truck and struck a match to light his cigarette. The match sent sparks that caught the cotton, and flames flashed up. To Elmo's dismay, the prisoners ran from the truck and the military guards backed off with no concern for the cotton. Fortunately, a couple of his regular hands had the presence of mind to turn the truck over, smother the flames, and save most of the cotton.

By mid-September, most Pickens County farmers had given up on the POWs as cotton pickers. They reported that few could pick a hundred pounds a day and that many could barely manage eighty pounds a day, as compared with "an ordinary negro" who, according to the county newspaper, could pick two hundred pounds without half trying.

As for the Germans, POW August Wanders made a notation in his diary that picking cotton was definitely not a job the prisoners wanted to do, but he added with resignation that at least it was a business and that they got paid for doing it. August Wanders was twenty-one years old when he arrived at Camp Aliceville sometime during the summer of 1943. He remembered that many of the guards were about the same age and that they sometimes looked the other way when prisoners tried tricks to lighten their work loads. He once told relatives that the POWs put stones in the bottom of their cotton sacks to make them heavier at weigh time.

It should be noted that the lack of success with POW pickers did not keep Pickens County from experiencing a bumper cotton harvest for the war effort. The cotton ginning report at the end of September 1943 showed 6,442 bales of cotton ginned in the county by September 1, as compared with only 1,335 bales by the same point in 1942. Later, in November, the numbers were even higher. Prior to November, 18,867 bales had been ginned, in comparison with 16,693 bales from the 1942 crop.

In early September, Colonel Prince's staff concluded that perhaps the prisoners would do better at a different type of harvest. On September 9, fifty-three truckloads of them left Camp Aliceville for Dothan, a timber and peanut growing area in southeast Alabama near the Florida state line. Dothan had once been a cotton town like Aliceville, but the boll weevil had ruined crops in the late 1800s, and Dothan had turned to peanuts instead. The change was so successful that the town began hosting the National Peanut Festival in 1938. Eventually, nearly 50 percent of all peanuts produced in the United States were being grown within a one hundred-mile radius of the town.

The POW convoy headed for Dothan that September morning in 1943 must have been an ironic sight. Camp Aliceville's shortage of guards had become critical by early September as the camp received more and more prisoners. In order to have enough guards for the Dothan project, a special contingent was sent over from Camp Shelby, Mississippi, to transport the German prisoners and set up the temporary branch camp. This special contingent was part of the 442nd Regimental Combat Team, a most unusual unit. Although no one would have guessed it in the fall of 1943, the 442nd was destined to become the most decorated combat unit in United States history.

The formation of the 442nd had been announced in February 1943 by President Roosevelt with the words, "Americanism is not, and never was, a matter of race or ancestry." These words were necessary because the 442nd was made up of two segments of American society not particularly popular at the time—second generation Japanese-American citizens from Hawaii and young volunteers from the mainland Japanese internment camps set up on the west coast in the spring of 1942.

These two groups collided psychologically when they arrived at Camp Shelby in June 1943 for training. The Hawaiians were more carefree and less concerned about proper behavior and proper speech. The mainland Japanese were quieter and more reserved—many were preoccupied with worries about families they'd left behind in the harsh environment of internment camps while they attempted to prove their loyalty and distinguish themselves in military service to America.

Inevitably, tensions grew. The Japanese made the Hawaiians feel inferior by criticizing their "barbaric" manners and pidgin speech (a curious mixture of English, Japanese, Chinese, Hawaiian, Filipino, and Spanish). The Japanese called the Hawaiians "buddhaheads" from the pidgin term *buta-head*, which meant "pig-headed." On the other hand, the Hawaiians considered the mainland Japanese unfriendly and snobbish and called them *kotonks* or "stoneheads."

Searching for a way to defuse the growing hostility between these two groups, the American commander arranged for the Hawaiian recruits to visit a Japanese internment camp in Arkansas one weekend. When the Hawaiians saw the oppression in the barbed wire encampments, they developed compassion for the mainland Japanese and worked harder to understand and accept them. The result was a cohesive military unit that fought so admirably in North Africa and Europe later in the war that President Truman honored them with a White House ceremony in 1945 and declared, "You fought not only the enemy, you fought prejudice, and you have won."

All that battle and glory was still ahead in September 1943 when the newly recruited Japanese and Hawaiians loaded muttering German POWs onto trucks and headed for Dothan. The Alabama peanut crop for 1943 was estimated to be worth $30 million, and a total of six tent camps were set up in southeastern Alabama to complete the harvest. Each morning, the German POWs headed out into the fields, ten to a crew with three Japanese-Americans to guard them—a sight that local residents could not have helped but find ironic and amusing. One newspaper article speculated that the Germans would not put much effort into picking peanuts, knowing they would be used in food and munitions preparation as part of the war effort against "their God-man Hitler."

The German POWs had been in Camp Aliceville for two months before they received any personal mail. Their first letters from Germany, some of which had been written and posted as far back as January, arrived in early August, and the event was duly recorded by August Wanders in his diary. August also noted the arrival on August 11 of the first package from the DRK (German Red Cross) with tobacco, thick German bread, and books for the POWs. On the same date, August noted that the first call for manuscripts for a poetry competition went out in the compounds of the camp.

Katie Emberger was still living with her parents in the German village of Bargau. Well over a year had passed since she'd fallen in love with young Hermann Blumhardt while he was stationed at the convent nearby, recuperating from the friendly fire wound he'd received in Russia. He and Katie had been engaged all the time that he fought in North Africa, but Hermann had not been granted his promised leave in May to come home and marry her. In fact, she'd heard nothing from him in several months and had no idea where he was.

Then one day near the end of summer, Hermann's parents received a telephone call informing them that their son was a prisoner of war in the United States. They made contact with Katie and told her they had no other information.

Katie remembers being relieved when she received this news. "I didn't know yet how the war was going to end—nobody knew—but I knew that he was not going to be killed. The future was very uncertain, but I knew that he was safe." She was not worried about how Hermann would be treated in America because her father's brother had moved to Michigan when she was a young girl, and she'd grown up with the many nice pictures and letters her uncle sent back to Germany.

When Hermann was able to write to her from Camp Aliceville, he wrote nothing about his surroundings. His letters were censored, and there were restrictions on what POWs could write home about. He wrote to Katie faithfully once a week, and she wrote back at least once a week, sometimes twice, knowing only that he was somewhere in America. "His letters were always just personal—really beautiful love letters," she says with a shy laugh. The letters were never sealed, and anybody could read them. "My mother thought she was being sneaky about reading all my mail, but once she slipped and mentioned something Hermann had written, and I asked her how she knew that. She just smiled and said, 'Oh, he writes so nice, so beautiful.'"

Tensions were growing inside the camp between fervent Nazi prisoners and those, like Erwin Schulz, who were just as fervent in their opposition to Nazi authority. Though American officers preferred that German NCOs—whether fervent Nazis or not—keep order in the compounds, they could no longer ignore the fact that some Nazis were clearly intimidating and threatening other prisoners.

In July, when the number of German POWs in the United States reached fifty-four thousand, the War Department sent a confidential letter to the various service commanders ordering that all "Nazi leaders, Gestapo agents, and extremists" be transferred to a segregation camp in Alva, Oklahoma. This letter urged camp personnel to be on the alert for Nazi political activity among prisoners and to report such activity to the camp commander. Initially, each camp commander sent the names of prisoners recommended for transfer to Camp Alva to the office of the Provost Marshal General in Washington for approval, but this process proved too slow. By October, the service commanders were given the authority to approve transfers.

On August 13, Colonel Prince received a communication recommending immediate transfer of two Camp Aliceville prisoners to Camp Alva. This order would have been in response to a list he'd sent through the Fourth Service Command to Washington, and it is entirely possible that this list had been generated soon after the complaints Erwin Schulz sent to Colonel Prince through Walter Meier back in July. The leader of

Company 8 in one of the compounds was recommended for transfer because his extreme Nazi views had caused so much trouble among prisoners that he'd been moved to a different compound, but he'd continued to cause unrest even after the move.

The leader of Company 7 in another compound had also voiced Nazi preferences and created ill feelings among the prisoners in his company. He'd gone "as far as to have his men fail to fall out for work details, fully expressed this thought to the men, that they were helping the war effort if they worked at all."

Thirteen days later (August 26), the commanding general of the Eighth Service Command received a form announcing that the commanding general of the Fourth Service Command had been authorized to transfer nine more prisoners from Camp Aliceville to Camp Alva. British intelligence reported that these nine were believed to be German officers masquerading as enlisted men in order to carry out subversive activities.

First Lieutenant Joseph B. McFeely was put in charge of the 324th MPEG guards assigned to escort these nine POWs to Oklahoma. He would be accompanied by seven enlisted men, creating a ratio of nearly one guard to one prisoner for the trip.

Another nine prisoners were scheduled for transfer to Camp Alva in a letter dated August 30. No specific reason for this transfer was given.

Not all prisoner transfers were to Camp Alva. As the United States government sorted out who was who among its captives, transfers took place for a number of reasons. In her book *Stalag, U.S.A.*, Judith Gansberg tells of one camp commander who contacted Maxwell McKnight at the Camp Operations Branch in Washington to report that he'd received a number of German prisoners who didn't speak German. The commander wasn't sure what they spoke, but he knew it wasn't German. The captives turned out to be Russians who'd been impressed into the German army to relieve a manpower shortage.

Wilhelm Westhoff wrote later that the removal of all of these soldiers from Camp Aliceville brought new unrest among the remaining POWs as they struggled to work out how they should relate to each other and to their captors in the prisoner of war setting. Westhoff was of the opinion that only strict organization and order could provide an atmosphere that would "give everyone air to breathe and strength to persevere."

While this transfer activity was going on, Colonel Prince was preparing for his second retirement from the military. Lieutenant Colonel William Waite arrived at Camp Aliceville on August 7 with orders to take command in September. Prince was to take the title of Vice Commander on September 20, remain for a short transition period and then, finally and again, retire to his home in Los Angeles.

Like Prince, Waite was a career army officer who'd been ready for retirement when the war began. Waite had served in the Philippines in the early 1900s and then in Russia during World War I. He'd been called back to active duty in 1940 after seven years of retirement and came to Aliceville from the position of Executive Officer at the Key West Barracks in Florida.

On August 29, 1943, Mr. Alfred Cardinaux, a member of the Swiss Legation, inspected Camp Aliceville in the company of a representative of the International Red Cross Committee. Under the terms of the 1929 Geneva Convention, Switzerland had been designated the protecting nation for all prisoners of war, and American officials were concerned that the findings of these inspections be favorable because they did not want reprisals against American prisoners in German camps.

Cardinaux began his report with general information, noting that Camp Aliceville now had 5,608 German prisoners—the 6 medical officers, 1,082 NCOs, 24 sanitary personnel who worked in the camp hospital, and 4,495 regular soldiers. He reported that the prisoners were housed in standard American army-type barracks and that the housing quarters were extremely clean. He wrote that the prisoners put their bedding out in the sunshine once a week and scrubbed the floors of the barracks with soap and water each day.

At the time of Cardinaux's visit, there were 219 patients in the hospital, 50 with war wounds. There were two cases of malaria, Horst Uhse probably being one of them. One prisoner, Gunter Höver, had died earlier that week from complications of trenchmouth (Vincent's Angina) and respiratory infection.

Cardinaux indicated he was pleased with the camp conditions in general. He wrote that the prisoners enjoyed ham and eggs for breakfast several times a week and that they were building a baker's oven. The concrete laundry tubs were now available in the shower barracks, and a stage had been built in each recreation hall. No books had arrived yet, but the prisoners were trying to organize a school that would grow once study supplies arrived. The canteen was well stocked, and prisoners could drink the non-alcoholic beverages Will Peebles delivered and also one bottle of beer a day at the canteen counter. They could also buy cigarettes, tobacco, and toilet articles. Both Protestant and Catholic "divine services" were celebrated on Sundays, and gardens were springing up around the barracks—some were even decorated with works of sculpture.

The "General Remarks" section of Cardinaux's report adds an interesting perspective about the difficulties of Sergeant-Major Walter Meier's position as camp spokesman. Cardinaux notes that the International Red Cross Committee representative accompanying him had been able to move freely about the camp and to talk with Walter without American witnesses. The American officials had told Cardinaux how pleased they were with Walter's cooperation and that he'd organized the camp in a "very satisfactory manner." However, Cardinaux also reported that, earlier in the summer, some of the prisoners had resented Walter's collaboration with the Americans and that they'd accused him of showing "a pro-American spirit." Apparently, Walter had resigned when this happened, but when an election was held for a new spokesman, he was reelected, almost unanimously. Since then, Cardinaux reported, the prisoners had realized that their spokesman was working in their best interest, and there had been no further complaints.

Wilhelm Westhoff also wrote of the difficulties Walter Meier encountered as he tried to provide good leadership and run interference between the POWs and their American captors. "He took the animosities of many upon himself, and everyone's bad tempers raged at him. Often, waves of fire and fury seemed almost to swallow him up, but steadfastly and logically, our Walter sought his way and did not tire in spite of all the hostility. He discovered friends and comrades, true helpers. A few crises had to be overcome, but the whole camp became a calm and well-adjusted community in which we could aspire to the building of a culturally worthwhile life."

As Sergeant-Major Walter Meier had pointed out to Wilhelm Stüdl on that quiet evening in the Compound D library earlier in the month, a culturally worthwhile life seems to have been of utmost importance to these German POWs, no matter what their circumstances. Various calendar records show this to be true. A variety show was produced and presented in Compound D on August 28. With the arrival of more books and study materials from the YMCA, the first "school" opened in Compound A on September 20. A poetry competition was held during August, and during September, Compound F put on both an art exhibition and a fairly sophisticated drama production. The play, which may have been produced from memory, was Johann Peter Hebel's *Schätzlein des rheinischen Hausfreundes* (The Little Treasure Box of the Rhenish Family Friend). This play, the first of many produced within Camp Aliceville, was written by one of Germany's most widely read writers, a man who lived from 1760 to 1826. August Wanders commented in his diary that, after the first visit from the International Red Cross and the Swiss Legation, it appeared to him that much more support for sport and cultural activities began to arrive from the YMCA and other groups.

It was around the middle of August that Wilhelm Schlegel arrived at Camp Aliceville after a voyage to New York from Glasgow, Scotland, aboard the *Louis Pasteur*. Having been deloused and disinfected in Camp Shanks like all the others, he rode the train down to Alabama under heavy guard and was impressed by the luxury of the Pullman car in which he rode. Wilhelm remembers the American faces that stared as the Germans passed slowly through train stations along the way. The Americans seemed surprised that the Nazi soldiers they could see through the windows looked human.

Upon arrival, Wilhelm was marched from the train depot to the camp. He marched in formation, carefully carrying his backpack and scrutinizing the faces of the soldiers who stood along the route with guns at their hips. "How will we be accepted by these people?" he wondered.

After processing, Wilhelm was assigned to Company 19 in Compound E. Because of his *Unteroffizier* (NCO) status, he was not required to work—at least not until almost two years later—after the signing of the unconditional surrender of all German forces. At Camp Aliceville in August 1943, Wilhelm was impressed with the clean bathrooms and showers and with the food he had to admit was better than what he'd eaten as a soldier in the German army. "The land of milk and honey" was the phrase that kept running through his head in the first few days as he tried to remember how long it had been since he'd had such good lodging and food.

Unlike Hermann Blumhardt, Wilhelm Schlegel was able to send a postcard to his mother that announced not only his status as a prisoner of war but also his location at Aliceville in Alabama. The postcard listed his health as *gut* and gave his birth date and place (*Asslar Kr. Wetzlar 14.3.1918*). It listed his POW number (4WG-4806) and was dated August 13, 1943.

With a capacity of 6,000, the Prisoner of War camp at Aliceville is the largest of its kind in the United States. It was the first to be completed of 72 over the country, and has its full quota of prisoners, mostly Germans from Rommel's crack army of North Africa. They are mostly young and strong men, well developed and perfectly drilled. While the camp is officered by United States military officers, the prison body is self governing, with its own men in charge of affairs in the compound. They discipline the men while in the compound, and seldom is a matter of discipline referred to the ranking officers in the camp.

• November 4, 1943 •
The Pickens County Herald and West Alabamian

CHAPTER NINE
Routine and Creativity

On Thursday, September 9, the county newspaper carried a front-page story about the unconditional surrender of Italy at eleven o'clock the previous morning. "German high officials (who'd been caught by surprise) went into a rage, declaring that it was the most treacherous thing ever to occur in all history." The Italian people, however, were celebrating in the streets of Rome. Certainly, newspaper editor Jack Pratt was celebrating, too. His oldest son, Jack Jr., had been serving in Italy since early October.

President Roosevelt warned in a worldwide hook-up that "this was but the beginning of the bitter conflict" and that ultimate victory would continue to require tremendous effort both on the battlefront and at home. The POW camps in America would not be closing soon.

That same week, August Wanders recorded two significant dates in his diary. The first was September 10, date of the first "marriage" at Camp Aliceville—a proxy ceremony for fifteen POWs. Proxy weddings, legal according to German law and arranged through the Swiss legation, allowed a German POW to sign a letter and marry his sweetheart back home with a POW friend standing in. Since Alfred Cardinaux, a member of the Swiss legation, had just visited Camp Aliceville on August 29, it is likely he carried with him the necessary paperwork for these fifteen marriages.

By October 1944, more than sixty such marriages would be performed within the camp. The primary purpose would have been to assure benefit status and other legal advantages for the wife at home, but they also provided a wonderful excuse for a party. Arnold Krammer includes a photo of a POW wedding by proxy in his book, *Nazi Prisoners of War in America*. In it, a groom dressed in his best uniform is surrounded by colorful carnations, a decorated wedding cake, a framed photograph of the bride, and smiling comrades offering congratulations. In *Stalag U.S.A.*, Judith Gansberg describes a double wedding by proxy at Camp Shelby in Mississippi in November 1943. The mess hall there was decorated for the occasion, complete with white tablecloths usually reserved for the officers. The compound chorus sang, someone recited a poem, and the camp spokesman made a speech. The camp band played the *Rosenkavalier* waltz for the two bridegrooms, and American officials even provided a quarter liter of wine for each. One of the grooms was given an elaborately dressed broom for his bed as a substitute for his missing wife.

August Wanders also recorded the death of Otto Ulrich from septicemia (blood poisoning) related to a leg injury that did not heal. Otto cut his leg on a piece of wire fencing at the compound athletic field and waited too long to report the injury. It became infected and eventually developed gangrene. When he finally entered the camp hospital, Captain Klippen recommended amputation, but Otto refused and died there on September 12.

Colonel William Waite took full command of Camp Aliceville on September 20. He told his staff he'd concluded that the camp's American officers and enlisted men sometimes underrated the importance of their service. This was fairly common, not only among military personnel who felt they'd been passed over for more exciting duty overseas but also among journalists and the general public who tended to downplay the significance of and the skill levels of soldiers on duty on the home front. Colonel Waite reminded the men that their job was vital to the war effort and that he expected every officer and every enlisted man to give it his very best.

Week after week, the Frisco trains continued to chug and hiss up to the depot at Aliceville to deliver newly processed POWs—462 during the first week of October alone, as Germans captured in the invasion of Sicily and then Italy made the Atlantic crossing. Seasoned POWs were boarding trains out of Aliceville on a regular basis, too, and for a variety of reasons. In the middle of October, Colonel Waite sent fifty more to Camp Alva, suggesting that the July transfers had not stamped out radical Nazi activity within the compounds. His memo gave no specific reason, stating only that the prisoners were being transferred "for the benefit of the service."

Camp Alva was known as the *Nazilager* (Nazi Camp). Some referred to it as the "Devil's Island" or "Alcatraz" of the War Department's POW system because its primary purpose was to segregate hard-core Nazi POWs from the general prison populations in camps like Aliceville. The *Nazilager* opened on July 31, a mile south of Alva, Oklahoma, west of Highway 281 on land now occupied by an airport and fairgrounds. Camp Alva had much greater security priorities than other camps. Like Aliceville, it could house six thousand POWs.

The terms "Nazi" and "anti-Nazi" covered a wide spectrum of belief and behavior among the POWs, and the War Department continued to puzzle over proper classifications.

Camp commanders had trouble deciding which Nazis were fanatical enough to warrant transfer to Camp Alva and which were simply well disciplined soldiers who could, as the county newspaper described it, keep the prison body self-governing "with its own men in charge of affairs in the compound" so that they would discipline their men and seldom find it necessary to refer problems to American officers.

By mid-October, it became clear that this "self-governing" system posed a serious safety threat to certain POWs, and nineteen Aliceville prisoners were recommended for transfer to the anti-Nazi Camp McCain near Elliott in Grenada County, Mississippi, for their own protection. Their documented grievance reports dramatically illustrate the pressures some Camp Aliceville prisoners endured at the hands of the "more moderate" Nazis who remained in the camp compounds. Colonel Waite's memo directing their transfers to Camp McCain details a number of these incidents including these:

1. One evening Siegried Wienhold made the mistake of expressing personal views not in keeping with the Nazi ideals of the German NCO in his compound. From then on, he was a marked man who knew what could happen. One night, while huddled on his cot, he'd listened in silence as another prisoner was surrounded in the darkness and beaten senseless for expressing a dissident opinion. But as much as Siegried despised the Nazi NCO and his thugs, he felt no certainty that he could trust the Americans. He was not sure they recognized or understood the frightening dynamics among the prisoners. Finally, taking a risk, he reported his fears to an American intelligence officer inspecting the compound. To his relief, the

officer allowed him to tell his story and then reported to Colonel Waite that Siegried was "beyond doubt" an anti-Nazi who needed to be protected.

2. During the night of October 15, several of the camp's *Lagergestapo* isolated three more prisoners whose views they considered unacceptable—Franz Hermann, Anton Hoffmann, and Alfred Knoph. The three had already tensed themselves for the coming blows when an American officer entered the compound unexpectedly and realized what was happening. He removed the three to headquarters for their own safety and reported to Colonel Waite that, in his opinion, word of the incident would spread quickly and that these three men would no longer be safe anywhere within the enclosures at Aliceville.

3. Erich Jarass told his compound's intelligence officer that he was terrified every night when the lights went out in his barracks. He was convinced the Nazis would sneak in and do him bodily harm because his views were "definitely not in accord with Nazi ideals."

After documenting these and several other incidents, Colonel Waite ended his memo with the following comment: "Keeping the above men at this camp now is rather difficult for all of the strictly [*sic*] Nazis are on the lookout for they definitely do not like the anti-Nazis, and these men may be accosted at any time and will be beaten badly, possibly killed, and therefore permission is requested to send them to prisoner of war Camp McCain, Mississippi, at once." The transfer of these men took place at the end of October.

The POW quarters at Camp McCain had been expanded hurriedly in the fall of 1943 to accommodate anti-Nazi POWs being sent from camps like Aliceville. In contrast to the strict authoritarianism of the German army, Camp McCain tried to operate on the basic concepts of civil liberty. Its prisoners were allowed to hold a general election for their camp spokesman, and they established a democratic camp constitution.

Erwin Schulz's name does not appear in Colonel Waite's October 17 memo, but he was also transferred to Camp McCain in either October or November. When Erwin arrived in Mississippi, he met a number of men he'd known in North Africa before he deserted and surrendered to the Moroccans who turned him over to the French. Erwin has written that he was initially elected camp spokesman but was later replaced because of "some differences and conflicts." His pre-war experience with labor disputes in Germany echoes through the terminology he uses to describe how issues were handled at Camp McCain. "I felt like a shop steward, settling differences in a factory," he wrote. "The Americans wanted quiet and order, and as few problems as possible."

Erwin stated that Nazis were not a significant element at Camp McCain, but that he and others wanted to inform the outside world about how Nazis were dominating and tormenting prisoners in other camps around the country. Without the knowledge of American officials, a small group, including Erwin, began to communicate with sympathetic German Americans and well-known journalists. It would take until the spring of 1944, but eventually this group and others would catch the attention of a number of prominent people and create a profound effect on the POW system in the United States.

Colonel Waite's memo documents threats and violence, but there is no concrete evidence that deaths resulted from Nazi intimidation at Camp Aliceville. One of the American medical officers, Captain Stephen Fleck, hinted at murders and "forced suicides," but official camp records do not confirm this. Captain Fleck told a magazine interviewer that prisoners were sometimes beaten with cooking utensils and that some deaths classified as suicides were actually murders committed by Nazis. "Nobody would squeal," he said, "because the squealer likely would face a similar fate."

Medical officer Arthur Klippen recalled things differently. He wrote to historian E. B. Walker in 1988, "I do not accept the premise of rampant murders. There were fights among themselves surely, but nothing that came to my attention.... Regarding your question about violent deaths, other than the two who were shot in an escape attempt, I vaguely recall a suicide by hanging."

Chaplain's assistant Jack Sisty does not mention murders, but he does remember rumors about beatings in the camp. "We heard that the camp's Nazi leaders would fill socks with gravel and use them as weapons to keep the others in line."

Seeing the Nazi intimidation of others in his compound convinced Hermann Blumhardt not to speak out about his personal political views. "As a POW, you were really walking a fine line," he has said. "On the one hand, you were still a soldier, a German soldier, so these fanatics were constantly reminding us, 'You should make as much trouble as you can. And you should be a nuisance.' I could not come right out and confess I never was Nazi because some in the camp were beaten."

When E.B. Walker reviewed the interment register of the German-Italian POW cemetery at Fort McClellan, he concluded that six prisoners died during incarceration at Camp Aliceville. All were buried at Aliceville, under Gerald Stabler's supervision, but moved to Fort McClellan cemetery later in the war. Rolf Schneider and Friedrich Rauschenberg were the two shot in August while attempting to escape. As already mentioned, Gunter Höver died of complications from trenchmouth and Otto Ulrich from blood poisoning. Albert Barthelmess died of a coronary occlusion in December 1944. The only officially recorded suicide at Camp Aliceville, Kurt Knoph, occurred in May 1945, and a number of sources suggest this man hanged himself in his cell in the psychiatric ward of the camp hospital.

Arnold Krammer has written that vigilantes in some POW camps called themselves "the holy ghost." They would sneak into a barracks under cover of darkness, pull a pillowcase over someone's head, and beat them mercilessly. "There were also cases where they would take them into the latrine or closet, hang them, and make it look like a suicide, pin a note on them, saying, 'I'm despondent and I want to kill myself.'"

The History Channel reported about Nazi terror in the camps in its January 2002 documentary. "[T]he POWs had more to fear from their own people than from their American captors. Since the United States had a shortage of German translators to send into the camps, the War Department decided to let the prisoners police themselves. In doing so, hard line Nazi operatives took over in the camps, intimidating others with threats and beatings."

In that documentary, Heino Erichsen shared his eye witness account of what was certainly the most widely reported incident of POW abuse by Nazi vigilantes. Heino was interned at Camp Hearne in Texas with a POW corporal named Hugo Krauss. Hugo was born in Germany but came to the United States with his parents in 1928. He was raised in New York City but returned to Germany in 1939 as a supporter of the Nazi party. He joined the German army voluntarily and served in Russia before being captured in North Africa. Hugo spoke excellent English and sometimes listened to American radio instead of joining others in singing militant German marching songs after dinner in his compound mess hall.

Heino Erichsen remembered that one morning in December 1943, Hugo got into a shouting match and claimed that the German war reports were lies. American radio broadcasts at that time would have been boasting of Allied successes in Italy and of the increasing number of Allied bombing raids over Germany. The Allies, Hugo concluded, deserved to win the war.

Hugo's disbelief of German war propaganda sealed his fate. According to Heino, when the lights went out at ten o'clock that night, "a bunch of guys came in and said, 'everybody stay in their bunks.' There was a scuffle, and then there was beating. Seven POWs savagely beat Krauss with pipes, clubs, and a board with four-inch spikes." While Heino and others crouched in terrified silence, Hugo suffered three skull fractures that led to the bruising of his brain, two broken arms, and multiple lacerations and bruises to the rest of his body. "We were all too scared to do anything," said Heino, "[A]nd then he died within a day or two [on December 18] in the camp hospital outside. There was a stunning shock amongst most of us, but also fear to say anything because, if somebody could do that, you better don't say a word."

Not all vigilante groups in the POW camps were prosecuted, but those who attacked and killed Hugo Krauss were. The American government tried and convicted the seven POWs who beat him. Each was sentenced to life imprisonment at hard labor. The sentences were confirmed in March 1946 by the government's reviewing authority, and the convicted POWs were sent to the federal penitentiary at Leavenworth, Kansas. Later that year, when the evidence was reviewed again, two sentences were dismissed, and the others were reduced. Five of the seven remained in prison and were denied clemency in 1947 and 1948. In 1949, those five were paroled and returned to Germany after serving only three years.

Not long after Colonel Waite sent the nineteen prisoners to Camp McCain, five hundred seasoned POWs were shipped down from Aliceville to the newly opened "German Army" compound at Camp Blanding on the eastern shore of Kingsley Lake in northeast Florida. Rural, isolated, and huge (one hundred-fifty thousand acres), Camp Blanding was an ideal place to hold prisoners of war without much media and public attention. It had been housing a small number of U-boat captives since September 1942.

The first 250 from Aliceville arrived on November 5, along with 250 from Camp Opelika in eastern Alabama. A week later, 250 more from each of these two camps arrived. One of the

Blanding camp commanders wrote that it seemed to him most of the POWs from Aliceville were "either wounded or troublemakers" and sometimes a combination of the two.

As mentioned earlier (see Chapter Eight), four of these transferred POWs testified to the German government about their prisoner of war experiences after they were repatriated in March 1944. One of them, a private in the tank corps of the Hermann Göring Division (the same division Walter Felholter served in) reported that troubles at Camp Aliceville began when POWs were ordered to pick cotton. Although local newspapers and the comments of several former POWs indicate that prisoners did pick cotton in the Aliceville area, at least for a week or two, this private told German authorities that the camp spokesman refused the work order on the prisoners' behalf. He said the spokesman cited the Geneva Convention, which did not allow a country to force POWs to do work related to the war effort. The private testified that prisoner resistance to the cotton-picking order resulted in "their segregation in a branch camp of the Aliceville base camp and subsequent transfer to Camp Blanding."

The United States did not consider agriculture, including cotton farming, an area off limits to POW labor. In fact, American farms used more POW contract labor than any other area of the economy during World War II—more than logging, food processing, meatpacking, or railroad work. POWs were credited with helping prevent potential losses of cotton, peanuts, and a number of other crops when army inductions and high salaries in war plants drained American manpower from the countryside.

It is interesting to consider how the tank corps private's testimony fits with other information about the picking of cotton by Camp Aliceville POWs. An entry in August Wanders' diary on October 3, 1943, reads, "1,000 men ordered to pick cotton until December 1, 1943." This entry corresponds with POW contract labor records showing that POWs picked more than six million pounds of seed cotton in Mississippi between October and December 1943. It also corresponds with documentation for the 436th MPEG unit that states they returned to Aliceville in December from at least a month's guard duty in Belzoni, Mississippi. Since branch POW camps were always labor camps, it is likely that the segregated branch camp the tank corps private referred to was a cotton picking camp in Mississippi.

This same private also testified about conflicts between Nazi POWs and communist-leaning POWs at both Aliceville and Blanding. He told the German government in March 1944 that members of the so-called punishment battalions (like Erwin Schulz) "separated themselves from their fellow prisoners, formed soldiers' councils, and attempted to replace camp leaders." Then, with an element of bravado, he suggested that the German army should never use such battalions—made up of political prisoners and common criminals—against English and American armies because they would desert too quickly and then offer to help the enemy.

Sometime in the fall of 1943, an unusually large number of prisoners at Camp Aliceville began complaining of sore throats and fever. "My heart is pounding, and I'm weak all over," was the usual complaint to the medical staff. At first, the American medical officers—Major Arthur Klippen, Captain Stephen Fleck, and Captain John Kellam—were not sure what they were dealing with. They ran a number of bacteriological tests and eventually concluded that the disease was pharyngeal diphtheria.

Diphtheria is a highly infectious disease that creates a false membrane in the upper parts of the throat. Pharyngeal diphtheria is the most common form. It usually appears in winter months and is spread by droplets when an infected person coughs or sneezes. The incubation period is about three days. If a patient who has diphtheria symptoms develops respiratory problems, he must receive intensive hospital care. The disease can be fatal if not treated.

When the first official diagnosis was made at Camp Aliceville, the army doctors ordered Schick tests to determine who among the six thousand people at the camp—both Germans and Americans—had immunity to the disease. The doctors were surprised to find that more than twelve hundred people tested positive, a discovery that mandated an immediate program of immunization with diphtheria toxoid. *Alabama Heritage* magazine states that this was done in the early fall, with the aid of the German doctors, and that a new, lower dosage proved effective even though some adults suffered adverse reactions and had to be hospitalized for a short time. Many of the German POWs distrusted the toxoid and insisted they'd already been immunized for diphtheria, but this was not likely since such immunizations had not been routine in the German army. The memories of Walter Felholter and Hermann Blumhardt suggest either that the diphtheria outbreak occurred in December instead of September, or that a second outbreak occurred late in the year. On December 4, Hermann Blumhardt wrote in the small notebook he kept that his friend Walter Felholter was being moved to the camp hospital because he had diphtheria. Little did Hermann realize when he made that notation that, when Walter moved out of Compound C, forty-six years would pass before the two men would meet again.

Walter agrees that he left the compound and entered the hospital in December. His sore throat became worse and worse. "I couldn't swallow, and it was all swollen." The doctor came to the compound once a week to treat illnesses, but Walter was sick enough that he was admitted to the post hospital. When he was taken there by an American guard, he carried with him the English book he'd recently purchased at the camp canteen so he could continue to study the language.

At first, Walter was very sick, but gradually his condition improved, and he found that he rather liked being confined to the camp hospital. The food prepared by Elma Henders and her crew of German POW cooks was excellent, work details were not required, and he had plenty of time and solitude for what he most enjoyed doing—reading whatever he could and learning English.

Back in Compound C, Hermann continued to write to his sweetheart, Katie, in Germany. Katie wrote back at least once a week and sometimes twice. Her letters arrived in batches that Hermann read over and over. Once he wrote to Katie asking for the address of her uncle up in Michigan. He'd heard from other POWs that German-Americans could get passes to visit if they knew the location of prisoners, and he thought if he wrote, perhaps the uncle would come down to see him. Soon Katie answered. In her letter, she wrote, "I'm going to write you the address of my uncle." Then she put a colon, and everything after that had been snipped out neatly by the censors.

Hermann laughs at himself when he thinks back on the incident. "If I had been on the ball, I would have done as the English say—if you don't succeed at first, try, try, try again. They didn't read and censor every letter, and eventually it would have gone through, but I was stupid enough to give up."

While the prisoner transfers and the diphtheria epidemic were rebalancing the population of Camp Aliceville in the fall of 1943, cultural opportunities for prisoners continued to appear. Compound A dedicated an open-air theater on October 3, and Compound F opened its book bindery on October 7. Compound C staged an operetta called *Alt Berlin* beginning October 13, and Compound F opened its second art show on October 15, along with a variety show called *Eintopf* (HodgePodge) on October 24.

Local civilians and many of the camp military personnel were busy with another focus—the annual fall ritual of high school football. In the daytime, heavy summer heat and humidity continue into September and October in Alabama, but around the end of August, the nights begin to cool, and those first crisp evenings trigger football mania in small towns like Aliceville.

Coach R. W. Brandon and the Aliceville High School Yellow Jackets were about to enjoy the first of a series of fantastic seasons even though some of the team's best potential players had already left or were preparing to leave for military service. The season began with the defeat of archrival Carrollton on Friday, September 23, by a shutout score of 13-0. The game was played on Aliceville's newly lighted field, thanks to Alabama Power Company and the local school board. Adults paid fifty cents to attend, but school children and uniformed military personnel from Camp Aliceville paid thirty cents.

Right half back Murphy Windle Jr. was captain of the 1943 team. The eleven first team players also included Bubber Craft, Roy Dean, J.B. Driver, James Henders, Charles Turnipseed, Chester Graham, Lofton Davis, James Cox, George Frank Herndon, and Joe McDaniel. Of these eleven, three (J.B. Driver, Charles Turnipseed, and Murphy Windle) would eventually be listed among the more than four thousand Alabamians who gave their lives in defense of their country during World War II.

Energizing spectators on the football field sidelines were newly elected cheerleaders Eva Mae Hamlin, Margaret Lee Sommer, Frances Russell, Theron Cox, and Stuart Sterling. Janie Ruth McCaa led the marching band as drum majorette. She and Alice Williams had tied in the school vote for this position, so the two drew straws. Janie picked the longer one, so the amicable solution was that she would lead the band in 1943, and Alice would do the honors in 1944.

When Jimmy Summerville, whose father, Homer, owned the Sinclair Service Station in Aliceville, thinks back on growing up in Alabama, his favorite memory is the community spirit and the camaraderie of the Yellow Jacket football team during the 1940s. "The whole community was involved behind the team. After every home game, they'd block off Broad and Third and play records for a street dance right in the middle of town. Just a good get together is what it was—a great time."

By the end of October, the Yellow Jackets had tallied an amazing record—undefeated, untied, and unscored upon. Guards from the POW camp got caught up in the high school football fervor, too. Some even served as referees. One MPEG commented that "the only thing the town did that created a lot of interest was its fabulous football team. I went to Tuscaloosa once to watch them play—all the townspeople would go wherever they played (in spite of gas rationing)."

Another soldier remembered that those coming to Aliceville from larger cities were surprised to discover a local football team that could probably outplay the teams back home. "The Aliceville Yellow Jackets are without a doubt one of the best trained and [most] capable teams we have seen in a long while," he said.

Karl Stegall was a young boy when he rode into Aliceville with his parents one Friday evening for a football game. The family lived thirty miles away, but Karl's mother had been born and raised in Aliceville, and his Aunt Thelma Bell McKee taught third and fourth grade at Aliceville Elementary School. The boy was already aware of the prisoner of war camp because he and his three brothers sometimes hurried to the back of their pasture to watch the trains loaded with prisoners as they made their way to Aliceville.

On this Friday evening, as the family drove into town, they found Highway 17 blocked by one of the POW trains, and Karl was fascinated as he peered through the backseat window and watched the MPs unloading prisoners for their march to the prison camp. The memory of those tired and dirty prisoners—many of whom did not look to him to be more than sixteen years of age—stayed with Karl throughout the war as his family received telegrams about the critical wounds two of his uncles received in European battles. When the war finally ended and the German prisoners headed home, Karl could not help but juxtapose them with his uncles' suffering and the suffering of the many American soldiers who never made it home.

Early in October, Jack Pratt began urging families to send the county newspaper the photographs and addresses of those serving in the armed forces. Jack planned a special Christmas issue of the newspaper that would honor as many as possible of the nearly fifteen hundred men and women from Pickens County who were in service.

The nearly one thousand American military personnel who'd descended on Aliceville the previous spring had been in town long enough that many serious romances had blossomed between Aliceville young women and soldiers from all over the country. After their bowling date back in May, 389th New York state native Stanley Pendrak had continued to see the pretty hair stylist who worked at the Aliceville Hotel. He and Jeanne Holiday were married in August.

Perhaps the romance and marriage that created the most attention was that of Bobbie Kirksey and Nat Aicklen. First Lieutenant Henry "Nat" Aicklen, recently promoted from second lieutenant, was the handsome Camp Aliceville Headquarters Administrator from San Antonio who fell in love with civilian payroll clerk Bobbie Kirksey at camp headquarters.

The two were part of Margie and Emmie Archibald's set of young friends who went to church together, enjoyed "silver and china" dinner parties, planned picnics at Lubbub Creek, and visited the night clubs over in Columbus, Mississippi, whenever they could scrape together enough gas ration coupons.

The county newspaper gushed with detail as it recounted the various events honoring the bride elect, "a favorite in social circles in West Alabama for several years." The round of parties began with an evening reception at the home of Emmie and Margie who received guests with their mother, Mrs. S.W. Archibald; the bride; her sister, Edwina; and her mother, Mrs. Wallace S. Kirksey. Bobbie's sister Edwina would marry another member of this young set of friends, Captain Lawrence L. Persons, the following March.

Seventy-five guests called between four and six on the evening of Wednesday, October 6, to enjoy coffee and sweets served from a table laid out with the heirloom silver Margie and Emmie enjoyed displaying whenever they entertained the young officers from the camp. Friends and young business associates of the bride stayed an extra hour to shower her with gifts of lacy lingerie.

The wedding took place on Wednesday evening, November 3, at the Aliceville Presbyterian Church with the ministers of both the Presbyterian and the Methodist churches performing the double ring ceremony. Bobbie Kirksey's wedding was characteristic of Southern small town weddings in the 1940s. Glossy, green-leaved vines of Southern Smilax draped the backdrop of the altar, which was adorned with alternating pots of ferns and Gothic candelabra. Bobbie's aunt, Mrs. Robert

J. Kirksey, sang "Oh Promise Me," and her cousin, Mrs. Woodford Abrams, played Lohengrin's wedding march on the organ. Her sister Edwina served as maid of honor in a heavenly blue velveteen and net dress flanked by bridesmaids Mary Emily Kirksey (her youngest sister), Emmie and Margie Archibald, and the groom's sister June in rose-toned dresses of the same style.

The bride wore white satin with long sleeves that tapered to points over each hand. As in most church weddings in that time and place, her gown had a full-length train and a full-length veil of illusion with lace insets. She carried a bouquet of roses, gardenias, and carnations centered with orchids and showered with tuberoses.

The groom's best man was Lieutenant Jack Daugherty from the POW camp headquarters staff. The ushers were all lieutenants from the camp—Bob Barnes, Lester Lombardi, Albert Setzer, and Walter Rosskopf, who would marry another member of this social set, June Kirksey Etheridge, in a similarly elaborate celebration the following February. The men wore their dress uniforms, and little Tommy Amason, ring bearer and nephew of the bride who would grow up to be a prominent Birmingham pediatrician, wore a miniature officer's uniform to match.

The Robert Kirkseys hosted a lovely reception following the six o'clock ceremony, decorating their home with candlelight and white chrysanthemums. Guests enjoyed pieces of the heart-shaped, three-tier wedding cake, with nuts from silver compotes and coffee from silver urns. After the new Mrs. Aicklen changed into her traveling costume—a teal blue dressmaker suit with model hat of blue feathers and a corsage of white orchids—the newlyweds left for a honeymoon trip to New Orleans. When they returned, they moved into an apartment on Third Avenue.

Among the many wedding gifts Bobbie and Nat took with them to their new home was a handcrafted, eight by ten-inch keepsake book with wooden covers hinged together by decorative pieces of leather. Neatly carved on the front cover were the words "Bobbie" and "Nat." In smaller letters on the back cover were the words, "Prisoner of War Camp Aliceville, Alabama 1943." The book was a gift from the German POWS and would remain in the Aicklen home throughout their married life.

The November 4 issue of the *Pickens County Herald and West Alabamian* carried an article headlined, "War Prison Camp Largest in Country." It explained to readers that POW camps in places like Aliceville allowed the Allies to feed and guard prisoners at less expense and less risk than if they'd been held in their conquered country. "The prisoners are living on the fat of the land, work when they want to, and enjoy the best food they have had in years. Under international agreement, prisoners of war must be fed the same food as is given to the home army, so they enjoy the same fine food that U.S. soldiers of the camp enjoy. And they are pretty well contented. Most of them had rather be where they are than where they were, and there's reason."

The article also recapped the economic impact of the camp. "It has given employment to hundreds of civilians at a better wage than they had ever had, and local markets have been patronized when possible. More than nine hundred soldiers and officers live in the county, and many of them have their families. They must be fed, housed, clothed locally, so thousands of dollars are spent weekly in the county, resulting directly from the Prison Camp."

Kay Fillingham had just become the wife of one of those nine hundred soldiers. She arrived in Aliceville with her newlywed husband, a second lieutenant just assigned to the 389th MPEG unit, shortly after their wedding in Chattanooga on November 5. Kay had been born in San Antonio but raised in Glendale, California. The war became very real for her when she was in high school. "Living on the west coast, we had to have a blackout room with shades that could be drawn. Some of the streets had even been camouflaged with paint. We had some drills, but of course, the Japanese never did come that far."

On a summer vacation to visit relatives back in Texas, Kay met Bob Fillingham, who was also from San Antonio. Kay was eighteen years old when she married Bob, knowing he was in the service and knowing there was a possibility he'd be gone from her before long. She remembers her first reaction to Aliceville, Alabama—very different from any place she'd ever known—the most isolated location the army could find, she thought, except maybe the desert. "The places we lived in were very primitive for me—an oil stove in one place, a wood stove in another. I had no idea how to cook so it was very hard." There was culture shock, too. She was amazed to see black women carrying laundry baskets on their heads and to see a rat run across the stage at the Palace Theater on her one and only visit there. "We never did see the end of that movie!" she remembers.

Kay and Bob moved into a rented room (with kitchen privileges) in a private home. "The upstairs bathroom didn't have a door on it, so I went to the one store in town and bought a curtain and put that up. The landlady was very nice. I don't remember her name, but we lived on a street that I later found out had once been called Millionaire Row."

Millionaire Row (now Third Avenue) was the first street laid out in Aliceville about 1903. Most of the twenty-two historic homes along it were constructed before 1915. Every home had a large porch with galleries built for two purposes—to escape the sweltering summer heat and to visit with neighbors in large rocking chairs. The nickname was a joke started by the mayor when he made the ironic comment that all Aliceville millionaires lived there. One of the early houses (moved in 1984 to become the Plantation Restaurant on Highway 14) was that of lumber company owner James Murphy Summerville, who had access to the very best materials for moldings, parquet-style ceilings, and wainscoting. James Summerville and his wife, Emma Chalmers, lived in the white pillared house with their eight children. Laura Gardner Kirksey, mother of Bobbie, Edwina, and Mary Emily, grew up on Millionaire Row in the T.W. Gardner home and was married in her uncle Henry Gardner's home on the same street.

The Fillinghams later lived in a two-bedroom apartment, also on Millionaire Row. "It was a vast improvement except for the oil stove. We shared a bath with the couple across the hall from us. In civilian life, he was an Irish policeman from Chicago, and they had two little children. There was an icebox in the hall, and every day a guy would come by with a big block of ice. It was all very different for me, but it was an adventure, really." She remembers concluding that the upstairs bathroom must have been added, cutting into the roof to make room for it. "The floor slanted, and when you sat in the tub, all of the water settled toward the front. There was a tall window right in front of the tub, and it gave me the feeling I was going to slide right out the window and land in the yard!"

The Fillinghams moved again to a private room and bath in a comfortable house with a landlady who had a reputation for grouchiness. Kay had permission to try her cooking skills on the wood stove in the kitchen but made do with a two-burner hot plate in their room.

Alabama is a major swath of the South's "tornado alley," and the landlady had had a tornado shelter built into the ground in her side yard. One night she and Kay and Bob spent several hours huddled inside. "She had everything down there you could need. We could have survived for days. The tornado didn't come, but it was scary, and I was glad to climb out again into fresh air." Kay can't remember why her husband became upset with the landlady when they were preparing to move out, but she does remember that he paid the last month's rent in pennies as an annoyance.

Kay and Bob became friends with Bobbie and Nat Aicklen and got together for picnics when they could. She still has one picture of the four of them together.

Kay worked in the Quartermaster's building at the POW camp with Earline Lewis. "I was stationed kind of at the front desk, and I had some contact with the prisoners because they would come in with work orders for supplies. Some of them would do the "*Heil Hitler*" at me right there. I was really upset about that, but my boss just told me to ignore it, so I had to ignore it. It was hard, and they were quite flirtatious, too."

Kay did notice that the Germans were wonderful workers. The camp always looked orderly, and she often saw the POWs playing soccer. "A lot of them were blond and tanned and trim," she says. "They certainly were treated well."

Sometimes on the weekends, Kay and Bob enjoyed an evening out at the Officers' Club. Kay thought it was fun to meet people from all over the country. She and Bob would go for dinner and dance to music played by the POW orchestra. "Their rhythm was not like the rhythm of our music, and we thought that was funny, but we enjoyed it."

Dinner at the Officers' Club suddenly lost its appeal for Kay one evening when she discovered that the chefs were POWs. "I thought they were going to poison me, and I wasn't the only one who felt that way. My husband laughed, but it made me uncomfortable to eat that food." Realizing Kay was truly upset, Bob stood up and suggested they take a couple days off—head for a lodge across the Mississippi River, a few hours away. "As we left the club, I could hear the faint musical strains of 'Pistol Packin' Mama' being sung by a German prisoner. It was a good effort, but it didn't measure up. He was caressing the microphone like Frank Sinatra early in his career. We hurriedly packed a few things and were on our way, leaving all thoughts of war and prison camp behind us."

They took a room in the lodge at Choctaw Lake. It was early morning when they arrived. The air was frosty, but the sun soon warmed it. Kay couldn't stop staring into the crystal clear water that seemed to wash her cares away. She hoped moments like this would be more plentiful in her life someday. Time was precious, not knowing when Bob's orders for overseas duty might arrive. At seven that evening, they sat down to a leisurely, delicious dinner in the dining room of the lodge. Kay is sure that just knowing the chefs were not German prisoners added to her enjoyment.

Back in Aliceville, Bob got a telephone call very late one night and jumped up with his pistol. Kay was terrified when he explained that a prisoner had escaped. Bob didn't talk to her much about the camp—a lot of office work and some guard duty were all he ever mentioned. "I don't know if he just didn't want me to know what was going on out there or what—at least the bad part. He was a very protective man, very young, but one of those very stable young men."

Early in 1944, not long after the trip to Choctaw Lake, Bob suffered an acute appendectomy and was rushed to Tuscaloosa for surgery. Following his recovery, he was transferred to Miami Beach and later shipped to Germany. One letter he wrote from overseas gave Kay additional insight into how her husband had felt about his stint in Alabama. "Even Aliceville would look good to me compared to where I am now," he wrote. Bob Fillingham spent two years in Europe. Kay returned to San Antonio and lived with his parents while working at a bank.

The first edition of the *Camptown Crier* appeared at Camp Aliceville on November 15. Camp commanders believed a community-style newspaper would improve morale among the soldiers stationed there, but the camp had no funds for a newspaper, so the Aliceville Rotary Club agreed to sponsor it by soliciting advertising to cover the cost of each issue. Advertisements for the same businesses that regularly supported other civic efforts filled the back page—MS&C Hardware Company, the Aliceville Coca-Cola Bottling Company, Sam Wise, Summerville Service Station, Mack's Bowling Alley, D.E. Day City Grocery, the People's Café, and Jones Drug Store, among others.

The Rotary Club specified that no soldier should be required to pay for a copy. It held a naming contest at the high school, and Miss Nancy Jenkins submitted the winning name. The *Camptown Crier* Board of Officers included Captain L.H. Beasley, Lieutenant Joseph E.Vincent, and Chaplains Hinnebusch and Jungmeyer. Lieutenant Lawrence Persons was added later as technical advisor.

The front page of the first issue carried a profile of the 305th MPEG unit and one of Colonel Waite that described his long service in the army, including a stint in the Philippines where he "fought the treacherous Moro, a savage whose murderous fury is comparable to that of a wild beast." Colonel Waite had also commanded a prisoner of war camp in Russia during World War I and served on a French mission sent to investigate the deaths of Czar Nicholas and his family in 1917.

There were social notes about weddings and anniversaries of soldiers, a sports column, and a feature about the Stardusters dance band with the announcement that the band's former vocalist, Dot Latham, was now serving with the Navy's WAVES in New York City. "Good luck, Dottie" the article said. "Long may you wave!" Burt Martin's wife, LaVeda, had stepped in to do the band's vocals. Burt was a guitar player with the 436th, and he and LaVeda had been a team on the radio before the war. She'd been an acrobat before that. Now she sang with the Stardusters at Camp Aliceville and also played the accordion.

The people of the town of Reform took out a full page ad in the *Pickens County Herald and West Alabamian* on Thanksgiving Day 1943 to honor the boys of their community who were serving overseas. It featured photos of James Scott Browning, still a prisoner of war in occupied China, and Luther D. Orr, still a prisoner of war in Japan.

Mary Lu Turner put on her Sunday best dress and walked with her parents through the guard gates to Thanksgiving dinner in the camp hospital dining room. All the people her mother worked with were there with their families, and it was a very nice affair. There were printed menus and floral arrangements on the tables, which were covered with white cloths. Mary Lu loved the festive atmosphere and felt quite grownup as she sampled an appetizer of shrimp cocktail served with crackerettes. The tables were piled high with platters of roast turkey with oyster dressing, snowflake potatoes with giblet gravy, candied sweet potatoes, English peas (the little green ones she recognized from home rather than the pink and black ones more common in Alabama), and even wedges of iceberg lettuce with Thousand Island dressing. The desserts went on and on—mince pie, pumpkin pie, fruitcake, ice cream, and mixed nuts with assorted candies. There was fruit punch for the children and plenty of coffee, cigars, and cigarettes for the grownups.

The enlisted men celebrated, too. Stanley Pendrak had stayed up all night preparing enough turkeys, and there was plenty of cranberry sauce, dressing, corn, and English peas.

There is no record that the German POWs celebrated Thanksgiving that year—it was not a holiday they were familiar with, but they certainly sought out reasons to celebrate and relieve the boredom of their captivity whenever they could. On November 9, all of the compounds held festivities apparently meant to commemorate the founding of the confederation of Swiss cantons that later became the country of Switzerland. The open-air theater in Compound A presented the "Rütli" scene from Friedrich von Schiller's classic play, *Wilhelm Tell*, which recreates the historic meeting of Swiss representatives at Rütli Meadows on the shores of Lake Lucerne in 1307.

Later in November, *Totensonntag* (All Souls' Day or Festival of the Dead) became the occasion for the first parade at the camp. The compounds were still locked off from each other at that time, but each compound was allowed to have a parade and a celebration hour in the streets between its barracks. *Totensonntag* is a feast day of the Roman Catholic Church on which people pray for the souls of the faithful departed who might be suffering in purgatory. In evangelical churches, it is a day to remember and celebrate the lives of faithful people who have died. At Camp Aliceville, the POWs pronounced it a memorial day for their own fallen heroes.

Camp Aliceville was evolving into more of a community now that most of the outspoken troublemakers—both Nazis and anti-Nazis—had been transferred to other camps. Camp spokesman Walter Meier was still the only POW who could move freely in and out of all the compounds, but on November 24, the administration issued a new regulation allowing every POW the right to apply for a pass to confer with the camp spokesman.

That same week, Walter Meier issued the first edition of the *Allgemeinen Mitteilunger* (general announcements), which was distributed through all the compounds. It was more an announcement sheet than a full newspaper, but it detailed the various cultural, sports, educational, and religious activities—schedules, scores, and some commentary. The *Allgemeinen Mitteilunger* was duplicated on equipment belonging to the American administration of the camp, but Walter had been a typesetter and a printer in civilian life, a man who loved the beauty of the German language, and his dream was to publish a true newspaper. Nine more months would pass before he would find a way to acquire a printing press and make this dream reality.

On November 25, Werner Tobler arrived at Camp Aliceville to conduct the second inspection by the "Protecting Power" (Switzerland). A previous visit had been conducted by the Legation of Switzerland on July 26. Tobler was accompanied by Parker W. Buhrman from the United States Department of State. Buhrman filed a detailed report of this visit on January 6, 1944.

Buhrman's report noted that the appearance of the camp had been greatly improved since July. The POWs had hard-surfaced all of the roads and walkways within the camp and created drains of concrete or stone. The formerly swampy land on camp grounds had been drained, and additional areas of low-lying adjoining land were also being drained. The water supply came entirely from artesian wells, and the camp had an efficient underground sewage system, with settling basins leading to ultimate disposal in the Tombigbee River.

Camp Aliceville was still close to capacity, with 5,399 NCOs and enlisted men and six POW officers, including medical personnel and one chaplain. The hospital had 171 patients on the day of the visit, and Buhrman noted that most of these had relatively minor problems, including lingering complications from the malaria they'd contracted before arriving in the United States. They were cared for by four American physicians, one dentist, and one optician, with good cooperation from the German medical officers among the POWs. Prisoners told the inspector they were pleased with the medical attention they received.

Each compound now had its own large recreation area. In addition, a general recreation field had been constructed for inter-compound competitions and exhibition games on special days. The prisoners spent a great deal of time competing in organized football and fist ball games as well as boxing matches. The report mentioned the many theatricals being presented and the camp school, which now offered organized study courses in languages, mathematics, arithmetic, history, painting, woodworking, and drawing.

Hans Kopera, the Austrian motorcycle battalion member captured by Scottish Highlanders on Good Friday, was one of the Aliceville POWs who truly welcomed the establishment of the camp school. The war had cut short his dreams of becoming a physician, but Hans had a talent for drawing. He loved to sketch, and during the months he'd been in Aliceville, he'd created hilarious caricatures of other POWs and even of American officers in the camp. Whenever there was a birthday or other special occasion, his sketches were in demand as simple gifts.

Hans used the classes at Camp Aliceville to improve his English and his drawing abilities. When he heard that the camp hospital needed an interpreter for the surgical wing, he jumped at the chance and worked with others to encourage the German doctors to start medical classes as part of the camp education curriculum. By early 1944, he was spending his mornings sitting on a small, self-made chair studying everything from basic chemistry to histology, and his afternoons working as an interpreter. At night, he visited the X-ray lab to make sketches.

His diligence paid off. By the time he left Camp Aliceville, Hans had completed nearly two thousand medical drawings and the equivalent of three semesters of medical study. When he finally made it back to Austria, he was accepted at the University of Graz and given credit for his training at Camp Aliceville. He received his medical degree in the summer of 1951.

The drawing classes, like those Hans Kopera took, used staged scenes for still life practice—one of them a floral arrangement placed on a gate leg table partially covered by a striped cloth. A pottery class used native clays and a potter's wheel to create large vases, teapots, bowls, and beer steins. The math and language classes met in the mess halls between meals, studying books and charts sent by the Red Cross and the YMCA.

Sue Stabler marveled at the artwork the POWs were creating. "They were really artists. They made their costumes for everything. They could take nothing and come up with something of beauty. They even took the bones from the sides of beef they served, let them dry, and then carved them, and they looked just like ivory."

Sue remembers watching the POWs playing soccer. "They made their uniforms out of potato sacks. They put half the uniforms in the laundry with their denims to dye them blue. Then they picked red pokeberries when they worked out on the farms and used those to dye the other half pink." Sue laughs at the memory of watching those big German POWs out on the soccer field in baby blue and baby pink.

One of the theatricals presented was Heinrich von Kleist's 1806 comic masterpiece, *Der Zerbrochene Krug* (The Broken Jug). Several prisoners worked hard to fashion authentic costumes for this play, which is set in the Netherlands, and POWs took both male and female parts. The POW playing Mother Martha Rull, who comes before a local village judge to claim damages for a broken jug, wore wooden shoes, makeup, and the typical white "Dutch" cap with turned up corners. Camp spokesman Walter Meier played Adam, the judge (and also the culprit) who heard Mother Rull's complaint that a midnight visitor to her daughter's bedroom had broken the jug. Walter wore white stockings, breeches, a dress jacket and ruffled shirtfront, and even a wig—all fashioned from improvised items available in the camp. The elaborate set displayed the pivotal jug on a table underneath a chandelier and in front of a pillar wrapped with artificial leaves.

The library had accumulated a good collection of German and English books as well as German American language newspapers and copies of *The New York Times.* Religious services, conducted by a Catholic POW chaplain and two United States Army chaplains, were well attended.

Parker Buhrman's report analyzed the POW employment situation at Camp Aliceville, noting that there was no significant industry in the area and that local farms were small and usually operated by their owners. They could not employ large numbers of prisoners. Side labor camps were being set up in Alabama and in neighboring states, sometimes quite distant from the main camp. One was an agricultural and pulpwood camp for a thousand men in Indianola, Mississippi, almost two hundred miles due south of Aliceville.

POWs who worked for pay received eighty cents a day, and each POW also received three dollars per month in canteen coupons that could be used to buy snacks and toiletries. The report noted that nail files, scissors, and nail clippers were hard to obtain because of the scarcity of metal.

Prisoners reported to the inspector that they were generally pleased with the food, especially since they'd been allowed to receive more potatoes and bread instead of foods (like corn) that they were less familiar with. The inspector observed that most of the POWs had gained from five to ten pounds since arriving in the United States.

By November, winter weather was moving into Aliceville, and one problem mentioned in the report was the ongoing shortage of winter clothing. According to regulations, olive drab American uniforms had to be dyed a blue color before POWs could wear them. When wool uniforms were dyed, they tended to shrink one or two sizes, so the camp administration was having difficulty getting enough uniforms of the proper sizes. There was plenty of underwear, but overcoats and raincoats were also in short supply.

No POWs were under disciplinary punishment when the Swiss legation inspector visited. Five MPEG companies were in residence along with a processing company and a total of sixty-nine American officers. The report mentions the two shootings in August and notes that both clearly involved attempts to escape.

Buhrman summarized the comments of the Swiss representative—that he had found general orderliness and good behavior among the prisoners. However, Tobler had observed some confusion about whether prisoners could be required to work. Most prisoners seemed to have the impression they could volunteer to work but couldn't be required to work. Tobler discussed this with both Walter Meier and Colonel Waite. Both expressed the wish that work details could be mandatory, but apparently this had not been the general policy in the Fourth Service Command. "They [Meier and Waite] contend that German soldiers are accustomed to obeying orders and that when they are asked to turn out so many men on a voluntary basis, they prefer to direct the men to report rather than begging them to volunteer for work details. They believe that the present system tends to lax discipline in the camp."

Buhrman finished the report with his own personal observations, which included the notation that some prisoners were upset that those required to perform jobs within the camp, like shoe repair and tailoring, were not getting paid. He commented that neither Walter Meier nor any of the compound company leaders were getting paid either. He also listed several other complaints—shortages of paper and razor blades, for example—and stated that there was no evidence the camp administration was deliberately withholding these items. Colonel

Waite had told him he wanted to replace the army cots in the barracks as soon as possible with double-deck steel beds. Quite a few of the wooden cots had been destroyed, and Waite suspected prisoners were tearing them apart to use the materials for making other things they needed.

Buhrman also addressed Walter Meier's frustration about not having the means to maintain necessary discipline. Buhrman speculated that the camp commander might be reluctant to use measures available to him and suggested that "discipline in these camps would be greatly improved if it were clearly stated to the prisoners that they are required to work and have some system worked out under which they could be properly disciplined in the event of their declining to respond to work details." He ended the report by stating his observation that the prisoners held the camp administration in high regard and recognized that they had done everything they could for the welfare of the camp.

By the end of November, the dynamics of the war in Europe began to shift, and the Allies knew the time had come to move forward with plans for the invasion of northern France—the invasion they'd delayed the previous year. Victory was still not certain, but the possibilities were promising. Between November 28 and December 1, Roosevelt and Churchill met with Russian Premier Joseph Stalin in Tehran, the capital city of Iran. It was the first time Stalin was present at a meeting of what was clearly emerging as a three-power entity that would shape post-war Europe. The three men agreed to keep in close touch from that point forward. Their discussions at this Tehran Conference confirmed plans for Operation Overlord, the code name for D-Day, the invasion of France that would take place in June 1944.

In preparation for this invasion, the most experienced MPEG units were being recalled and retrained for duty overseas. The 425th, at Camp Aliceville only since September, had already departed for Fort Custer in Michigan. The 305th, which had come to Aliceville in the middle of a mud-slogging night the previous March, left Alabama for Fort Custer on December 1. As Bob Siddall, Byron Kauffman, Chet Eisenhauer, Joseph Samper, Joey Futchko, Hubert Jordan, and the rest of the 305th gathered their gear and lined up, the 389th field band showed their support as a guard of honor. The ten musicians raised their bugles and drums and belted out a series of military marches as they escorted the entire 305th through the camp gates and up the highway to the Aliceville depot.

At Fort Custer, the men of the 305th spent the next eight weeks training in Michigan's freezing snow and wet wind, then boarded a train for Boston. By April, they would be in France, taking part in what was known as the Redball Express—escorting convoys carrying food stuffs, medical supplies, gas, and ammunition to Allied soldiers at the front and then guarding the same convoys as they packed their empty supply trucks with enemy prisoners. They would guard these prisoners until they could be loaded onto transport ships headed for camps like Aliceville in the United States.

One morning in early December, a small, olive drab pickup truck packed tight with camera and recording equipment arrived at the Camp Aliceville guard gate. The four men inside showed identification and were allowed to proceed directly to the inner perimeter gates of the POW compounds. The leader of the four, an officer with credentials from the OWI (Office of

War Information), received permission to speak with Camp Spokesman Walter Meier.

The OWI officer explained, through an interpreter, that he wanted to set up cameras so his men could record messages from POWs to their families back in Germany. Each prisoner would be able to give his name, the state of his health, a brief Christmas greeting, and a comment about the treatment he was receiving. The messages would be broadcast by Voice of America and could be picked up by short-wave transmitters anywhere in Europe. It would be an opportunity for POWs to let their families know they were safe, even if those families were in areas where postal service was being disrupted.

Walter Meier listened to this explanation for a few seconds and then responded with two emphatic words—*Durchaus nicht!* (Absolutely not!). Even though the OWI officer assured Walter the interviews were strictly voluntary, he still refused the request. Walter knew civilians in Germany were forbidden to try to pick up such broadcasts and would jeopardize their safety if they did. He also suspected the American government had a propaganda motive for bothering to make them.

Walter's suspicion was correct. The OWI did have a motive other than simply informing German families that their captured soldiers were safe. Since Germany was losing more and more ground in Europe, it was thought such broadcasts might encourage disillusioned German soldiers to surrender if they believed America would treat them well. The tactic was similar to one the Germans had used in North Africa when they dropped leaflets over American and British troops promising "honourable and decent treatment to every American and

British soldier who realizes the futility of this struggle on African soil." The Allies had responded to that propaganda with their own leaflet drop to German soldiers that read, "*Die Toten kommen nicht nach Haus...Aber die Gefangenen bleiben am Leben und sehen die Heimat wieder.*" (The dead do not come home, but the prisoner remains alive and will see home again.)

Colonel Maxwell McKnight, who would help found the Special Projects Division education program for the War Department in 1944, wrote later that the recording team turned away at Camp Aliceville learned a lesson from their negative encounter with Walter Meier. From then on, when they traveled to other POW camps, they checked in first with the Camp Commander but never with the Camp Spokesman. Then they went directly into the compounds and began setting up their equipment. By the time the Camp Spokesman realized what they were doing, many of the curious POWs had already volunteered and recorded messages for their families back home.

On December 8, the Camp Aliceville Post Theater bustled with celebration as 134 civilian employees gathered to receive their Emblem for Civilian Service awards from the War Department. Employees like Earline Lewis and Elma Henders, Harvey Stapp and Jake McBride, Ward and Mary Turner, and Bobbie Kirksey—all those who'd completed six consecutive months of satisfactory service by November 1 (with an efficiency rating of "Good" or better) were eligible. Before the awards were handed out, everyone was required to view a twenty-minute showing of *Mr. Blabbermouth,* an OWI documentary that reminded civilians not to compromise the war effort with gossip about their jobs.

On Sunday, December 12, August Wanders wrote in his diary that the gates between the six compounds were opened for the first time, allowing prisoners to visit each other back and forth. This would become the practice for a few hours each Sunday. Also on this date, Compound B received a Christmas gift from Adolf Hitler—a sizeable check for more than $12,000—to provide Christmas gifts. The German government had transferred 1,440,000 francs to the Swiss Legation so that Christmas gifts "from the *Führer*" could be given to all POWs, and this was apparently part of that money. A week later, Pope Pius XII sent $1,000 as a Christmas gift.

The Aliceville Arts Club observed Alabama Day with great Southern pride on December 14 at the home of Mrs. W.E. Barrett. Among those attending were Mrs. B.F. Johnston, wife of sawmill owner Johnny Johnston, and Mrs. Gerald Stabler, wife of the funeral home director who'd been elected Mayor of Aliceville in November.

Mrs. Wallace Kirksey presided over a business session, and members responded to roll call by reciting the names of revered historical Alabamians. Plans for the upcoming formal dance for enlisted men at Camp Aliceville were discussed. One member was put in charge of making sure the high school gym would be bathed in soft blue light for the occasion, and another was sent out to gather enough mistletoe and holly for each doorway.

Jack Pratt's younger son, George, paid a visit home just in time to celebrate his eighteenth birthday with his family on December 18. George had been headed across the Pacific with the Merchant Marines when a boiler burst, and his ship had to limp back to San Francisco for repairs. While at home, George helped his father put together the special Service Men's Edition of the county newspaper and prepare it for mailing to a thousand servicemen all over the world.

When he headed back to San Francisco a week later, George told his father his true ambition was to head in the opposite direction and drive a landing barge in the "channel invasion" being orchestrated by General Eisenhower. "You never know what a youngster will do," Jack Pratt wrote in his column that week. "With one son on the Italian front for the past sixty days and another seeking the most dangerous job in the war, it kind of leaves a fellow with the jitters. But they have a duty to perform. Some mother's son must fill the hard places, so why should we complain? In war, all men are equal. I don't think I'd be proud of a son who looked for the safe and easy jobs in this war."

Within that week, and just before Christmas, the family of Lieutenant Richard Somerville received the news they'd been dreading for an entire year. Their son had been missing since November 1942 when his plane went down over the English Channel. Now the War Department was notifying them of that "hard place" Jack Pratt had written about—there was no hope of survival, and their son had been officially declared dead.

On Tuesday evening, December 21, the young ladies of Aliceville turned themselves out in fine fashion for the Aliceville Arts Club's formal dance to honor enlisted servicemen from the POW camp. As the newly appointed society editor for *The Camptown Crier*, Emmie Archibald covered the event for Camp Aliceville and wrote a front page story entitled, "GIs Yearn for

More Arts Club Formals." Emmie declared the evening "the most successful of the entertainments that have been provided for the soldiers at PWC since their arrival."

Even though this event did not take place at the Officers' Club, the Arts Club members made sure the evening began with an elegant Grand March followed by Christmas carols sung by a quartet from the 389th. Under the glow of the soft blue lights, the Stardusters dance band played waltzes and rhumbas and everything in between. Emmie wrote that the enlisted men wanted to be sure to thank Mrs. Kirksey, the Arts Club president, and Mrs. George N. Downer Jr., the dance committee chairman, for the wonderful party.

On Christmas Eve, the POWs in Compound A presented Bach's Christmas oratorio. The following day, there were feasts and celebrations throughout the camp, along with an all-day soccer competition pitting Compounds A, B, and C against Compounds D, E, and F.

Hermann Blumhardt did not have much Christmas spirit. The censored letters he received from Katie that week only made matters worse—it was good to hear from her, but her words made him ache to be back home. He was sitting on his cot feeling sorry for himself when a friend insisted he come to the mess hall and join the Christmas celebrations. "I was in no mood for a Christmas party," Hermann remembers, "but then I was glad I went." The American authorities had allowed a special holiday dinner to be prepared, and the men were even able to enjoy a few beers.

The 389th spent Christmas Day celebrating the anniversary of their MPEG unit activation at Camp McCain a year earlier.

Colonel Waite conducted a formal review of the company and handed out citations and good conduct ribbons. The company bugler played for the occasion.

The final 1943 edition of the *Pickens County Herald and West Alabamian* carried a column that appeared occasionally under the title, "What Pickens County Negroes Are Doing." It highlighted the fundraising efforts for a new auditorium at the Summerville School for Negroes in Aliceville. "While it is yet a very new institution, it [the school] has become part of the development of colored youths of Pickens County and adjoining counties." The article mentioned the large number from the student body who were serving in the United States armed forces. It also carried the photos of two young ladies, ages seventeen and fourteen, who'd won the ticket-selling competition for the auditorium fundraiser. Thelma Hughes of Pleasant Ridge had sold the most ($145 worth) and was crowned "Miss Summerville." Ineice Foster had sold $120 worth and received honorable mention. The article pointed out that many white citizens had also contributed to the fund and that it was hoped the auditorium could be built as soon as the war ended.

On December 28, Hans Kopera pondered the next long year of captivity that was probably ahead of him and wondered what it would bring. As always when his mood was one of contemplation, he reached for his sketchpad. He drew a tall figure in a top hat and too short pants holding aloft a tray with a roasted pig's head. *Neu Jahr 1944,* he printed down the side of the sketch. There was no particular symbolism. It was just a sketch to mark the so slow passing of time.

Anyone with any knowledge of German and Nazi mentality knows that this Nazi terror against those German prisoners who no longer wish to conform to Hitler's teaching could be stopped overnight by simply letting the Gestapo-minded prisoners know that this democracy simply will not tolerate such nonsense. There is nothing in the Geneva Convention against doing this.

• January 1944 •
William L. Shirer, *New York Tribune, Inc.*

PLATE 1 A view of Camp Aliceville prisoner barracks as they neared completion in late 1942. The "dead zone" and inner and outer perimeter fences are visible at left.

PLATE 2 A drawing of the Camp Aliceville Commandant's residential quarters, reputed by local residents to be the former home of Tom Parker. First occupied by Colonel Frederick A. Prince, the house stood in the shadow of one of the hexagonal guard towers.

PLATE 3 A drawing of one of the prisoner compounds showing the tarpaper-covered barracks atop low stilts, with landscaping planted by the POWs and drainage ditches completed by them.

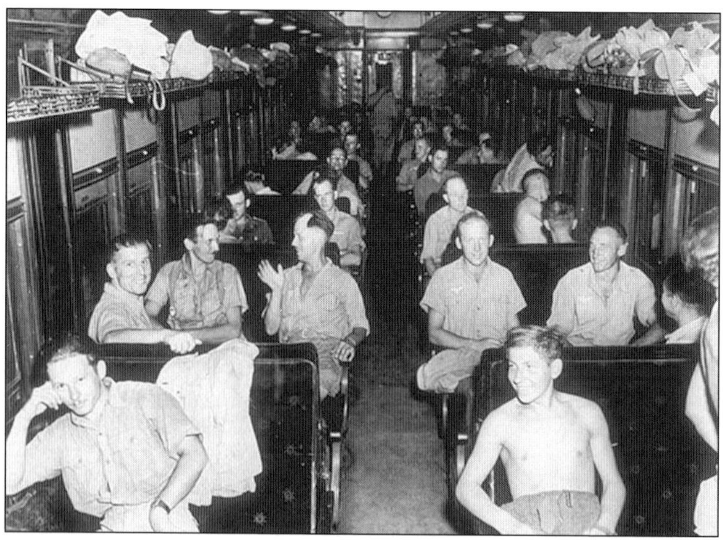

PLATE 4 Camp Aliceville POWs were surprised to discover the comfort of the passenger cars in which the American military transported them. Wilhelm Schlegel later described these Frisco passenger cars as "the Mercedes of trains."

PLATE 5 *(above)* On the morning of June 2, 1943, the first Frisco cars unloaded POWs near the depot in Aliceville. Exhausted prisoners stepped down from the cars and stared at their new surroundings, while inexperienced MPEG guards stood with their weapons at the ready.

PLATE 6 *(left)* Prisoner of War Horst Uhse arrived in Aliceville on June 3, 1943. Horst had battled jaundice and malaria following his capture in North Africa, but would be nursed back to health in Aliceville.

PLATE 7 In spite of a military directive to stay inside their homes, the citizens of Aliceville lined their yards and porches to watch the arriving German POWs form up, five across, on the highway in the middle of their town to begin their two-mile march to Camp Aliceville.

PLATE 8 An early roll call of POWs in front of the barracks in one of the compounds. The POW second from left wears denim pants painted with the white, five-inch letters P and W to make his status obvious.

PLATE 9 In the compound mess halls, POW cooks prepared meals from local produce and ample supplies brought in by train.

PLATE 10 By the spring of 1944, a greenhouse had been constructed in the shadow of one of the guard towers. It was the perfect place to nurture shrubbery and flowers to be used in landscaping the camp.

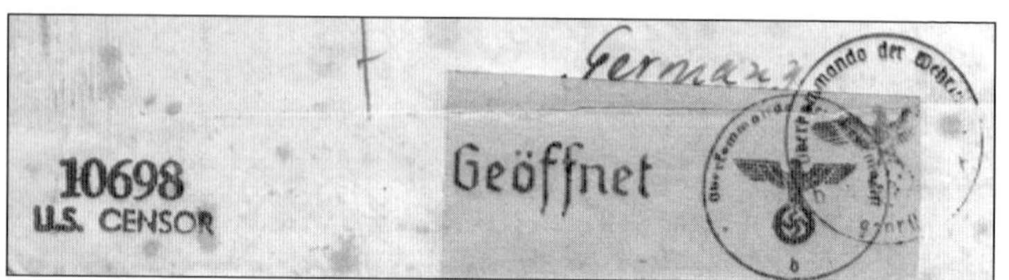

PLATE 11 The envelopes of mail received by POWs in Camp Aliceville bore two censor stamps like these, indicating that both the American and the German governments reviewed and censored the communications of the prisoners.

PLATE 12 Only two prisoners were shot while attempting to escape from Camp Aliceville. The foreground headstone here is that of Rolf Schneider, shot while attempting to cut through the fencing on the night of August 1, 1943. After the war, his body and those of all other prisoners buried at Camp Aliceville were moved to the German Italian Memorial Cemetery for prisoners of war at Fort McClellan.

PLATE 13 Diphtheria struck Camp Aliceville in the fall of 1943. Prisoners were treated in the post hospital, and these last four diphtheria carriers were among those quarantined in Compound B until they no longer tested positive for the disease. Walter Felholter, on the far right, used his time in quarantine to study English.

PLATE 14 Although POWs began organizing classes for each other soon after the camp opened, the "official" school in Camp Aliceville opened on February 24, 1944. Fifty-eight POW teachers offered classes in art, ethics, mathematics, English, and other subjects to more than nine hundred prisoners.

PLATE 15 Physical fitness was a priority with Camp Aliceville POWs. They built pits for broad and high jumping, laid out soccer fields, and cleared a track for running events. When the gates between compounds were opened, the compounds competed against each other in numerous events.

PLATE 16 Plays, sometimes recreated from memory, were popular in the camp. POWs played both men's and women's parts and created their costumes and the stage sets from items available within the camp. Camp Spokesman Walter Meier is shown behind a bench playing a judge.

PLATE 17 The POWs formed many musical groups within the camp, including a dance orchestra, choirs, glee clubs, and six bands. Many of their instruments were donated by the YMCA. Here, the POW orchestra plays for a dinner dance at the Officers' Club.

PLATE 18 In 1944, prisoners used profits from their canteens to purchase a huge printing press so they could print a camp newspaper (*Der Zaungast*), as well as calendars of events and programs for concerts. Here, a prisoner operates the press nicknamed "the Flying Dutchman."

Der Zaungast

Aliceville, den 3. Dezember 1944 Nummer 7

WOCHENZEITSCHRIFT DES KRIEGSGEFANGENENLAGERS ALICEVILLE · ALABAMA

Approved Periodical Number: „APN - 4 - 45 - M". Edited and published semi-monthly by and for the German Prisoners of War at Prisoner of War Camp Aliceville-Alabama. - Verantw. f. Inhalt: Lt. Busch - Satz und Druck: Lagerdruckerei

Ich schaute in eine Adventskerze und fragte: Warum ist Licht so schoen? Und es sprach in mir: Weil es Verwandlung ist.

Aus der festen dunklen Kerze wird erst ein Fluessiges, dann ein noch Zarteres, Edleres, Leuchtendes und doch ruhig Bestaendiges. Schoen ist alle Verwandlung von Stufe zu Stufe. Alles Grosse in der Natur, das Fruehlingwerden, die Sommerreife, der Purpur des Herbstes, ist Verwandlung. Alles Grosse im Menschenleben: Schmerz und Schauer der Geburt, Drang und Schwang der Jugend, die weitende Kraft der Liebe und die geballte des Kampfes, ist Verwandlung. Wehe dem Menschen, der sich nicht wandeln will; Starre ist sein Schicksal, Enge und Eigennutz sein Wesen, Armut und Leere sein Alter. Und die letzte und groesste Verwandlung, der Tod, findet ihn unbereitet. Drum will ich mich verwandeln lassen durch alles, was mir begegnet, durch das Glueck in schenkende Tat, durch den Schmerz in liebende Weisheit, durch den Feind in Festigkeit, durch die Stoesse in Kraft, durch das Unerwartete in Geistesgegenwart, durch das Schwierige in Beharrlichkeit, durch den Mangel in Freiheit, durch die Fuelle in Mass, durch das Unbegreifliche in Ehrfurcht und Froemmigkeit, durch die Menschen in Guete und Geduld. Dann wird mir auch der Tod zur milden Macht werden, die das Dunkel der Kerze in Licht verwandelt.

Warum ist Licht so schoen?

Weil es so still ist.

Ohne Laut vollzieht sich in ihm die grosse, die unaufhoerliche Wandlung. In seinem Umkreis ist alles Feier und Friede. Oft suchte mein Auge mitten im lauten Getuemmel eines menschenerfuellten Saales ein brennendes Licht und wurde stille wie eine Insel in ihrem Anschauen. Und alle Stille ist schoen. Ob sie als leiser Schnee vom Himmel faellt und die Erde beschwichtigt. Ob sie als weisser Nebel den Baum, das Haus, dich selber mit Schweigen umhuellt. Ob sie als Wolke am Himmel in stummer Erhabenheit ihre maechtigen Glanzgebirge baut. Oder ob sie in einer Menschenseele dem Kommen Gottes voranschwebt wie die Morgendaemmerung dem Anbruch des neuen Tages.

Warum ist Licht so schoen?

Weil es strahlt.

Es bleibt nicht haften an der Stelle, wo es brennt, es sendet sein Leuchten aus. Und der Widerschein der Waende, der Dinge, das Glaenzen still blickender Augen strahlt ihm Antwort. Sollte ich nicht Gleiches vermoegen? Ist meine Liebe, mein Denken, mein Wuenschen an den Punkt gebannt, wo ich weile? Koennte des Menschen Geist nicht strahlend weite Gegenwart sein? Wirkende Hilfe in die Ferne, in Bereiche, wo Brueder kaempfen, schaffen und leiden und der unsichtbaren Gefaehrten beduerfen? -

Warum ist Licht so schoen?

Weil es aufwaerts brennt.

Unbeirrbar sucht jede Flamme die Hoehe. Neige die Kerze zur Seite, ja wende sie kopfab der Erde zu, und sie wird dennoch die Richtung des Himmels suchen. Ins Licht schauend, fuehle ich den gleichen Zug, dasselbe

1

PLATE 19 The first issue of the POW newspaper *Der Zaungast* (Guest behind the Wire) appeared in Camp Aliceville on July 16, 1944. The front page shown here is from a December issue with an article about the season of Advent. A complete collection of issues can be seen at the Aliceville Museum.

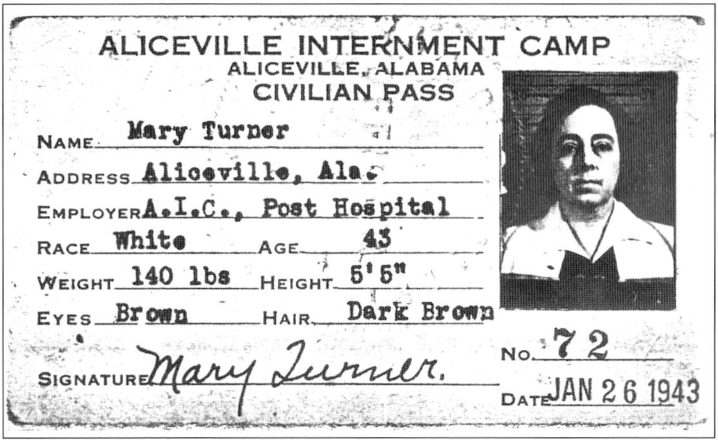

ALICEVILLE INTERNMENT CAMP
ALICEVILLE, ALABAMA
CIVILIAN PASS

NAME Mary Turner
ADDRESS Aliceville, Ala.
EMPLOYER A.I.C., Post Hospital
RACE White AGE 43
WEIGHT 140 lbs HEIGHT 5'5"
EYES Brown HAIR Dark Brown
NO. 72
SIGNATURE Mary Turner.
DATE JAN 26 1943

PLATE 20 Civilian employee Mary Turner had to show this ID card each time she passed through the camp guard gate to go to her job at the Aliceville Internment Camp Post Hospital.

PLATE 21 Major Karl H. Shriver was in charge of the construction of Camp Aliceville for the Army Corps of Engineers. He is shown here riding his beloved horse, Cokey, on a fall afternoon during the construction of the camp.

PLATE 22 Aliceville high school student Dot Latham and her friends loved the opportunity to dance all different styles with the soldiers at Camp Aliceville. Having a beautiful voice, Dot also sang popular hits with the Stardusters band at Camp Aliceville's NCO club before joining the WAVES.

PLATE 23 Sue and Gerald Stabler opened their home to Army Corps of Engineers personnel while Camp Aliceville was being constructed. As a local funeral home director, Gerald often helped provide dignified burial for prisoners who died in Camp Aliceville. As mayor, he sometimes heard from former POWs after the war ended and often sent care packages to them. In 1989, Sue organized the first reunion of MPEG guards and former POWs.

PLATE 24 Margie Archibald and her friends enjoyed entertaining the American officers who came to Camp Aliceville. She worked as a secretary in the camp, and is shown here with a sketch of herself created by one of the POWs.

PLATE 25 Former 389th MPEG guard Stanley Pendrak is shown here with former POW Walter Felholter and historian E.B. Walker in May 1982 when Walter first returned to Alabama to relive the memories of his detention in Camp Aliceville. L-R: E.B. Walker, Walter Felholter, and Stanley Pendrak.

PLATE 26 The first reunion of former Camp Aliceville MPEG guards, POWs, and townspeople took place in October 1989. In this photo, Hermann Blumhardt and Walter Felholter stand together at left as a former MPEG guard and a former POW hug each other in friendship not far from where the German POWs began their march to Camp Aliceville from the railroad depot in June 1943.

PLATE 27 *(above)* Former Museum Director Mary Bess Paluzzi receiving recognition at the 60th reunion of Camp Aliceville in March 2003. L-R: Walter Felholter, Ms. Paluzzi, Walter Schlegel, and Hermann Blumhardt.

PLATE 28 *(left)* Katie and Hermann Blumhardt at the March 2003 60th reunion, with photos of the camp in the background at the Museum.

PLATE 29 Mary Lu Turner Keef with the doll she cherished while living in Aliceville as a child during World War II. She has returned for several reunions and maintains close friendships with several Aliceville residents and also with former POW Hermann Blumhardt and his wife, Katie.

PLATE 30 As an American waist gunner shot down over Germany, Wendell Parrish experienced food shortages and primitive conditions in *Stalag Luft IV*, a sharp contrast to that of Camp Aliceville POWs. Wendell is shown here with his wife, Clem, during the 2003 reunion of Camp Aliceville.

PLATE 31 This photograph was sent to friends of the Aliceville Museum on August 5, 2002, showing the gingko tree planted by former POWs in front of the museum during a reunion in October 1995. "The world may be troubled, but there are still moments when peace can be found" was the message with it from then Museum Director Mary Bess Paluzzi. The gingko was the first tree to bud at Hiroshima after the destruction caused by the atomic bomb in August 1945.

CHAPTER TEN

Identity and Persecution

During the first six months of 1944, the population of Camp Aliceville consisted almost entirely of prisoners captured in North Africa. Wilhelm Schlegel, who'd come to Alabama from North Africa by way of Scotland in late August 1943, continued to be amazed at the quality of everyday life in the camp. Compared to his Spartan existence as a German soldier, it was truly, as he phrased it, "a land of milk and honey." There were opportunities to play competitive soccer and listen to fine music, to dine at a sumptuous, unrationed table, and to develop new friendships with other POWs. Most evenings after dinner in the mess hall, he lingered to join in the robust singing of German marching songs with others in Compound E—songs that never failed to heighten his sense of national pride.

Flamme empor, Flamme empor.
Steige mit loderndem Scheine
Auf die Gebirge vom Rhein…

Heilige Glut!
Rufe die Jugend zusammen
Dass bei den zischenden Flammen
Wachse der Mut.

(Flames rising, Flames rising,
Climbing with a brilliant blaze
On the mountains of the Rhine.

Holy passion!
    Call the youth together
    So that by the sizzling flames,
    Courage grows.)

The men sang these lyrics to a lusty melody composed by K.L. Gläser in 1791. The verses evoke a flickering campfire and a soldierly ritual of dedication:

See—we stand
True in the dedicated circle
To see you burn
To the glory of the Fatherland.

Brilliant gleam!
See, we singing pairs
Swear at the flaming altar
To be German!

On January 7, Wilhelm enjoyed a performance of *Monika*, an operetta by Austrian composer Niko Dostal, staged by the POWs themselves, which he and other NCOs were allowed to attend at the theater in Compound A. Wilhelm was quite impressed with what the men in Compound A had done to transform their plain POW recreation hall into a first-class facility with an excellent stage and orchestra pit. Using their own labor and materials paid for by profits from their canteen, the POWs had removed the wooden flooring, excavated so that the seating area could slope towards the stage, poured a concrete floor, and even constructed comfortable wooden seats. The building could accommodate an audience of 190. Wilhelm thoroughly enjoyed the operetta, almost forgetting he was watching the performance in a prisoner of war camp. He longed for the war to end and believed in his heart that Germany would triumph eventually, but if he had to be a prisoner, he could think of worse places than Camp Aliceville to pass the lonely months.

As the second full year of war began, many POW camp commanders were pressuring NCO prisoners to sign away their exemption status and work for eighty cents a day like enlisted prisoners. It was not that the War Department wanted to make money from prison labor. Despite the fact that employers like Pickens County cotton farmer Elmo Owen and Aliceville sawmill owner Johnny Johnston paid the government the prevailing community wage for prison labor while the government paid the prisoners only eighty cents a day, the government was not netting a profit. *The Birmingham Age-Herald* pointed out on January 15 that the United States Treasury expected to collect $2 million in 1944 from the "services of civilian detainees and prisoners of war," but the newspaper also pointed out that the costs of maintaining these people would "far exceed returns to the treasury from their labors." What the War Department wanted was to put more and more prisoners to work because the American economy needed them to get jobs done—jobs that were vacant because more and more American men were enlisting and being drafted.

The war in Europe had a growing appetite for newly trained American soldiers. The old Desert Fox nemesis from North Africa, Erwin Rommel, was now commanding more than fifty divisions of German troops in France. Hitler had sent Rommel to northern France in late 1943 when the threat of an Allied invasion there could no longer be ignored. He appointed Rommel Inspector of Coastal Defenses and later commander of Army Group B.

Rommel believed the only way to repel a landing in northern France would be to counterattack the beaches as soon after a landing as possible, but other commanders thought it more prudent to keep the *Panzer* divisions farther inland until an enemy line of advance became clear. Because Hitler was not sure where the Allies would land—perhaps Brest or Cherbourg or Le Havre (the only French ports close enough to English shipping and aircraft bases)—he chose to divide his six northern France *Panzer* divisions. He assigned three to Rommel and located the other three farther inland with orders not to release them without direct approval from his operations staff.

On January 16, General Eisenhower assumed his duties as leader of Operation Overlord, code name for the invasion Hitler anticipated—the one that was secretly planned to cross the English Channel, land at an unanticipated beachhead in France, and then push into the heart of Germany. Huge numbers of Allied troops were already gathering in England for this invasion. Once it occurred and the Allies began capturing Germans in France, the population of Camp Aliceville would take on a whole new dimension—a dimension that would lead to another conflict between two distinct factions among the German prisoners.

Back at the beginning of 1944 in Aliceville and other camps, many NCO POWs like Wilhelm Schlegel ignored pressure from camp commanders and refused to work. Some believed they would be aiding the enemy even in jobs approved by the Geneva Convention, and some believed they could make better use of their time studying English, staying fit and creative, and taking educational courses in the school the prisoners themselves were organizing.

The POWs opened their official school in Camp Aliceville on February 24 with fifty-eight teachers and more than nine hundred students among the prisoners. Volunteers had taught courses informally before this, but now, as camp spokesman Walter Meier had hoped, there would be credits for studies in the arts and in technical fields. Wilhelm Frederick Westhoff, who'd been a teacher in civilian life, was appointed Director of Studies for the camp school. He taught art classes along with two artists from Berlin, Dietrich Schulz and Hans Spetski.

Horst Uhse had recovered from the lingering symptoms of malaria by the time the camp school began offering classes. Although he spent most of his time playing in chess tournaments, he did sign up for courses that appealed to him. One favorite was "Fundamental Questions of Right and Wrong," which approached ethics like a chess game. "You could dissect it like a frog, and it taught me to analyze the difference between right and wrong, not only for World War II, but for all historical studies."

Wilhelm Schlegel had made the decision when he first arrived at Aliceville that he would not work willingly while serving as a POW. As an *Unteroffizier* (NCO), he believed this was his duty as well as his right. For the first few months, his decision was not a problem. There were enough enlisted POWs to satisfy local needs for pulpwood and farming labor. Besides, there didn't seem to be enough jobs available at the small farming and sawmill operations in the Camp Aliceville area to occupy even the enlisted prisoners who wanted to work.

Aliceville, like a number of other large POW camps built early in the war, was located in a relatively isolated area for security reasons. As the war dragged on and manpower needs became a critical issue, this concept seemed less and less like a good idea. As early as 1943, one Inspector General's report concluded that "prisoner of war camps with few exceptions were too large, too elaborately constructed, and poorly located with regard to fuller utilization of prisoners as labor…."

Such opinions may have been the reason for the news that shocked Wilhelm and others at Camp Aliceville the third week of January. A huge number of POWs were to be transferred from Aliceville to the custody of the Second Service Command and sent north to Fort Dix, near Trenton in central New Jersey. On January 17, Wilhelm was among the one thousand POWs lined up and marched under guard to Frisco passenger cars for the journey north. It would be six long months before he returned to Alabama.

At Fort Dix, these men entered a population of almost fifteen thousand prisoners—Germans and Italians held in separate compounds at the same base where thousands of American soldiers were undergoing final combat training before shipment across the Atlantic to England to prepare for the Normandy invasion. The Fort Dix compound had similar facilities to Aliceville, including laundry and showers, and well-equipped kitchens where prisoner cooks prepared good meals.

Like Aliceville, it had a camp orchestra, a theater, and opportunities for sports activities.

The jobs were different and more numerous in this more densely populated location. Enlisted men worked in warehouses, loading civilian equipment onto trains, and in canneries, processing fruits and vegetables. They were also used to fill labor positions at the military camp itself. NCO prisoners supervised many of these jobs, and Wilhelm may have been selected to go there because camp officials thought he would make a good labor supervisor in a different setting. However, Wilhelm stuck to his original decision. He would not work willingly in any capacity.

The transfers to Fort Dix were only the first of many that would occur during 1944 as Camp Aliceville evolved gradually from a general POW camp to one that specialized in non-commissioned officer POWs who refused to work. This transformation made sense to the Provost Marshal General's office because Camp Aliceville was not making a significant, year-round contribution to relieving the labor shortage in the country. By the time Wilhelm Schlegel returned in August, the transformation of Camp Aliceville to a segregation camp for defiant NCOs would be mostly complete.

Captain James S. Wilson visited Aliceville on January 19 and filed a lengthy report with the Provost Marshal General in Washington. During his visit, he discussed administrative problems with Colonel Waite and the rest of his staff, including Captain Scott Strohecker, the compound commander. Wilson reported that only five of the six compounds were in operation in January 1944, with a total of 4,392 prisoners. He mentioned the transfer of prisoners to Camp Blanding and to Fort Dix as explanation for the drop in population.

Wilson reported that all drainage ditches were now lined with stone and that concrete aprons had been poured around each mess hall to increase neatness and sanitary conditions. He also commented on the considerable profits from compound canteens that had been spent on beautifying the grounds. One project was a greenhouse with a slanted, framed glass roof and wall panels. Two prisoners experienced in nursery operation worked here full time, nurturing shrubbery and flowers for landscaping and decorating.

The POW camps used coupons as currency, both in the United States and in camps operated by other governments. The eighty cents a day prisoners earned was paid in coupons. Under the terms of the Geneva Convention, prisoners above the rank of corporal could refuse to work but were still paid thirty cents a day, also in coupons. Hermann Blumhardt remembers receiving and then "spending" these coupons, which changed color each month. They could be exchanged at the compound canteen for food, soap, toothpaste, tobacco, postcards, and stamps—even Hershey bars and beer, which could be sipped while standing at the canteen counter. At the end of a month, Hermann had to turn in any leftover coupons, but he was given credit in coupons printed in the next month's color.

Coupon profits (the difference between what the United States Army paid for items and the slightly higher value POWs paid) were calculated carefully. The POWs themselves decided what these profits would be used for—contributions to the German Red Cross or other German charities, shrubbery to beautify the camp, and eventually, even the printing press Walter Meier dreamed of.

Wilson listed the United States Army personnel records for the camp, including 69 officers and 245 enlisted men in the headquarters detachment. A total of 227 civilian employees provided clerical and other support. One of those civilian employees was an attractive young secretary at Headquarters Personnel named Martha Bonner Smith. Martha was a third cousin of Will Peebles. Everyone called her Ettie, and chaplain's assistant Jack Sisty soon found himself captivated by her quiet Southern charm. He found more and more excuses to ride his bicycle over to Headquarters Personnel so he could share good jokes with Ettie. The two dated throughout the spring and summer. They were married in August and moved into an apartment building for married soldiers across the highway from the camp.

When the war ended, Jack and Ettie returned to Jack's native New York City for a while, but then, like a number of other "transplanted Yankee" soldiers who married local women, returned to Aliceville and made it their permanent home. Jack served for ten years as director of the Aliceville Chamber of Commerce and contributed his excellent voice to the choir at the Methodist church. He also worked for Huyck Felt Company in Aliceville before completing his degree at the University of Alabama and working with the physically handicapped. Ettie taught high school in Aliceville for many years.

Another civilian employee was John Richey who was lured away from his twenty-eight-year job as cook at the Aliceville Hotel by Colonel Prince not long after the POW camp opened. Colonel Prince hired him first as bartender for the officers' club, making him the highest-ranked African American employee at the camp. John worked nights, swapping stories with the camp officers, and spent his days building a house for himself and his family. One of his jobs was emptying the eighteen slot machines that were part of the club's entertainment, as they were on many military bases during World War II. John once told an interviewer that the officers' club at Camp Aliceville was a "regular little Las Vegas" and that he often deposited as much as two thousand dollars a week from those machines in the camp account at the Aliceville Bank & Trust Company.

During the second year of the war, Colonel Prince transferred John to the position of chef at the camp hospital. The colonel remembered the wonderful hams and pastries John had prepared at the hotel, and he wanted these for the hospital mess hall (which was also, of course, where the officers ate). John Richey spent the rest of the war supervising nineteen German POWs who worked with him in the hospital kitchen. He often scrambled as many as thirty-nine dozen eggs and cooked thirty-two slabs of bacon for breakfast.

John Richey's association with the POWs was a good one, in spite of the language barrier. They laughed together as they worked, and the Germans even "initiated" John into something (he was not quite sure what) by hitting him on the backside with a board. One of them painted his portrait in oil on a piece of cardboard—a full-faced black man in his tall chef's hat and white tunic. The POWs gave John other pieces of artwork, too, including a pen and ink drawing of a street scene in Germany and a plaster casting of a fifteenth-century sailing ship. The ship was glazed in dark brown and gold and set in a handmade wooden frame.

In early 1944, the guard detachment at Camp Aliceville included five MPEG units with a total of 675 enlisted men. During the January 19 inspection tour, Colonel Waite complained to Captain Wilson that even though he'd requested "general service men" to replace the many guard unit members being alerted for overseas duty, those who'd been sent as replacements were "far below average and of no value for guard purposes." Waite observed that the IQ level for new guards reporting to Camp Aliceville ranged from a high of 122 to an almost incomprehensible low of 21.

Perhaps it was this frustrating situation that led to the decision on February 11 to replace American guards at the inner gates between the five compounds that were still open. German NCO POWs would now guard these gates, and the POWs would be able to move freely from one compound to another during daylight hours any day of the week. The camp commanders already admired the military discipline and intelligence of the German NCO prisoners, and it is likely they concluded that these Germans, whether Nazi or not, could do a far better job of policing the inner perimeter gates than newly drafted American soldiers with low levels of ability and no military experience. August Wanders noted this change in his diary and commented that the decision would allow the camp to become a more close-knit community.

In typical military fashion, the rest of Wilson's report belabored the minute details of one issue—he went on for two full pages (typed in tight, non-double-spaced paragraphs) about the prisoner of war canteen funds and the difficulties encountered in keeping track of this money when POWs (like those sent to Fort Dix) were transferred from one camp to another.

With the inner compound gates now open during the day, two POWs were often seen wandering all over the camp with sketchpads under their arms. Here and there, one of them would stop, take up a position, and begin to sketch. The two POWs, Hans Fanselow and Hermann Kalbe, both excellent artists, had obtained permission from camp authorities to produce fifty pen and ink sketches of scenes at Camp Aliceville. Long after the war ended and the two artists had left Alabama, reproductions of their sketches would continue to provide a detailed record of how the camp appeared to those who lived and worked there in the 1940s.

Hans and Hermann sketched everything. One detailed drawing shows the small guard shack and pass gate at the main entrance with its neatly printed sign: "Prisoner of War Camp, Aliceville, Alabama." The AT&N railroad tracks run in front of it, and the storm drain tunnel under the road into the camp is visible. Another drawing, titled *Wohnung des Kommandeurs* (Camp Commander's Home), depicts Tom Parker's former house with striped awnings shading several windows, window boxes overflowing with flowers no doubt cared for by POWs, and a screened porch on the side. Towering ominously behind the house, now occupied by Colonel Waite and his wife, is one of the large hexagonal guard towers with its ladder and searchlight in clear view.

Hans Fanselow identified his drawings with a tiny "HFW' in one corner. He seemed to favor more white space and fewer lines to create an image. One of his drawings shows a grouping of the one-story duplexes built for civilian personnel like Ward Turner and his family. Hans sketched rocking chairs at the front doors, and the railroad tracks running by only a few yards away. A 1939 Ford and a pre-war Plymouth are parked in front of one duplex. Another drawing is of the rows of barracks in Compound D with wooden stairs leading up to each door. There are trees and shrubs in the barracks yards, and in the distance near the barbed wire, men in shorts and t-shirts playing soccer.

Hermann Kalbe signed each of his drawings with a rather large "HKalbe44," in a stylized design. His drawings are busier, some with people in them, and more shading of images. One Hkalbe44 image portrays the interior of a POW barracks. Cots have been replaced by sturdy wooden beds with mattresses rolled up for the day. Two-door wooden cabinets with clothes bars underneath alternate with windows along the walls. Two prisoners are playing cards next to the potbellied stove and its pile of split kindling.

Another Hkalbe44 scene depicts the outdoor orchestra shell built by the prisoners in Compound A. The shell is big enough to accommodate a full orchestra of forty musicians. Hermann has sketched it with a concert in progress and a crowd of POWs enjoying the music from the rows of amphitheater seats made of bricks created in the camp's kiln. Some of the listeners wear the denim caps Colonel Prince ordered for them. Some wear only t-shirts, but the backs of others clearly display the large letters "P" and "W" painted on their work shirts.

On January 23, William L. Shirer wrote an article for the *New York Tribune* suggesting it would be in America's best interests to "evangelize" its German prisoners. He quoted an American Army chaplain who'd worked with POWs in Texas as saying that if this was not done, "they [the POWs] will return to Germany after the war with nothing but contempt for our ideals, more than eager to fight another war."

"I may be wrong," Shirer wrote, "but inasmuch as President Roosevelt says we are going to stamp out Nazism in Germany and Vice President Wallace says we are going to re-educate the 'master race,' I've been wondering whether it wouldn't be possible, and perhaps even desirable, to begin right here at home with the specimens we have in the German prisoner of war camps."

Shirer knew the German mind and heritage well. After graduation from Coe College in Iowa in 1925, he'd worked his way across the Atlantic pitching hay on a cattle boat and spent the next twelve years covering significant European events for major newspapers, including Lindbergh's solo trans-Atlantic flight and League of Nations meetings in Geneva.

For three years, beginning in 1934, Shirer served as a correspondent for the Universal News Service in Berlin. With growing apprehension, he covered the massive Nazi party rally in Nuremberg that year and wrote about the puppy-like devotion of the crowds to Hitler, this "vulgar, uneducated, fanatically bigoted Austrian." Shirer said the rallies reminded him of Holy Rollers he'd once seen in rural Arkansas with the same "crazed expression[s] on their faces."

After stints in Vienna and Geneva in 1937 and 1938, Shirer returned to Berlin and again reported from there until his return to the United States in December 1940. He wrote about how eager Germans were to overcome the humiliation of defeat in World War I and how German churches initially welcomed Hitler as the deliverer of a restored moral order. He wrote about young people who, like POW Hermann Blumhardt, were torn between believing that Hitler would restore national pride and prosperity and a sense of growing apprehension about the human rights cost of Hitler's plans.

Late in 1940, Shirer knew he needed to leave Berlin. Although he'd been careful to hide his subtle reports of German aggression in American slang unfamiliar to British-trained German censors, the German high command had begun to object to his reporting. Shirer was relieved when his request to leave Germany was granted. He wanted to take his extensive diaries with him but knew there was "enough in them to get me hanged—if the Gestapo ever discovered them." Eventually, he smuggled them out in two steel suitcases, hidden under piles of radio broadcast scripts already stamped with approval by the German military censors. These diaries later created the framework for Shirer's best-known work, *The Rise and Fall of the Third Reich*, which he published in 1960.

In his January 1944 article for *The New York Tribune,* Shirer estimated there were forty-five thousand German POWs in America. He based this estimate on press reports, but the War Department Monthly Progress Reports show that the total was far higher by January 1944—124,880 German POWs in the continental United States along with 49,826 Italians, and 116 Japanese, for a total POW population of 174,822.

Shirer described the German POWs as living in "a weird super-Nazi world of their own" and wrote that American commanders did little about it except when news of the "Gestapo-like kangaroo courts" in the camps leaked out to the general public. He suggested the world might experience another whole generation of bitter Germans seeking revenge in a third war if something wasn't done to change their point of view.

Shirer went on to report a number of frightening incidents, including the death of an Austrian POW who committed suicide after writing to his wife and child that he was afraid the Nazis would kill him. Another POW in West Virginia had listened to a news report about the eastern front in Europe and then drawn a map for other prisoners, speculating about how much ground the Germans had apparently lost. In the morning, this prisoner was found badly beaten. Shirer noted that the commanding officer of the West Virginia camp did not consider re-education of prisoners a good idea. Like many commanders, he was against forcing new opinions on his captives because he feared any perceived violation of the Geneva Convention might endanger American POWs in German camps.

Shirer held the exact opposite opinion—that if commanders let Nazi prisoners know their intimidation tactics would not be tolerated, terror in the camps might stop overnight. He based this conclusion on his knowledge of German respect for authority—even the authority of captors—writing, "…if firmness—with strict justice—were shown, there would be little trouble and little dissension." He continued, "Firmness is what Germans like and expect and respect. And a beginning might thus be made with some of the problem children of our time."

Shirer anticipated that critics would object to his ideas about firmness and education on grounds that such measures might violate the Geneva Convention, so he sat down and read all ninety-seven articles himself. He concluded that, in general, he approved of America's generous "Christian" or "Golden Rule" interpretation of the Geneva Convention—giving prisoners the same food and sanitary facilities as our own soldiers—but he criticized American Army authorities for tolerating fanatical Nazism in the camps.

He also reported that the Provost Marshal General's office had rejected a request by a group of German POWs for a subscription to a German language publication in New York that projected an anti-Nazi point of view. "I cannot find a single word in any of them (the ninety-seven articles) which could be construed as preventing the American authorities from allowing German prisoners to read anti-Nazi publications if they request them." Besides, he pointed out, there was already plenty of political dissension in the camps, as reports of beatings and forced suicides confirmed.

Articles and editorial columns on this subject began appearing more frequently in American newspapers in early 1944, suggesting perhaps that the letter-writing campaign Erwin Schulz and other anti-Nazi POWs had launched the previous fall was reaching sympathetic German Americans and prominent journalists.

An article in *The New York Times* on February 24 featured Gerhard H. Seger, editor of the German language newspaper

Neue Volkszeitung and a former member of the German *Reichstag.* He had addressed a group of American newspapermen in Baltimore and told them he knew the Nazis were already organized in the POW camps. "Any German prisoner who shows any interest in democracy or America is punished by his fellow prisoners," said Seger, who'd been sentenced to a German concentration camp in 1933 for anti-Nazi activities. He told the newspapermen prisoners in POW camps had been beaten by other prisoners simply for reading his newspaper and that one man had been hanged for circulating the German language paper and expressing democratic opinions. Fortunately, he said, the man was found by American authorities and cut loose before he died.

Seger suggested that the only solution to this problem was a program of re-education "as permitted under the Geneva Convention." He also expressed the opinion that, in some cases, even this might be fruitless.

Public opinion flared further in April when well-known radio news commentator Gabriel Heater suggested in one of his broadcasts that American guards were expected to salute German and Japanese officer prisoners. After the broadcast, the Provost Marshal General's office was flooded with letters forwarded by congressmen who received complaints from Heater's loyal listeners. The War Department issued a statement clarifying that the Geneva Convention did not require saluting but admitted that apparently some camp commanders had allowed it.

Also in April, columnist Dorothy Thompson spoke out against American treatment of POWs. "It is clear," she wrote, "that we are going farther than the obligations of the Geneva

Convention." Repeating the accusation about the hated Nazi salutes, she pointed out that the "Heil, Hitler!" salute was a Nazi party custom, not a tradition of the German army.

In her column, which The Bell Syndicate released for publication in the *Birmingham Age-Herald* and many other newspapers on April 24, Thompson expressed the opinion that permission given by camp commanders for political Nazi celebrations and Nazi salutes only strengthened the power of fanatics over other prisoners. She even pointed out that prisoners who died were buried in coffins draped in the Swastika flag.

"Men live in symbols," she wrote. "The disintegration of Nazi morale may come with defeat. But these prisoners will not be present there [in Germany]. They will go home in excellent health, having been very well fed and cared for. And meanwhile, on American soil, we shall have kept alive all the symbols of their party dictatorship." Her column prompted the War Department to issue a brief press statement denying that the army "coddled prisoners."

Sometime in the spring of 1944, publicity about this issue caught the ear of Eleanor Roosevelt, a determined woman who never shied from an issue she considered important. Several journalists contacted Mrs. Roosevelt directly, and these contacts prompted the First Lady to look into the matter herself. Author Judith Gansberg interviewed Maxwell S. McKnight in 1975 and wrote of his encounter with the President's wife in her book *Stalag, U.S.A.*

According to Gansberg, McKnight and his wife were invited to dinner at the White House. Suddenly, in the middle of the meal, the First Lady turned to McKnight and said, "I'm so glad you're here tonight. I've been hearing the most horrible stories from Dorothy Thompson and Dorothy Bromley and others about all the killings that are going on in our camps with these Nazi prisoners. I was told you would be able to tell me whether there was truth to these stories."

McKnight was not sure what he was authorized to tell the President's wife, and she did not press him, but the next morning he went to the office of the Assistant Provost Marshal General, who gave him permission to be honest with Mrs. Roosevelt about the problems in the camps and also about the proposed re-education plan that had been rejected almost a year earlier.

A few days later, McKnight had tea with Mrs. Roosevelt on the South Portico of the White House and told her what he knew. "I've got to talk to Franklin," she said. "Right in our backyard, to have these Nazis moved in and controlling the whole thought process!"

Eleanor did speak to Franklin. Soon Henry Stimson, the Secretary of War, was busy corresponding with Edward Stettinius, the Secretary of State, about how to revive the re-education plan that had been gathering dust on a shelf in Washington for almost a year. On March 30, Stimson and Stettinius agreed to implement a program for POWs based on this re-education plan. It helped that the new PMG, Major General Archer L. Lerch, was more receptive than his predecessor. "We anticipated the problem all along," Lerch told the President and First Lady with a straight face and then appointed Colonel Edward Davison to head the program. Davison would be assisted by Maxwell McKnight and an international staff of college professors, lawyers, and scholars.

It would take until August for the objectives of the new program to be laid out. Simply stated, the goal would be to use literature, film, newspapers, music, art, sports, and academic courses to familiarize POWs with the point of view of the Allies, particularly American democratic ideals. The hope was that this could be done by presenting information objectively, while carefully selecting which information would correct distorted impressions about America and the other Allies without seeming to force anti-Nazi propaganda on the prisoners.

It is ironic that journalistic pressure compelled the government to dust off, polish up, and implement this program because the War Department decided to keep it secret from the public, at least until the Allies achieved victory in Europe. The primary reason was fear that prisoners might read about it in American newspapers and then, recognizing its propaganda-related motives, resist. Another reason was the ongoing fear of violating the Geneva Convention, which was vague on the issue. Because the plan was deliberately kept secret, public criticism of POW treatment in the United States continued.

For L.D. Orr of Reform, Alabama, who was beginning his third year as an American POW in Japanese custody, issues surrounding the Geneva Convention had little relevance. American officials hoped their policies of good treatment for German POWs would have a positive effect for American POWs in Germany, but they were not so optimistic about Americans held in Japanese territories. In 1942, the Japanese had made verbal promises to abide by the Convention, but they had never signed it, and records clearly show that POW treatment in their camps was often incredibly cruel.

By February 1944, L.D. and eighty other American prisoners had been moved from cramped living quarters under the seats of the Itchioka sports stadium in Osaka to Hirohata camp so they could work as stevedores unloading cargo and ore ships for the Seitetsu Steel Mill. Some worked in blast furnaces, clearing slag. Frank Nichols Jr., who was in the Hirohata camp with L.D., has told an interviewer that infections, dysentery, and malnutrition plagued the camp.

One bitterly cold morning in February, Japanese guards at Hirohata called a shakedown inspection because they'd caught several prisoners hoarding food. While the other prisoners stood at attention, guards stripped the offenders naked and made them stand barefoot in the snow. Then they beat them on their buttocks—with a hawser-type rope, a length of hose, and a wooden stick—until their skin was raw.

When the guards realized the prisoners could no longer feel the pain of the beating, they made them climb into a large concrete tub of freezing cold water. There were several of these tubs scattered around the camp to provide water in case of a fire. The Japanese believed the cold water would restore feeling, so after several minutes, they hauled the men back out, made them stand in rank again, and continued beating them. This went on for an hour before the prisoners were dismissed and returned to their barracks.

According to Franks Nichols, "The Japs insisted, under the pain of such punishment, that the prisoners should never steal, lie, or gamble. For the POWs, this was simply accepted as a challenge…." Those who were beaten were quite defiant in spite of their suffering. When they returned to the barracks, they gritted their teeth and smiled, announcing that they'd hoard the food again the next day, only not get caught this time.

L.D. Orr was beaten while in the Hirohata camp—either in this incident or in others—severely enough that, when he was liberated in September 1945 and finally returned to Alabama, he was never again able to work full-time.

While the War Department fine-tuned its plans for a re-education program, it was also under pressure from many congressmen and interest groups to expand the POW labor program. In February, the commanding generals of the various Service Commands met in Dallas to consider the growing manpower shortage in the country, along with other problems related to prisoners of war. One outcome of this conference was the decision to move as many POWs as possible out of large, isolated camps like Aliceville and into smaller enclosures and branch camps where they could supplement civilian labor more effectively. The thinking was that this would also make the camps and their surrounding communities safer because there would be fewer huge concentrations of prisoners.

Even before the Dallas meeting, *The Birmingham News* reported in December 1943 that five new branch camps would open in Alabama to provide labor for agriculture and pulpwood work, and also for the processing of fertilizer. The newspaper emphasized that the POWs would not displace Alabama citizens but rather fill jobs where labor was not available or could not be recruited easily.

Branch camps began opening in Alabama soon after the meeting in Dallas. August Wanders noted in his diary that a hundred Aliceville POWs were sent to Greenville, Alabama, on February 23. Greenville became a permanent branch camp where POWs worked year-round in the lumber and wood products industries.

Four days later, on February 27, August Wanders recorded that five hundred more POWs left Aliceville—this time to activate a labor camp on the grounds of Camp Rucker, a military base created in April 1942 in southeast Alabama between the towns of Ozark and Enterprise. Records show this POW camp was thrown together quickly after the Dallas meeting. It remained active until March 1946, supplying much needed labor for farms and lumber operations.

Some of the Aliceville POWs sent to Camp Rucker were "loaned out" each morning to work on the farm of Robert Lee Hodges in nearby Geneva County. Hodges told his grandson the prisoners seemed happy to have something to do to relieve the tedium of their captivity. Many had been pilots, and some had even been educated in the United States before the war. Hodges befriended a few prisoners and, until his death several years after the war, corresponded with them.

Other POWs harvested peanuts or climbed into the back of Manonia Snell's grandfather's truck to become part of the logging crew for his sawmill in Dale County. After the war, an Alabama soldier who returned to the Camp Rucker area was upset when he discovered POWs had had decent accommodations and had been paid for work on farms. He didn't like the fact that they'd had hot showers and movies while American soldiers were eating K rations in hand-dug fox holes.

Later in the year, Stanley Pendrak traveled to Camp Rucker with a group of eighty POWs who were sent down temporarily to help with a pulpwood project. He was in charge of the kitchen for the group and found them to be pleasant and cooperative. "Once they got away from the main group (back in Aliceville), they weren't too hard to put up with," he has said. "A lot of them were young—nineteen or twenty—and they were easy to get along with. They liked getting in the kitchen and helping with the cooking, and none of 'em tried to escape or nothin' like that. We were there about thirty days."

Branch camps were also set up near the Alabama towns of Dublin, Loxley, Clanton, and Chathom. In July 1944, the *Birmingham Post* would report that Alabama was housing prisoners in five permanent and five temporary branch camps. By the time the war ended, the state had hosted a total of five permanent base camps—Aliceville, Opelika, Fort McClellan, Fort (Camp) Rucker, and Siebert—along with approximately twenty smaller branch camps.

Aliceville POWs were also transferred out of Alabama in 1944, to smaller branch labor camps in other southeastern states. On February 9, eighty Aliceville POWs were moved to Camp Stewart in Georgia, an army base about forty miles southwest of Savannah not far from the Atlantic coast. Camp Stewart had been built in 1940 as a training center for anti-aircraft artillery, but beginning in 1943 it also became a holding camp for POWs. Italians and Germans were held in separate compounds and provided much needed labor for base operations, construction projects, and area farms. If the POWs sent to Camp Stewart had thought it hot and steamy in Aliceville, they certainly found it doubly so near Savannah, Georgia.

Those sent to Camp Stewart were lucky, however, in comparison with the three hundred Aliceville POWs who left for Clewiston, Florida, eight days later. Clewiston was a branch of Camp Blanding set up in February 1944 near the southwest shore of Lake Okeechobee. The WMC (War Manpower Commission) in Atlanta had asked for two thousand POWs to help harvest sugar cane in the Clewiston area, but inspection reports indicate that as late as April, the only POWs occupying this camp and cutting sugar cane were the three hundred sent from Aliceville. According to a speech one of the camp officers gave to a local Kiwanis Club in June 1944, these prisoners were all former members of Rommel's Corps, "of high intelligence and fine physical fitness, and considered themselves Hitler's elite." There were no anti-Nazis among them.

Hubert Prosch was one of the Aliceville POWs sent to Clewiston. He might have had a good first impression of the place when he saw the small, whitewashed wooden building with a green roof that would be his new home, but that impression would have faded quickly once he entered the surrounding sugar cane fields. One International Red Cross report labeled Clewiston "the worst camp in America." The Aliceville transfers worked eight hours a day under a blazing sun, using machetes to cut nine thousand pounds of cane a day from stalks that often reached fifteen feet in height. Summer temperatures hovered at or above 100 degrees. During dry spells, the POWs labored in swirling clouds of dust.

Compound B at Camp Aliceville was becoming something of a ghost town. Although a few barracks were occupied, many were empty because of the frequent transfers of POWs to labor camps like Greenville and Clewiston. At the end of February, one of the empty barracks suddenly acquired a select and cloistered contingent of prisoners, and Walter Felholter was among them. Walter had only been seriously sick with diphtheria for a few weeks in December, but he'd continued to test positive as a carrier. Throughout January, he spent his time reading and studying or playing cards and chess with the other remaining diphtheria patients.

Every Wednesday and Saturday morning, nurses came into the ward to collect throat cultures. If a prisoner tested negative for the disease three cultures in a row, he was considered cured and returned to his regular barracks.

When a wave of influenza hit Camp Aliceville in February, Walter was one of only fifteen diphtheria-positive patients still in the hospital. Because their beds were needed for the influenza patients, he and fourteen others were moved into quarantine in an empty Compound B barracks. They were not allowed to do any work—even cleaning. Other prisoners were sent in to clean the barracks while they were at meals. Because they were still considered contagious in close contact, the men ate together in the Compound B mess hall when all other POWs were finished.

After their transfer to the quarantined barracks, Walter and three others discussed the frequent stories they were hearing about prisoner transfers to labor camps and came up with a plan for continuing their quiet and pleasant status in Compound B indefinitely. Each Wednesday and Saturday, when they returned to the hospital for throat swabs, the four would switch their glass slides before the nurse came in to label them, making sure no one who'd already received two negative evaluations was likely to receive a third (confirming he no longer had the disease). In this way, the four of them became the last "four positives" in the camp and stayed on in Compound B until May. "We liked to stay in the hospital," Walter has said, "because we didn't have to work then. Otherwise, we had to truck somewhere to pick cotton or something else."

Camp Spokesman Walter Meier's dream of a newspaper for the POWs at Camp Aliceville took a giant step closer to reality on February 21 when an ancient printing press was purchased with profits from the compound canteens. "To get that for the men—that is my mission, the single true duty—from that not even the red tape can dissuade me," Walter once said of his efforts to establish the newspaper.

An article published later in the year implies that POWs Walter Meier and Wilhelm Stüdl rode along with camp guards when they made the day-long drive to the small town of Jasper (north of Birmingham in Walker County) to purchase the press. Wilhelm wrote later that he and Walter jammed themselves into the vehicle between the parts of their "Flying Dutchman" (the printing press) during the chilly evening return drive to Camp Aliceville. The choice of metaphor is interesting. According to legend, the *Flying Dutchman* was a glowing ghost ship doomed to sail with its crew forever, never putting in to shore and never reaching home, led by a captain who swore he would never retreat in the face of a storm and would eventually round the Cape of Good Hope, even if it took until Judgment Day.

The hulking press was set up in one of the buildings in Compound B. It took several months to assemble it, oil it, and make sure it would function. During this time, book binding supplies arrived in the camp, and a bindery was also established in Compound B. Because of his printing training back in Stuttgart, Hermann Blumhardt was one of those who helped set up the press. Though it would also be used to print diaries and calendars, concert programs, and sports award certificates, the primary function of "the Flying Dutchman" would be to lay ink on paper to create issues of a regular newspaper for the POWs of Camp Aliceville. The first issue of *Der Zaungast* (The Guest Behind the Fence) would finally appear on July 16.

Transfers out of Camp Aliceville continued steadily in March. On March 15, a total of five hundred were sent to Camp Van Dorn near Centreville, Mississippi. Among them was Bruno Schneider, an *Afrikakorps* POW who'd arrived in Aliceville with the very first prisoners on June 2, 1943. Bruno was known among his fellow captives for a poem he wrote that captured the essence and personal experience of a POW camp in southwest Alabama. Dr. Paul G. Reitzer later translated Bruno's poem as follows:

The Frogs of Alabama

Alabama, this distant land
Well known to the infantryman
There in a prison camp to stay
To while away many a day.

The camp lies near a place that's swampy,
On leveled land that now is stumpy.
All sides secured by rows of wire
To include a safety zone as specs require.

The men complain about their grog,
But even more about the Alabama frog.
While both serve to annoy each day,
What more is there for one to say?

When daily tasks in heat are met,
The men are usually drenched with sweat.
The P.O.W. responds to evening call,
Above the searchlight scans them all.

An evening concert becomes a fair,
Having really something there.
Much nicer than jazz and flute,
And doesn't cost a cent to boot.

Eventually, his home comes to mind,
About that girlfriend left behind.
Perhaps she's at her window true
And hears the inner crying, too.

Bruno Schneider remained at Camp Van Dorn until May 9, 1945, when he was transferred to Camp Shelby, also in Mississippi. From there, he returned to Camp Shanks in New York and then was shipped to additional labor camps in England. During his time in the United States, Bruno accumulated $204.46 in earnings as a POW. On March 14, 1946, before leaving for England, the United States War Department presented him with a check for this amount—a check he would keep with him as a remembrance for more than fifty years.

Another five hundred POWs left Camp Aliceville on March 16 for Davis, North Carolina, and five hundred more left for Camp McCain in Mississippi on March 19. A military directive dated March 13 states that those being sent to Camp McCain would be expected to perform labor previously done by anti-Nazi prisoners. All anti-Nazi prisoners except those in the officers' compound were being transferred out of Camp McCain. Aliceville was not to send NCOs to Camp McCain unless they were willing to perform non-supervisory work or, when necessary, supervisory work with the two transferred POW companies.

Erwin Schulz was one of the anti-Nazis shipped out of Camp McCain just before the two new companies of prisoners arrived from Camp Aliceville. He was sent, with several hundred others, to a German POW compound attached to the American army base at Fort Devens in Massachusetts, northwest of Boston. At the outbreak of World War II, Fort Devens had become a reception center for New England draftees in the United States Army. The base was used to train American military chaplains, cooks, and nurses as well as combat soldiers. Later in the war, it held more than five thousand POWs. Fort Devens was a designated anti-Nazi compound similar to Camp Campbell in Kentucky. Most of the early arrivals were, like Erwin, former members of the 999th "punishment battalion" Hitler had formed in 1942.

During the two months he spent at Fort Devens, Erwin studied when he was not working in a Quartermaster Corps warehouse. He took courses the German POWs had helped design, in "safe" subjects like English, French, mathematics, and American history and noted later in his own writings that there was "nothing in the study plan about trade unions or desirable social reforms" and "nothing about the history of the Weimar Republic or anything controversial."

Erwin was not among the first group of POWs who volunteered to leave Fort Devens for a woodcutting camp in New Hampshire, but he was among a group of 250 who headed there in mid-May 1944. Camp Stark was smaller—a former Civilian Conservation Corps camp now enclosed by a high fence and four guard towers. He later described the group of men who occupied nine narrow wooden buildings in this much more primitive setting as a mixture of Communists, Social Democrats, trade unionists, and others with no specific political ties, along with a few prisoners the American authorities considered common criminals.

At first, Erwin loved the surroundings—cutting down trees in a shady forest where the air was crisp and clear with no hint of the thick humidity left behind in Alabama and Mississippi. "The war will soon be over," he thought, "and this is a great place to spend our remaining time."

Working to supply pulpwood for The Brown Company was hard and dangerous, and hordes of black flies attacked savagely as spring turned to summer, but most of the men liked being in a smaller camp even though it was even more isolated than Aliceville had been. Because of the strenuous activity, they were fed up to five thousand calories a day. Erwin remained in Camp Stark until the war ended in Europe the following May.

The last two major transfers out of Camp Aliceville in the spring of 1944 were 250 to Camp Gordon Johnston in Florida on March 20, and 750 to Camp Sutton in North Carolina on March 25. Like Camp Blanding, Camp Gordon Johnston was a large POW camp attached to a military base. It was located in the Florida Panhandle, near the small town of Carrabelle, about sixty miles southwest of Tallahassee on the Gulf Coast. The white sandy soil of the area made crop cultivation impossible and did not allow for an efficient sewerage system. The accommodations were so crude that one American soldier dubbed the place, "Hell-By-the-Sea, Carrabelle, Florida."

One of the prisoners who left Camp Aliceville for Camp Gordon Johnston in March 1944 was Hermann Blumhardt. He was given a choice because Camp Spokesman Walter Meier wanted him to remain at Aliceville and continue to help with the printing press. After careful consideration, Hermann decided to make the transfer to Florida with his company because he didn't want to be separated from this group in which he now had close friends.

The POW section of Camp Gordon Johnston started out as a branch-type camp with fifty tents that housed five to six men each. One large tent served as kitchen and mess hall. There were also two latrines, a shower house, an infirmary, and a canteen. The soil was so sandy that a sports field could not be built, and even though the camp was only a few hundred yards from the Gulf, the prisoners could not swim because the undercurrents were too treacherous. Most of the prisoners sent to Camp Gordon Johnston worked in the American military sector—in the kitchens, the post hospital, the warehouses, the machine shop, and the repair shops for military equipment. Fourteen of them formed a detail to do drainage work designed to prevent mosquito infestation.

Even with the primitive conditions, Hermann did not mind the transfer because food was plentiful, as it had been in Camp Aliceville, and because he now had the opportunity to work daily eight-hour shifts and earn eighty cents a day. "Now we could go to the canteen and buy extras," he has said. "One prisoner bought eight bottles of beer at ten cents each almost every day, and that made him really happy!"

One afternoon an American sergeant came into the tent camp looking for five prisoners to work in the military base bakery. Hermann volunteered because he was tired of his current job of picking up cigarette butts and waste paper around the camp hospital. Friends told him he was crazy to volunteer to work in a hot bakery, but Hermann found that he liked the work. He welcomed the friendliness of the guards there and practiced his English with them whenever he could. He would spend almost two years working in the bakery at Camp Gordon Johnston before being transferred to another camp called Telogia.

Camp Aliceville POWs shipped to Camp Sutton near Monroe, North Carolina, included Herbert Knopf and Werner Meier. Camp Sutton was opened in March 1942 to train American soldiers—including Jack Pratt Jr. of Pickens County, Alabama, who arrived there in June 1942. From 1944 to 1946, Camp Sutton also served as a German POW camp.

When Herbert Knopf boarded the troop train for North Carolina, he watched the scrub pines whiz by the windows and thought back on his memories of Camp Aliceville. It had not been a bad place even though it was a prison camp. He'd been there for almost a year, one of the first POWs to arrive, and he'd watched as the various sports and cultural activities developed—the choirs and theater groups, and just before he left, the weekly showings of German movies. He supposed his best memory of Camp Aliceville would always be the great soccer competitions when the players of Compounds A and B and C faced off against the players of Compounds D and E and F. Even inside the barbed wire, it had been a wonderful sports rivalry.

Herbert would spend a year at Camp Sutton and then be sent to Camp Newton Stewart in Scotland. He would not return home to Germany until 1947.

Feldwebel Werner Meier had also been one of the first six hundred POWs to arrive at Camp Aliceville. He'd been a Stuka pilot in the *Luftwaffe* in France and Russia and then had served with ground forces in North Africa before being captured when Tunis fell to the Allies. Although he'd spent almost an entire year functioning well inside the wire at Camp Aliceville, Werner Meier survived only a little more than three months at Camp Sutton before becoming that camp's only attempted escapee. On July 11, he was shot and killed while trying to leave the camp. He was buried with military honors at Camp Buttner on July 13. Werner's brother would fight the Americans at Normandy that spring and again at the Battle of the Bulge later in the year. He, too, would become a prisoner of the Americans but would remain in Europe and survive.

By the end of March, more than four thousand German POWs had been transferred out of Camp Aliceville, leaving several compounds vacant. The profile of the camp was changing. August Wanders noted in his diary on April 5 that the

9th Company in his compound had been disciplined with *Verpflegungsentzug* (food deprivation). This usually meant several days on bread and water. He also noted that, in response and in support of the men in 9th Company, the rest of the prisoners in the compound had gone on a brief hunger strike. He made no mention of the reason for the punishment.

Lieutenant Colonel Waite sent a memo to Washington on April 7, commenting on the disposition of his current prisoners. One hundred and forty-three NCO prisoners refused to supervise other prisoners or to do regular labor themselves. These men had been isolated in one compound (probably D or E) away from the rest of the camp. The colonel believed eight of these were "head troublemakers" and that if these eight could be transferred to a camp solely designed for "this type of habitual troublemaker," the other one hundred and thirty-five might change their minds and agree to work.

Beginning in April, German cultural films were shown in the camp each week. August Wanders noted in his diary that the first, a travel documentary about a mountain village in Europe, was shown on April 9. Incredible as it would have seemed to the average American citizen—then or now—Adolf Hitler's birthday was celebrated on American soil in the Compound A open-air theater on April 20.

Then, on May 1, there was a huge May Day celebration. This was not the medieval English festival familiar to Americans as a celebration of spring—a Maypole bedecked in flowers and streamers with children dancing around and in and out to create a colorful pattern on the pole. May Day, as traditionally celebrated in Germany, was more closely related to International

Workers Day, a commemoration of the social and economic accomplishments of the labor movement in the late 1800s—the kind of celebration Erwin Schulz would have participated in. Although this movement eventually led to the eight-hour workday in the United States, Americans in the twentieth century were reluctant to celebrate it because of its associations with socialism and communism. In many countries, it involved mass demonstrations and political rallies by working class citizens.

In twentieth century Germany, May Day had a controversial history. In 1929, the social democratic government in power prohibited annual May Day workers' demonstrations in Berlin, but the Communist Party—the strongest party in Berlin at that time—called for demonstrations anyway. The result was that Berlin police fired eleven thousand rounds of live ammunition, and thirty-two workers and bystanders were killed. When the Nazis came to power a few years later, they adapted May Day to their own purposes, declaring it a public holiday and calling it a "day of work."

Walter Felholter remembers how May Day was celebrated in Germany during the time of Hitler. "You didn't see anything about working people—only people in uniform who were hired to march with signs and sing. Then they all gathered in a big open place while political speeches were made by high SS and SA men. Afterwards, the hired ones yelled 'Bravo!' and clapped."

At Camp Aliceville in 1944, the celebration included a procession of occupational groups represented among the prisoners, followed by the planting of a May tree at the open air stage in Compound A and a band concert. Most of the morning was taken up with enthusiastic soccer and other sports competitions. In the afternoon, the POWs sipped coffee at the open-air stage and then visited colorful booths and munched on potato pancakes.

Walter Felholter, who'd just been released from quarantine in Compound B, volunteered to help with the May Day festivities. Walter and the other three remaining "positives" from the diphtheria epidemic had no longer been able to trade negative test slides for positives ones, so they'd been declared cured and returned to the general population of the camp.

At the conclusion of the May Day celebration, camp spokesman Walter Meier rewarded Walter Felholter with a journal-type book—a book no doubt printed on the camp's new printing press. "To Private First Class Walter Felholter," it was inscribed in German, "for the work he did for all of us in planning the activities of May Day." It was dated May 3, 1944. Felholter remembers that the May Day celebration at Camp Aliceville included speeches by at least two officers among the POWs. The men wore their uniforms, just as they did on Sundays, rather than their POW clothes.

After Rudolf Fischer, a representative of the Swiss legation, inspected Camp Aliceville on May 14, he reported to Lieutenant Colonel William Waite that he'd heard no complaints from prisoners. This was the first visit from a representative of the "protecting power" since November 1943. Fischer was accompanied by Parker W. Buhrman who filed his own report with the United States Department of State on June 12.

Buhrman noted that there'd been no deaths in Camp Aliceville since the November visit. The educational programs had been disrupted somewhat with the transfer of so many prisoners to other camps, but classes were continuing, with about 25 percent of the POWs involved in some kind of study—

English, art, manual training, military science, commercial practice, or agriculture. A number of students like Hans Kopera were taking premedical courses.

The report to the State Department listed 1,596 prisoners, with 972 employed for pay doing post maintenance, cutting pulpwood, or working in the camp's automobile repair shop. In addition, many prisoners were involved in camp maintenance in a "non-pay status." Camp Aliceville had 321 German NCOs. Its eleven German officers were all medical personnel.

No prisoners at Camp Aliceville were under disciplinary punishment at the time of this visit, and Buhrman commented that the discipline appeared to be excellent. "The men are generally cooperative and go about their work in an orderly manner. The camp administration is strict but altogether just and fair. The camp gives every appearance of being well seasoned as to officer and guard personnel."

Only two problems were noted. The first involved a POW priest who appeared to have the rank of a German Army chaplain but was suspected of having been a political police agent in the Germany army. Buhrman wrote that this priest was unacceptable because he concerned himself more with National Socialist ideologies than with the religious needs of the prisoners. The camp had recently acquired a Lutheran POW chaplain and a Lutheran United States Army chaplain to assist with religious life.

The other problem was the same one that had existed for quite some time, both at Camp Aliceville and at other camps around the country. The German NCOs who had declined to work themselves were deliberately discouraging other prisoners from working, insisting that any work constituted aid to the enemy. Buhrman concluded his report with a comment that echoed the memo Colonel Waite had sent to Washington on April 7: "It is important that the leaders of this movement be removed from this camp without delay and it is highly desirable that all the non-commissioned officers in this camp who have declined to volunteer for work should be removed to some camp where they can no longer discourage other prisoners in the performance of the work details to which they are assigned."

By the time Paul Schyder inspected Camp Aliceville for the International Red Cross Committee on June 5 and 6, the population had dwindled even further. Only Compound A was occupied, with a total of 892 prisoners, but this number appears to have included 148 POWs living and working in the Greenville branch camp. Walter Meier was still the camp spokesman, and Schyder noted that he was not able to speak to Meier without American witnesses.

There was now a large library with two thousand books. Most of the POWs had radios available to them, and many subscribed to American publications like *The New York Times, The Chicago Tribune, The Birmingham News,* and *The Saturday Evening Post.* Contrary to August Wanders' notes about weekly German films being shown, Schyder reported that only American films were shown. A chapel had been built and was now being used for services celebrated by both Catholic and Protestant POW chaplains, under the supervision of an American chaplain.

Schyder mentioned that on one of the days he conducted his inspection, a group of seventy prisoners had been given permission to go swimming in a nearby lake. Accompanied by guards, they were transported to the lake by bus and allowed to spend one hour in the water. August Wanders confirms in his diary that this was the first swimming outing for Camp Aliceville POWs. Even in June, the heat would have been oppressive in Aliceville, and the prisoners must have welcomed this opportunity. Schyder also notes in his report that the prisoners had arranged small "rooms" underneath their barracks, which were built on stilts. They'd made tables and benches and planted shade-loving flowers. It was a cool place to sit on a hot June day.

Five hundred prisoners were working for pay at this time. Schyder noted that the camp had its own shoemaker, tailor, and bookbindery. He also mentioned that the print shop was currently closed for repairs.

He ended his report with a comment about how many prisoners had already been transferred out of Camp Aliceville and predicted that there would soon be very few prisoners remaining. Most of the rest, he wrote, would be sent to Camp McCain.

The American guard contingent had changed, too. Many of the MPEG units had left to train for overseas duty, and they were not being replaced because the POW population was so much smaller. The 305th had left in December, and all other MPEG units except the 436th had been disbanded or moved in April. Only the 436th and smaller, independent groups of guards remained. The 436th would leave Aliceville on June 9 for Camp Kilmer and then for overseas duty. The *Camptown Crier,* a publication designed to encourage community and morale among the enlisted men at the camp, ceased publication in early 1944 after only four issues because there was no longer enough news to justify it.

It is too bad that I was captured. Soon it will be over and my comrades will be back home—maybe in a few weeks. But now I am a prisoner and it will take much longer.

• July 22, 1944 •
a Nazi paratrooper under guard near Saint-Lo,
as quoted in "German Prisoners Rejoice
at News of Attempt on Hitler"
by Hal Boyle for the Associated Press
The Birmingham Age-Herald

CHAPTER ELEVEN
The D-Day Effect

On May 2, 1944, after completing Officers' Candidate School, Robert Hugh Kirksey and thirty-two other members of the Citadel Class of '44 learned they were headed to Camp Claiborne in central Louisiana to become part of the 84th Infantry Division of the United States Army. It was almost a year since Robert Hugh had stood with his father on the side of Highway 17 to watch the first German POWs march through Aliceville with their chins up in spite of their fatigue. Since then, he'd been to Fort McClellan for basic training and back to The Citadel for additional class work while eagerly awaiting his slot in Officers' Candidate School. In late December 1943, he'd reported to Fort Benning for training as a second lieutenant.

Robert Hugh was proud of his new officer status. While home on leave before heading for Louisiana, he wore his uniform almost constantly—to church, to meals, to visits with family friends. When asked about the colorful insignia patch on his uniform, he explained that it was a white axe stuck into a white log on a red background. The 84th had carried the nickname "Railsplitters" since World War I because most of its original members were from Abraham Lincoln's home state of Illinois.

Robert Hugh was keenly aware that before long he, like so many other young men from Aliceville and the rest of Pickens County, would be heading overseas. He was also aware that the town of Aliceville continued to experience its share of losses from the war. In early February, Dr. T.R. McLellan had been advised by the War Department that his son, Beverly, was missing in action over Germany. Beverly was an aerial gunner and radio operator stationed in England who'd once written home that he was ready and willing to drop one of the "big capsules" on Berlin or Tokyo. No other information was available.

There was good news, too. Family relationships were evolving in spite of, and also because of, the war. Two more local young ladies—both cousins of Robert Hugh—were now the wives of officers stationed at Camp Aliceville. On February 6, June Kirksey Etheridge had become the bride of Lieutenant Walter Joseph Rosskopf in a Sunday afternoon ceremony at her mother's home. Robert Hugh's father gave her in marriage because her father had passed away. During the ceremony, June's aunt (Robert Hugh's mother), sang the two "must-have" wedding songs of the 1940s—"Because" and "Ah, Sweet Mystery of Life," which she performed as a duet with Captain Lawrence Persons.

Margie Archibald stood by, smiling with satisfaction at how wonderfully romance had blossomed in the small social set she'd help create with her sister Emmie and other Aliceville young ladies. All those Sunday dinners with the good silver and china and all those picnics down by Lubbob Creek had already charmed a number of the POW camp officers. Captain Persons would be the next groom among the group, and he, too, would join the extended Kirksey family when he married the Wallace Kirkseys' daughter Edwina. Margie remembered how amused she'd been the first time Larry Persons showed up at Aliceville

Bank & Trust in his armored car with rifle-toting MPs to collect cash for the POW camp payroll.

Lieutenant J.E. Daugherty served as best man for Walter Rosskopf just as he had for Nat Aicklen when he married Bobbie Kirksey the previous November. Margie loved the Venus blue suit and the small fuchsia hat and veil June Etheridge chose for her wedding costume, and she thought June showed such good taste in wearing, as her only jewelry, the gold nugget bracelet that had been in the Rosskopf family for generations. June was a graduate of the Aliceville schools. She'd been employed by the FBI in Washington before returning home to accept a position at the POW camp when it opened. Walter was a graduate of the Engineering and Technical School of Oakland, California, and had been an architect in Oakland before entering the service. The new Lieutenant and Mrs. Rosskopf took a wedding trip to New Orleans and then returned to Aliceville to live, but only briefly. Lieutenant Rosskopf was soon transferred to Camp Gordon Johnston—the bare bones camp on the Florida Gulf Coast where Hermann Blumhardt and more than two hundred other transfer POWs from Camp Aliceville were now living and working. June joined her husband there in early summer and, like war brides across the country, made the best of things.

Just a week after the Rosskopf wedding, Bobbie Kirksey Aicklen's younger sister, Edwina, married Captain Lawrence Longshore Persons at a ceremony in Montgomery. Edwina had been doing secretarial work since her graduation from high school in 1940. The county newspaper described her, like her sister Bobbie, as "a favorite in the social circles in West Alabama and Mississippi." and also as "one of the most popular and best loved students of Aliceville High School." Larry Persons had been born in the Philippine Islands while his father was stationed there. He'd grown up mostly in the United States and was following his father's footsteps in a regular army career.

In March, Pickens County residents buzzed with news of the May/December wedding of another local young woman. Crooks Steele had married the gentlemanly army colonel who'd ridden his black horse, Cokey, all over Aliceville while supervising construction of the POW camp two years earlier. Fifty-seven-year-old Lieutenant Colonel Karl Shriver had kept in close contact with his Aliceville acquaintances (especially Crooks Steele) after he left for Tuscaloosa to oversee construction of Northington General Hospital, which opened in September 1943 to specialize in skin grafts and reconstructive surgery, often for battlefield burn victims. After that project, Shriver reported to the Bahamas to build military airport runways.

Crooks Steele's wedding took place in Miami, but she and Colonel Shriver then visited her parents in Pleasant Ridge, near Aliceville, and were entertained at numerous dinner parties, including one given by Miss Minnie Merle Brandon, whose sister Lillian—Pickens County's very first WAAC—would later marry Crooks Steele's brother. Minnie Merle herself would soon marry a dashing young MPEG from Camp Aliceville named B.B. Stevens, who visited her café and captured her heart.

The "Local News" article announcing the wedding of Crooks Steele reported that the bride had also been entertained lavishly in the Bahamas by Lieutenant Colonel Shriver's many friends there. Among those friends were the Duke and Duchess of Windsor, England's former King Edward VIII and his American divorcee wife, Wallis Simpson. On one of those occasions, Crooks posed for a photo in a tropical garden. She wore a knee-length black dress with white lace top and a gardenia in her upswept dark hair. Colonel Shriver, in his dress white uniform, looked on admiringly. Another photo shows the colonel in his khaki uniform standing next to the impeccably dressed Duke of Windsor, who served as Governor of the Bahamas from 1940 to 1945.

Following the visit with Crooks' parents and the round of celebration parties in Aliceville and Pleasant Ridge, Lieutenant Colonel Shriver left for overseas duty on April 28. He would not return to the United States and to Aliceville until the Allies had secured most of Europe almost a year later. Crooks would remain in Alabama, playing bridge with her friend Sue Stabler and listening anxiously to the war news from Europe.

Second Lieutenant Alva Temple wrote to Jack Pratt on March 31 to thank him for the souvenir copy of *The Pickens County Herald and West Alabamian*—the special edition Jack had printed at Christmastime with photos of all the local soldiers. Alva Temple was the only commissioned officer among African American Pickens County soldiers in service. "Here in Italy," he wrote from his base with the 99th Fighter Squadron, "we are always thrilled to receive news from our home towns back in the states. It is our determination to continue to fight until the war has been brought to a victorious end."

Jack Pratt published this letter in his "News of Interest to and from the Boys in Service" column on April 27, under the headline, "Pickens Negro Boy Writes from Italy." He commented that Alva, "like hundreds of others of our [*sic*] negroes" is making a good soldier.

Alva's squadron of Tuskegee airmen was now attached to the 79th Fighter Group, which had involved them fully in the Anzio Campaign at the end of January 1944. During this campaign, the squadron was so successful that German *Luftwaffe* pilots began referring to them as the *Schwarze Vogelmenschen* (Black Birdmen). When Alva wrote the thank-you note to his hometown newspaper at the end of March, the Anzio Campaign was continuing, and the Tuskegee airmen were flying C-51 Mustangs on bomber escort duty over Italy, working hard to help bring the war to a victorious end.

Robert Hugh Kirksey's ten-day leave among family and friends in Aliceville went by quickly. Around May 15, his father drove him to Meridian, Mississippi, so he could catch a train to Alexandria, Louisiana, and then a bus to Camp Claiborne. During this journey, Robert Hugh wondered which overseas duty assignment was in his future. Would he be shipping out for the Pacific to fight the Japanese? To the Mediterranean for the battles in Italy? Or maybe to England to prepare for the Allied invasion of northern Europe? He knew instinctively that the Citadel Class of 1944 would make valiant contributions to the war effort, but he did not yet know that his class would sustain more casualties than any Citadel class in history—a total of thirty-four killed in action.

Wendell Parrish was not a native of Aliceville. He'd been born in Clanton, Alabama, and then grown up in Selma, a small city on the Alabama River in Dallas County. Selma was near Craig Field, which was built just before World War II to help train the growing number of airmen in the American military. Long after the war, Selma's Edmund Pettus Bridge would become a lasting landmark of the civil rights movement during Voting Rights Act demonstrations there in 1965. Also, long after the war, Wendell Parrish's life would become entwined with Aliceville and, ironically, with the legacy of its German POW camp.

In May 1944, Wendell was a twenty-year-old armorer and waist gunner in the United States Army. He was married and enthusiastic about becoming a father for the first time. He'd just completed a course of flight training at Avon Park Army Airfield in central Florida with a ten-man crew led by a former flight instructor who'd finally been assigned to combat duty. During training, the crew became like a close-knit family. They were from all over the country—Massachusetts, Pennsylvania, West Virginia, North Carolina, and Alabama—and their morale was high when they arrived at Hunter Field near Savannah, Georgia, for overseas processing.

The morning they were assigned to a "spanking new" B-17G, Wendell stood in awe as he gazed up at the mighty, four-engine bomber that was to become the crew's weapon for daytime bombing raids on German industrial targets. The looming gray giant was almost twenty feet tall and weighed more than seventy thousand pounds.

Wendell was even more impressed with the sturdy bomber when the crew flew it to Grenier Field in New Hampshire on May 19. They spent one night there and then flew on to Gander, Newfoundland. Their next hop was a long one—all the way to Nutts Corner, Ireland. During the flight, Wendell stared nervously at the pile of extra gas tanks wedged into the bomb bay to assure sufficient fuel. He knew they were an important insurance policy. "Flying that northern route, if you went down, you were gone because no help was coming in those days," he told an old friend.

The crew left Nutts Corner on May 23, traveling by boat and train, until they reached Stone, England, early on the morning of May 25. Here they discovered, to their great disappointment, that their brand new bomber was needed immediately but that they themselves would have to submit to another two weeks of processing before they could fly their first mission.

During those two impatient weeks, the term "D-Day" and the code names "Omaha Beach" and "Utah Beach" would permanently enter the world's vocabulary. General Eisenhower's Operation Overlord preparations became the Normandy invasion on the morning of June 6, 1944—D-Day. It was the largest amphibious landing in military history, eventually involving nearly three million troops who crossed the English Channel to occupied France, contributing directly to the final defeat of Germany less than a year later.

Robert Hugh Kirksey was still at Camp Claiborne when confirmation of the D-Day landings reached the United States. He knew that his boyhood friend, Francis Gardner Park, was a rifle platoon leader in the 116th Infantry Regiment, a part of the

29th Infantry Division, and he worried that Francis had been involved in the invasion. Robert Hugh thought about the time, years ago, when Francis's older brother had duped the two of them into washing dogs for a small circus that visited Aliceville. The brother collected pay for the dog washing but only gave Francis and Robert Hugh two fake butcher-paper passes that did not admit them to the circus.

Robert Hugh remembered the regulation-size Ping-Pong table he and the Park brothers had labored to build from flooring scraps and the long summer hours they'd spent batting tiny white balls back and forth on the Parks' side porch. So much had happened since those good times and, more recently, since he and Francis had made trips up to Tuscaloosa together to play golf on the old Meadowbrook course.

Having just been designated a rifle platoon leader himself, Robert Hugh worried about his friend because he knew the rumor that the life expectancy of a combat rifle platoon leader on the battlefield was something like thirty minutes. When he picked up the newspaper the next morning, he worried even more. The 29th Division was described as one of the spearhead units landing at Omaha Beach— right in the face of concrete encased machine-gun placements that rained fire down upon them from higher ground.

All over the country, civilians and soldiers awaited details about the fate of the brave men who'd stormed the beaches in France. The death toll was high—somewhere near two thousand just at Omaha Beach, according to most estimates—and the foothold was fragile, but at least a second front had been established against Hitler's stranglehold on Europe.

Newspapers reported day after day about the difficulties encountered in pressing inland in German-occupied northern France. Robert Hugh soon learned that his friend Francis had made it ashore and was part of the troops who managed to establish a two-mile deep beachhead between nine in the morning and nightfall on June 6. But then, on June 17 after surviving all of that, Francis was killed in action, just nine days after his twenty-fourth birthday. His death was a huge blow to the close-knit community of Aliceville. The county newspaper noted that Francis Park had grown up next door to his cousin, Lieutenant Richard Somerville, who'd been lost on a flight over German-held territory just before Christmas in 1942.

"Oh, how I wished I could be home in Aliceville," Robert Hugh wrote in his memoirs. "His [Francis's] brother, James Verner [the one who'd pulled the circus dog washing stunt], was in the South Pacific, and his other brother, Somerville, was in England. I just wished I could be in Aliceville with their mother, for just a little while."

The Griffin family of Aliceville had a son who landed on the beaches at Normandy on June 6, too. John Griffin was twenty years old, working as a welder for Ingalls Shipbuilding in Pascagoula, Mississippi, when he was drafted. He became a private in the 1340th Combat Engineer Regiment and was sent to Liverpool, England, for intensive training in how to search for and eliminate mines.

When he boarded an LST (Landing Ship Tank) on the morning of June 5, 1944, he did not know where he was going, but it was not long before he could guess. "They gave us seasick pills, but I was so nervous that I threw mine away. You'd look out on the sea and all you could see were ships from one side of the English Channel to the other. You could walk on them. I've never seen that many ships in my life."

John was part of the third wave to hit Omaha Beach the next morning. "The LST we were in couldn't take us all the way to the beach, so it stopped short and dropped us off. We were in water up to our necks; we had to swim to the beach." A chilling sight awaited them on shore—bodies everywhere that they had to step over before they reached the point, about three hundred yards inland, where they began to search for land mines. "The Germans were shooting at us the whole time." As John probed the sand with his bayonet, hoping not to find a booby-trapped mine, a sergeant behind him told him to hurry up. "I'm taking my time," John told him. "This is my life!"

John's regiment remained at Omaha Beach for several days, participating in burial teams that moved American bodies into trenches dug by bulldozers. The army knew who was being buried because they had the dog tags, and later the bodies would be reburied with full military honors in the Omaha Beach Cemetery.

When they left Omaha Beach, the 1340th moved ahead of the advancing army, clearing many land mines—especially Teller mines that were designed to damage vehicles. "I liked removing Teller mines," John remembered. "They had a post and you'd tie a rope around that post, get a ways off and pull it. If it was booby-trapped, it would go off." John Griffin would continue moving with the 1340th and helping protect American forces until early November.

Exactly a month after D-Day, Alabama launched its part of the Fifth War Loan Drive, seeking a quota of $102,000 to support the war. The United States Treasury ran an ad in the *Pickens County Herald and West Alabamian* reminding citizens to support the country's war effort. "Right now, while you are reading this, men are dying—American men, giving their lives to establish beachheads from which they can sweep on to Victory." These words rang true for far too many local families. "You're an American—you have a duty, too! Here's *your* chance to do your share—to fight by their side on every bitter beachhead in the world."

Aliceville residents did their share with a huge auction to kick off their new war bond campaign. Jack Pratt called the sales along with an experienced auctioneer from Fayette. Sam Wise donated a man's suit that raised $1,000, and somebody paid $5,000 for a bale of cotton. More than fifty items were donated and sold, including a white Leghorn rooster and a Perfection mattress. District War Bond Chairman U. B. Sullivan congratulated the district on July 18, announcing that the Carrollton District, including Aliceville, had oversubscribed its quota and had been the first district in Alabama to reach its quota.

The guard detail at Camp Aliceville changed almost completely that summer. Stanley Pendrak left his wife, Jeanne, with her family and her beauty shop and shipped out for Europe in July. He was proud of the work he'd done at Camp Aliceville and at Camp Rucker. He was also proud of the fact that the United States Army was following the Geneva Convention 100 percent in its treatment of prisoners. His assignment overseas would eventually take him to a place near Munich called Dachau, and what he saw there would be the starkest contrast he could possibly imagine to what he had experienced in Aliceville.

Gene Dakan and the 436th were already overseas. In July, they escorted twenty-two hundred newly captured German prisoners from northern France to Boston and then returned to Europe for additional guard duty.

For the July Fourth weekend, Margie and Emmie Archibald put together a holiday trip for their group of friends that included many officers from Camp Aliceville. Pooling gas ration coupons, the young people drove over to Lake Choctaw in Mississippi—the vacation spot Bob Fillingham had taken his wife, Kay, to when she became so upset while eating food prepared by POWs at the Camp Aliceville Officers' Club. Nat and Bobbie Aicklen went along on the trip, and so did Misses Lorene Day and Myrtis Wheeler. Lieutenants Albert Seltzer and Bennie Maschellins shared the driving duties. The group enjoyed the many coves that offered clear, cool water for swimming and also a wonderful candlelit dinner at the lodge.

On the night before Robert Hugh's friend Francis Park battled his way ashore in Normandy, a German soldier named Ernst Schacht stood watch near the coast. He was one of thousands of German soldiers for whom the Normandy invasion would mark the end of their military service to Germany and to its *Führer*—thousands who would, like the POWs captured in North Africa, make their way across the Atlantic. During the summer of 1944, they would add a new element and a new attitude to the already large prisoner of war populations in the United States, and Aliceville would become home to many of them.

Ernst Schacht's post was on a small rise just above the swampy delta of the Vire River where it flowed north from the town of Saint-Lo and emptied out into the English Channel between two beaches prominently code-named on secret Allied military maps. Heavy clouds cloaked the sky, and gusts of wind blew incessant rain showers into a swirling mist before Ernst's face. He stood with his wireless communication equipment at the ready under a canvas tarp and listened to steady shelling in the distance.

Ernst had begun his service to the German government in the same way Wilhelm Schlegel, Walter Felholter, Hermann Blumhardt, and so many other young men had—in RAD, the auxiliary civilian corps that supported the German armed forces. Reluctantly, he'd worked in RAD from October 1940 until late 1941, when he'd been drafted into the *Wehrmacht*. Like Wilhelm Schlegel and Walter Felholter, he was trained in wireless communications.

Ernst served the German army first in Russia, with troops that swept onto the Crimean peninsula and battered the besieged city of Sevastopol with artillery barrages and bombing raids throughout the winter. He and his fellow German soldiers were impressed by Sevastopol's stubborn Russian citizens who moved underground into caves and shelters and continued to manufacture shells and mortars to supply the defenders of their city.

When Sevastopol fell in July 1942, Ernst was sent to the northern front near Leningrad. The German siege of that city had begun in September 1941 and would last until January 1944. Hitler predicted that, once surrounded, Leningrad would fall like a leaf, but its citizens were also stubborn in spite of severe starvation and exposure. They resisted enough to keep German troops out of the heart of their city.

Ernst remained near Leningrad for only a few months in the late summer and early fall of 1942 before developing the yellow pallor of hepatitis. He was sent to a military hospital and, after recovery, to a base in Celle, a beautiful historic town in the Lower Saxony region of northern Germany. He spent a year there as a military instructor.

Late in 1943, Ernst received orders to join one of the new regiments that would become part of Field Marshal Erwin Rommel's Coastal Defense forces in northern France. For the first half of 1944, Ernst's regiment trained and drilled and waited, while Allied troops on the other side of the English Channel trained and drilled and waited for the opportune moment to cross the channel and confront them.

As Ernst stood watch in the nighttime rainfall on June 5, his mind drifted back to the peaceful year he'd spent teaching survival techniques to new recruits in Celle. He reached deep into a pocket of his damp uniform and fingered the last letter he'd received from Wilfriede several weeks before. There was no need to pull it out. He knew it by heart. He'd met her one day on a narrow street in Celle. Their love had grown during that somewhat sheltered year, and she'd promised to wait for him. He wondered now how long it would be before he would see her again, or if he ever would. If it weren't for the war, they'd be married by now and starting a family life together.

Suddenly, late in the night and in spite of the rain, Allied planes emerged from the clouds directly above the small rise between the two beaches and began dropping paratroopers very close to Ernst's position. He sounded the alarm, and his unit quickly captured several American soldiers as they struggled out of their chutes.

Ernst remained at his watch post. Just before dawn, when he sensed a change he could not define, he climbed a tree and gasped at what he saw below in the pale gray light—hundreds of ships of all sizes and shapes rocking in the waves of the channel as far as he could see. The invasion, he thought. The Allied invasion had finally begun.

Later that morning, Ernst's unit captured another group of Americans, hiding in wait for them as they struggled up the hill. Ernst braced for more fighting, but nothing happened until the following morning, June 7, when gliders swooped silently overhead and dropped more Allied paratroopers within cannon range. Up to that point, the unit had not been attacked, but when they fired their cannon, incoming Americans pinpointed them and set upon them violently. The German unit retreated, taking their prisoners with them but leaving Ernst and five others to defend the bunker as best they could. These men held out for some time but then determined that further resistance would serve no purpose. When Ernst Schacht finally raised his arms high in surrender, the main thought in his head was that he'd fulfilled his duty. Whatever happened next, he'd done that.

Ernst's captors motioned for him and the others to march downhill towards the beach. The men were herded into a long, sandy trench between two makeshift strings of barbed wire, just a few feet from the water's edge. They huddled there, under the watchful eye of Allied guards with rifles. Later, with gestures, they were made to understand that they should slosh out into the choppy waves. More gestures from behind pointed rifles told them to climb aboard one of the bobbing landing craft that had shuttled the Americans across the channel. After a chilly, nauseous crossing, Ernst arrived in an English port and was taken to an interrogation camp. Several days later, probably at Liverpool, he boarded the USS *Wakefield* and began his journey across the Atlantic to Boston. From there, like North Africa captives before him, he traveled by train down to Camp Aliceville.

Günther Peter Ertel also found himself on the northern coast of France by the spring of 1944. It was the second time he'd been stationed there. At age nineteen, Günther had received his notice to join the RAD labor force. Only six months later, he'd been drafted into the *Wehrmacht* and stood by as the more experienced soldiers in his barracks were ordered to pack up and help invade Poland on September 1, 1939.

Günther was left behind. He hated the army, and it showed. "Only the best were sent to the front then, and I was not the best," he has said. Günther did not regret missing out on the brutal *Blitzkrieg* assault that completely destroyed the Polish air force and resulted in the capture of most of the Polish army. Two days after the *Blitzkrieg* began, France and Great Britain (which had guaranteed Poland's borders in treaties) declared war on Germany. Canada entered the war a few days later. Poland offered little resistance and surrendered at the beginning of October.

By May 1940, when Hitler launched an offensive into Holland and Belgium with his sights set on France, Günther Ertel was not left behind. "Everyone was called out then. They needed every man, even me." Günther first experienced combat against British troops defending Belgium. "They were very disciplined fighters. We highly admired them."

German troops pressed on into France, and Günther was with them. He remembers feeling embarrassed at fighting against the French because he spoke their language and admired their culture. He was stationed near Calais, overlooking the Strait of Dover, the narrowest point of the channel between France and England, and not far from Dunkirk where Field Marshal Rommel's divisions had cornered the Allies weeks earlier, forcing them to evacuate three hundred thousand soldiers back to England in a humiliating ragtag rescue.

By the spring of 1940, any hint of French culture had been bombed to bits in Calais. The city had become a German command post, bleak with hulking metal. Günther was now a member of a combat engineering unit training for *Unternehmen Seelöwe* (Operation Sea Lion), Germany's never-carried-out plan to invade Great Britain. Günther knew that, if *Seelöwe* took place, his chances of survival were slim. "We would have been the first to go there in the strong boats," he has said. Combat engineers—the soldiers who secured roads and bridges and laid land mines—were always first in and last out in an invasion. "Our losses would have been horrendous."

Operation Sea Lion never occurred. British planes destroyed many of the boats the Germans planned to use, and the *Luftwaffe* did not succeed in clearing the skies over England. "We had to have total air superiority, but we didn't," Günther has said.

Hitler came to believe that Great Britain would recognize her hopeless situation once all of her European allies surrendered. He concluded that the defiant island nation north of Europe would surrender once Russia was defeated, so he ordered the Sea Lion troops shipped east by train to prepare for the invasion of Russia. This proved disastrous for the unit of combat engineers. Four months later, in June 1941, Günther was one of only eight men left in his company of 120. All the rest were dead, badly wounded, or in captivity.

Günther now became a platoon leader on the Russian front. Like Robert Hugh Kirksey back at Camp Claiborne in the American infantry, Günther knew this was a dangerous designation. "It was a formality. They made you a platoon leader one day, then sent you home dead the next." He never wore the platoon leader insignia on his uniform because he knew it was a favorite target for Russian sharpshooters.

Günther managed to survive the terrible Russian winter of 1943, though he watched many of his comrades freeze to death or become so cold they couldn't fight. By the time he was shipped back to France in the spring of 1944, he was totally discouraged with the war and wondering why he was still alive. Stationed again on the edge of the narrow channel that separated France from England, he was struck by the contrast four years of war had wrought. In May 1940, the Allies had been backed into a corner in this place and had retreated to England in disgrace. Now, four years later, they had regrouped and gathered strength with America in the war. As most everyone on both sides agreed, the Allies were poised to launch a very aggressive assault somewhere near where Günther was posted.

Field Marshall Erwin Rommel was back in northern France, too. Although charged by Hitler with defending the French coast, Rommel failed to convince other German commanders to lay plans for stopping an Allied invasion on the beaches themselves. He could not persuade them to deploy *Panzers* in small units as close to the coast as possible. When D-Day came, some German tank units inflicted serious damage on the invading forces, but Hitler's refusal to release the inland tank units soon enough—combined with superior Allied air support and the overwhelming numbers of their troops—allowed the Allies to secure their beachheads and begin to advance.

Not long after the invasion began, Günther Ertel received a letter from his wife—a letter in which she wrote, quite recklessly, "When you see the first American, throw away your gun and just give yourself up." He was careful to burn the letter before prying eyes could discover the treasonable advice it contained, but day after day, he could not forget its words. He wondered why his wife, who was enduring the war back in Munich with their toddler son, assumed the Americans would treat him well. In later years, whenever he thought back, he also wondered how big a part her words played in his actions on June 16.

Northern France was swarming with Americans who'd battled their way ashore ten days earlier, and Günther spotted a group of them as he and sixteen others were changing position. "I can only think that maybe in my subconscious I deliberately went in the wrong direction, right into the Americans. I walked knowingly with my gun not hidden in readiness, which I would never have done in Russia." He stared at the enemy weapons pointed at him and braced himself to die, but no shots were fired. Then, to his relief, he heard the words, "Hands up!"

As he raised his hands, Günther thought about his wife and son and prayed that his wife had been right. He also prayed that, for her sake and his son's sake, the Americans would reach Munich before the Russians did.

No matter where the Allies actually carried out their D-Day landings, both Hitler and Rommel believed the first strategic objective would be the port city of Cherbourg on the Cotentin peninsula—a logical port for shipping soldiers and equipment directly from the United States. Siege and occupation were nothing new to this city built on the site of a Roman camp. The British had claimed it numerous times since the 1200s, and now it had been occupied and fortified by the conquering Germans since 1940. Hitler issued orders to his commanders to defend Cherbourg to the last bunker and, if defeated, to leave the Allies only ruins where the harbor had been.

During the third week of June, one of the *Wehrmacht* soldiers defending the outskirts of Cherbourg was thirty-year-old Reinhold Wilhelm Schulte who, like Ernst Schacht, had already been stationed in northern France for several months with

Rommel's Coastal Defense forces. Reinhold carried a beloved photo of himself in his dress uniform with his wife, Herta, standing behind him and his young son Dieter seated on his lap. The photo had been taken in January 1942 just before Reinhold left for the Russian front to join a machine gun battalion ordered to fortify a major railroad line to Moscow.

A soldier's life was certainly not what Reinhold would have chosen for himself under more peaceful circumstances. Neither was a position in manufacturing, even though he'd been born in the industry-rich Ruhr Valley. From the time of his fifteenth birthday, he'd trained and worked as a gardener and landscaper. Nurturing plant life was much more to his liking than pointing guns or building machines, but such a career had not been possible in Germany in the late 1930s. Instead, Reinhold fulfilled his RAD labor requirement, as ordered, and then transferred south to Passau in Bavaria for basic military training.

Life returned to normal for a time after that. Reinhold married Herta in early 1940, and the couple moved in with his parents. For almost a year, Reinhold was able to do the work he loved with a landscape gardening and tree nursery business in Osnabrück in northwest Germany, but then he was called to active military duty. Now, following D-Day, his machine gun battalion was among the thousands of troops attempting to keep the Allies from capturing Cherbourg.

They would not succeed. The Allies had drawn a line across the Cotentin peninsula much as they had done when they captured Wilhelm Schlegel and thousands of others on the Cape Bon peninsula in North Africa a year earlier. By June 20, three divisions of Allied troops approached Cherbourg, and Reinhold was captured on that day. As he made the choppy channel crossing to England, his thoughts turned to the safety of his family. With the obvious Allied successes in Normandy, the bombings at home would only increase. Herta and young Dieter, as well as both sets of grandparents, were caught in Germany's most industrial region in the Ruhr Valley, and Reinhold knew from Herta's letters that they'd already grown accustomed to racing for air raid shelters several times a day when the sirens wailed. Reinhold was sure things would only get worse now.

At the time of the D-Day landings, the German navy controlled many of the coastal artillery batteries that stood several kilometers apart along France's northern coastline between Le Havre and Cherbourg, and these came into play as the Allied troops advanced steadily towards the coveted harbor. The original defense bunkers had been open concrete pits equipped with machine gun, mortar, and anti-aircraft gun positions, all connected by trenches and ringed with minefields and a network of barbed wire.

After heavy Allied bombardments along the coast in late 1943, Rommel had ordered these bunker pits encased in thick concrete casemates, but the work was far from complete by D-Day. As a consequence, most of the bunkers offered only weak resistance, and many of them were easily overcome by Allied troops.

Franz August Hinz was an artillery mate in a bunker nicknamed *Kleiner Hund* (Little Dog). Thirty-two-year old Franz had been born in Königsberg, a city in East Prussia (now part of

Poland), near the Baltic Sea. As a boy, he'd been a carpenter's apprentice but then followed his heart to the nearby sea and become a ship's steward. Later, he'd attended helmsman's school and worked for a variety of shipping firms before being drafted into the German navy.

In mid-June 1944, when he and the other defenders of Little Dog surrendered in exhaustion, they were sent to a prisoner of war camp in England. Unlike Ernst Schacht, Günther Peter Ertel, and Reinhold Schulte, Franz would spend a year in England before arriving in Camp Aliceville.

By June 23, American troops had broken through the outer defenses of Cherbourg. The city's German commander ignored a formal demand for surrender and issued orders for the harbor installations to be destroyed. Horst Spieker, a printer from Berlin, was with the German air forces that tried to give cover for this destruction, but artillery barrages from offshore Allied battleships were too strong. Horst's plane went down, and he was captured on June 25, one day before the German commander finally surrendered the city. Horst ended up aboard the *Argentina*, which arrived in Staten Island, New York, on July 14.

Werner Kaiser was also in the Cherbourg area. His entire division had retreated in the direction of that city after being driven out of coastal defense positions. When it became clear that the Allies had cut off the tip of the peninsula, Werner and his comrades faced two probable choices in the coming days—death or prisoner of war camp. Werner, twenty-two years old and newly engaged to a young woman back in his hometown of Hannover, considered himself too young and too strong to submit to either of these choices, so he talked another young soldier into risking a break with him through the Allied lines.

Grabbing only some crisp bread and their pistols, the two young soldiers waited until dark on the evening of June 23, and then began moving south, out of the area already controlled by the Allies. In the daytime, they hid and slept in clumps of bushes, hardly daring to breathe as enemy units passed right by where they were resting. For two nights, they traveled undetected, but just before dawn on the third morning, their luck ran out when they were spotted by a group of American soldiers hiding in a roadside ditch. The Americans shouted for them to stop walking and raise their hands over their heads. "You are lucky," one of the captors announced in German. "For you, the war is over."

The two German infantrymen ended up in Liverpool and were marched aboard the *Mauritania* for the journey to New York. They would spend the next ten days lying in hammocks in a sardine-can-crowded room directly above the engines of the *Mauritania*. They would be allowed on deck once a day for a few gulps of fresh air.

The war was just beginning for American waist gunner Wendell Parrish when German infantryman Werner Kaiser and his friend surrendered. Wendell was now stationed at Kettering Air Base in England. He and his crewmates had nicknamed their new plane The Fightin' Cock and decorated its fuselage with the image of a bright red gamecock wearing a pair of boxing gloves. They climbed aboard the B-17 for their first combat mission on June 22 and dropped six huge bombs on German robot installations near Calais. Wendell's crewmate, William E. Black, wrote in his diary that evening, "We were only up four hours, and only over enemy territory about 15 minutes. Flak was light but accurate. We got six holes in the ship but no one injured. Just 34 more [missions] to go—if the quota isn't raised again." Wendell hoped those thirty-four missions would pass quickly and without injury so he could return home to his wife and the child who would be born by that time.

On June 24, the crew of The Fightin' Cock flew their second mission and bombed synthetic oil factories in Bremen. The next day, they dropped ten bombs on a small German airfield in Toulouse, France. Then the rains came in, and they were grounded for several days.

Back in Alabama on June 28, August Wanders recorded the arrival of the first D-Day POWs at Camp Aliceville. Ernst Schacht was among the 450 prisoners who arrived by train from Boston early that morning. The county newspaper reported that these prisoners were of all ages, some as young as fifteen. A few spoke English and told their guards they were glad to be safe in America.

When Ernst stepped down from one of the Frisco passenger cars and marched out to the camp gates, he was pleasantly surprised to find a well-landscaped and well-organized POW community amid the cotton fields and pine forests of Pickens County. He'd had no idea what to expect as the train wound its way south. The compound was brutally hot, but the good drainage ditches dug by the POWs already in residence had vastly improved both the mud and the mosquito issues since the first prisoners arrived a year earlier.

Ernst ignored the derogatory comments of some North Africa POWs who taunted the new arrivals and questioned their bravery. He threw himself into worthwhile activities, which were plentiful by the time he arrived. One of his favorite pastimes was watching the movies shown at least once a week. Some were German films, and some were American, but he enjoyed both.

Ernst had always been interested in theater. While at Camp Aliceville, he welcomed the opportunity to appear in productions like *Windstark 10 (Wind Strength Ten Knots)*, in which he played a sailor. Keeping busy was good, but it did not entirely erase the *Heimweh* he felt whenever he thought about Wilfriede, his sweetheart back in Germany. The first time he read Heinrich Most's poem—about the girlfriend left behind, sitting by the window—he felt it had been written just for him.

Werner Kaiser reached Aliceville from New York City at about the same time. He'd thought it a good sign when his captors allowed him to send a postcard to his parents notifying them of his status as a POW. The American guards gave him clean, new clothing. It was lightweight like German uniforms used in the tropics, and Werner understood why after his three-day train ride to Alabama. Although the POW camp at Aliceville provided good food and medical care, July temperatures in the tarpaper covered barracks often topped one hundred degrees—even at night. The air sat thick and moist in his lungs whenever he took a breath.

Walter Felholter remembers when those first Normandy POWs arrived at Camp Aliceville. It was late June. Like most of the prisoners captured in North Africa, Walter continued to believe Germany would eventually win the war. The camp now provided American newspapers, but many of the prisoners still viewed much of what these contained as Allied propaganda designed to energize American patriotism and discourage German morale. "We didn't know anything about what had happened in Russia, especially in Stalingrad, and we always believed what Hitler told to everyone and what Goebbels told to everyone."

Stalingrad is perhaps the saddest example of Hitler's stubborn refusal to pull back when common sense would dictate. In the fall of 1942, he'd sent an army of more than five hundred thousand men to attack Stalingrad, an oil-shipping city on the Volga River in the Russian Caucasus. The city was defended by sixteen Soviet divisions. By November, after intense house-to-house fighting, the Germans held a tenuous foothold in most of the city. They were not, however, prepared for a long winter siege. Even though the Soviet garrison received fresh supplies from across the Volga while *Wehrmacht* soldiers shivered in summer uniforms and grew thin on reduced food supplies, Hitler ignored the advice of his general staff and refused to pull back.

The result was a bitter winter standoff—with staggering losses on both sides. It was the same winter in the same country that Günther Peter Ertel had survived while many in his unit froze to death. Finally, in February 1943, General Friedrich Paulus surrendered what was left of the German troops. Hours before the surrender, Hitler promoted Paulus to the rank of Field Marshal. Since no German Field Marshal had ever surrendered, it was clear that Hitler expected Paulus to take his own life in disgrace, but instead, while in Russian captivity, Paulus became an outspoken critic of the Nazi government and eventually testified at the Nürnberg trials after the war ended.

Most estimates put the loss of human life in this barbaric five-month battle at more than one million people. The Germans lost three hundred thousand men, along with four hundred-fifty thousand Romanians, Hungarians, and Italians fighting with them. The Russians lost seven hundred-fifty thousand, including many civilian residents of the city. In addition, more than one hundred thousand German soldiers were taken prisoner, including twenty-two generals considered fine prizes by the Russians. In stark contrast to American POW camp survival rates, fewer than five thousand of these German captives survived imprisonment to see their homeland again.

After the German surrender, the Soviets liberated Stalingrad, began an aggressive drive westward towards Nazi-occupied Europe, and remained on the offensive against Germany for the rest of the war. This was also the point at which Erwin Rommel and the *Afrikakorps* began to face setbacks in North Africa. President Roosevelt and Prime Minister Winston Churchill, who were meeting in Casablanca at the time, began calling for Germany's unconditional surrender on all fronts.

Walter Felholter's comment about what "Goebbels told to everyone" is a reference to Dr. Paul Joseph Goebbels, who served as Hitler's Propaganda Minister. Goebbels is often cited as the model for Squealer in George Orwell's *Animal Farm*, published in 1945—the pig who used propaganda to convince the other farm animals that the pigs' activities were not corrupt.

On February 18, 1943, after General Paulus's humiliating surrender in Russia, Goebbels gave his *Sportpalast* speech to motivate the German people to support the country's war machine in "total war" even though the tide was turning towards an Allied victory. The speech signaled the first admission of military difficulties by the German government, but Goebbels used the slogan, "Let the storm break loose!" to rally German people to fight harder for victory. He promised them that harsh austerity measures being put in place were only temporary. The severe rationing announced in that speech in February 1943 took five months to implement and did not bring victory. Sadly for the German civilian population, severe shortages of food and basic necessities would continue and grow worse in the country for several years, even after the war ended.

Walter Felholter had little opportunity to talk with the new Normandy POWs about the war in Europe because he was transferred to Camp McCain almost immediately after they arrived. He does remember hearing their discouraging reports—Germany was losing ground in Europe, supplies were dwindling, morale was low, people at home were starving. He and others in his compound wondered if perhaps these new prisoners, who had so recently fought in France, were not such good soldiers as the North Africa men had been. "Maybe they hadn't fought hard enough to win, and they had early put their hands up. That's what we thought about them," he said in later years. Walter was not a Nazi party member, but he had taken pride in his military service even though he, too, had surrendered.

Walter never drew any more conclusions about what he was hearing. Within days, he was en route to Camp McCain in

Mississippi. His relaxing days of reading, studying, and playing chess in the infirmary and then in the diphtheria-quarantined barracks at Camp Aliceville were over. At Camp McCain, Walter was put to work in the kitchen that served mess halls for American servicemen in training. In September, he was moved again, this time to Camp Shelby where the work became even more strenuous. He was now ordered to pick peanuts—the nuts used to make the peanut butter that had been his first taste of food at Camp Aliceville, and then when that harvest was complete, to pick tung nuts.

Walter had never heard of tung nuts, but he soon learned that the trees they grew on had been imported to the United States from China in the 1930s and were being cultivated successfully on huge plantations along the Gulf Coast. The American automobile industry used the oil from tung nuts to prevent rust and reduce friction on engine parts. The oil was also used to coat the insides of cans, insulate electric circuits, and manufacture high-quality paints. It was an excellent finishing product for fine wood.

During most of October, Walter stayed in a branch camp and spent his days among the endless rows of tung trees on plantations near the Mississippi Gulf Coast. The nuts looked a little like chestnuts. When they fell to the ground, the POWs picked them up in baskets. "We were supposed to pick twenty baskets a day," Walter remembers. "To get finished earlier, we put not only tung nuts but also soil in those baskets. Then the truck would come by for us and count how many baskets we'd picked and write the number down by our name."

During his transfer to Mississippi, Walter may have crossed paths with another North Africa POW, Fritz Hagmann, who was transported at about this time from Camp Shelby to Camp Aliceville. Fritz was a sergeant, and therefore, part of the regrouping that sent non-working NCOs to Aliceville in mid-1944. A War Department directive ordered all non-working German NCOs in the First through Fourth Service Commands above the rank of corporal to be sent to Camp Aliceville.

Fritz Hagmann had been captured by the British in North Africa in May 1943. When he came to Camp Aliceville, he apparently agreed to work in spite of his rank because he participated in work details under the supervision of T.J. Hester, a civilian employee of the Engineers and Maintenance department at the camp. When Fritz finally returned to Germany, he wrote to T.J. Hester and told him what good memories he had of working with him during his captivity.

Günther Peter Ertel arrived in Aliceville after Walter Felholter left in the middle of July. Like Ernst Schacht, he signed up for as many activities as he could—playing in the orchestra and acting in plays. Günther also took advantage of the school now operating on a daily basis with German instructors who'd been proficient in their fields at home. He studied English and French. "I stayed busy all day long," he told a reporter years later. "I've never been so busy in my life. I never felt a minute of being bored or lonely. I was trying to make the best of the time I had."

One hot afternoon, Günther sat by an open barracks window with an old violin braced under his chin. As he practiced a piece for an upcoming camp concert, he watched the armed MPEG guards scanning Compound A from their perch on the wooden surveillance tower. Odd, he thought, but I feel as if I'm in heaven—even if this version of heaven is surrounded by barbed wire. Camp Aliceville was heaven, in a way, after three years on the Russian front and then the devastation in France. "If not for the concern for my family, I would have even been happy."

Günther had not wanted to be a soldier in the first place, but if he couldn't be at home in Germany, in peacetime, then he, too, would make the most of the time he spent in this place. There had to be a good reason why he had survived, time after time against illogical odds, and he promised himself that he would use this odd interval to better himself for the future.

Günther did his best to avoid the taunts of some North Africa POWs. He also took careful pains to avoid confrontations with overly fanatical Nazis. There were fifty guys in each barracks, and it would not be wise to make any remark that would rub the Nazis the wrong way. Just as on the battlefield, a group of them would kill you or at least beat you up rather than discuss things, and the Americans couldn't get there fast enough to help. It was a danger he sensed and tried to ignore.

One of Gunther's acquaintances in Camp Aliceville was Horst Spieker. They had not fought together in France—Horst was in the air force and Günther was a combat engineer, but in Compound B, Company 7, they shared stories of their war experiences and concern for their families back home. Horst had worked in his father's printing business in Berlin before the war. He may have been the one who talked Gunther into writing articles for *Der Zaungast,* the weekly POW newspaper camp spokesman Walter Meier finally launched that summer.

When Reinhold Schulte came to Camp Aliceville, he found peace in carving a chess set for himself. There were many men in his barracks who loved the game, and it was never difficult to find a match. Reinhold obtained a chunk of yellow pine from the woodworking shop and spent many evenings carving it intricately into a box to hold his chess men. Carving was not a skill he'd learned before coming to the POW camp, but Reinhold found that focusing on it soothed him and occupied his thoughts. He kept the box in the chest at the end of his bunk and pulled it out for a match whenever he could.

Reinhold also immersed himself in the thriving horticulture of the camp, using the skills he'd learned at home in Westphalia to help landscape the barracks and the pathways of his compound. He worried constantly about his wife and son, knowing from American newspapers that the Ruhr Valley was a constant Allied bombing target because of its industry. He did not yet know that Herta and Dieter had fled the Ruhr River valley and taken refuge with relatives in a house on a hill in Bad Öynhausen. Here, they still looked down on a factory town in the valley below but were no longer bomb targets themselves.

Werner Kaiser was relieved when he finally reached Camp Aliceville in mid-July. After the crowded, noisy conditions aboard the *Mauritania* and the uncertainty of the three-day train ride to an unknown destination, the mundane daily routines of the camp were welcome. Werner didn't mind falling in for a head count twice each day. There appeared to be plenty of food, and it was good to have a solid roof over his head and excellent medical care.

Werner was surprised to find weekly church services and plenty of plays and concerts to enjoy, as well as weekly soccer competitions. He was also grateful for the opportunity to write postcards home on a regular basis. Like Günther Ertel, he might have been completely happy in this place if he hadn't been concerned about his fiancée and his parents back in Hannover.

...Immediately, the thought flashed in my mind, "What if they are going to the German Prisoner of War Camp in Aliceville, Alabama. Here we are, reluctantly headed for their homeland; and there they are reluctantly headed, perhaps, for ours. The pathos of war was etched in my mind and I can see those German faces clearly in my mind, even today.

• Robert Hugh Kirksey •
"Off To Europe—Thank Goodness"
With Me

CHAPTER TWELVE
European Front

Not long after August Wanders began noting the arrival of D-Day POWs at Camp Aliceville, the weather in England cleared, and Wendell Parrish's B-17 took off for its seventh mission—on the seventh day of the seventh month of 1944. Just as it reached its target area, over Leipzig, Wendell heard the sound of anti-aircraft fire and then the sputtering of first one and then another engine. The plane lost altitude rapidly, but the pilot managed to level off at eight thousand feet—point blank range for German ground fighters.

Most German fighter planes had been eliminated by that point in 1944, but anti-aircraft guns were firing strongly. As the B-17 crossed the coast of Holland, Wendell heard more sputtering sounds that signaled the Germans had knocked out a third engine. The plane headed feebly out over the North Sea and kept flying "long after all the laws of engineering and aeronautics declaimed that it should have crashed," as Wendell's crewmate William Black described it.

After radioing an SOS to a British base, the crew ditched halfway between enemy-held Europe and the friendly shores of England. Fortunately, they were picked up by a high-speed British launch before the Germans could reach them.

After flying two more missions, they were given a week of "Flak Leave" at an elegant English manor house, where they wined and dined, rode horses and bicycles, played softball and poker, and caught up on the latest movies. The week was over all too quickly, and the crew flew six more missions in late July and early August. With each successful run, Wendell breathed a sigh of relief as he counted off the remaining missions of his duty commitment and the few remaining weeks until the birth of his first child.

On July 17, while Wendell was enjoying the hospitality of the English manor house, a Royal Canadian Air Force Spitfire pilot named Charley Fox strafed an unidentified black car near the Normandy coast across the channel in France. Charley, the son of an Irish immigrant to Canada, would eventually receive the Distinguished Flying Cross for destroying or damaging 153 enemy vehicles during World War II. On this day, one of the passengers in the car he strafed turned out to be Field Marshall Erwin Rommel, who was seriously injured in the attack and hospitalized with major head injuries.

Three days later, as Rommel began a long and slow recovery, Adolf Hitler held a staff meeting at his heavily fortified and guarded *Wolfsschanze* military headquarters in East Prussia (now part of Poland). Just before the meeting, a German army colonel named Claus von Stauffenberg placed a briefcase containing a bomb near Hitler's position in the war room. Stauffenberg slipped outside and watched to make sure the explosion took place. He then hurried to the nearby airfield and flew to Berlin, confident his next task would be to supervise a transition of power from Hitler to the group of high-ranking military and civilian officials who'd planned the bombing. These Germans had come to believe their country's only hope was to remove the Nazis from power.

Hitler survived the explosion because he was standing next to a heavy oak table. The table deflected the blast that killed four of the twenty-four people attending the staff meeting. Hitler's wrath at the botched attempt on his life led to horrible reprisals. The primary leaders of the plot, including Count von Stauffenberg and three others, were caught that very evening and shot by firing squad in the courtyard of the War Ministry building in Berlin. Hitler then moved to smother any remaining whiff of resistance, eventually ordering the execution of more than four thousand people believed to have been involved.

In the United States, seven hours behind European time, news of the attempt on Hitler's life headlined the afternoon newspapers on July 20. "Fuehrer Burned, Bruised in Try at Assassination" reported *The Birmingham News*.

Gerald Stabler, now the mayor of Aliceville, heard about the assassination attempt while on a fishing trip in Florida with George Downer, Joe Cunningham, and Harold Speed. Early newspaper and radio coverage in the United States and other Allied countries was based on press releases from the official German news agency DNR. They made no mention of where the bombing took place. *The Birmingham News* speculated incorrectly, based on unidentified sources in London, that the blast might have occurred in Breda, Holland—Rommel's field headquarters. The London source suggested the plot might have developed because of disagreements between Rommel and another military commander about where to deploy *Panzers* before the Normandy invasion.

Sue Stabler heard the news on the radio in Aliceville. Margie Archibald heard it on the radio, too. She was enjoying a long weekend visit with Captain Larry Persons and his wife, Edwina, near Fort Oglethorpe in Georgia, where they were now stationed. One broadcast quoted what German stations had reported to the civilian population in Germany—that the attack involved Allied sympathizers.

American newspapers reported all kinds of speculation during the next few days. An NBC news reporter radioed from Turkey of widespread rumors there that Hitler had been arrested. Travelers reaching Sweden from German cities told of at least one hundred prominent German generals being executed on Hitler's orders. Some sources reported hearing a mysterious broadcast from Frankfurt in which a solitary voice declared, "Let Hitler know this much for certain—there is more than one Stauffenberg. Stauffenbergs are here in the thousands."

August Wanders does not mention this incident in his diary. What the POWs just arriving at Camp Aliceville from Cherbourg and LeHavre thought about the attempt on Hitler's life is not known, but they did have access by this time to American newspapers and radio broadcasts. A reading room had been opened, offering current editions of thirty-four American magazines and newspapers. Radios were also available.

On July 22, an American reporter traveling with troops in Normandy reported the reaction of six prisoners who had not yet been shipped to the United States. Five of them were Austrians who shook hands and slapped each other cheerfully on the back. "Too bad they didn't get him," said one of them as they sat under guard in a barn near Saint Lo. "But they will," said another. "This is the beginning of the end. Hitler is kaput—finished. There will be more attempts."

Reporter Hal Boyle wrote for the Associated Press that another of the prisoners in the barn—a young paratrooper who looked "like a typical Nazi fanatic"—made the comment that many soldiers were just waiting for the internal collapse of their country. "It will come soon now. Morale is terrible because of your bombings, and people are discontented over the severe new rationing [the rationing propaganda minister Goebbels had announced] imposed now after we have been fighting so long."

Whether or not Rommel helped plan the attempt on Hitler's life has never been clearly proved, but as the investigation spread, Hitler came to believe his trusted Desert Fox field marshal had been involved. Hitler was well aware of Rommel's popularity with the German people, and so he considered carefully and for some time before deciding how to punish him. He would not take action until October.

Wilhelm Schlegel returned to Camp Aliceville from Fort Dix late in the summer. This time, he was assigned to Compound D, Company 16—most certainly a compound designated for NCOs who would not accept work assignments. Shortly after his return, word spread that a group of prisoners from Normandy would be assigned there. As they came through the gate, Wilhelm watched and listened with a mixture of disbelief and frustration. "What we heard, we could not believe. These comrades were downtrodden. They hung their heads and saw no future." This was not the attitude of a German soldier! Wilhelm was indignant that such men had been allowed to wear the uniform.

North Africa POWs like Wilhelm Schlegel were reluctant to accept the pessimistic reports and predictions of defeat expressed by the Normandy POWs. They still held fast to the belief that their country would be victorious. The clash of attitudes was serious and widespread. As time went on, there were loud arguments and even fist fights. Eventually, camp administrators were forced to separate the two groups. Years later, Wilhelm recalled this period with the comment that it took a long time for him and his North Africa comrades to understand the situation. "We had not yet seen the bombed cities or the suffering of the civilian population of Germany—the women and children."

August Wanders makes mention in his diary that there was a great soccer competition on August 13, with Normandy POWs competing against North Africa POWs. He does not mention who won, but this was probably an attempt by the camp administration to turn personal animosities into more healthy sports competitiveness.

Camp spokesman Walter Meier's beloved printing press finally began printing a camp newspaper near the end of the summer in 1944. It was an event Hermann Blumhardt had worked for but had not been able to see accomplished because of his decision to transfer with his unit to Camp Gordon Johnston. As one POW described the scene on the day the first issue was printed, "two printers threw themselves onto the colossus of the 'Flying Dutchman' that soon set its limbs in motion with a clattering noise.... Both press operators—one could compare them to careful horse grooms—were convinced that the press would endure." Three typesetters stood at their stations and began setting out letters in rank and file, sorting each one individually.

Only a few issues of the first edition were printed, and these were distributed only to those who contributed to it or helped assemble it. The editorial staff announced that no further editions could be printed until an APN (Approved Periodical Number) was received from the American government. This (APN-4-45-M) was apparently obtained at the beginning of September, and from then on almost until the camp closed, *Der Zaungast* appeared each week. Judging from the number of POWs who saved all issues and stuffed them into their one duffel bag when they left Camp Aliceville, its publication meant a great deal to them.

There has been speculation down through the years about the exact meaning of the newspaper's name. Most agree it was intended to mean "Guest Behind the Wire." The phrase "behind the wire" is often used to refer to prisoner of war and internment camps. The German word *Zaun* means "fence" in English, and the German word *Gast* means "guest." However, speculation has arisen because there is an idiomatic meaning for the compound word *Zaungast*, which translates roughly as "intruder" or "onlooker." In everyday German usage, the word *Zaungast* would refer to someone who stands by and watches without taking action. Perhaps the POWs chose this name because it could also be an ironic description of their POW role while the war continued.

The issue of *Der Zaungast* published on August 4, 1944, was largely a tribute to Camp Spokesman Walter Meier because August 4 was his twenty-ninth birthday. In one article, POW Wilhelm Stüdl praised the spokesman, reflecting the attitude of many prisoners who had at first been suspicious of Walter's leadership and his communication with the American captors. "All who know your honorable endeavors and your indefatigable caring, wish you from the heart that this new year of your life will begin, not with petty work, but rather with better assumptions—that it will be easier and more cheerful than the past year and a prelude to a happy return home."

Wilhelm Westhoff also wrote an article titled "The Way to Order," in which he recapped the history of the camp and expressed the very German editorial opinion that maintaining "soldierly order" was the only way to live. Westhoff praised Walter Meier dramatically for the "monstrous amount" of work he'd done to turn the POW camp into a thriving community. "Often, waves of fire and fury seemed almost to swallow him up, but steadfastly and logically, our Walter sought his way and did not tire in spite of all the hostility. He discovered friends and comrades, true helpers. A few crises had to be overcome, but the whole camp became a calm and well-adjusted community in which we could aspire to the building of a culturally worthwhile life."

Westhoff's article refers to the removal of many soldiers from Camp Aliceville (during the first half of 1944) and says this brought new unrest but also united more closely the group left behind. "Everyone had to fit into the soldierly order of the prisoner of war camp," he wrote. "Most did it willingly.... Some complied in spite of their desire to resist. Others, however, took the consequences and left the camp."

Westhoff predicted that the arrival of "new comrades from the fighting front [Normandy]" would not pass smoothly. He reminded those who'd been in Camp Aliceville longer that it was their responsibility to help these new arrivals come to inner peace and become accustomed to their new condition. "Only organization and order can give everyone air to breathe and strength to persevere."

The second issue of *Der Zaungast*, also distributed on a limited basis, contained a note that four marriages by proxy had been celebrated for POWs the previous Sunday [August 6]. "We wish these comrades everything good in this step," the newspaper stated.

This issue carried an article about a memorial service held on August 6 to honor four POWs who had died in August and September the previous year. The service began at 8:30 in the morning with all the companies of Compound A lining up in an open square. The band played "Largo" by Handel, and a POW recited a poem by Rilke. The choirs of Compounds B and D sang "Death is a Reaper," which was noted as an appropriate transition to a speech given by camp spokesman Walter Meier. Sergeant Major Meier called the names of the dead and mentioned particularly the great urge for freedom that had caused Rolf Schneider and Friedrich Rauschenberg to try to escape.

This issue also contained announcements of when various religious services were held, when the canteens were open, and when various groups—like all the prisoners from the Hildesheim area of Germany—were getting together to chat about home. It contained numerous articles about sports activities and a German film review.

On the other side of the Atlantic, very early on the morning of August 9, Wendell Parrish left England for his sixteenth bombing mission—this time aboard a B-17 nicknamed Big Barnsmell after the stinky fellow in the "L'il Abner" cartoon who brewed up Kickapoo joy juice. There were only nine in the B-17 crew this time—partly to make room for a larger bomb load and partly to conserve manpower. Big Barnsmell was headed again for Leipzig, a major industrial city in east central Germany, when heavy clouds and turbulence disoriented the navigator. Instead of passing south of Aachen near the Belgian and Dutch borders with Germany, he sent the B-17 directly over Aachen—the worst location outside Berlin for anti-aircraft fire.

Big Barnsmell took a direct hit, ripping off the nose and killing the pilot, the navigator, and the bombardier outright. The other six parachuted out. Five, including Wendell, were captured within minutes by waiting German SS troops who beat them during interrogation and held them for three days in a dank room infested with fleas and lice. On one of those days, in clear violation of Geneva Convention standards, the five men were ordered to remove their shoes and march barefoot through the streets of Aachen while civilians pelted them with bricks from bomb-shattered buildings. The sixth crewmember was captured a day or so later.

At one staging area, a captured American colonel distributed Red Cross parcels. Each contained soap, a razor, long johns and a wool shirt, pants, and an overcoat. This same colonel arranged for Wendell to send a cable, letting his pregnant wife know he'd been captured. The Red Cross cable went through Lisbon and then to Washington, and did not reach Selma, Alabama, until September 4.

After official processing as POWs, Wendell and the others were transported first to *Stalag Luft VI* and then to *Stalag Luft IV* at about the same time that Wendell's wife received the cable about his capture. This trip was made, not in passenger cars with upholstered seats like those of the Frisco Railroad but rather, like the French railroads in North Africa, "in filthy, stinking boxcars" with one slop bucket for "forty to fifty miserable souls" who struggled with gnawing pains of hunger and dysentery.

*Stalag Luft IV (*the word *Luft* meaning "air" in English and signifying a POW camp for airmen) was near the Baltic Sea in East Prussia. It was no Camp Aliceville. The prisoners lived in wooden barracks, but they had no plumbing. At first, they slept on the floor, but then one day, a load of wood and a small box of nails arrived and they were able to build crude bunks for themselves. Wendell learned to choke down dry German black bread with imitation coffee each morning. In the evening, a bucket of gritty, boiled potatoes arrived, sometimes accompanied by a pile of kohlrabies (turnip cabbages) dumped on the ground. These, the men ate raw.

During the first week at *Stalag Luft IV*, Wendell received a Red Cross package containing a can of Spam, some powdered milk, a dehydrated chocolate bar, some crackers and cheese, and two packs of cigarettes. The second week, there was one package for each two men. Two weeks later, near the beginning of October, four men shared one package, but after that, no more Red Cross packages arrived to supplement the two meager meals per day. Wendell's weight began to drop from a fit and trim 148 pounds. By the time he was finally released, he would weigh less than 100 pounds. He hoped the Red Cross cable about his captivity had reached his wife, but he had no way of knowing. No mail arrived for the American POWs at *Stalag Luft IV.* Wendell knew his baby must have been born by this time, and he hoped his wife and child were doing well.

Not long after Wendell Parrish's B-17 was shot down, on one of the hottest days in August, Robert Hugh Kirksey left Louisiana's Camp Claiborne on a troop train headed for Camp Kilmer in New Jersey. The 84th was finally headed overseas—in sweltering wool uniforms. On September 18, to the sounds of an army band playing "Over There" on the dock in New York City, the men marched up the gangplank of a converted German cruise ship that had been confiscated at the end of World War I. For the next twelve days, they battled seasickness and tried to guess exactly where they were being sent. It had been planned that the 84th would be the first division to land at the now restored harbor in Cherbourg, but that harbor was overcrowded, so the ship was diverted to the British Isles.

Early in October, the ship moved up the Firth of Clyde and docked near Glasgow, Scotland. Robert Hugh watched from the deck as two men at a sentinel post on shore waved a huge British Union Jack and then a huge American flag in greeting. "I shall never forget that stirring sight," Robert Hugh wrote later. "It was like receiving a sincere greeting at the home of a cousin."

Scotland was indeed like the home of a cousin to him, with ancestors named Kirksey, Robertson, and McLeod.

There was little time in Scotland. Within hours, members of the 84th boarded troop trains and headed south. Late the next afternoon, they steamed into the railway station in Birmingham, England—the industrial center for which Alabama's largest city was named. Robert Hugh noticed, as he looked out the window, that another train, headed north, was stopped on the track just opposite. "Look!" someone shouted. "They're German prisoners!" The coincidence stunned Robert Hugh more than anyone else. What an odd juxtaposition, he thought as he stared deep into the German faces staring back at him. He couldn't help wondering if those particular prisoners would end up in Camp Aliceville.

The POWs already living in Camp Aliceville—both North Africa and Normandy captives—continued to build their "culturally worthwhile life" and to expand their educational opportunities. Alvin Tepelmann was captured in central Italy and arrived in July. A former railroad employee, he'd been drafted in 1941 at the age of twenty. During his captivity in Aliceville, he made a concentrated effort to further his education, taking courses in physics, economics, and technical drafting. Studying drafting and physics without a slide rule was difficult, so Alvin went to the woodshop in his compound and asked for a piece of cedar. Then he went to the camp library and looked up the logarithmic scale. With a little creativity and diligence, he used a razor blade to fashion a slide rule and then used pen and ink to mark it. When he finally returned home in 1946, the handmade slide rule went with him.

By the summer of 1944, Camp Aliceville had one entire barracks building designated for classrooms and more than nine hundred POWs registered for classes in a wide range of subjects on a variety of educational levels. The quality of learning suffered somewhat with the frequent transfers that removed qualified instructors, but new ones began to arrive from the battlefields in Normandy and classes continued. The theater in Compound A had an orchestra pit and all of the necessary equipment and instruments for the performance of classic plays and concerts. A chapel had been built, and services were celebrated there each week by both Catholic and Protestant POW chaplains under the supervision of an American chaplain.

Late in the summer, the War Department's re-education program was finally dusted off and polished up enough to begin implementation. With a brighter light at the end of the long, dark war tunnel in Europe, some in Washington were ready to focus on influencing the attitudes of POWs who would likely return to Germany in the not too distant future. As General S.L.A. Marshall had originally suggested more than a year earlier (see Chapter Six), it would be good for America to separate out the worst Nazis and then begin offering education courses for the "amenable ones" with an emphasis on democratic theory and practice.

The Secretary of State and the Secretary of War had lobbied hard for this program in spite of the fact that President Roosevelt and others in Washington, including Roosevelt's confidant and Secretary of the Treasury Henry Morgenthau, were reflecting that the First World War had not destroyed German aggression. They believed the only solution was to destroy German industry completely, dismember the government, and "return the Germans to their primeval agrarian origins to start all over again."

It was more likely public pressure—and that of his wife—to do something about the Nazi issues in the POW camps than a desire to rehabilitate Germans that convinced President Roosevelt to approve the re-education program. It may also have been the growing realization that communism might become a threat in postwar Europe.

On August 23, the Provost Marshal General's Office created a subcommittee to establish policies and procedures. Colonel Edward Davison was put in charge of the POWSPD (Prisoners of War Special Projects Division). Maxwell McKnight, the officer Eleanor Roosevelt had summoned to dinner when she heard of Nazi abuse in the camps, would be Davison's assistant.

A War Department memo outlined the objective: "to give the prisoners of war the facts, objectively presented but so selected and assembled as to correct misinformation and prejudices...." This would be done under the guise of providing objective intellectual diversions, including movies that disproved Nazi charges about America and German language books that stressed Christian ethics. The lofty thinking was that if facts were presented clearly, ...perhaps the German prisoners of war might understand and believe historical and ethical truth as generally conceived by Western civilization, might come to respect the American people and their ideological values, and upon repatriation to Germany might form the nucleus of a new German ideology which will reject militarism and totalitarian controls and will advocate a democratic system of government.

There was still the risk of retaliation—mistreatment and Nazi indoctrination of American POWs in Germany—but the War Department had studied the Geneva Convention thoroughly and concluded that Article XVII gave them a big enough loophole to create something called the Intellectual Diversion Program. Article XVII included the phrase, "so far as possible, belligerents shall encourage intellectual diversions and sports organized by the prisoners."

The American press and the public, totally unaware of the top-secret program, continued to criticize War Department policy. They continued to accuse the government of coddling Nazi prisoners and demanded that something be done about the growing Nazi influence in the camps.

Gerhard Seger, the German American newspaper editor in New York who had warned about Nazi control in the camps back in February (see Chapter Ten), had formed a committee late in the spring to seek some sort of re-education program for Nazi prisoners. The committee's members included an impressive collection of Americans, including syndicated columnist Dorothy Thompson and world-famous German author Thomas Mann, who was living in exile in the United States. Seger and his committee received a great deal of publicity just as the War Department was trying to keep its re-education efforts secret. Seger publicly demanded a joint session of the Senate and House Military Affairs committees and also a meeting with General George C. Marshall.

Eventually, the War Department took Seger aside and assured him that such a plan was being undertaken but that no civilians would be allowed to participate and that it would not be publicized. They explained to Seger that if the POWs read about the program in newspapers, they would not want to participate. The War Department representatives must have been convincing because Seger backed down from his demands. Some POW newspapers continued to reprint stories about Seger, but this does not appear to have hurt the Intellectual Diversion Program.

William Shirer—the newspaper columnist who had suggested that if German POWs were not re-educated they might go home and start World War III (see Chapter Ten)—was another thorn in the side of the new program. Shirer continued to write about getting tough with Nazi prisoners and made the Special Projects Division nervous for a time. However, by fall, the SPD decided Shirer's articles were more help than hindrance. Any suspicious POW who read a newspaper column by Shirer would be convinced that the United States Army was doing absolutely nothing to influence the thinking of POWs.

While the War Department stayed silent about the launching of its re-education program, it did make an effort to publicize how well POWs were being used to ease the labor shortage across the country. An article in the *Birmingham Post* on July 15 noted that the prisoner of war program in the Fourth Service Command was being expanded with more branch camps. According to Captain Richard E. Smith, the reason for this expansion was "not merely the anticipation of additional prisoners being sent into this country but rather to increase the working efficiency of the men as laborers by having camps situated near the places where the need for their services is greatest." Captain Smith commented that the prisoners being held in Alabama were willing to work and were interested in their jobs. He noted that many were mechanically inclined and enjoyed working with machinery.

Another article appeared in *The Birmingham Age-Herald* in September noting that the forty thousand prisoners held by the Fourth Service Command had performed labor worth more than $3 million from May through July. Major General Frederick E. Uhl reported that private contractors had paid the United States Treasury $418,628 above the amounts that would be paid out to the prisoners in canteen coupons—money that would help cover the cost of their care. The main point was that instead of being coddled, prisoners were being put to work and were performing jobs that would help save the American economy.

On September 6, the re-education program was officially inaugurated. Its greatest effects would not be felt in Camp Aliceville until November, but subtle changes began taking place in August and September that suggest some of its policies were already being implemented. On August 1, a study room stocked with two thousand textbooks opened in Compound A—the textbooks no doubt selected and/or reviewed carefully by the camp staff to reflect American values. On August 14, the camp received a microphone and two record players that would make it easier to stage major cultural performances on the stage in Compound A.

On September 4, the official prison school, which would issue credit certificates for completed studies, opened in Camp Aliceville. Classes of all kinds had been conducted at the camp ever since those early weeks in June 1943 when Walter Felholter and Hermann Blumhardt decided to study English, but both camp spokesman Walter Meier and the American officers of the camp wanted to establish an official school accredited enough that the

POWs would be able to apply what they learned in Aliceville towards degrees and work permits when they returned home.

Certainly, the government's plans for the re-education program played a large role in promoting the opening of the official camp school at this time. Forty different day classes, 82 evening classes, and 46 study groups would now be offered by 179 POW instructors. More than twenty-four hundred POWs signed up to attend.

The Intellectual Diversion Program would also encourage opportunities for self-study in democracy, history, civics, and the English language. Idealistically, the Provost Marshal General's Office suggested that "The success of this type of re-education is guaranteed by the essential truth of the materials presented.... Truth, unlike false propaganda, speaks for itself and is sustained by events."

It is interesting to note that the Approved Periodical Number for *Der Zaungast* came through at exactly the same time as the official inauguration of the re-education program. Another commitment of the Intellectual Diversion Program was to encourage (and closely monitor) individual camp newspapers and also to create a national German POW newspaper (*Der Ruf*—The Call) that would give anti-Nazi prisoners a forum for their views. The PMGO also made a point of reminding those implementing the re-education program that, although POWs were to be sent home to Germany with a sense of respect and appreciation for the United States and its values, they were not to be encouraged to remain here or to return as immigrants once they were released.

Whether or not the replacement of Sergeant Major Walter Meier as camp spokesman was connected to the inauguration of the re-education program is not clear. Sometime between mid-September and mid-October, Walter Meier was replaced by *Hauptwachtmeister* (Master Sergeant) Johannes Bogdan, who had been a minister in civilian life.

When October arrived, Adolf Hitler and the "German People's Court" made their decision about the fate of Field Marshal Erwin Rommel. Two SS generals arrived at his home on October 14 and offered him two distasteful options. Rommel chose the second option and explained to his fifteen-year-old son Manfred,

> I have just had to tell your mother that I shall be dead in a quarter of an hour. To die by the hand of one's own people is hard. But the house is surrounded and Hitler is charging me with high treason. In view of my services in Africa, I am to have the chance of dying by poison. The two generals have brought it with them. It's fatal in three seconds. If I accept, none of the usual steps will be taken against my family. I'd be given a state funeral. It's all been prepared to the last detail. In a quarter of an hour, you will receive a call from the hospital in Ulm to say that I've had a brain seizure on the way to a conference.

Rommel then left the house with his son, who remembers how loud the gravel crunched under their feet as they went through the garden gate. The two generals saluted and said, "Herr Field Marshal." Rommel then shoved his Marshal's baton under his left arm, shook his son's hand, and got into the waiting car. Manfred watched the car drive quickly off up a hill. He learned later that it stopped just a few hundred yards away so Rommel could end his life with a cyanide pill. Hitler ordered a period of national mourning throughout Germany, and Rommel was buried with full military honors.

It was announced that Rommel died of complications from the wounds he'd received in July when the Canadian Air Force Spitfire pilot strafed his staff car in Normandy. Rommel's family and close friends knew the truth, but they were threatened with severe punishment if they revealed it in any way.

Heinrich Most remembers that prisoners at Camp Aliceville were shocked to learn of the death of the fifty-three-year-old field marshal. The news spread like wildfire, and POWs had no trouble getting permission to hold a memorial service for Rommel because American staff members were also deeply touched by his death. Even though he was an enemy, Rommel was greatly admired for his intelligence and strategy. American newspapers wrote of him:

> His name will always remain bound to the two-year heroic fight of the German tank corps in Africa.... He was the master of mobile warfare, the brilliant tactician, a general of headstrong will and magnificent capabilities—experienced, strong and brave, quick and fearless, German in his thoroughness in the planning of lightning quick decisions in battle—above all, a leader who inspired his troops to the highest accomplishments.

On Wednesday evening, October 25, 1944, huge searchlights—probably borrowed from the guard towers—illuminated the soccer field in Compound D. The bright lights swept a hastily erected speakers' platform and paused on each sweep to highlight a gigantic portrait of Rommel painted that week by POW artists who depicted the Desert Fox in full uniform with all of his war decorations.

According to Heinrich Most, several American officers attended the memorial service with their families, and a number of Aliceville citizens also attended. Members of the former *Afrikakorps* marched onto the soccer field dressed in their preserved uniforms and polished boots to pay their respects to the fallen leader. The service began with a speech by the new camp spokesman, Johannes Bogdan. A Catholic priest and a Lutheran minister who served as POW chaplains offered prayers, and everyone present joined in reciting The Lord's Prayer—in German and in English. One of the American officers (which one is not recorded) also gave a brief speech and emphasized, like the other speakers, the merits of Rommel the man and his leadership qualities.

The camp orchestra played off and on throughout the service and ended it with accompaniment for the singing of "*Ich Hatt einen Kameraden*," (Once I Had a Comrade), which was always sung at German military funerals.

This song, roughly translated below, evoked for German soldiers the close dedication they felt to each other on the battlefield:

Ich hatt einen Kameraden, einen bessern finst du nit

Die Trommel schlug zum Streite, er ging an meiner Seite im gleichen Schritt und Tritt.

Eine Kugel kam geflogen, gilt sie mir oder gilt sie dir?
Ihn hat es weggerissen, er liegt zu meinen Füssen, als war's ein Stück von mir.

Once I had a comrade, and a better one you could not find.
The drum beat to battle, and he was at my side, marching in the same rhythm.
A bullet came flying—meant for me or meant for you?
It snatched him away, and he lay at my feet as if he were a part of me.

The issue of *Der Zaungast* published a few days later contained two articles about Field Marshal Rommel. One was a general remembrance of his life. The other recounted the memorial service, noting that "if ever there was a relationship between leader and followers in battle, pure and clearly formed, it was with the great general and his troops in North Africa. He could require gallant determination and often superhuman actions from his regiments because he was, in all things, a soldierly example." The author of this piece, who signed it simply "B.," was probably Camp Spokesman Bogdan. He wrote that when the assembled POWs began singing *"Ich Hatt einen Kameraden,"* all of them thought about how difficult the struggle had become now for their country. Thoughts about Rommel, he wrote, should remind the POWs to be victors over the pressures of everyday life in captivity.

Apparently two Aliceville POWs found the pressures of captivity too much to handle. On Monday evening, October 16, during the week before the Rommel memorial service, Hans Becker and Claus Hoyer managed to slip out of Camp Aliceville and make their way to the swamps of the Tombigbee River seven miles away. There is no record of exactly how they escaped, but perhaps the borrowing of searchlights and the preoccupation of camp personnel with planning the memorial service made it easier.

The *Pickens County Herald and West Alabamian* went to press while the two POWs were still at large. The newspaper printed physical descriptions and noted that both had recently been transferred to Camp Aliceville. Neither spoke any English. The newspaper also reported that, on Tuesday morning, Becker and Hoyer had asked for food at the home of a negro [*sic*] living eight miles south of the camp.

After sixty hours of battling mammoth mosquitoes and increasing hunger, and listening to haunting owl hoots echoing over the swamps in the darkness, the two POWs surrendered willingly just before sundown on Wednesday evening.

The headline in the *Birmingham Post* on Friday, October 20, read "Tight FBI Net Foils Flight of War Prisoners." Special Agent R.J. Abbaticchio Jr. told the newspaper he was proud that the capture of Becker and Hoyer preserved the record of the Alabama FBI—no POWs had escaped and crossed the Alabama state line since the prisoner of war camps opened. He described an intensive search by FBI agents and military authorities on Tuesday and Wednesday.

Abbaticchio praised the cooperation of local law enforcement officers and patriotic citizens in recapturing the only six prisoners who had escaped from any of the nine permanent POW camps in Alabama. He described the aftermath of an escape earlier that summer when Dothan area citizens chased down a German prisoner in a wooded area and surrounded him with dogs, rakes, pitchforks, and whatever else was handy until military authorities arrived.

"Recaptured prisoners of war give many explanations for their escapes," Mr. Abbaticchio explained. "One declared that he had an uncontrollable longing to get out in the woods and pick wild flowers. He had a bouquet in his hands when captured. Another said he wanted to go sightseeing so that when he returned to Germany after the end of the war he would be able to tell his friends what he saw in America."

The War Department's re-education program went into full operation at Camp Aliceville in November with the appointment of Lieutenant Harrison W. Gessling as AEO (Assistant Executive Officer)—the title that designated (but did not identify for the public or the POWs) the person who would become the backbone of the educational program at each POW camp. Lieutenant Gessling spoke fluent German. He was one of 150 AEOs appointed to camps across the country. Part of his job was to gain gradual control of classroom activities, carefully reviewing all books that came into the camp and seeking opportunities to include information about democratic theory in subject matter.

A new camp commander, Colonel R.S. Grier, arrived at Camp Aliceville in October or November. Though he would not officially replace Colonel Waite until January, Grier—formerly commanding officer at Camp McCain in Mississippi—was obviously part of the transition to a re-education based camp system. Historian E.B. Walker has noted that Grier had a reputation for "being fair yet demanding," and that he was "well versed in the intent and purpose of the Intellectual Diversion Program."

When Werner Tobler revisited Camp Aliceville for the Legation of Switzerland on November 3 and 4, he reported that the camp was again nearing full capacity with close to six thousand POWs in residence. Tobler also reported that Aliceville was now almost entirely "a non-working non-com camp" with no more outside work contracts like those with Johnny Johnston's sawmill or Elmo Owens' cotton fields. Tobler commented that most of the NCOs were not willing to work and that the sixty-five men who were working for pay were all working inside the camp. He expected that an additional forty men were about to be employed for pay as teachers in the expanding educational program.

One of the tragedies of Aliceville's World War II experience began to unfold on November 2 when John Griffin was captured during the Battle of Hürtgen Forest. John's combat engineering regiment had cleared mines and built Bailey bridges from Omaha Beach all the way to Paris before moving east through Belgium to this triangular section of forest just over the German border. Although the Battle of the Bulge, which came a little later, received far more publicity, the series of battles fought in the Hürtgen Forest between September and December 1944 was just as bloody and costly. The ground was frozen, and snow hid many ingenious booby traps and mines that men like John Griffin were expected to find and disarm. The area included parts of the *Westwall* (the Siegfried Line) system of trenches, bunkers, and pillboxes that Wilhelm Schlegel and Hermann Blumhardt had helped dismantle as part of their RAD service. The Germans had abandoned the Siegfried Line after their successful invasion of France but were now reoccupying and defending it as they fled Allied troops advancing from Normandy.

As Carl Heintze described them for a California newspaper fifty-six years later, these were battles often fought on both sides by replacement infantrymen with little combat experience. "Tragically, everyone fought in what was described by one participant as a green hell for the wrong reasons in the most difficult of climates and places.... Unlike D-Day it was neither a turning point nor the beginning or the end of anything."

It was during one of these battles that shrapnel from an exploding mine tore into John Griffin's leg. He went down and was soon captured by German troops. A German doctor in a field hospital probably saved John's life when he removed the shrapnel and treated the wound before John was shipped to a German POW camp. He would remain there until the camp was liberated by Russian troops many months later.

John Griffin had a sister named Bee who was a nurse in the hospital at Camp Aliceville. He also had a younger brother, Thomas Napoleon Griffin, who was known to everyone as Nap. On November 9, when news of John's capture reached Aliceville, a German POW named Hulwaz presented Bee Griffin (now Bee Griffin Musso) with a beautiful and serene painting of a waterfall. The gift was perhaps meant to help her deal with the anxiety of knowing her brother had been wounded and captured. Nap Griffin decided immediately that he could not sit in high school classrooms for another semester while his brother was a prisoner overseas—even though he knew he could get an army deferment because of his brother's service. Nap withdrew from school and enlisted, hoping he would be shipped to Germany and could somehow search for his brother.

Just a few days before John Griffin's capture in the Hürtgen Forest, Robert Hugh Kirksey and his "Railsplitters" unit of the 84th Infantry crossed the English Channel on an elderly Belgian ship named the *Leopoldville.* This ship got them safely to the landing area at Omaha Beach but was destroyed two months later, on Christmas Eve, by a single torpedo from a German U-boat. The ship sank five miles from Cherbourg, with a loss of 760 lives.

Robert Hugh saw great devastation during the next ten days as the 84th moved two hundred miles east towards Germany. He remembers the impact of realizing that he was now headed directly to a place where artillery shells and bullets were being fired—"where people were planning to kill you; and you had to kill them, or be killed yourself."

Allied commanders had been energized by the successful landings in Normandy, but in the late fall and winter of 1944, their troops were bogging down in the push to invade Germany itself. Robert Hugh discovered that his platoon was to take part in a large-scale attack on the German fortifications known as The Siegfried Line (the *Westwall*), not too far north of where John Griffin had been captured. In his memoirs, Robert Hugh summed up the situation they faced: "We would be the attackers. They would be the defenders, skillfully entrenched in their interconnecting system of concrete and steel bunkers, with their trenches and communication lines running in between. They would be on the high ground. We would be coming across the open ground and running uphill."

When the attack began on November 21, the objective was a pillbox up a hill on the other side of a sugar beet field. Robert Hugh and his platoon began the assault but did not receive expected cover from artillery or flame-throwing tanks that were bogged down in rain and mud. Eventually, Robert Hugh and five others were trapped under a small overhang below the pillboxes. When a German mortar shell exploded almost on top of them, Robert Hugh was wounded more seriously than he realized. He gave the order for each man to make it back across the field on his own.

Robert Hugh Kirksey had a wound in his jaw and nerve damage in his left arm. He was evacuated the next morning on the hood of a jeep and then traveled by army ambulance to a field hospital in Holland. Eventually, he would receive both the Silver Star and the Purple Heart for his service.

As he bumped along in the back of the ambulance on November 22, Robert Hugh was surprised to discover several wounded German prisoners lined up side by side with wounded American soldiers. "Less than twelve hours ago, we were dedicated to killing each other," he thought. "Now they lie us down, side by side."

Every day let us work for peace with our mind and heart. Each person should begin with himself.

• inscription on the Bridge at Remagen •
rededicated in 1980 as a Memorial to Peace
honoring American, Belgian, British, and German
soldiers who died there.
Thomas Napoleon Griffin of Aliceville, Alabama
was one of those soldiers. Former German POWs
Bruno Schneider and Theo Klein adopted
this inscription as a theme for their lives.

CHAPTER THIRTEEN
Balloons and Perspectives

By December 1944, Margie Archibald had left her job at Aliceville Bank and Trust to become a civilian employee at Camp Aliceville. She worked in the camp hospital where Mary Lu Turner's mother worked. Margie had to check in at the main guard gate each morning and then walk on through a double-fenced walkway to the hospital.

She was always properly dressed for work—high-heeled shoes and a tailored suit or dress—and she was often running late. She remembers hurrying along many mornings while prisoners reporting to the hospital for treatment were walking the same route on the outside of the protected walkway.

One morning, she became aware that a POW with a big, shiny black crow on his shoulder was watching her. He'd caught the crow and turned it into a pet, and he'd often bragged about teaching it to speak German. Margie saw the POW whisper something to the crow. Suddenly it flew over the protective fences, landed on Margie's shoulder, and began to peck at her hair. While the Germans stood by and laughed, she froze. "It scared me to death," she has said. "The one German we were allowed to talk to was the Master Sergeant who worked in the hospital. He heard the laughter and came outside, and then he just blessed them out, and they called the crow away."

Margie remembers that the camp hospital had separate wards for prisoners and for soldiers needing treatment. The building also had a personnel office, the surgeon's office, a finance office, and a huge mess hall with beautiful scenic murals on the walls, painted by prisoners. The American medical doctors ate at tables on one side of the mess hall, and the German doctors on the other. It was the same with patients who were well enough to come to the mess hall for meals—American patients ate on one side and German patients on the other.

Civilian employees of the hospital—like Margie Archibald, Mary Turner, and Sue Stabler, who'd taken a job as a typist—ate lunch in the middle section of the mess hall and enjoyed it. "We didn't have coffee at home, we didn't have sugar, or very little, and no steaks, so we just felt like we were really something to have that great meal there."

Elma Henders was still the dietician, and Margie often went to the kitchen on her break to have coffee with Elma. When the camp first opened, the POWs who worked in the kitchen had been mortified to discover they would be working for a woman, but now they were as gracious as could be, and they worked hard, too. Margie smiled as she watched them fall all over themselves to open the refrigerator door for Elma or carry the larger crates of produce.

One morning, as the two young women visited, sipping precious cups of coffee at a small side table, one of the POWs approached and mumbled in heavily accented English, "*Fräulein*, I have a picture of you, and I need to show it to you. Your mouth is too big, I think."

This was after the crow incident, and the man's approach scared Margie. She couldn't imagine what he meant. "No, you don't," she said. She stood up to leave, and the POW became flustered. He motioned for another prisoner to join the conversation and began speaking in quick German.

"Please, Miss," the other POW explained in better English. "He wants to tell you that the American officer you are dating gave him your snapshot and asked him to do a sketch of you, but he thinks he has done it with the mouth too big."

The sketch was to have been a surprise. No longer frightened, Margie looked at the delicately penciled portrait and was pleased with the way it highlighted her long curly hair and her fine cheekbones. She didn't think it made her mouth look too big. She accepted the portrait, and it was something she kept among her belongings long after the camp closed.

Corporal George Bristow arrived at Camp Aliceville in December 1944 when more large groups of POWs were being processed in from the battlefields in France. George had had rheumatic fever as a child and was not rated for combat. When his unit of the 100th Division left Tennessee to ship out for overseas, he worked for a while in an officers' mess and then was sent to Aliceville. Because he could not climb up and down from the surveillance towers, he was assigned to maintain order in two of the compounds.

Some of the POWs worked all over the camp grounds during the day, tending gardens or doing maintenance and other jobs. In the evening, one of George's responsibilities was a roll call to make sure everyone was back in his compound. Occasionally, one or two POWs would be missing.

George says it was not difficult to find them. They all knew that the "Toonerville Trolley" (the cartoon strip nickname for the AT&N Railroad line that ran right in front of the camp) chugged on down to New Orleans after it passed through Aliceville. If the POWs managed to slip out of camp, they always walked close to the road that followed those tracks. "We'd call in the FBI and go after them. We were always pretty sure just where they would go, and sure enough, we'd run across a farm or two, check the barn, and there they'd be."

George developed a good rapport with his German charges. They often cooked breakfast for him in their company mess hall. He had a small office at the front of one compound and a German assistant who spoke English. The assistant was quite young. One day he asked George the question other POWs had asked after traveling by train from New York down to Aliceville. "How did you rebuild your cities so well and so quickly?" Like other German soldiers, he'd been told that the German Air Force had repeatedly bombed American cities and caused severe damage.

George enjoyed visiting with prisoners all over the camp. "Each compound had some kind of specialty. One had a place where plays could be presented, and another had the band shell. Another had the sports area for soccer, which was very, very popular. Whenever there was an event, they'd have quite a turnout."

POW artist Hermann Kalbe once gave him a hand-painted picture of a Camp Aliceville guard tower with flowers growing beneath it. Kalbe had painted it on a shirt cardboard. "It's beautiful. His name is on the back, and it is dated 1945." George also kept a desk nameplate another POW made for him and a small vanity box. "They never asked for anything in return. They were paid by the government, and they had their own PX where they could buy what they wanted."

The camp commanders cautioned him and other soldiers to stay out of the "colored section" of town, and he remembers that some did and some didn't. Once, George took a truckload of eight or nine Germans through Aliceville to a nursery so they could buy shrubbery for camp landscaping. He sat up front with the driver, and the Germans were in the back. When they stopped at the nursery, out near a cotton field, one of the POWs asked George if he could walk over to the other side of the hill. "I'll come right back," he said. George knew what the prisoner had in mind. He wanted the chance to visit the women working in the fields. "I told him no, and that was the end of that. I never had any other trouble there."

On December 4, a thirty-seven-year-old POW named Albert Heinrich Barthelmess collapsed in the shower room of his compound and died of a heart attack. As with other deaths at Camp Aliceville, Gerald Stabler was called to prepare the body for burial. He also helped the POWs hold a brief funeral service in the small area at the back of the camp set aside as a cemetery. After the war, all bodies in this cemetery were exhumed and transferred to the German-Italian Cemetery at Fort McClellan in northern Alabama.

Gerald became well acquainted with a small group of POWs who volunteered for funeral detail whenever there was a death. When one of them saw the "Stabler" nameplate on the hearse Gerald drove, he asked about it, and Gerald told him his ancestors had come to America from Germany. The POW nodded. "We have many Stablers at home," he said.

Christmas 1944 passed in Camp Aliceville with little mention. One of the POWs—perhaps Wilhelm Schlegel—kept a mimeographed copy of the program for a service titled "*Kriegsweihnachten* 1944" (Wartime Christmas 1944) with his copies of *Der Zaungast*. The single sheet is decorated with two Christmas tree sketches and shows that candles were lit, and Christmas music, including Charles Francois Gounod's "Ave Maria" and "*Hohe Nacht der Klaren Sterne*" (Holy Night of the Clear Stars) set to music by Beethoven, were performed—perhaps by the camp orchestra and at least one of the several choirs. There was a sermon, and those attending the service sang the traditional carols "*Stille Nacht, Heilige Nacht*" (Silent Night) and "*O Tannebaum*" (Oh, Christmas Tree).

August Wanders was in the hospital with gastritis most of the month and did not record details about the holiday in his diary. Special packages from home—even those mailed in September and October—did not reach the camp until January and even later. Wilhelm Schlegel mentions receiving three packages from his mother on January 16. She'd mailed the Christmas one on October 18. The anonymous poem about Aliceville found among Maxwell McKnight's personal papers contains a verse (translated) about this situation:

> Aliceville in Alabama, where the mail is always late,
> And a Christmas card in April is always up to date,
> Where we never have a payday and we never have a cent
> But we never miss the money,'cause we'd never get it spent.

Günther Ertel remembers a letter his wife wrote at Christmas 1944 (though he does not say when he received it). It was his first mail after coming to Camp Aliceville. "The best present ever I got was when I knew you were in the Aliceville prison camp," she wrote. "Now I knew I have not lost my husband."

For the people of Aliceville, Christmas 1944 was a time to stretch rationed sugar and meats as far as possible to create festive meals. Local citizens did not enjoy the same food supplies that the POW camp did. It was a time to pray that, when Christmas 1945 arrived, the war might well be a thing of the past and the many local soldiers might finally be home.

Robert Hugh Kirksey spent his first Christmas away from Aliceville in a military hospital just outside Salisbury in England. He could see the steeple of the town's medieval cathedral from his window and could have visited Stonehenge ten miles away, but even though he was well enough, he did not feel an urge for sightseeing. On Christmas morning, he enjoyed listening to a group of English school children singing Christmas carols up and down the hospital hallways. He still had trouble eating because of his jaw wound and would not receive further treatment for his arm until he finally returned to the United States in February.

Mary Lu Turner Keef remembers that her fifth grade class at Aliceville Elementary School held a gift exchange on the last day before Christmas vacation. Everyone had a great time playing Santa and passing out gifts to each other until the teacher realized that one poorly dressed little girl in the class had not received—or given—any gifts at all. The teacher scolded the rest of the class for not including her and gave the girl a quarter so she could go into Aliceville after school and buy something for herself. "I learned a lesson that day that has stuck with me through life," Mary Lu remembers. "It was the first time I realized that some people are truly less fortunate than others—I mean, sometimes during the war, we only had a bowl of rice with raisins in it for supper, but we always had a roof over our head and didn't want for much of anything. Many times, especially at Christmas, I wonder where that little girl is, and my heart aches to think how cruel we were without realizing it."

Beginning in mid-December 1944, a series of mischievous incidents occurred at Camp Aliceville. These incidents have been recorded in various ways, depending on perspective and individual memory. Wilhelm Schlegel wrote in his diary that one of the men from his barracks (Company 16 in Compound D) "went over to the Americans" along with two other POWs from Company 13 on December 12. Basically, this meant the men had decided to become anti-Nazi and therefore were considered turncoats, which put them in danger of physical harm in their own compound.

In order to protect the three men until they could be transferred to an anti-Nazi camp, the American guards locked them in a detention barracks, which was fenced off by itself in the same block of buildings as the camp morgue, the dental clinic, the boiler house, and some of the administration offices. Since the "jail" had no kitchen facilities, Compound D company kitchens were expected to continue to supply meals for these men. Wilhelm Schlegel wrote in his diary that "naturally" the cooks for Company 16 and Company 13 refused to do so. From their point of view, it was a matter of national pride not to feed "deserters."

When word came down that these two companies would be punished with bread and water rations beginning the next morning, the men began to hoard whatever they could. "They tried to hide a lot of food—under the beds and stuff—so we had to call in the guards," George Bristow remembers. "The guards looked high and low for food in the barracks, and of course, if they found it, they took it away. They kept checking for several days." Some of the guards overstepped their orders and slit open bedding or tore up personal items as they searched. "They did so much damage, and it was utterly ridiculous what they did, but I guess they felt happy doing it."

The gates into Compound D were closed the next morning for the first time in almost exactly a year, and Lieutenant Gessling, current Assistant Executive Officer of Camp Aliceville, spoke to an assembly of POWs from all six compounds at noon. The situation seemed to calm down, at least for a week or two.

Then, on December 30, tensions flared once more. The gates between the various compounds were shut again, and American guards were sent in to replace POWs who'd been handling internal security. Companies 13 and 16 were again placed on bread and water rations while Companies 14 and 15, whose kitchens were close by, continued to receive full provisions. Earline Lewis Jones remembers this incident because she was the person in the Quartermaster's Office who was notified not to supply anything but bread and water to the two companies.

"That was the punishment for little things that happened around the compounds, but it didn't ever last too many days," she has said.

As a disciplinary action, a two-and-a-half hour roll call was held at noon on December 30 and another roll call at five o'clock that evening. In defiance, several members of Company 13 did not step up. Four American officers came in to restore order, and one POW threw bread at the feet of an American sergeant. Wilhelm Schlegel commented in his diary that this was nonsense—not a good thing to do.

That evening, the Company 14 kitchen managed to slip good noodle soup and cutlets to the two bread and water companies. The Company 14 kitchen also provided donuts made with flour, which Wilhelm and the others ate with coffee before dawn the next morning.

On New Year's Eve day, the prisoners of Company 16 played handball against the prisoners of Company 14. Wilhelm described the game as a contest of "the hungry against the full" and wrote that the game ended in a 13 to 13 tie.

About 8:30 that evening, after the sun dropped below the horizon, a shadowy figure slipped out of the mess hall in Compound F with a small sack over his shoulder. There was no "dead zone" along the fences between the compounds, and this figure knew exactly where he could slip easily underneath the single fence behind the mess hall and into Compound E. His name was Heinrich Müller. He'd only been in Camp Aliceville since the summer, having been captured at Normandy, but he knew that Wilhelm Schlegel, who was from the same area of Germany that he was, was in Compound D.

Heinrich walked calmly and quickly between the barracks and across the grounds of Compound E and then made a quick slip under another single fence and into Compound D. He'd heard about the bread and water punishment and was worried about his friend from home. Heinrich delivered bread, two tins of milk, and some cornflakes because he was afraid Wilhelm was starving to death. He also delivered cans of potatoes with sauce and sausage.

After the "feast," Heinrich hurried away to his own compound. Wilhelm watched him slip back under the fences and then wrote in his diary that he wished Heinrich everything good in the New Year.

George Bristow and the other American guards did not allow the residents of the two companies in Compound D to celebrate New Year's Eve. All appeared to be quiet and calm as they patrolled. About midnight, in the darkness inside the barracks, the company leader for Company 13 moved through the barracks and wished all of his men *Ein Glückliches Neues Jahr.*

When dawn came—for the new day and for the new year of 1945—it appeared that, in spite of the order not to celebrate, some mischief had been afoot during the night, and not just in Compound D. Someone (Wilhelm did not record who) had managed to unfurl a flag bearing a Nazi swastika from the railing of the guard tower at the end of the street that went down between the compounds. Wilhelm did record that an American guard brought the flag down quickly and made a point of using it to shine his shoes. Under their breath, the German POWs had a good chuckle over this, which they viewed as a little New Year's fun with their captors in spite of the order not to celebrate.

The American guards, who were charged with keeping order, were not so quick to see the humor. For Americans, the swastika (*Hakenkreuz*)—a rigid cross with arms bent at right angles in a clockwise direction—was a flash point symbol of the enemy and of the fascism and racism they associated with Hitler. Its display, unlike other symbols of German heritage, was forbidden in the camps.

Determining that the swastika flag had been unfurled by someone from Compound F, the guards located the spokesman for that compound and locked him up in the detention barracks as punishment. They also took action against Company 13 in Compound D, confiscating the mattresses of those who'd refused to step up for roll call the previous day and posting a guard outside the company's barracks to quell further nonsense.

The POWs, like adolescents who've discovered how to yank the chain of their elders, decided to carry their fun a bit further. August Wanders does not record the next incident in his diary, but his daughter Ellen distinctly remembers stories he told her about the balloons that floated through the skies over Aliceville in early January 1945. She says the POWs in Compound F were sitting around thinking about what they could do to create a little more mischief. "So they started to make balloons, and they painted the balloons with the faces of three men—Hitler, Göring, and someone else, I don't remember who." Ellen says they sent the lighted balloons up into the sky and considered it great fun. "They were kidding around, but they were also careful not to tell anybody who did it. It was a secret, and none of them were caught."

Wilhelm Schlegel wrote that a balloon went up at 12:30 on the afternoon of January 3 with a large swastika flag hanging beneath it. It came, he wrote, from Compound F. Robert Mitterwallner remembers the balloon incident, too. He says those who created the balloons used FLIT oil as fuel to get them up in the air. He also remembers that the American guards in charge of Compounds E and F got in trouble with their commanders for allowing the incident to happen.

FLIT, an insecticide used to control adult mosquitoes, would have been ubiquitous at Camp Aliceville and anywhere else in the town of Aliceville. It could be sprayed into the air and also sprayed on surfaces where mosquitoes might land.

Another probably exaggerated version of these incidents is recorded by a man named W. Sell who wrote that his father told him the stories. As Sell relates it, his father and other POWs created a kite with a small box attached to it and two long strings hanging down. On a nice, windy afternoon, they began flying the kite from an open area in their compound. The guards were watching and seemed pleased that the men were amusing themselves with harmless fun.

After about twenty minutes, when the kite was high over the camp, one of the POWs handed the second string to a guard and asked him to pull it. When the guard did, thousands of tiny paper swastikas (which the prisoners had sat up cutting out by hand during the previous several evenings) floated down over the camp and even out over the town of Aliceville. According to Sell, the camp commander was furious, especially after townspeople began calling and complaining. When he marched into the compound and demanded to know who was responsible, the POWs pointed to the oblivious guard who was still holding the string. They were laughing so hard, they had tears in their eyes.

Wilhelm Schlegel makes a brief reference to kites in his diary as well. He says that after the Compound F spokesman was locked up and the mattresses confiscated in Company 13, the POWs in Compounds B and E "let the kites fly," perhaps as a gesture of support for the other compounds.

Sell says the POWs struck again a little later, this time sending up a balloon they'd made from four stolen bed sheets, three buckets of paint, a wooden bucket, and some coal. They applied enough coats of paint to the sheets to keep the hot air from escaping through them. They filled the bucket with coals, attached the sheet balloon, lit the coals, and sent it off with a large, homemade Nazi flag flying on top. Sell's father told him the balloon performed better than expected, sailing off over Aliceville and then some fifty miles away where the United States Air Corps finally shot it down and then returned for a victory roll over Camp Aliceville. Although rations were temporarily reduced to half, the POWs considered the fun worth the punishment.

Exactly what happened—or how many times—will probably never be unraveled from the amusing stories passed down by former POWs and former guards, but the nature of the incidents certainly rings true. Wilhelm Schlegel noted in his diary that Colonel Waite was replaced on January 1 as a direct result of the New Year's Eve mischief. He stated that a Major Braun would take his place.

It probably appeared that way to the POWs, who were delighted to believe their mischief had created such havoc; however, camp records do not support this version of the end of Colonel Waite's military career. Colonel R.S. Grier had arrived at Camp Aliceville in October as the announced successor to Colonel Waite. It was a similar transition to the one from Colonel Prince to Colonel Waite in September 1943 when Colonel Waite spent several weeks observing the camp operation before officially becoming commander.

Colonel Grier assumed formal command of Camp Aliceville on January 10, and Colonel Waite retired from active duty at that point. Wilhelm Schlegel's reference to a "Major Braun" taking Colonel Waite's place probably refers to Major W. R. Brown who was and had been the camp's executive officer since the previous year.

In Wilhelm's version of these incidents, Heinrich Müller supplied a second food contribution to his friend on the evening of January 4, this time a tin of milk and a slice of bread and butter sent through a POW named Gustav Becker. Undoubtedly, others received supplies in similar ways.

The bread and water punishment ended on January 6, and once again, the gates of Compound D were opened. The men of Company 13 were allowed to return to the dining room that evening. Before the meal, their company leader offered thanks for the comradely behavior of those in Compound F who had smuggled provisions to them throughout the punishment. He expressed hope that there were no more turncoats in Company 13.

In northern Europe, what came to be called the Battle of the Bulge began on December 16 with a surprise German counter-offensive in a region called the Ardennes. Colonel Karl Shriver, who had overseen the construction of Camp Aliceville, saw action in this battle.

Taking advantage of foggy weather that grounded Allied aircraft, the Germans broke through a thinly held American front and pushed nearly thirty miles back into Belgium. Their goal was to divide American and British troops and retake the port of Antwerp. They succeeded in creating a "bulge" in the Allied line of advance, but when the skies cleared and Allied planes again took to the air just before Christmas, the German advance slowed. Captain Stephen Fleck, who had treated Camp Aliceville POWs for diphtheria, had been sent to Europe by this time and was put in charge of more than eighty thousand German POWs captured during this fighting.

There was no immediate Allied victory, however. It took until the end of January to eliminate the "bulge," and Allied troops did not attempt to enter Germany again until February.

On December 17, a massacre of American combat prisoners occurred near the town of Malmedy in Belgium. Although there are conflicting accounts of what actually happened, it is clear that approximately 150 American soldiers who'd been disarmed by German SS troops were standing in a snowy field near a crossroads in zero degree winter weather. They were standing with their hands in the air when their captors opened fire, killing at least eighty of them. Exactly why this happened is also unclear, but news of the Malmedy massacre, as it came to be called, spread quickly among Allied troops. The order came down to shoot all SS troops on sight.

As the war moved into 1945, it was this incident along with a number of others that caused American officials to lose faith in their policy of treating German POWs fairly. The "Golden Rule" of the Geneva Convention was tarnishing.

Wendell Parrish of Selma, Alabama, was still being held at *Stalag Luft IV* in East Prussia. As an Air Force staff sergeant, he was not required to work. He and the others in his compound sometimes batted around the one softball or kicked the one soccer ball, but they spent most of their days walking in circles in the cold to keep warm and talking about home. Wendell's crewmate William Black wrote of this time: "The human mind knows no bounds when it comes to exercising the imagination, and while some few were surrendering to despair and hopelessness, a greater number of us managed to create a state of make-believe in which we acted out various and sundry roles depicting a far better, happier existence than that with which we were actually coping."

There were no organized activities, but the Red Cross had stocked a library, so Wendell often read three or four books a day, huddled on his bunk. He also wrote a postcard to his wife each week and put it in the sack of outgoing mail.

Once, the camp commander allowed the men to bank some snow and add water to create an ice pond. There were two pairs of ice skates for the two thousand men in that compound, and they took turns passing long hours on the ice.

Wendell's wife only received two of the cards he sent during the whole time he was in captivity. She'd been notified on

September 4 that he was a POW in Germany, two days after she gave birth to a healthy son. Wendell knew nothing about the child because he did not receive any of her letters. In fact, she'd sent far more than letters—packages once each week containing gloves and sweaters and other items she thought might be of use. Wendell received none of the packages.

To some extent, he was able to keep up with news of the war because British Intelligence bribed a German guard to use a fake fountain pen for smuggling in news reports from the British Broadcasting Corporation. Wendell's crewmate William Black described how this worked:

> At intervals of about once a week we would receive these reports which would be passed from room to room and read in low tones by one of our number, while precautions were being taken to assure that our guards were not eavesdropping. When all had heard the reports read, they were burned.

Because of these reports, there was a good deal of hope of rescue, except when news of the Battle of the Bulge reached the camp. Morale sank at that point until news began to trickle in late in January that the Allies were finally recapturing territory they'd lost temporarily.

Like Camp Aliceville, *Stalag Luft IV* had a "dead zone" perimeter twenty feet from the outer fence. Any prisoner who entered that zone could be shot on sight. Also like Aliceville, there were barbed wire inner fences that separated the four compounds, which held a total of eight thousand prisoners.

On Christmas Day 1944, the German commander decided to let the prisoners celebrate by walking to the barbed wire inner fence and visiting with POWs in the other compounds. This was not a small thing to the prisoners of *Stalag Luft IV*. The men greeted each other eagerly, each group having known about the others but having had no contact. From time to time, "Ohio" would ring out across the wire or "Kansas" as each POW searched for some small touch from home.

When Wendell stepped up and hollered out "Alabama," he heard a voice in another compound shout back, "What city?" When he hollered back "Selma," he was dumbfounded to see Charlie Cosby, a boy he'd grown up with, emerge from the ragtag crowd pressing near the other side of the barbed wire. Charlie had been shot down in October.

The coincidence was almost too much, but there was more. "Wendell, you have a son," his classmate shouted back. "I saw your wife and the boy just before I came over here, and they're doing fine." That news was the finest Christmas present Wendell ever received. Relief and hope filled his heart. Later in the day came another present—the first set of Red Cross packages he and the others in his compound had received since October.

The German POWs in Camp Aliceville were allowed to hold their New Year's celebration on January 20, after calm had been restored. Wilhelm Schlegel wrote that Company 16 beat Company 13 two goals to one in a game of soccer that day. "In the evening," he added, "we held our New Year's program which had been denied to us at New Year's. The evening was very nice."

The next day, Captain William F. Raugast arrived at Camp Aliceville for an inspection. The Field Service Report of his visit focused on the Intellectual Diversion Program and its effect on the camp. Aliceville was currently holding 5,931 German NCOs and seven officers (the medical team).

Captain Raugast reported that Colonel Grier was "well versed in the intent and purpose of this program" and that he was giving the new AEO (Assistant Executive Officer), Captain Raymond A. Speiser, a free hand in carrying it out. Speiser was one of the AEOs specially trained by the office of the Provost Marshal General in Washington to implement new "democratic principles education" in the camp. He spoke fluent German and was supposed to appear to the POWs as simply an interpreter and an assistant to Colonel Grier.

According to Raugast's report, the new Intellectual Diversion Program was progressing "exceedingly well." Most prisoners had shown an interest in furthering their studies. Adequate classroom facilities, textbooks, and visual aids were available, and the POWs had indicated a desire for lectures to be given in English so they could improve their understanding of the language. A nearby university was providing five short-subject films each week on musical and scientific topics for use in the program. Even though Captain Speiser was in charge, the POWs had their own Director of Studies. Wilhelm Frederick Westhoff, a POW who wrote frequently for *Der Zaungast,* had been a teacher in civilian life and seemed to have accepted this position eagerly. He also taught art as part of the accredited education program. Raugast stated that Westhoff was a university graduate and worked well with the camp administration.

The report declared the library and reading room facilities at Camp Aliceville inadequate but noted a plan underway to move two unused barracks into one of the compounds to house a library. At the time of the report, Camp Aliceville had six thousand volumes, and 60 percent of these were in constant circulation. The PMGO had asked Captain Speiser to submit a list of all books no later than February 5 for review—no doubt to make sure the books complied with the goals of the new Intellectual Diversion Program.

Captain Raugast commented that plenty of newspapers and magazines were available, but he recommended that books from the Modern Library, Pocketbook Editions, and the Infantry Journal-Penguin Series be offered for sale in the camp canteens. These would have been primarily literary classics in American and British literature.

The report mentioned Johannes Bogdan, the camp spokesman who had replaced Walter Meier, and commented that Bogdan had been a minister in civilian life and was cooperative with the camp administration. It also noted that the "general appearance, attitude and morals" of guard personnel were good and that they had their own adequate recreational facilities. A number of orientation courses (presumably about the Intellectual Diversion Program) had been conducted and would continue to be conducted.

The remainder of the report dealt with the camp in general, noting that prisoners now enjoyed two movies each week—one German and one American. It mentioned *Sprachrohr*, the general event calendar published by the POWs, and *Der Zaungast*, which it described as a general information newspaper that included creative writing and articles that were not political in nature.

Indoor and outdoor recreation facilities were well supported by the prisoners. Their main hobbies included woodcarving, wood burning, pottery making, theater, and puppetry as well as leatherwork, sculpture, gardening, and coppersmithing. Captain Raugast noted that there were many artists and painters among the prisoners and suggested arrangements be made to display their work publicly. In addition, the camp now supported a forty-piece orchestra, six smaller bands, and six glee clubs.

On February 6, Wilhelm Schlegel recorded in his diary that Lieutenant Gessling gave a lecture to a large group of POWs about education and the American school system. In the afternoon, an American cultural film was shown.

On that same day in Europe, it was clear that American and British troops were beginning to squeeze Germany from the West while Russian troops closed in from the East. At *Stalag Luft IV*, American POWs had been listening to the thunder of artillery for several days. All of them knew that sound could carry only a certain distance. "Somebody's fighting only twenty miles from here!" Wendell Parrish exclaimed, and he was right. The Russian army was headed in their direction.

During the next several days, German guards loaded the most seriously wounded prisoners onto trains heading west. Then, late on the night of February 6, guards burst into the barracks and announced that the rest of the camp was also evacuating. The prisoners were told to hurry to the warehouse and pack up all the food they could carry. Wendell remembers his bitter surprise when he stepped inside the camp warehouse and stared at the Red Cross packages stacked high against every wall. "There was enough food in there to feed our whole camp for two years."

At midnight, the American prisoners and their guards marched out of *Stalag Luft IV* in four groups—each headed generally west and away from advancing Russian troops. Incredibly, they marched for more than eleven terrible weeks, managing something less than twenty miles a day, often in cold and snow, taking refuge in barns and other structures during the day and trudging on each night. Wendell has estimated they covered something close to eight hundred miles. Other records suggest it was at least six hundred miles between February 6 and April 26.

The details of this dismal and disheartening march—which meandered in a crazy loop that eventually retraced earlier steps—are often unspeakable, like those of the Bataan march in Japan. Wendell remembers that many men died for health reasons—diseases like pneumonia, diphtheria, pellagra, typhus, trench foot, and tuberculosis—brought on by near starvation and lack of sanitation. Stragglers were sometimes led into the woods by guards. As one of the marchers later recalled, "There was a shot, and the German guard came back to the formation alone."

After the first three weeks, guards began disappearing. "The Germans knew by that time that it was lost. They would throw their rifles into the woods and take off," Wendell has said. The prisoners marched on, sticking together and eventually, with great relief and gratitude, encountering the Timberwolf Division of the United States Army which had just taken the German city of Halle after a bitter, five-day struggle. Those few German guards who were still with the American prisoners laid down their weapons and surrendered.

During the first week of February, President Roosevelt traveled to Yalta in the Russian Crimea to confer with Prime Minister Winston Churchill of Great Britain and Premier Joseph Stalin of the USSR. This conference is usually considered the high point of unity among the Allies. When it ended on February 11, a communication known as the Yalta Declaration declared the Allied goal "to destroy German militarism and to ensure that Germany will never again be able to disturb the peace of the world." It promised swift punishment for war criminals and reparations, along with a plan to divide up the postwar occupation of Germany and plan for free elections in former satellites of the Axis powers. There was mention of a "conference of United Nations" to be held in San Francisco in April. Agreed upon at Yalta but not announced until later was the Soviet commitment to declare war on Japan within ninety days of the end of the war in Europe.

The war experiences of the Griffin brothers from Aliceville—John and Nap—were unfolding in Germany at about the same time. John Griffin, who'd been captured in the Battle of Hürtgen Forest, remained inside a German POW camp when Wendell Parrish embarked on the terrible march that eventually led to his liberation. John's younger brother, Nap, who'd enlisted straight from high school in his strong desire to find his brother, had indeed been sent to Germany, but he had not found his brother.

Nap was with American troops when they moved east towards the Rhine River—a natural and psychological barrier to conquering the heartland of Germany. Hitler had ordered the bridges across the Rhine blown up as a defensive measure, but the one near the small town of Remagen, south of Bonn, had been left open so retreating German troops could use it to save some of their tanks and bigger guns from capture by the Allies.

On March 7, an advance unit of the 9th United States Armored Division discovered the bridge. They captured it during intense fighting and in spite of German demolition efforts to destroy it. For the next ten days, before it collapsed into the river, this bridge was used to transport elements of the United States First Army across the Rhine. They set up a sprawling bridgehead between Bonn and Koblenz before the majority of British and American troops crossed on pontoon bridges at other points. The final battles of the war in Europe were beginning.

In a sad irony, Nap Griffin reached the Rhine River at Remagen on March 24 and was killed in fighting there before discovering the whereabouts of his brother. John Griffin was freed in April when a unit of Russian troops liberated the camp where he was being held. In 1955, the National Guard Armory in Aliceville (now the city hall building) was named Fort Griffin in honor of Thomas Napoleon Griffin and his sacrifice for the country and for his family.

In the spring of 1945, a number of factors combined and culminated in drastic changes to the administration of POW camps in the United States. One of those factors was the realization, with the liberation of German POW camps in Europe, that many American POWs, like Wendell Parrish, had received treatment far below the standards of the Geneva Convention. Another factor was the escalating demand for labor to replace the manpower being sent to Europe in the last great push to end that segment of the war.

Some effects of these changes at Camp Aliceville are evident in a report filed on March 11 with the Labor and Liaison Branch of the Provost Marshal General's office. The report clarified that all "troublemaking and non-signing NCOs" in the Fourth Service Command were now being sent either to Aliceville (which was at near capacity again) or to Camp Opelika, also in Alabama.

Major Frank L. Brown, who filed the report, suggested implementing a number of measures to induce these NCOs to sign work contracts. First, he wanted "luxuries" like beer and soft drinks, fruit, and unrationed access to cigarettes removed from the canteens of those who refused to sign. He wanted stricter segregation of troublemakers from potential signers and, where possible and legal, reductions in food supplies. The report notes that a site inside the American sector of the camp was being enclosed with wire so German POWs who signed up to work could be protected there until they could be shipped to branch camps. This enclosure would hold three barracks initially but could be expanded to ten barracks by utilizing nearby vacant buildings.

Major Brown noted that Colonel Grier had changed the utilization of the POWs a great deal since his arrival at Camp Aliceville by substituting POW labor for American labor within the camp. He stated that many POWs were willing to work even though they were psychologically opposed to signing work contracts and that many more of them might sign if they could be guaranteed segregation from the "troublemakers."

He concluded his report with the comment, "The labor potential of this camp is at least 75% of the population (PW), providing the camp CO is given the necessary authority to bear down and make it worthwhile to sign up. SC Hq would have to provide the outlets for the signed POWs as soon as they are recruited." These "outlets" would have been branch camps like the ones at Greenville and Dothan.

At about this same time, George Bristow and another guard drove one of the bands from Camp Aliceville down to the branch camp at Dothan for a performance. The band was excellent and in demand because many of its members had been professional musicians in Germany before the war. The POW musicians rode in the open back of the truck and had great fun waving to the puzzled people in the towns they traveled through. "There was nothing to stop them from jumping out of the truck," George remembers. "We had guns up front, but if we came to a town and there was a red light, they could have jumped and taken off, but at that particular point, they were smart enough to know it wouldn't work."

George was surprised at the luxury and lax security when they arrived at the branch camp. During the week, these prisoners worked hard in the fields, but on Saturdays when the weather was warm enough, they often went swimming and picnicking. Sundays, they went to the movies in town with their guards.

The guards at Camp Aliceville had always been warned not to trust POWs with money for any reason because they would pool it and give to someone who spoke English and could realistically escape. For this reason, George was amazed when he asked for a soft drink, and a POW at the canteen put his hand into his own pocket and pulled out a handful of coins to make change. "I was shocked. I couldn't believe it," George remembers.

On Sunday afternoon, the band and the guards enjoyed a big dinner with the branch camp POWs. Then the band set up for their performance. "Everybody was sitting under the trees, listening to the music, and it was hard to believe, in that setting, that we were at war." The branch camp POWs had set up a bar for the afternoon, and it was surprisingly well stocked. George considered this ridiculous and wondered how an American serviceman, returning from a rough time overseas, would have felt about seeing that. Of course, when the concert was over, those boys in the band had to jump back in the truck so their guards could take them back to Aliceville.

At the end of March, Birmingham news reporter Jack House returned to Camp Aliceville for the first time since he'd covered the arrival of the first German POWs in June 1943. He published an article in *The Birmingham News* on March 25 under the headline, "Nazi Prisoners of War in Alabama Still Bow Before Shrine of Militarism." The subhead read, "Indoctrinated with

Prussian Superman Theory, They Cling to Hope They May Yet Win the War."

On this visit, Jack was amazed at the great physical changes compared with what he viewed as only trivial changes in the mental attitude of the prisoners. In appearance, the camp had gone from "nothing less than a mudhole, a plowed-up cornfield surrounded by swamp lands" to "a well-irrigated and handsomely groomed village of green-painted barracks with green lawns." But the prisoners, he observed, were still as "military-minded" as they had been the day they arrived. Camp Commander Colonel Grier agreed with this assessment.

"Despite good treatment," Jack wrote, "the best provided by the Geneva Convention rules, the prisoners held here and elsewhere in Alabama are as much German soldiers now as they were when firing on British and American troops. They have no more love for the Americans today than they had when they first came to this strange land." This may have been true of many prisoners, but others would prove, again and again, once the war ended and they left Alabama, that the good treatment they received at Camp Aliceville and from the people of Aliceville created fond and even loving memories that would profoundly affect them and even the next generation of their families.

In April, disciplinary supervision tightened even more at Camp Aliceville and at other POW camps around the country. In another effort to induce more German prisoners to sign work contracts, the United States Army sent a directive requiring all German NCOS to prove their rank. Those who could not were "busted" to the rank of private and expected to work.

Karl Berning, an NCO captured in North Africa, was one of the five hundred POWs who did have the paperwork to prove their status. He wrote to his wife on April 8 and expressed the deep concern many POWs felt for their families as they realized that the war was now raging in their hometowns and villages. He expressed his concern "that I am not able to be there with you in these difficult days and lend a helping hand." He reminded her that she was a good German wife and should believe with him in an eventual day of deliverance. He told her he continued to do well at Camp Aliceville but that he worried most now about her safety.

Reinhold Schulte continued to worry about his wife, Herta, and their son, Dieter, who had fled their home in the Ruhr River valley to stay with relatives in Bad Öynhausen. They were out of the industrial area but could still look down and see a factory in the valley below them. One afternoon, as they were sitting outside, Allied bombers came at them, as if directly out of the bright spring sunshine, and began pounding the factory in the valley below. Dieter, who was five years old at the time, remembers this vividly. "The terrifying thing was that, normally, when there was an attack like that, you'd hear the sirens before it started. This time the sirens didn't start until after the attack."

There was a definite sense from that point forward that individuals in Germany were totally on their own as far as protecting themselves. A few days later, the first American soldiers moved through Bad Öynhausen. It was an advance unit of all African-American soldiers, and Dieter laughs as he remembers that he concluded that morning that all American soldiers were black.

German civilians had been ordered to stay inside and keep their doors shut, but that was more self-discipline than a little boy could stand. "I peeked out to see what was happening. A tank was parked outside the house, and the turret gun was pointing right at me. That ended my curiosity."

The death of President Franklin Delano Roosevelt on April 12 was a shock to the American public and to soldiers fighting the war. Roosevelt had been re-elected three times and served longer than any other United States President. He suffered a cerebral hemorrhage at his retreat in Warm Springs, Georgia, and died knowing that victory for the Allies was all but certain. A funeral train transported Roosevelt's body from Warm Springs to Washington and then on to his home in Hyde Park, New York, where he was laid to rest in the rose garden of the Roosevelt family estate.

When Margie Archibald arrived for work that morning at the POW camp hospital, the American personnel and the German POWs already knew the President had died. She remembers a German sergeant who worked there telling her that the POWs were worried about what would happen to them now that Roosevelt was dead. They seemed to think he'd been largely responsible for their good treatment and good meals, and they feared their protection might change drastically now that he was gone. In reality, it was far more the concern of Eleanor Roosevelt that had influenced treatment in the camps, and it was primarily the discovery of terrible conditions in concentration camps and in labor camps in Germany that brought reprisals against German POWs in this country as the war came to an end.

Hitler hoped that perhaps the death of Roosevelt would cause a rift between the western powers and the Soviet Union. Those relations were weakening, but they remained intact. During April, the United States Fifth and the British Eighth armies reached the Po River in Italy, and the Russians began their advance on Berlin. The United States Seventh Army captured Nürnberg. On April 25, American and Russian troops clasped hands on a bridge over the Elbe River at Torgau while the last remnants of the German army battled hard to avoid being captured by the Russians, whom they feared far more than the Americans. After naming Grand Admiral Karl Doenitz as his successor, Hitler committed suicide on April 30.

There was no choice now. Doenitz sent his representative, General Alfred Jodl, to sign the unconditional surrender of all German armed forces at Eisenhower's headquarters in the French city of Rheims on May 7. At last, Roosevelt and Churchill had attained the goal they'd committed to at Casablanca in January 1943. Official ratification of the surrender occurred at one minute past midnight on May 8, with a second signing in Berlin that included Soviet representatives.

Heinrich Most remembers vividly the ongoing effects of the German surrender on life in Camp Aliceville. No more eggs or cigarettes were provided, and all meals were smaller and not nearly as good. When movies were shown, they were usually what the POWs called *Knochenfilmen* (bone films), which depicted the utter horror of concentration camps like Dachau and Auschwitz. As the weeks went by, all recreation programs stopped, and companies were transferred out to branch labor camps on a regular basis, whether the POWs had signed work contracts or not.

Even those who remained in Camp Aliceville were induced to work because, if they did not, privileges were withheld. Wilhelm Schlegel remembers local farmers picking him and other prisoners up each morning that summer for peanut or cotton harvests or to pick apricots and cut timber.

The Aliceville camp newspaper, *Der Zaungast*, continued to publish because it had been approved by the Intellectual Diversion Program. An article titled *Ein Brief* (A Letter) appeared in the May 13, 1945 issue. It was based on a letter Günther Ertel had composed for his wife on a rainy Sunday afternoon. He was not able to mail it to her because, after Germany surrendered, the United States government declared it was no longer necessary for a third party (the Legation of Switzerland) to represent German interests in the United States. It was the Swiss Legation that had handled the exchange of mail between the two countries.

Although the International Red Cross eventually assumed most of the duties formerly performed by the Swiss Legation, it took some time. The June 15 issue of *Der Zaungast* printed the text of a telegram from the International Red Cross asking German POWs to please be patient while it worked out the logistics for mail and complaints.

Günther Ertel's letter to his wife described a rainy Sunday afternoon in their lives before the tumult and the separation of war. "Since it is Sunday and a great blessed stillness has spread out around me," he wrote, "I want to, in this hour, reach into my heart with my pen. I want you, my brave wife, to remember one of those Sundays that still shines in our hearts today."

Günther went on to describe a hike he and his sweetheart had made along the banks of the Isar River "on a rainy day exactly like today, a day on which a person must wander if he loves to see Nature set free from people." He described the rustle and murmur of the rain sounding in soothing accord with a choir of bird voices and talked about how the two of them had enjoyed themselves "like children, untroubled by the noisy crowds of Munich tourists" at other points along the river. He reminded her how they had moved along arm in arm, "the sole possessors of this beautiful piece of earth on the shore of the lively, splashing Isar, totally surrendered to the carefree essence of the moment."

Near the end of the letter, he referred to the sad fact that time and space were now placed hostilely between the two of them and told her that "whenever I look for the happiest pages in the book of my life, I must appreciate how very much we all are children of our homeland." He wrote that, even in the turmoil of world events and his existence in a strange land, he held tight "to all the great and small things of life" that his homeland had taught him.

Günther ended his letter with the following description, which suggests he was already certain this letter would never reach his wife through any postal system. "Now it has grown towards dusk outside. The monotonous drumming of the rain on the roof and walls of these lightweight wooden barracks has died away completely. The written page of this warm stream of memories from brighter hours slips gently from my hands. I hope the playful evening wind will take it and carry it away—far away—to you?"

Hundreds of thousands of refugees will die of starvation in Europe during the next year, and it will take from five to ten years to rebuild the cities that were destroyed in Germany.

• Lieutenant Colonel Karl H. Shriver •
Unidentified clipping titled
"Colonel Shriver Back from Front"
in the files of his daughter,
Scarlett Shriver Parker

CHAPTER FOURTEEN
End of the Golden Rule

By the middle of May, one week after the war ended in Europe, all golden rule-type bargains were off for the German POWs. The concentration camps and prisoner of war camps in Europe had been liberated, and American soldiers like Wendell Parrish and Newt Davidson were headed home to share descriptions of their difficult captivity with family and friends. "It wasn't that bad, but we took our beatings," Wendell has said. "Everybody got a beating, and we didn't have any food. I went in at 145 pounds and came out about 92 pounds."

After their rescue by the United States Army Timberwolf Division, Wendell and other *Stalag Luft IV* prisoners had been sent to Allied army camps named for cigarette brands Lucky Strike, Chesterfield, and Camel. "We were a pitiful sight. They wouldn't let us go home looking like that. They wanted to fatten us up first so folks at home wouldn't see us in the condition we were in."

After feasting on cake and ice cream and any other high calorie foods he wanted, Wendell boarded a Liberty ship with two hundred other ex-POWs for the journey home. One night, after dark, they pulled into New York harbor and docked. "We woke up the next morning and could see the Statue of Liberty. We knew then we were home, and it was emotional."

Wendell flew to Montgomery, where his wife was waiting to greet him. He felt a sense of reacquainting with his sweetheart because he hadn't been married that long before he went overseas. The next day he went home to Selma, Alabama, and met his ten-month-old son for the first time.

With repercussions for American prisoners in German POW camps no longer an issue, the United States War Department changed its attitude about prisoner administration: in retaliation, let's now do to German prisoners at least an approximation of what Germans did to many American prisoners—hard work, little food, the bare necessities of existence, and little, if any, contact with loved ones.

Camp Aliceville and others like it became less hospitable hosts. Gone were the Hershey bars and the beer, the slabs of beef and the scrambled eggs, and the weekly mail. Non-working NCOs began receiving ten cents a day in canteen coupons instead of thirty, and they could use them only for toiletries. A small amount of tobacco was still available, but smokers had to roll their own cigarettes.

The camp spokesman at Aliceville did his best to continue representing his fellow POWs after the war ended. In the May 27 issue of *Der Zaungast,* Johannes Bogdan wrote about a conversation he'd had with an American government representative. Bogdan had somehow contacted the State Department in Washington, D. C. after discovering that the scheduled visit of a Swiss Embassy representative to Camp Aliceville had been cancelled. The camp spokesman did not indicate whether this conversation took place at Camp Aliceville, by telephone, or in another manner, but he did outline the answers Eldon F. Nelson gave to many of his questions about how German POW connections to their homeland and their families would now be handled.

Nelson assured Bogdan that, once a postal system was reestablished in occupied Germany, POWs would again be able to write to their relatives. He also assured him that the *Alliierter Kontrollrat* (the Allied Control Council now administering affairs in occupied Germany) would not permit German citizens to starve and would initiate a rebuilding program as soon as possible. Nelson promised to ask that his agency forward money earned by POWs to their relatives in Germany and agreed to arrange for a supplemental delivery of potatoes to Camp Aliceville in order to bring the calorie level back to what was stipulated by the Geneva Convention. (The POWs had complained, and Colonel Grier had confirmed, that new diet guidelines did not meet the required calorie level for working prisoners of war.) Nelson also reminded the camp spokesman that POWs should carefully safeguard any diplomas and certificates earned through the camp school because the Allied Control Council would recognize these when the POWs returned home looking for work.

Bogdan ended his article by suggesting several guidelines for POW behavior in the coming months:

- Political debates only lead to division among us.
- Whatever is ahead, we are now under the control of the American government.
- If we maintain order with small things, this will lead to order with more important things.
- Theft has become more prevalent recently, and we all need to work together to make this a non-occurrence.

- We should assist each other in tackling common concerns in a true spirit of togetherness.
- We should let our common suffering and misfortune unite us so that we will be prepared for the tasks awaiting us at home. A new Germany must be created!

Skepticism and fear about what that "new Germany" might become was what had prompted the implementation of the Intellectual Diversion Program in the POW camps—an attempt to persuade German prisoners to believe in democracy before they returned home. Ironically, it was this same skepticism and fear, based on knowledge of Hitler's rise to power after World War I, that had prompted the drafting of the retaliatory Morgenthau Plan, which would have reduced Germany to industrial ruin again after World War II.

It would take time for bitterness against the enemy to abate, but most American and other Allied leadership came to believe that helping Germany rebuild on a broader base was not only the right thing to do but that it also made sense economically and politically. As the United States, Great Britain, and France detected more and more differences between their approach to the redevelopment of Europe and that of the Soviet Union (which leaned towards recruitment for socialism and communism), these countries began to consider it even more important to weave what became West Germany into the economic and political fabric of Western Europe.

Part of that commitment was the European Recovery Program, or the Marshall Plan, as it became known. Announced in June 1947, this plan appropriated more than $13 billion in

American aid to be distributed primarily to Great Britain, France, Italy, and West Germany—in that order. However, from May 1945 until the Marshall Plan became effective in 1947 and until currency reform was introduced in 1948, the desperate postwar conditions in Germany improved only very slowly.

In the spring of 1945, the YMCA never wavered in its efforts to provide what it could for POWs remaining in American camps. On May 19 and 20, Camp Aliceville received two visitors—YMCA inspector Dr. Edoard Patte and the Reverend Nothacksberger from the World Council of Churches, who came to present awards for a YMCA competition. *Der Zaungast* reported that Camp Aliceville had made more progress with its educational program than any other Fourth Service Command camp, largely because of YMCA donations. Johannes Bogdan assured readers that the YMCA would continue to support the camp in any way it could. However, he expressed concern that the continuous transfer of POWs out of Camp Aliceville was making it difficult to conduct a consistent program of education and activities that would benefit prisoners once they were released.

One POW who benefited greatly from the educational program at Camp Aliceville was Hans Kopera, the Austrian who served as an interpreter in the camp hospital and studied medical subjects under the German doctor prisoners. When Hans returned to Austria after the war, he entered medical school at the University of Graz and was credited one full year of study in recognition of his military service and of the training he'd received at Camp Aliceville. He became a medical doctor in the summer of 1951 and was named head of the Clinical Pharmacology Unit at Graz in 1973.

Hans has said, however, that his journey from Camp Aliceville back to Austria was a long and often frustrating one. When the war ended, he was shuttled from one temporary camp to another. His NCO exemption from work details was revoked, and he was often expected to survive on as little as six hundred to eight hundred calories a day while performing heavy labor. Although American authorities attributed the food and work changes to shortages caused by the war, Hans Kopera and most German POWs believed that the harsher treatment was a form of retribution brought about by discovery of Nazi atrocities in concentration camps and poor treatment of American prisoners by German captors. "If they changed our thinking in the course of the years in America," Hans has said, "they spoiled a lot by the bitter end."

Karl Silberreis, who was captured in Tunis in May 1943, has praised the YMCA supplies and the educational opportunities he took advantage of at Camp Aliceville. "I studied languages, I studied history, and I studied modern German literature as well as English literature." Many of his instructors were German POWs, including one who'd been a guest lecturer at Oxford University in England before the war.

Karl remembers that lights went out in the camp barracks at ten o'clock but that lights in the latrines stayed on most of the night. Sometimes he and others went there after dark so they could study and learn vocabulary. He's very appreciative of the books provided by the YMCA. "I also studied American history—the colonial period—in English."

Hermann Blumhardt and Horst Uhse, who'd both been transferred from Camp Aliceville to Camp Gordon Johnston in Florida, also experienced drastic changes in their camp once the war ended. On the day Germany surrendered, their edgy camp commander ordered machine guns set up at every corner in case of trouble.

"Life was not the same anymore," says Horst as he describes Camp Gordon Johnston in May 1945. When the POWs suspected their canteen was about to close, they emptied it of everything from chocolate to cigarettes and buried what they could. They even nailed bacon and ham to the bottoms of the mess hall tables. Guards with steel pokers found some items, but they missed the bacon.

The bakery where Hermann worked closed down, and the American soldiers with whom he'd enjoyed practicing his English were discharged. "My morale went to an all-time low again, especially with the announcement that the mail to Germany would be cut off," says Hermann. His morale had stayed high not only because of good treatment and opportunities from the Americans, but also because Katie's letters had given him a link to home and a hope for the future.

Then came another huge disappointment. With the war over, both Hermann and Horst expected to be going home soon, but this was not the case. Instead, they were sent to a tent camp called Telogia to cut timber. "The quota was three cords a day," says Horst. "If you cut less than that, you worked on the weekend—both Saturday and Sunday. I worked every weekend."

If Hermann didn't make his quota on a given day, he had to walk back to camp from the woods—a distance of ten to fifteen miles—then sleep in the open on the athletic field. "This was our 'punishment' for losing the war. Double the workload and half the rations we'd had at Aliceville."

Horst Uhse was transferred out of Telogia after a few months. He spent three days at Fort Benning in Georgia, a few days back up at Camp Shanks in New York where his American stay had begun, then eighteen more months of captivity in England before returning home. Hermann Blumhardt remained at Telogia, cutting wood and chopping sugar cane. Katie has said their last year of separation was the longest because they could not exchange letters. "I had no idea where he was after the war was over. There were others in my village whose husbands and sweethearts came home earlier, but Hermann just didn't come home for another whole year."

Conditions in Germany were desperate—in Katie's opinion, worse after the war because there were no supplies of anything. "We got a ration card for 900 calories a day, and we got by. We had our own garden, and there was the black market if you had something you could trade, but we didn't have anything. Somehow my mother put food on the table every day, though."

Finally, in June 1946, Hermann left the United States and was transported to Le Havre. He considers himself extremely lucky that he was not transferred from there to two more years of hard labor in a French coal mine. This was not an unfounded fear. After some soul searching and careful consideration, the United States War Department had agreed in November 1944 to release large numbers of its prisoners for labor details in Great Britain and France, and also in Holland, Belgium, Luxembourg, Yugoslavia, and Greece to help with rebuilding after the war. France alone demanded 1.75 million prisoners but agreed in June 1945 to accept 1.3 million. The first 375,000 prisoners transferred to French custody came from among those captured near the end of the war but never transported to the United States. However, POWs like Hermann, who had served in camps on American soil, were also handed over for additional labor.

Hermann has said that when his group checked in at Camp Bolbec in northern France, the new American administrator there "realized the injustices done to the German POWs" and did not force them to spend more time working in French coal mines under terrible conditions. The International Red Cross may also have intervened. The Red Cross reported to the United States War Department in the summer of 1945 that France was not maintaining prisoners according to standards of the Geneva Convention—even allowing starvation conditions at French depots where prisoners were held. The French government claimed its prisoners were in poor health because the only ones the United States turned over to them were already in the worst physical condition.

That fall, General Eisenhower ordered all transfers halted for almost two months until the French agreed to improve POW conditions. Eisenhower was finally satisfied in November when France submitted guarantees and allowed regular monitoring by the International Red Cross. Eventually, the United States transferred seven hundred thousand POWs to France, forty thousand to Belgium, ten thousand to Holland, and seven thousand to Luxembourg, but it is difficult to calculate how many of these prisoners first served time in POW camps in America.

Hermann was released at Camp Bolbec in June 1946, but he was not offered any way to contact his family. He was sent by freight train to Nürnberg, where he received his discharge papers. Then he boarded a bus and headed for Bargau. He would see Katie first and then go to Stuttgart for a reunion with his family.

Katie was in Stuttgart-Hofen that week, visiting Hermann's sister. It was only thirty-five miles from Bargau, but at that time, a two-hour train ride away. Hermann's sister asked her to stay another day, but Katie shook her head. "I'm going home," she said. "I have this feeling—it's like I know Hermann is coming home."

The sister shrugged. "You are driving yourself crazy with this," she said.

But Katie felt certain. "No, I definitely feel something." She took the train for Bargau that afternoon.

The next day was beautiful, and late in the day, Katie sat on a bench with her own sister outside her family's home. She watched calmly as the local bus approached, bringing workers home to the village from the next town. "We knew the bus driver—everybody in Bargau knew everybody—and the bus drove by us very slow and almost stopped." Katie's sister asked her if she knew why everyone on the bus was looking over at them.

Katie knew exactly why. She'd had that feeling, and it had been exact. "Because my Hermann is on that bus. I see him." She rose calmly and walked the one block down to the bus station, and there he came. "That's the truth," she said years later. "That's exactly how it happened."

Hermann and Katie Blumhardt were married on September 10, 1946. "It was high time we got married." Hermann has said.

"But we hardly knew each other," says Katie. "I was nineteen when I met him, and twenty-three when he came home."

"Yes," says Hermann. Like Wendell Parrish, he needed to reacquaint himself with his sweetheart after four long years, "but it didn't take long for that old spark to come back. It had been there all along." They were married in the Catholic Church in Bargau.

The lady who owned the local restaurant/butcher shop offered to host a reception. "She was such a good woman, and she did her best," says Katie. Providing for wedding guests was difficult in postwar Germany, but the family used their ration credits and invited a small number of neighbors and family. Almost 150 guests showed up—just wanting to be there and help celebrate. "They paid for their own drinks, and if they wanted something to eat, they were not taxed from our wedding party. They paid their own way," Katie has said. "They just wanted to be there."

A friend played the accordion, and someone brought a drum, so there was plenty of dancing. Hermann wore Katie's brother-in-law's suit, and Katie wore a dress fashioned by a seamstress from the material of one dress that belonged to her sister and one dress that belonged to her sister-in-law. The top was lacy, and it had a long skirt. Katie borrowed dress shoes from a friend and remembers that her feet hurt all day because they didn't fit.

Afterwards, Hermann and Katie wanted a wedding photograph, so they drove in a borrowed car to a studio in town, but the photographer would not take the little money Hermann had. In 1946, it was worth almost nothing. "You got something to trade?" the photographer asked. "A pound of meat or something?" Hermann shook his head. "Sorry," said the photographer. "No picture."

Hermann found work almost immediately as a typesetter in Stuttgart. He felt a lump rise in his throat each day as he walked the streets of the city on his way to and from work—buildings bombed and skeletal, money worthless, and people with blank looks on their faces as they searched for necessities. Katie had wanted to stay in Bargau, where she had a large family and everybody knew everybody, but no jobs were available there.

As early as one hour after he returned to Germany, Hermann talked to Katie about the possibility of moving to America. He'd come to admire the country whenever he practiced his English with American people, but Katie was adamant. She couldn't leave her mother and her family. Besides, the American government had made it clear at the end of the war—POWs were not eligible for citizenship in the United States.

Just as they did with the wedding clothes, she and Hermann borrowed what they needed to set up housekeeping. Someone lent them a wardrobe, and Katie's grandmother lent them beds. Hermann worked in Stuttgart from 1946 to 1949, and during that time, he and Katie had two children. From time to time, Hermann spoke again about someday moving to America. Katie always listened, but she kept saying she couldn't possibly go. She was surprised when her mother told her that if Hermann was determined to go, maybe she should consider it. "You go where your husband goes," she said.

Another time Katie suggested maybe Hermann should go ahead if he wanted to—find a job and a place to live and then send for her and the children. Katie's mother again offered good advice—either you all go or no one goes, she said. But when these discussions were taking place, they were not practical. No POWs were being allowed to return to the United States and apply for citizenship.

Please w/d

– we have the new 2012 reissue.

JC 8/1/24

NOTE TO LIBRARY:

REGARDING PROCESSING

_______CIP cataloging is only cataloging available for this title.
___✓___There is not a MARC record available for this title.
_______Due to the format of this book, we have not attached a polyester cover
_______Due to the size/format of this book, we are unable to:
 _______Supply a jacket cover.
 _______Property stamp.
 _______Attach a pocket/check out card/date due slip.

REGARDING BINDING

_______The paperback cover was damaged during the binding process. Therefore, this book had to be bound in Cloth.
_______The bindery erroneously bound this book in Vinabind instead of Cloth.
_______Unsuitable for Vinabind. Book has been bound in Cloth.
_______Unsuitable for binding.
_______Perforated pages. Unsuitable for binding.
_______Book is too thick. Unsuitable for binding.
_______Book is too thin. Unsuitable for binding.
_______Narrow margins. Unsuitable for binding.
_______Fold out pages and/or covers. Unsuitable for binding.
_______Not bound. Binding could damage attached item in book
_______Not bound per customer request.
_______Other:____

MIDWEST LIBRARY SERVICE

Hermann remembers discovering a distinct downside to being a former POW in postwar Germany. "We were in daily contact with Allied soldiers and became a convenient target to take revenge on and let out anger and frustration. We were the scapegoats." He is referring to the attitudes of some British and American soldiers who treated POWs harshly when they had the opportunity—as a kind of personal payback for Holocaust atrocities committed by SS troops even though most *Wehrmacht* soldiers had not had involvement with or knowledge of the extermination camps. Still, Hermann didn't complain. He was home and had a job and was beginning a good life with Katie.

Walter Felholter, who'd lived in the same barracks with Hermann at Camp Aliceville before he contracted diphtheria, also ended up cutting wood in 1945. He was sent to Camp Richton in Mississippi—a small camp for about two hundred POWs assigned to the pulpwood industry. In February 1946, Walter returned to Camp Shelby and then to Camp Shanks in New York. After twelve days at sea, he arrived at Antwerp, Belgium, and began another series of assignments in labor camps—two in Belgium, three in England. His last stop was Cambridge.

Early in March 1947—almost two years after the war ended, Walter went home to his parents in Germany. He spent six months doing an apprenticeship in the undertaking business and then was able to continue the engineering courses he'd begun before the war. In February 1949, he received his certificate as a qualified engineer but found the job market difficult. After two months, he was hired as a construction engineer in a factory in Osnabrück that manufactured gas meter and gas pressure regulators.

Throughout this period, Walter stayed in touch with Lieselotte Custor, the young woman he'd met in the Catholic bookstore in Friedberg in 1940. They made plans for the future while he worked for stability in his life. Finally, in May 1950, Walter left his job in Osnabrück and moved to Friedberg to marry Lieselotte. Her father owned a small soap factory and retail store, and Walter worked with him in that business for ten years until he died.

In March 1960, engineering finally became the focus of Walter's career. He went to work for an engineering firm and later became the city engineer for Friedberg, where he and Lieselotte lived. In this job, from which he retired in 1987, Walter supervised all city operations having to do with water, gas, heat, and general maintenance. He and Lieselotte celebrated their fiftieth wedding anniversary on May 25, 2000.

Werner Kaiser, the German NCO who'd come to Camp Aliceville after trying to break through the Allied encirclement of Cherbourg, was transferred to the branch labor camp at Greenville soon after the war ended. He remembers several immediate changes at Aliceville just before that—food reduction, increased workload, and the beginning of an almost yearlong ban on correspondence. At Greenville, Werner was ordered to pick a minimum of 180 pounds of cotton per day or lose his free time. This was almost impossible for a man not used to the heat or this type of work. He remembers working side by side with African Americans in temperatures often well above 100 degrees.

Because he spoke English, Werner served as an interpreter and sometimes gained a few small privileges, but like the other

POWs, he slept in a tent that did little to keep out rain, wind, and heat. He would gladly have returned to the tightly built barracks of Camp Aliceville. When the cotton harvest of 1945 ended, he was transferred to Memphis, where he worked in a warehouse.

Like Hermann Blumhardt and Walter Felholter, Werner was hopeful of returning home when he crossed the Atlantic in the spring of 1946, but instead, he was sent to Brussels, where he spent two months enduring what he has referred to as the "notorious hunger brigade." This meant living in a foxhole and surviving on small amounts of terrible food—theoretically, a punishment for German aggression, but also a violation of Geneva Convention guidelines. When Werner was transferred to England, he remembers thinking the change would be good because nothing could be worse than where he was.

He has described his experience in England as fair. Although he longed to return home and resume his civilian life, he worked another entire year in a plant nursery near Cheltenham in the Cotswold before beginning the long process of repatriation that moved him through several more POW camps in England and Germany. He finally returned to Hannover on September 7, 1947.

There are conflicting accounts about the poor treatment of German POWs in Belgium and in other European countries after the war. Werner Kaiser's experience was similar to that of another German soldier named Siebenbrot who was interviewed by Martin Schenkel in 1999. Siebenbrot had also ended up in a POW camp near Brussels after leaving the United States. He, too, says the food was terrible and points out that he and others who'd been well fed in camps in America endured the punishment better than recently captured German soldiers already weak from battlefield food shortages. Siebenbrot, who spent six weeks near Brussels before going to England, stated that anyone who had a blanket or a tent in this camp was lucky.

In a nonfiction book titled *Other Losses*, Canadian novelist James Bacques alleged in 1989 that General Eisenhower, as head of the American occupation army in Germany, deliberately starved hundreds of thousands of German POWs to death. Although Allied soldiers sometimes mistreated German POWs after the war, claims of a calculated death plan have not been substantiated by other historians. Bacques suggested there'd been no food shortage in Europe and that plentiful food had been withheld from war prisoners as an act of retaliation. He went so far as to suggest that Americans "should take down every statue of Eisenhower, and every photograph of him and annul his memory from American history as best they can, except to say, 'Here was a man who did very evil things that we're ashamed of.'"

Historian Stephen Ambrose refuted these claims in a *New York Times* review of Bacques' book titled "Ike and the Disappearing Atrocities." Ambrose acknowledged that Eisenhower's bitterness towards German soldiers grew in the spring of 1945 after he signed tens of thousands of condolence letters to American families and after visiting concentration camps as they were liberated. However, Ambrose says there's no evidence to support Bacques' claims of a broad and deliberate plan on Eisenhower's part to exterminate German POWs. Instead, he says, American officers in postwar Europe followed a policy crafted by Eisenhower's superiors to treat German POWs roughly in order to emphasize their defeat and impress upon them that they'd brought their situation on themselves. One aspect of that policy was that German POWs were not to be fed at a higher level than German civilians or civilians of liberated countries—something POWs themselves, with numerous family members among those civilians, would have agreed with. Another aspect of the policy, which Eisenhower helped implement, was the sincere effort to "de-Nazify" prisoners as much as possible before sending them home.

There is no question that food and basic necessity shortages existed in postwar Germany. The infrastructure had been destroyed, and little farmland was under cultivation. Werner Kaiser's fiancée, Waltraud, had been a kindergarten teacher until late in the war. When the school where she taught closed, she could not find work and had difficulty getting food because ration coupons could not be obtained without a job. Eventually she secured a position as a nanny and lived with the family whose children she cared for. She remembers friends keeping rabbits and hens on their balconies, even in the city, as they tried to survive. There was almost no electricity or gas, and those who had the means added fireplaces to their homes and then scavenged for fuel. Some schools opened their kitchens so people could prepare warm meals.

When Werner returned in 1947, the couple married almost immediately so they could live together at the house of her employer. Inflation was rampant in postwar Germany, and it was normal to pay as much as one hundred marks for a piece of sausage. Cigarettes were the currency of the black market, and Werner was able to have cartons sent occasionally from contacts in America. Whenever cigarettes arrived, Werner traded them for meat.

Hannover had been damaged heavily during the war, but the people of the city used the stone debris to begin rebuilding, including a soccer stadium still in use today. It was crowded in the eleven-square-foot room Werner and Waltraud shared, especially after the birth of their first child. With the help of friends, they built a small stone house in a garden allotment. When inflation and the black market disappeared with currency reform on June 21, 1948, Werner found work, and the couple began a new life with eighty-nine new German marks in their pockets.

German Army draftee Leopold Dolfuss, one of the Austrians captured at Tunis in April 1943, was cutting wood at Camp Butner in North Carolina in the summer of 1945. He'd been transferred there from Camp Aliceville a year earlier. He has described the wood cutting, which he was called on to do from time to time, as "very exertious" and has said he preferred his more regular POW job of milking cows on a dairy farm, something he was used to doing on his parents' farm at home. Leopold also has said he was treated fairly in North Carolina. He was only required to stay within Camp Butner at night.

Leopold continued to milk cows and cut wood in North Carolina for a full year after the war ended. Then, near the end of May 1946, he left the United States and, like Hermann Blumhardt, arrived at Le Havre two weeks later. Perhaps because he was Austrian and not a "dedicated Nazi," he was released immediately without being required to perform additional POW labor. Finally a free man again, he traveled by train to Salzburg, Austria, and then on foot to his home village of Texing on June 21. He took over management of his parents' small farm, married, had two daughters, and worked as a postman until he retired in 1979.

In retirement, Leopold became a Red Cross volunteer, transporting outpatients to the hospital and moving patients around within the hospital. In 2002, he was honored by the Red Cross in Texing for having completed more than a thousand assignments as a volunteer.

Most Americans who remember the hundreds of thousands of Germans held in POW camps across the United States (more than 422,000 in July 1945) make the assumption that once hostilities ended, these enemy soldiers simply went home and rebuilt their lives. In reality, their experience was much more complicated. Like Walter Felholter and Werner Kaiser, many were transferred from camp to camp in the United States and then in England, France, or other devastated European countries before returning to Germany.

Anti-Nazi "punishment battalion" prisoners like Erwin Schulz believed they'd already served enough time, considering the combined total of their jail time under Hitler before the war and their POW time in the United States. The International Red Cross planned at one point to recommend that these prisoners be granted early release and returned quickly to Germany, but even this decision involved complications. There was concern about their safety if former Nazi prisoners caught up with them at home. There was also concern that they might contribute to the development of communism in the Russian sector that became East Germany.

Erwin Schulz was sent to Belgium in the spring of 1946 and then to another POW camp in Shelby, England. He worked there as a typist, preparing daily menus for the officers' mess. "Some of us wrote letters to top [British] government officials and to certain members of the British labor movement asking them to exert pressure so we could be sent home as victims of fascism." Erwin finally returned to Germany in October 1946 and settled in the German Democratic Republic (East Germany), where he continued to be viewed with suspicion—this time because communist leaders feared he'd been contaminated by Western political ideas.

Before their official release, even those who managed to set foot on their home soil in 1945 and 1946 maneuvered through endless piles of paperwork and usually spent time under American military supervision, working to rebuild the infrastructure in Germany.

Of the POWs profiled in this book, Günther Peter Ertel is the only one who made it all the way home during 1945. Singled out by the AEO Lieutenant at Camp Aliceville as "academically promising and educated," he was sent to Fort Getty in Rhode Island not long after he wrote the letter to his wife, Johanna, reminiscing about their rainy afternoon along the Isar River near Munich. This was the letter he'd allowed *Der Zaungast* to publish when the POW postal system shut down.

Fort Getty housed an Administration School (code named Project II) set up to train "the cream of the POW population" with the idea that they could help administer the new Military Government in Germany. From May through June, Günther studied English three hours each weekday morning in a small class of eleven prisoners. He also listened to college-level lectures on American history, German history, and military law. After completing the sixty-day program, he bided his time with other graduates at Fort Getty while waiting to be repatriated.

In October, General Eisenhower sent word from Europe that he needed all of the graduates (approximately eleven hundred) immediately to fill minor German government posts. Günther's morale was high when he and the others boarded ships to cross the Atlantic. He was still wearing the khaki shirt, jacket, and trousers of his most recent captivity with the big "PW" painted on them in large, unmistakable letters. What he was wearing didn't matter. Not only was he finally going home, but he was to have a job waiting for him—a job that would help set a good future course for himself and for Germany.

Unfortunately—but not unpredictably—only a few graduate prisoners obtained the jobs they'd been trained for. Tremendous bureaucratic confusion clogged the new German occupation government, and low level officials considered themselves too busy to understand and deal with Project II. Günther was deeply disappointed, but his disappointment was small next to the indescribable joy of holding Johanna in his arms again and hugging his son, Robert. Finally, there was an end to what had often seemed to him "a world-without-end of tears and anguish" during four long years of war. Günther looked only to the future after that and to the responsibility of providing for his family. Eventually, he found work with the State Department of the United States.

Reinhold Schulte, who'd been captured while trying to defend Cherbourg from the Allies in June 1944, returned to Germany in 1946. On the trip home, he carried with him several copies of *Der Zaungast* and also, carefully wrapped in paper, the chess set box he'd carved from southern yellow pine during his stay in Camp Aliceville. From November 1946 to October 1954, he worked as a gardener and landscaper for British Army headquarters in Bad Öynhausen in the Westfalen region of Germany. Reinhold told his wife, Herta, and his son, Dieter, that he'd been treated well in Alabama and that he'd eaten well. Like Hermann Blumhardt, he considered returning someday. He thought America might offer his son a good future.

When Germany surrendered, the Swiss legation withdrew from its role as intermediary, leaving German POWs in a kind of legal limbo. Because an internationally recognized German government no longer existed, German affairs in Europe and in the United States came under the administration of the *Alliierter Kontrollrat*, which felt no obligation to concern itself with the Geneva Convention. Amenities taken almost for granted by POWs and their camp spokesmen disappeared. Recreational and cultural activities were curtailed, mail was suspended, and meals were reduced to a bare minimum.

From their distant vantage point, prisoners still in Camp Aliceville in the summer of 1945 felt great concern about the welfare of their families and the future of their country. News trickling out of Germany indicated the civilian population there was in desperate need. There was no fuel for cooking what little food there was. Children begged to eat the toothpaste in the few CARE packages that arrived because they hadn't tasted sweets in so long. Underwear was shredded from being washed so many times, and jobs were few because so few companies had the resources to operate.

The final issue of *Der Zaungast* appeared on July 1. Its front page contained a message from the staff to the dwindling number of POWs who remained at Camp Aliceville. "Many of our comrades have left our camp," it said, "and soon it will be our turn. For almost a year, our camp newspaper has tried hard to find something in the monotony of our small world to hold on to, to relieve the sadness of the situation, and to remind us of what is worth remembering and what is best forgotten."

The staff took satisfaction in pointing out that the newspaper had had more than two thousand subscriptions while it was in publication. "We wish our readers good health in their last days in the camp and hope that we will soon have [a] happy return to our homeland."

More and more Camp Aliceville POWs were yielding to incentives to sign work contracts. One June issue of *Der Zaungast* listed a number of transfers, including 500 prisoners to Memphis, Tennessee, at the end of April, 1,350 to various military bases and hospitals in South Carolina during May, and 500 to Jacksonville, Florida, in June.

Karl Silberreis was one of the Aliceville POWs sent to North Carolina in May 1945. Leaving his YMCA studies behind, he spent another year in North Carolina, working as a "kp pusher." Because he spoke English, he was put in charge of fifty other prisoners who worked as cook assistants in an American base mess hall. "This was when the war was over, and it was a bit difficult," he has said. "The food was super compared to what our people at home had to eat, but we did have it a bit rough. We'd get maybe two pieces of bread covered with lettuce."

Karl cringed each time he collected all the kitchen waste and finally asked a supervisor if the prisoners could at least have the food the Americans were throwing away. "At first, they didn't agree, but I knew our kitchen was the best when there was an inspection. I rotated my people, eight days on pots and pans, eight days on the chow line, eight days cleaning tables, so I never had any problems. Everyone knew [each job] was only eight days." After a while, the American supervisor told Karl he could save some of the leftovers for himself and his workers.

"We were very much treated like human beings in North Carolina," he says. He and the kitchen supervisor became acquaintances. Karl was a good athlete, and the supervisor suggested Karl come out with him on a Sunday afternoon to play American football. "He knew I was kicking the ball very fast and throwing the ball very fast, but I said, 'Well, I can't get out of the camp.'" The supervisor gave Karl his overcoat, and he went out on Sundays and played football with the Americans.

One day, the supervisor told him his sister wanted to meet Karl because he'd told his parents so much about the POWs. The sister came and watched the football game the next several Sundays.

Then came the day the supervisor told Karl he'd give him his military uniform—the green trousers, the combat uniform. "You go with my sister and leave the camp, disappear," he said. Karl, who was already married, shook his head. He hoped his freedom would come soon in a more legitimate way.

Karl Silberreis returned to Germany late in 1946. Before the war, he'd worked for Höchst, a chemical plant based in Frankfurt, but he was not able to return to his old job as a sales representative. Instead, he applied for a job in civil aviation and, because of his diligent study of English at Aliceville, was soon hired by British European Airways in what became West Germany. Karl was fortunate to have this job, not only because he received a regular salary but also because the company supplied him with a CARE-type parcel each month. It contained coffee, milk, other kinds of food, and sometimes even a blanket at a time when such basic necessities were almost non-existent in many parts of the country.

Karl settled in Frankfurt, happy to be through with the war and to have some sort of a future in business. The one remaining loose end in his life was the reunification of his family. By the time he returned, the Potsdam Conference (1945) had partitioned Germany with the eastern sector under Russian control, and Karl's wife was still in that sector. It took quite a bit of maneuvering through the bureaucracies of the various controlling powers, but eventually Karl managed to bring his wife to Frankfurt. By 1952, he was a town supervisor with British European Airways. He joined BOAC in 1955 and worked with them until 1974, building their image and business in Germany.

As Camp Aliceville moved steadily towards a complete shutdown after the war, the campus of Northington General Hospital in Tuscaloosa became a permanent branch camp for POWs. Between May 28 and June 13, 1945, more than two hundred Camp Aliceville prisoners were transferred to Northington and put to work in the kitchens and laundries of the hospital. They lived in temporary wooden barracks enclosed by barbed wire on the hospital grounds, approximately three miles from the campus of the University of Alabama, near property later occupied by Shelton State Technical Institute.

Northington General had been built under the direction of Colonel Shriver in the months after he completed Camp Aliceville. It opened to patients in September 1943 and sometimes received soldiers with severe burns directly from the battlefield. The hospital had one thousand beds and specialized in plastic surgery.

One of the final issues of *Der Zaungast* reported that at first sight, the POWs sent to Northington were not impressed with their new camp. It didn't look like much on the outside, but the Germans were optimistic about sprucing it up in the coming weeks.

Birmingham bookseller Jim Reed remembers the beautiful rose bushes prisoners planted and cared for along the fences of their small compound. He was three years old in 1944 when his family moved to a modest asbestos-shingled bungalow on Eastwood Avenue, just across the street from the huge Northington campus where his father worked as a carpenter. Jim's physical memories of the hospital complex are fragmented—spotlights scanning the skies for enemy planes, guard towers at the corners of the fencing, an occasional air raid siren, and the rose bushes.

He remembers that children were taught to hate—absolutely hate—Japanese and Germans. "They were the al Quaida, the Taliban, yet my daddy would come home and talk to us about these wonderful young [German] men he worked with."

Over the next two years, Jim and his friends played war in the shadow of the hospital—blowing up make-believe Germans with toy hand grenades but making sure they came back to life quickly so they could be killed again. After a while, the children shifted to killing more Japanese than Germans with their "air Lugers and John Wayne-style machine guns" because no Japanese were tending rose bushes right across the street.

What Jim remembers most about Northington is the stories his father told at dinnertime, and the handmade gifts the POWs presented to his father—a small wooden nameplate for his desk, a painting, a thick curved bottle hand painted with the picture of a little girl on it, and a copper beer mug. Jim's father told him most of the Germans were draftees who just wanted to go home. "They didn't have any particular reason to try to escape because they would have been pretty obvious in America. The Germans got up every day and cleaned. They had the habit of scrubbing everything with water, and finally the guards had to tell them—slow down, don't clean so much. They'd scrubbed the floors of the barracks so much they were rotting." German POWs remained in the temporary camp at Northington Hospital until the spring of 1946.

As the population of Camp Aliceville trickled out to branch camps and other base camps in the summer of 1945, civilian employees began to leave, too. Elma Henders quit her job as nutritionist a short while before the hospital closed. The German POWs who worked with her gave a tea party in her honor, using precious rationed supplies to create a beautiful and delicious cake and bringing summer roses from the camp greenhouse to decorate a table. They invited the hospital employees and all the Germans who worked in the kitchen. "It was beautifully done, and I thought it was so nice of them," Elma said.

Ward and Mary Turner were discharged from their jobs in early July. "I can still remember the day we left," their daughter, Mary Lu, has said. "Riding down the driveway with my doll in my lap, and all the people standing out in back of my father's building waving. We all had tears in our eyes." Adelaide Morrow and Claude Earl Martin would have been among those waving good-bye, and perhaps Earline Lewis and Will Peebles.

Mary Lu remembers her father driving through Aliceville one last time before heading north to take a job as an insurance salesman in Rochester, New York—up Red Hill he drove to where she'd cooled off on hot summer afternoons under splashes from the town water tower, past the school where she'd participated in scrap metal drives and piano recitals, past Sam Wise's store that always smelled like new clothes, and past the Palace Theater, where she'd enjoyed movies with her school friends on Saturdays. A large, unique chunk of her childhood was ending, but it would become the stuff of memories that would stay with Mary Lu for a lifetime.

On July 7, POW Horst Spieker left Camp Aliceville for the Indiantown Gap Military Reserve in Pennsylvania. There, like Günther Ertel, he participated in a postwar re-education program for qualified prisoners. He also worked as a kitchen helper and waiter in an officers' mess. On February 25, 1946, Horst left the United States on board the *Aiken Victory,* which docked at Antwerp, Belgium. "In Antwerp, the American officer in charge delivered us 'erroneously' to the British military authorities who put us to work for another eighteen months." Horst finally returned to Berlin, which was now in ruins, on

September 21, 1947—eight years and ten days after he'd been drafted into the *Luftwaffe* on September 11, 1939.

Horst Spieker's comment about being "erroneously" delivered to the British was sarcastic, but the fact was that at least 150,000 of the POWs who'd been held in the United States were "British-owned" from the beginning (see Chapter One). Now that the war was over, Great Britain insisted on reclaiming at least 130,000 of those prisoners. The British wanted to put them to work on labor-short English farms and in repairing war damage in British territories. After centuries of wars back and forth, Europe was used to agreements about reparations and considered this part of the peace process.

Among other prisoners who spent a year or more working in England was Ernst Schacht, the Aliceville POW who'd climbed a tree to witness part of the invasion at Normandy. In July 1945, Ernst left Aliceville for Camp Springs, Maryland, where he spent nine months working at Andrews Field near Washington, D.C. His job there, which he has described as pleasant, was serving as interpreter at the officers' club. In March 1946, Ernst was sent to England and spent the next year and a half working on farms. Although he was still not home, he remembers this time as peaceful. He and other POWs were allowed contact with the English and made friends among families in the Society of Friends (Quakers). The English government allowed the Quakers to invite German POWs to share meals with them and allowed the POWs to leave camp when they were invited.

Finally, in September 1947, Ernst was given permission to call his parents in Germany and tell them he was about to be repatriated. A member of a charity organization called TOCH arranged for him to place the call. He reached home in Hamburg on September 15, 1947—one month less than seven years after he left.

Ernst worked hard to help his father rebuild his textile shop after the war. In July 1950, he married Wilfriede—the girl he'd met on a narrow street in Celle while recuperating from a war wound in 1942. They had two sons and eventually five grandchildren, building a life centered around their textile shop and their interests in classical music, theater, and nature conservation. By 1985, their youngest son was running the shop, and they were able to retire with a good pension. In 2000, their son built a flat for them on his property, and they celebrated their fiftieth wedding anniversary surrounded by family.

Bruno Schneider, who wrote the often quoted poem "Frogs of Alabama" about Camp Aliceville, also spent time working in England. When he finally returned to Germany in 1947, he carried with him the United States Treasury check for $204.40—his accumulated earnings at the rate of eighty cents a day for work he'd done at Camp Aliceville, Camp Van Dorn, and Camp Shelby. There was no point in trying to cash the check in Germany with the rampant inflation, so he tucked it away with the mementoes of his stay in America.

Like Leopold Dolfuss, Bruno went to work for the local postal service. He married a woman named Rosemarie and had two children, Meta and Ben. He also became active in the political life of the town of Spessart in Bavaria and served as its mayor for forty-two years, from 1952 to 1994. When he died in 2004, the notice of Bruno Schneider's death listed his honors as follows: retired

Mayor of Spessart, Recipient of the German Service Cross and the Baron von Stein Plaque, and also—Honorary Citizen of the State of Alabama—recognition given to him when he made a return visit to Aliceville many years after the war.

Franz August Hinz, who'd been captured at Normandy in the bunker nicknamed "Little Dog," also served additional time in England after the war. He'd been there before, spending a year working on English farms before being sent to Aliceville. In 1947, when he was released, Franz went to Saxony where his wife was living with her parents. With them, he endured months of terrible cold and hunger. Eventually, he left his wife with her family and traveled alone to the western sector, where he found work as a miner. In 1948, he was able to bring his wife from the Russian sector and begin a new life in West Germany.

Like the British, the French also considered themselves deserving of postwar POW labor. They had plenty of war damage to repair, and there were plenty of farm jobs to be done. Besides, why should German soldiers who had devastated France be allowed to pick up their lives so easily and so quickly? The least they could do was spend a year or two relieving the French labor shortage before they went home to peaceful lives.

Most candidates for French labor brigades came from the ranks of prisoners captured and held in Europe as the German military collapsed, but the United States did supplement with fifty-five thousand German POWs who'd been held in America. One of those "supplemental" prisoners was Wilhelm Schlegel, the last of the POWs profiled in this book to return to Germany.

Once the war ended, Wilhelm found it impossible to stick to his commitment not to work. Between May 1945 and March

1946, he worked at a number of branch camps and in a variety of jobs in American agriculture—picking cotton, harvesting peanuts and peaches, and baling hay. He even went into the forest, like so many Aliceville POWs before him, to fell trees for the pulpwood industry. "Everyone had to work then," he has said. "They picked us up at camp each day and sent us out somewhere."

Finally, in early March 1946, Wilhelm boarded a ship in New York, believing like so many others that he was about to be released from his status as a prisoner of war. In the one duffel bag he was allowed to carry with him, he'd tucked away his copies of *Der Zaungast* and the diary he'd kept. Both would serve to remind him in years to come of the bittersweet time he'd spent in Alabama.

Freedom was not, however, as imminent as he'd hoped. When the ship docked in Le Havre, Wilhelm discovered that his POW days were far from over. Instead of returning home, he was sent first to Attichy, in Picardy, and assigned to a transfer camp attached to "US Army France." Then, on March 14, the date of his twenty-eighth birthday, Wilhelm was transferred officially from American to French custody.

From there, he endured a long series of work assignments, moving in and out of a base camp at Dunkirk—first on a farm near Merville and later at a chicory harvest near Lille. He worked on a farm near Roye on the Somme River and then with street construction for the firm of Pont & Chausses. When he was relocated to a depot at Hesdin in November 1947, he thought he was about to be discharged and anticipated spending Christmas back home in Asslar with his mother.

But the French were not quite through with him, and Wilhelm spent Christmas in yet another labor camp—his ninth holiday away from home and family and career. Finally, on January 26, 1948, not long before his thirtieth birthday, he was granted a formal discharge and reunited with his widowed mother. Wilhelm was grateful to be able to return to his banking job in Asslar, bringing with him many lessons in leadership he'd learned in battle and in captivity. He was in no hurry to begin a romantic relationship. Instead, he enjoyed the peace of "stretching my feet under my mother's table" and did not marry until 1954.

Wilhelm is certain his mother would have been pleased if he'd given her a daughter-in-law and grandchildren earlier, but he also admits that just the right amount of time passed before he met the woman who would become his wife. Otti had been born in Düsseldorf in 1928. She and her family fled that city when it was bombed. Eventually, Otti's relatives brought her to Asslar, where she met Wilhelm. They were married on May 15, 1954, in the *Evangelische Kirche.* Their first son, Klaus-Dieter, was born April 13, 1957, just six months before Wilhelm's mother died. Their second son, Werner, was born July 4, 1962.

Almost 178,000 of the POWs held in America during World War II spent at least one additional year—and in some cases, like Wilhelm Schlegel, even longer—in British and French labor camps after the war. Another two hundred thousand were sent directly back to Germany (and Austria) in 1946 and 1947 when repatriation agreements were worked out with the occupying governments in the various sectors.

Both the American government and the American public were deeply divided about the issue of whether to repatriate war prisoners and send them home or keep them working in America until the economy returned to a peacetime footing. Many wanted prisoners returned to Europe as soon as possible—either to their own countries or to labor brigades in war-torn European countries. They didn't want war reminders remaining in their communities, and they wanted jobs available immediately when American soldiers returned.

Others were hesitant to send prisoners back to Europe for a variety of reasons. Some feared Nazi prisoners might corrupt efforts to create a democratic Germany—especially since so many American newspapers kept reporting that Nazi prisoners had been allowed to continue honoring Hitler while in the American camps. In addition, the Allied Control Council was not overjoyed at the prospect of sending thousands of POWs home to an unstable environment of drastic food and fuel shortages in Germany. The Allied Control Council was finding it difficult enough to work with the civilian population in picking up the pieces of their lives.

On July 9, 1945, Fritz Hagmann, one of the remaining POWs at Camp Aliceville, was notified that his NCO rank had been revoked because he could not produce the correct paperwork to prove his status. He was immediately transferred to Fort Meade in Maryland and then to Camp Shanks in New York. On the train ride north, Fritz thought back over the year he'd spent in Aliceville after his transfer there from Camp Shelby. It had been a difficult but not an entirely unpleasant one. The highlight had certainly been his gentle friendship with Mr. T.L. Hester, the kind civilian American who supervised POW work details for the camp's engineering department. Once, Fritz had injured his foot while digging a ditch, and another time he'd somehow contracted food poisoning. Both times, Mr. Hester had interceded for him and signed his work detail record authorizing treatment. Mr. Hester had a son in the American army, and Fritz hoped he would make it home safely.

Fritz Hagmann remained on a work detail at Camp Shanks for almost another entire year, until May 1946. Then, with great anticipation, he boarded a ship and crossed the Atlantic where he was, like Horst Spieker and Bruno Schneider, designated a "British-owned" prisoner and spent another year working in England before returning home. When he was finally repatriated on June 17, 1947, Fritz carried his duffel bag containing the German-English dictionary he'd used while at Camp Aliceville. He settled in Tübingen and wrote, just four weeks later, to Mr. T. L. Hester in Alabama, telling him that he often thought back on the nice work group at Camp Aliceville. In careful and halting English, he told Mr. Hester there was only one way to describe Germany in 1947—"terrible conditions everywhere."

In early September 1945, Pickens County's two American POWs in Japanese custody were freed. James Scott Browning had been moved from the Chinese mainland to Japan in July 1945 to perform slave labor in the coal mines on Hokkaido. His first hint of relief came when B-29s began dropping food parcels to the camp on August 28. A rescue team arrived at Hokodate #3 POW camp (Utashinai) on September 11, and James Scott left the camp behind on September 17. L.D. Orr was also rescued in September 1945 after Japanese guards fled the Hirohata camp. He was placed on disability and returned to his parents' farm.

By the fall of 1945, all prisoners and most military personnel had left Camp Aliceville. Many prisoners remained in the United States, continuing to provide much needed labor in agriculture and industry, but the government began taking steps to end its role as POW custodian. At the end of March 1946, only 140,606 prisoners remained in the United States. At the end of May, that number had dropped to 37,491. Finally, on July 23, the last 1,388 regular prisoners of war on American soil marched up the gangplank at Camp Shanks for the voyage home. The only POWs remaining in American custody were 141 prisoners serving criminal justice terms (like those who beat Hugo Krauss to death at Camp Hearne in Texas), 134 being cared for in hospitals or psychiatric wards, and 25 missing escapees.

Three of the Aliceville prisoners profiled in this book eventually returned to the United States and became citizens. The first was Hermann Blumhardt, who went to apply the very next day in 1948 after he heard a speech by President Truman suggesting German immigrants would be welcome. "I was always listening to the American Forces Network on the radio in Stuttgart, and they said President Truman had lifted the ban on German immigration. My first thing was to go to the American Consulate and ask for permission to come to the United States."

A woman there told Hermann he needed a sponsor, so he and Katie contacted her uncle in Niles, Michigan, and he agreed to sponsor them. They waited and waited, but the paperwork did not come. Then, in December, they learned that the uncle had died. Before his death, however, he'd asked his wife, Katie's Aunt Agnes, to promise him she'd try to follow through and get "that young family over to America." Aunt Agnes had limited financial means, but she enlisted her brother's help and arranged for the sponsorship.

Once the paperwork was approved, Hermann discovered there were long waiting lists at German ports, but he was able to arrange passage instead from Le Havre, in France, and took his wife and two-year-old daughter there in the fall of 1949. Paying $600, they boarded the *Mauritania*, the ship that had taken POW Werner Kaiser to New York after his capture near Cherbourg in June 1944. The Blumhardts arrived in New York on October 14.

Katie remembers the beautiful fall afternoon when they arrived in Niles after a nineteen-hour train ride from New York. The small train depot was empty because no one had known exactly when they were coming. Hermann flagged a taxi, and off they went to Aunt Agnes' home. Katie remembers thinking, "Oh my goodness, what have I done?"

The fearful feelings melted immediately when they reached her aunt's home, where she and Hermann and their daughter stayed until they could find a place of their own. There were many people of German ancestry in the community, and they made the Blumhardts feel welcome. Katie's first trip to the A&P amazed her. "All the fruit, and all the vegetables—my eyes just about popped out."

One stipulation of Hermann's sponsorship was that he could not have a pre-arranged job waiting for him in Michigan, but Aunt Agnes unwittingly solved the job search when she called a reporter at the *Niles Daily Star* to come to the house for an interview. The article that appeared on October 24, 1949, was headlined "Prisoner Returns with His Family: German is Sold on U. S. During War Prison Stay." It outlined Hermann's career in the German army and his capture in North Africa. "During his confinement, he got acquainted with the United States through books and camp training courses and learned to speak English quite well," it said. "Today, in Niles, Blumhardt contemplates his future and is confident he will obtain a job and be able to care well for his family."

Hermann was surprised at the interest in a former prisoner of war returning to the United States. Even the Associated Press called and printed a story that appeared in newspapers all over Michigan.

The reporter from the local paper not only interviewed Hermann and Katie, but he also offered Hermann a job as a linotype operator. Herman worked for the *Niles Daily Star* for the next five-and-a-half years and then worked another thirty-one years for the *South Bend Tribune.*

At Thanksgiving, a month after their arrival in Michigan, Katie was overwhelmed by all the food on the table. "I felt like I'd gone to heaven, you know. We hadn't had milk for years and years, just the little with the ration card, and that was for the children in the family. And we didn't see meat for a long time in Germany. I liked the pies right away. I had never eaten pumpkin pie in my life, or mincemeat pie. I liked it all."

Günther Peter Ertel came to the United States in July 1953. He settled in Ohio with his wife, Johanna, and his two sons, Ernest and Robert. For a while, Günther worked in the daytime and went to college at night. Later he worked for a chemical export business in Akron, advanced to the position of vice president, and then retired after twenty-seven years at the age of seventy-one. His son Kenneth, "the true Yankee in the family," was born in Richfield, Ohio, where the family lived and became active in the United Church of Christ. Günther and Johanna celebrated their golden wedding anniversary there in December 1990 by renewing their vows. "At one time in my life," Günther wrote in his autobiography, "I thought God had forgotten me and would abandon me unfeelingly to a depressing fate. I must ask his forgiveness for the weakness of my faith and give thanks for every minute of my happy days."

Reinhold Schulte, the former POW who'd worked as a landscaper for British Army headquarters in Germany, brought his wife and two sons to the United States in 1954. When he packed for their trip, he made sure the hand-carved box and chess set from Camp Aliceville were in the luggage. The family had relatives in the Chicago area, and Reinhold was able to continue working as a landscaper until he retired in 1986. He and Herta then moved to Lake Geneva, Wisconsin, but Reinhold suffered a stroke in 1989 and went into a coma. He died in May 1993.

Reinhold's son, Dieter, had been a small child the day he concluded that all American soldiers were black when he peeked out as American tanks rolled by. He was fourteen when the family left Germany. It was a difficult age for such a transition, but Dieter handled it well. "It's kind of hard to deny that you're German with a name like Dieter," he has said. "Being in a school that had a large Jewish population, some of my relatives were concerned about name calling, but that never happened."

Dieter became a teacher and later a coordinator of student transportation for a kindergarten through eighth-grade school. His brother, Hartmut, returned to Germany to work as a freelance translator. When their father died, Hartmut inherited his chess set and Dieter inherited the carved box from Aliceville.

With its former inmates scattered to other camps, Camp Aliceville was officially deactivated on September 30, 1945. Almost immediately, the physical property began to disappear. The Army Corps of Engineers took possession and initiated a lengthy, methodical disposal of everything from screen doors and tons of nails to mirrors and laundry equipment. Their goal was to dismantle whatever could be dismantled, stack and grade the material, and then sell it all off to retrieve the cost of the demolition. Historian E.B. Walker has noted that more than two hundred Pickens County residents were employed in 1945 and 1946 to help with the demolition—certainly welcome jobs since the camp itself was no longer hiring.

It took more than a year to dismantle the camp that had risen from the pastures and swampland of Doc and Nannie Parker's farm in the fall of 1942, and there were priorities about who was entitled to the pickings. In November 1946, the National Housing Authority enjoyed a ten-day "set aside" period to choose what it wanted. Then the War Assets Administration offered other priority holders like government agencies and builders of veterans' housing the opportunity to buy what they wanted.

Last in line were Pickens County residents who were allowed to bring in wagons and trucks to haul away scrap—

mostly kindling and firewood, pieces of clay pipe and metal stove pipe—for about a dollar a load. Records show that approximately one thousand such loads were hauled away.

Once the barracks-type buildings and their contents were sold off, the various utility systems disappeared, too. An advertisement in the *Birmingham Age-Herald* on February 20, 1947 listed for sale, among other things, more than eighteen thousand linear feet of asbestos pipe from the water system, twenty-two thousand linear feet of street light circuits, and twenty-two thousand feet of telephone system drop wire.

Even the deceased prisoners, buried so carefully and honorably by Gerald Stabler and a funeral detail crew of POWs, were exhumed from their quiet graveyard with its white picket fence. Gerald was under the impression their bodies would be sent to a receiving station and then shipped to their homeland, but that is not what happened. The bodies were instead reburied under white marble, military-style headstones in the German-Italian Cemetery at Fort McClellan in Anniston, Alabama, along with the bodies of POWs who died at other camps in Alabama and Mississippi.

When the last of the American military personnel moved on to assignments at other bases in 1946, a few civilian employees remained on the Army payroll to oversee the final demise of the camp. Claude Earl Martin became the "store manager." Grady Coleman stayed on, and so did Jake McBride and Margie Archibald, the last woman to work at Camp Aliceville. Margie had come a long way since the spring morning in 1943 when she'd returned so reluctantly to her father's hometown. After leaving her job at Aliceville Bank and Trust in late 1944, she'd worked as a secretary at the Camp Aliceville hospital. She'd also helped out in other departments—personnel, finance, and supply.

When a supervisor arrived from Mobile to oversee demolition and salvage operations, the Army Corps of Engineers hired Margie as his assistant. She worked in the building that had been the fire department when the camp was active. One of her jobs was handling the auction bids that came in for various buildings and equipment. "I was busy then," she has said. "When people bought these buildings, they'd tear them down [and take away the materials]."

Margie was eager to see if she could make a profit on something auctioned off from the camp. She pooled her personal resources with two local businessmen and bid on part of the hospital property, missing the winning bid by just fifteen dollars. Because of war supply demands, electrical and plumbing supplies were difficult to obtain in the United States. "They were just sick because one of them was a plumber and one an electrician, and they could have used all that."

Next, Margie bid by herself on all the plants still landscaping the empty spaces where the barracks had been. "I bought all of that shrubbery for $85, and then I sold it piece by piece to individuals. It took me two years, and I may have made $400. I thought I was quite the businesswoman."

After the last salvage had been hauled away, Claude Earl Martin gathered up a number of unclaimed pieces of POW craftwork that had been removed from the dusty shelves and corners of the camp workshops—a cedar chest, a carved wooden crest, a small weathervane with revolving figures, and a lighted wooden box with a silhouetted Nativity scene created from tissue paper. It didn't make sense to throw away such beautiful pieces, so he took them home with him and tucked them away in his attic.

Sue Stabler remembers how the camp disappeared, almost like Brigadoon, back into the soil and the undergrowth after the deactivation. "Grass and weeds quickly cluttered the lots of lawns and beds of flowers so carefully tended by the German inmates in the compounds," she wrote. "The scene of so much activity for a span of three years reverted to nature."

Eventually, 133.72 acres of the camp property became part of the City of Aliceville. Although the area's economy remained agricultural, forward-thinking Coca-Cola bottler George Downer worked with the federal government to arrange the transfer, hoping the land would someday have value as an industrial development site.

Even though kudzu vines groped forward to reclaim the well-built amphitheater seating and the handmade brick drainage conduits, they could not strangle the memories. Aliceville citizens who'd had contact with the prisoners told their families how surprised they'd been to discover the basic humanity they had in common with the men they'd once regarded as Hitler's super soldiers—love of family and music, of mountains and children, of sports and games and a good, hearty laugh.

Aliceville families and former guards continued to display in their homes the many works of art prisoners had crafted for them. Nat and Bobbie Aicklen often showed friends the leather book they'd received as a wedding gift, along with a clay beer stein, a leather album containing a complete set of the Camp

Aliceville sketches drawn by Herman Kalbe and Hans Fanselow, and an intricately tooled leather attaché case in which Nat kept his military records.

MPEG Guard George Bristow kept a watercolor painting of the main guard tower, two carved picture frames, and three ceramic tiles painted with decorative scenes. Grady Coleman preserved several of the wall murals painted by POWs when the mess halls were demolished, and his daughter kept the jewelry box a POW made for her when she was six years old. Colonel Shriver and his wife displayed in their garden two white pillars and statues of the seven dwarfs POWs had made and presented to him, and Woodrow Wheat, who'd worked as an electrician at the camp, cherished the lovely portrait of his daughter Janice, painted for him by a POW artist named Waysemr when Woodrow gave him art supplies and a small black-and-white photo.

Most of the German POWs, whatever their other war experiences, told their families they'd been treated well in Aliceville, Alabama, in spite of the heat and the mosquitoes and the homesickness. They'd been given decent and abundant food, sturdy shelter, good medical care, and opportunities to further their education. Here and there, they'd developed tentative friendships with hardworking Americans like funeral director and mayor Gerald Stabler and sawmill owner Johnny Johnston. What stood out for some was the golden rule attitude exemplified by one Aliceville resident who offered a glass of sweet tea to a POW on a humid afternoon when he was mowing her lawn. Someone in town criticized the woman for being kind to an enemy, but she replied that she certainly hoped a German woman would offer a glass of tea to an American POW doing chores around her home.

Like Brigadoon, Camp Aliceville had been, to some extent, a remote refuge from the troubles of the world. Once the kudzu reclaimed it, the camp itself never came to life again, but every so often a polite letter in halting English arrived for Mayor Stabler or someone else in the community. Every so often, someone appeared as if from nowhere and inquired at the post office or the drugstore about where the camp had been. Much later, whole families would find their way down through Pickens County to Aliceville, seeking a link to the memories of a father or grandfather who had been a POW and then gone back to Germany to nurture a loving family and contribute to a good community. Forty-five years would pass before a formal reunion took place on the site of the former POW camp, but every so often before that, people from both sides of the barbed wire would remember and connect.

We ought to be humane and generous in this matter because we are Americans, and because we have always believed as a nation in decency, humanity, humaneness and a break for the underdog—which war prisoners certainly are. If we should take to maltreating war prisoners, we would betray something fine in our national make-up; and the consequences of that betrayal would kick back in our own teeth.

• August 12, 1944 •
Editorial in *Collier's* magazine

CHAPTER FIFTEEN
Post-war Relationships

When the war ended and the prisoner of war camp closed its gates, the hustle and bustle of Aliceville reverted rather quickly to its pre-war pace and population. Gone were the military payroll transactions that had busied the tellers at Aliceville Bank and Trust. Gone were the good jobs at the quartermaster's office and in the motor pool, and gone was the windfall of extra customers patronizing Minnie Merle Brandon's café, Simon Jones' drugstore, and Sam Wise's clothing store.

There were valiant efforts to transform post-war Aliceville into a thriving center for industry and commerce, and some of these succeeded, but never on the big city scale Margie Archibald had envisioned when she returned to her father's hometown in 1943. The Aliceville Chamber of Commerce organized in July 1945 and spearheaded a campaign to bring a cold storage/quick freeze plant, a brick making plant, and other businesses to the area. George N. Downer, who was about to put up a new building for Aliceville's successful Coca-Cola bottling works, served as Chamber president with Robert Hugh Kirksey's father as vice president and Margie Archibald's sister Emmie as full-time secretary. They shared office space with the Red Cross recreation center that remained open for military personnel staying on to close the camp.

As mayor, Gerald Stabler courted business prospects with information about Aliceville's railroad and bus-truck transportation network, its moderate climate, its pure water supply and good health facilities, and its "flaming community spirit." Gerald and the Chamber pressed state and federal officials to move forward with development of the Tombigbee River by building a waterway to connect it to the Tennessee River.

Although Congress approved the concept for the Tennessee-Tombigbee Waterway in 1946, thirty-seven years would pass before the project was finally funded and operational. One publication suggests it ran into opposition from the railroad industry and from other regions of the country eager for federal development funds.

After the war, even Karl H. Shriver, who'd supervised the building of Camp Aliceville and then Northington Hospital for the Army Corps of Engineers, became a promoter of Aliceville industry. He and Crooks built their California-style home, Steelecrest, at Pleasant Ridge near Aliceville. Their daughter, Scarlett, was born in 1946.

In 1949, retired Colonel Shriver began working with the Alabama State Planning Board to help sell West Alabama to prospective industries. "I decided this state had a wonderful future from an economic and industrial standpoint," the former Pennsylvanian told a newspaper reporter. "Since 1942, Alabama has progressed wonderfully and in my opinion has only started to become one of the outstanding states in the nation." He mentioned the Tombigbee River plans and the area's abundant underground water supply as major reasons for his enthusiasm.

While the town struggled to prosper, the POW camp property sank further and further into weeds and oblivion. However, some Aliceville residents continued to display the artwork they'd rescued from the closing camp and often reminisced about the economic heyday they'd enjoyed when the camp was in operation.

Occasional letters from overseas kept memories of the German POWs fresh. Early in 1947, Mayor Gerald Stabler received the first of nine letters from Gerhard Stroh, a Camp Aliceville POW waiting in the French sector until he could return to his home near Tübingen in Germany. After leaving Camp Aliceville in May 1945, Stroh had worked for a while with a transportation corps in Charleston, South Carolina, before leaving the United States in November.

Stroh addressed his letter to the Mayor of Aliceville and asked for pictures of the camp and the town. Gerald wrote back that he would send the pictures. On April 27, Stroh wrote again. "Yes, you were right," he wrote in apparent response to comments from Gerald. "When we were in Aliceville, we were all in very good condition. We were well feeded [*sic*] and well dressed. The Americans treated us in the best manner."

He concluded this letter with the comment, "When I was a prisoner, I had more to eat than today when I am a free man and I was also better dressed."

Stroh wrote again in June, saying he often thought about the time he'd spent as a prisoner of war in Alabama. "In this time, I was never hungry. I always had enough to eat. However, today in Germany I am always hungry.... There is little bread; we have no potatoes, no flour, and no sugar. We have also very little fat and dripping.... We hope it will be better in autumn, when the harvest is brought in." He mentioned that he'd been quite young when he became a soldier and that all of his civilian clothes were too small.

In a letter dated July 8, 1947, Stroh noted that many Americans sent gift parcels to their relatives in Germany but that he had no relatives in the United States. Gerald wrote back, saying he and Sue would very much like to send a package and asking what was most needed.

It was almost a year before another letter arrived with suggestions. That letter, dated June 22, 1948, began with a reference to the currency reform that had finally occurred in Germany. "We are very hopeful and think we will [be] getting better very soon," wrote Stroh. He offered details about his family—his sixty-year-old father and fifty-five-year-old mother, his twenty-five-year-old sister, and now his sweetheart whom he hoped to marry in the coming year. "May I be so imprudent and tell you what I am wanting? But, send me only things, which do not have too high prices. I would like to have a little soap, because we have only a soap, which is very bad. I would like also a little lard and perhaps some other provisions if you like to send me. When you have old shirts for me or old shoes for my bride and a pair of stockings for my bride and my sister, I would be very glad also. Do not think that I am in imprudent [*sic*]. Think, that there is a lack in all things and I will be glad what you will ever send, to eat or to dress."

When Sue Stabler read this letter, she immediately found a large box and began packing it with lard, sugar, soap, and underwear. Gerald shipped it as soon as it was filled.

A grateful reply arrived in July. "I received your gift parcel with great joy," Stroh wrote. "The provisions were a great help for myself and my family in these days of need and hunger. We all would starve when the USA would not help." He went on to express concern about the political situation, saying that German people were afraid because they didn't know what the Russians planned to do. "I hope the Americans will help the European peoples in each regard, for the American frontier is Europe." He signed the letter, "I remain, my dear Sir, your sincere friend Gerhard Stroh."

The Stablers heard from at least one other former POW—Johannes Peters, who wrote to them from the British Zone on September 15, 1947. "For a long time I was PW in the camp," he wrote. "Often I have gone through your town. I am sorry that I was not able to speak often with the American people, but I can say, that I have been treated there very well." Peters told the Stablers that he and his family had lost everything as a result of the war. "Often I must think on the good lie [*sic*], we have had in your country. Although I was a PW at that time, I have not to take care for clothing and food. Both are very scanty here."

Johnny Johnston, who'd employed so many of the Aliceville POWs at his sawmill, received a letter from Werner Stein in June 1947. "To let you know that I didn't get lost in the meantime," Stein wrote. "I finally traced my steps back home and write my first letter to you from Germany." Stein had left the United States in the spring of 1946 and spent another ten months working in England as a POW before he "finally achieved a normal status as a free citizen again."

Stein did not hear anything from his wife and children for an entire year when the war ended, but he wrote now that he'd been fortunate to find them relatively healthy in spite of the current conditions in Germany. He'd spent his first few weeks at home playing and rolling with his two little daughters, "the youngest of whom I hadn't seen at all, and thinking often of your sweet little Carin who probably has become a little lady by now." (This reference is to Johnny's second child.) Stein said he'd told his wife all about America, "our grand camp at Aliceville there and my work in the woods there." He said he was glad he'd saved souvenir pictures to show her.

Stein told Johnny he'd reestablished contact with most of the men from the theater group at Camp Aliceville and that most were back home now, living in the American and British zones of postwar Germany. He mentioned that the artist named Hummel, who had painted portraits of Johnny and his children, was still in England and not happy about it. He was painting and doing portraits there as he had at Camp Aliceville, "but not under those splendid circumstances he and we experienced in the States."

Stein expressed a desire to hear about Johnny's business and family life and about "what's going on in the woods." He said he would not go into great detail about the postwar situation in Germany because he didn't like to lament and because he believed American newspapers were covering it fully. He did say that everything was far from normal, "especially the food situation" and that he didn't expect much improvement in the Russian zone, where he was living. He continued to remember "with great pleasure" the barbecue Johnny had hosted for his POW workers before the military authorities informed him he wasn't allowed to entertain the prisoners. He wrote that the barbecue had now become a pleasant mirage in his mind, given his present situation.

Finally, Stein humbled himself at the end of his letter. "Dear Mr. Johnston," he wrote. "When we left you promised to help us in distress. I didn't think then that I'd be forced to ask for your help. But now I dare to ask for it because of our children. Will you do them a favor, Sir, by sending us a box of coffee? Not because we've become caffeine addicts, but you can barter anything for coffee here especially fats from our farmers who are the only ones left in Germany who can afford luxuries at present."

His final sentence was a clear window into the new political tensions festering in postwar Germany in 1947. "I am not yet back to teaching because they (i.e., our present German authorities) first expect me to turn Communist, therefore I still prefer to work in the building industry with shovel and pick for minimum wages. If you like, I'll give you a more lengthy account next time." He closed his letter with "My kindest regards to you, your wife and children, Sincerely yours, Werner Stein."

Although this is the only letter the family still has, Johnny's son, Pep, remembers that his father continued to correspond with Werner Stein and that he kept trying to find Hummel, the artist. He knows they eventually connected, but he has no copies of their correspondence. "It was just like they weren't really thought of as enemies after they got here and they all went to work," he says of the POWs who worked for his father.

A fourth letter that has survived was written to Claude Earl Martin on July 30, 1947, by former POW Georg Trzakas from the British zone. This letter illustrates again the level of respect and friendship between some of the POWs and their American civilian work detail leaders during their time in Aliceville. Trzakas wrote to thank Claude Earl for a letter and a food parcel. "I was happy to have once again a good breakfast," he wrote. "It had a good taste."

Claude Earl, who worked as a civilian employee of the Army Corps of Engineers during the war, had apparently asked for the man's shoe size. "That is 9-9 ?," Trzakas wrote. "I need some underwear and a pants [*sic*], maybe you can send me an old overcoat for working."

Trzakas had been a glass painter before the war, but he was now taking any kind of work he could find. "In Germany we have much work, but we are missing material, tools, and work clothing. We have no glass," he wrote. He also said he missed the nice water color brushes Claude Earl had let him use at his home. "I should like to return to Aliceville and work for you again. I remember when I got so often some sweets from you and the other detail leaders." He wrote at the end that he would be thankful for whatever Claude Earl could send him and that he hoped the conditions he was living under were clear.

T.L. Hester had supervised POW work details for the Engineers and Maintenance department at Camp Aliceville, and he, too, had established personal relationships with a number of the prisoners who worked for him—prisoners like Fritz Hagmann who wrote to him after the war (see Chapter Fourteen) about the terrible conditions in Germany and about his good memories of the "nice work group" in Aliceville. Sometime during the war, another POW had drawn up plans for a stone house that Hester eventually built. Located at 209 15th Street, it remains the only stone house in Aliceville.

In addition to the letter from Fritz Hagmann, Hester heard from three other former POWs after the war—Heinz Dorn of Dortmund, Hans Hohn of Dahn, and Wilhelm F. Hönnicke of Bayreuth. Heinz Dorn's postwar letter was translated in 2004 and appeared in the Aliceville Museum newsletter. Dorn greeted Mr. Hester and said he hoped he was in good health. "I have finally arrived back in Germany," he wrote, "but my health is not as good as it was in Aliceville." He spoke of others he'd known at the camp and then made a personal request. "I want to write the entire truth to you, just as it is, no exaggerations. I recently returned home from internment. I am sick and have lost my belongings and home to the bombings, and on top of everything else, I am very hungry. I am asking you from man to man, with as much dignity as possible, if it would be possible for you to send me a package? I would be very, very happy if you could help me. Please do not be angry with me Mr. Hester. It is only the absolute desperation that forces me to ask." Heinz Dorn closed his letter with best wishes for Mr. Hester's health and with heartfelt greetings.

In June 1948, the town of Aliceville bought 133 acres of the POW camp property and extended the town limits to include the site, hoping to turn it into a thriving industrial park. Will Peebles remembers that George Downer was instrumental in securing this land for the city. Government policy dictated that the original landowners had first choice to redeem their land, but one family chose not to do this. George Downer flew to Washington, D.C., to negotiate with Alabama senators, Army officials, and others and was successful in obtaining ownership of this acreage for the City of Aliceville for the price of one dollar. This, however, was not the end of the negotiations.

"Mr. Downer flew back to Aliceville," Will Peebles remembers, "but before his arrival, Mayor Gerald Stabler received a telegram [from Washington] stating the deal had fallen through. Mayor Stabler revealed this news to Mr. Downer as soon as he arrived back in town. No time was lost until his wife had repacked his bags and had plane reservations for later that night. Mr. Downer told Mayor Stabler that he would not return from Washington until he had the land deed in his possession. He also told him he would pay all of his expenses since the city could not afford to pay for the second trip. About ten days later, he returned home to Aliceville, deed in hand."

The Birmingham News reported in February 1953 that George N. Downer Jr. and Tom Parker were using some of this property for a thriving poultry business. The city was busy recruiting other businesses for the site.

In the early 1950s, Aliceville's population hovered around three thousand. Agriculture continued to be the basis for the town's economy, as it had been before the war. The town had fourteen churches representing eight denominations. It supported an elementary school and a high school for white students and another elementary and high school for black students.

American soldiers from Aliceville were coming home and getting on with their lives. Some chose to make their careers in military service. Frank Chappell, whose father and uncle founded the Aliceville Iron Works, had flown seventy-six combat missions during the war. He took an air staff assignment at the

Pentagon and continued to be a part of the Air Force until 1970. He then worked another eighteen years as an engineer for the Fairfax County, Virginia, Department of Public Works.

Alva Temple, who'd flown 120 missions with the Tuskegee Airmen of the 99th Pursuit Squadron, also chose a military career. He spent twenty years in the United States Air Force and then returned to Columbus, Mississippi, where he opened a service station.

Robert Hugh Kirksey completed his undergraduate degree at The Citadel after the war, married, and went to law school at the University of Alabama. Eventually, he became an attorney in Aliceville and then Judge of Probate in Pickens County.

In the 1960s, when America became involved in the Vietnam War and began sending Pickens County draftees off to the other side of the world, Judge Kirksey initiated a special ceremony at the courthouse in Carrollton. "We try not to make it a tear-jerker," he said. "Our main point is to let these boys know that Pickens cares about them. We try not to have a lot of speechmaking." Acting on a suggestion from his friend, retired Army colonel David Ross, Judge Kirksey had refreshments served and presented each new soldier with an overnight zipper bag presented by the City of Gordo, a nail clip and key ring from Carrollton, a personal grooming kit from Aliceville, a ballpoint pen from Reform, a pearl-handle pocket knife from the Commissioner's Court, and a New Testament from the local Ministerial Association.

Wendell Parrish, who'd been a POW in Germany, returned to his hometown of Selma, Alabama, after the war and became director of YMCA programs there. In 1968, he moved to Aliceville to assume leadership of the local Chamber of Commerce. J.T. Junkins, who'd been a fascinated thirteen-year-old when the MPEG guards began riding around Aliceville in their jeeps, grew up and became a member of the Aliceville City Council.

Construction on the Tennessee-Tombigbee Waterway began in 1971 but took twelve years to complete. During that time, Aliceville businesses did a good job of providing employment. Aliceville Cotton Mills, Inc. spun yarn for Fruit of the Loom products, and Huyck Felt Company manufactured industrial felts for the fast-growing southern paper mill industry. Rico Liquids opened a plant to manufacture and process feeds and supplements for cattle and horses, and Aliceville Veneers began shipping box veneer to nine states for fruit and vegetable crates. The town also supported several sawmills and an aircraft painting shop.

Over in Reform, Westinghouse Electric Corporation built a Lamp Division plant to make Christmas tree lights, photoflash bulbs, and decorative lamp bulbs. Stevens Fashions built a plant in Carrollton to supply knit goods to Butte Knit and Jonathan Logan, and Gordo had X-L Manufacturing, which made topcoats and jackets for national markets.

During these years, there were no formal remembrances of the POW camp that had dominated the life and economy of Aliceville during the war, but occasionally, as time ticked forward, a person or two would make their way back down the winding roads of Pickens County to Aliceville—between gently rolling hills and past spindly trunks of scrub pine, between patches of black water swamp and past huge, reddish hills where fire ants staked their claim—to search for remains of the camp that could spark old war memories.

One afternoon in 1962, Harvey Stapp got a telephone call from the desk clerk at a local motel. A man staying there had inquired about Harvey and said he used to know him at the prisoner of war camp. When Mr. Harvey went by the motel the next morning, he discovered that the guest was a former POW who had since become a Catholic priest.

Mary Lu Turner Keef remembers that her parents drove down through Alabama and passed through Aliceville while traveling in the early 1970s. They didn't stay. There wasn't much of the old camp to see, and the people they'd known when they worked there were mostly gone back to other parts of the country.

One afternoon in February 1975, while the Vietnam War was slogging to an end, City Council member David Stringfellow noticed two strangers as he stepped into the Aliceville post office. One of them asked in thickly accented English if David had lived in Aliceville a long time. "Oh yes," he replied, and the two began to talk.

After a few minutes, the other stranger, a doctor from Birmingham, explained that the man with the accent had been a POW in Aliceville during the war and had flown to Birmingham from Austria for a medical meeting. The Birmingham doctor had volunteered to drive him down to Aliceville to revisit the camp. Dr. Hans Kopera then introduced himself. He was now a lecturer and director of clinical pharmacology at the University of Graz in Austria.

David Stringfellow spent the rest of the afternoon taking the two men on a tour of the former POW campsite. There wasn't much to see, but David located one of the old buildings, and Dr.

Kopera took a picture of it. Memories of the two years he'd spent in Camp Aliceville began to spill out—the valuable medical studies he'd begun there and the caricatures he'd often created as a hobby.

At the end of the afternoon, Hans Kopera and his medical colleague thanked David Stringfellow and drove back to Birmingham. A few weeks later, a letter arrived at the City Council chambers. "Thanks to the City of Aliceville" was written at the top. In it, Dr. Kopera expressed his heartfelt thanks to those who'd made him feel welcome when he visited to renew old memories:

> I have to admit that I did it with some excitement and expected more of the camp than I finally found, however, what I did not expect and actually found was the extremely kind reception by people with whom I talked in Aliceville. In particular, one of your town councilmen was so kind to even give us a sort of "sightseeing tour." I believe this attitude towards a former prisoner of war excellently demonstrates how much the thinking of people has changed to the better. The ready acceptance which I have found in your town by members of the younger and older generation convinced me once more that the desire to promote understanding between nations has become strong enough to suppress or perhaps even forget bad experiences of periods full of insanity and lack of humanity. I can assure you I was happy to be back in this part of America and to meet so many friendly people.

This, I thought, I should let you know. With best regards from a friend.

The letter was signed by Dr. H. Kopera (former 4WG 25 38).

In 1981, historian E.B. Walker's son Chip chose Camp Aliceville as the subject for a history assignment at Birmingham-Southern College. Chip did extensive research and interviewed a number of people who'd been associated with the camp. His paper, which focused on the music, art, theater, and creative writing of the German prisoners, was later published in *The Alabama Review* under the title, "German Creative Activities 1943-1946."

During this research, E.B. and his son visited Aliceville, and Tommy McKinstry Jr. took them on a brief tour of the POW campsite. A few concrete foundations were still in place along with a part of the kiln prisoners had used to make brick for drainage ditches and other projects. The stone chimney and fireplace from the old Enlisted Men's Club were still standing, and Tommy poked back a few weeds to show what was left of the gate posts that had marked the entrance to the Post Engineer area of the camp. Knocked over and damaged by truck traffic, they lay almost completely hidden in underbrush, but E.B. and his son could picture how they'd once stood because they'd seen them in a copy of the sketch collection created by POWs Herman Kalbe and Hans Fanselow during the war.

When Chip went on to graduate school, he left his Camp Aliceville research materials at home with his father, who remained interested in the subject and began to collect additional information about the camp. E.B. Walker's interest increased the following February when a letter was forwarded to him in Birmingham from the Aliceville Chamber of Commerce—a letter written by a former German POW who hoped to revisit Camp Aliceville in April 1982. This German city engineer, who in his retirement had decided to visit all the places he'd experienced earlier in his life, had addressed his inquiry to the Chamber of Commerce, or to the Mayor of Aliceville, if no Chamber existed. He'd written that he wanted to revisit the place where he'd been held prisoner in Alabama and that he would like to meet with a person who could talk about the camp. Someone in Aliceville—probably Tommy McKinstry—forwarded the letter to E.B. Walker.

Because time was short, E.B. immediately sent a one-sentence telegram to the man in Germany. "Please call me when you are in the United States," it read. He included his telephone number and address.

The German man wanting to visit Aliceville was none other than Walter Felholter, the North Africa captive who'd been one of the last four "diphtheria positives" in 1944. His oldest daughter was living in Kentucky for a year while her husband pursued graduate work in agriculture at the University of Lexington, and Walter and his wife were coming to visit them and their three-year-old granddaughter.

Walter received E.B. Walker's telegram just before he left for the United States and wrote back immediately, listing his four-week itinerary and giving the telephone number of the professor he'd be staying with in Kentucky. When he arrived in Lexington, the professor's wife said, "There was a phone call for you, Walter. You should call back at once."

Walter returned E.B.'s call, and the two agreed to meet in Cullman, Alabama, on May 9. Walter wanted to visit Cullman because it had been founded in the 1870s by a German entrepreneur. The two men had lunch in a restaurant there—probably the All Steak, a Cullman landmark—and had a good talk. E.B. had a tape recorder and asked all sorts of questions about Walter's memories. Then he asked, "Do you want me to go with you tomorrow to Aliceville?" Walter said yes, he'd like that, and they agreed to meet at a gas station in Birmingham.

The next day was Sunday. Walter went first to attend church at St. Bernard's Abbey, the Benedictine monastic community near Cullman. Time passed quickly there. After the service, many people wanted to shake hands and share stories about their own German ancestors. They insisted that Walter visit the Ave Maria Grotto—the park and hillside where, during the 1930s, Brother Joseph Zoettle had patiently created more than a hundred miniature reproductions of some of the most famous buildings and shrines in the world—the temple in Jerusalem, St. Peter's Basilica and the Coliseum in Rome, the Spanish missions of the American Southwest, and the shrines at Fatima and Lourdes.

Walter was late getting to Birmingham, but he did manage to connect with E.B. Walker, who suggested that Walter ride with him to Aliceville so they could continue to talk. Walter's daughter would follow in the rental car. Walter remembers that he and E.B. had another very good discussion.

When they arrived in Aliceville, E.B. Walker drove to the home of a man who was originally from New York state and had been a guard at the camp. He'd married an Aliceville woman and come back there to live after the war. Now he owned his own grocery store, with an excellent butcher shop, in Aliceville, and his wife owned her own beauty salon a half block from where she'd worked during the war at the Aliceville Hotel.

Within a few minutes, Walter Felholter, the former POW, and Stanley Pendrak, the former 389th MPEG guard, were busy comparing notes on their memories of the camp while E.B. Walker, the teenager who'd watched the first trainload of POWs move through Birmingham on its way down to Aliceville, listened in fascination.

The three men drove out to the campsite. Walter tried to pinpoint where his quarantine barracks in Compound B had been, but it was impossible to tell. "Don't go in there," Stanley warned, pointing to the overgrown bushes and trees. "It's full of snakes." Stanley showed them a site at the end of Aliceville's main street where two plaster monuments created by German POWs had been installed. He also drove them to the Stapp home, where a four-foot tall golden eagle sculpture created by a POW was on display atop a five-foot concrete base.

Like Hans Kopera, Walter Felholter found few physical remains of the camp, but he did find warm-hearted local people who seemed pleased that he'd come back to visit. Like E.B. Walker, Walter loved history, and the two men remained in contact after the visit to Aliceville. "He sent me books," Walter has said. One of them was Arnold Krammer's *Nazi Prisoners of War in America*, which had been published in 1979. Walter wrote back to E.B. that he liked the book but not the title. "We are not the Nazi prisoners," he wrote. "We are German prisoners, but not Nazis—we were not all Nazis."

It was 1988 before former POW Günther Peter Ertel made the drive down to Aliceville from Ohio, where he'd been living and working since 1953. He was now vice president of a chemical export business near Richfield in northern Ohio and considered himself richly blessed to have made a good life for himself and his family in America after the war.

When he and Johanna made their visit on April 15, a number of copies of the old camp newspaper *Der Zaungast* had been donated to the local Aliceville library. As the couple leafed through the carefully preserved old issues spread out over the checkout desk, Günther suddenly became very excited. "Look, Johanna!" he said. "It's the letter I wrote for you!" He'd forgotten it completely in the intervening years.

Johanna didn't know what he was talking about, but Günther quickly described the letter he'd written about their walk in the rain along the Isar River near Munich. "It was almost the end of the war, and they stopped the POW mail right after I wrote it," he said. "When I couldn't send it to you, I gave it to the newspaper editor, and he published it, and here it is, after all these years."

Johanna leaned over the counter and read, with tears in her eyes, while the Aliceville librarian, Ethelda Potts, looked on with tears in her eyes, too. Johanna read and translated Günther's memory of how they'd wandered like children along the river that day and how they'd strolled arm in arm, "the sole possessors of this beautiful piece of earth" before the madness of the war.

When he'd submitted the letter for publication as an essay in *Der Zaungast,* Günther had added a wish that the "playful evening wind" would carry "the written page of this warm stream of memories from brighter hours" far away to Johanna. It had taken a long time, but the words had come full circle, and here she was now, reading them aloud in Aliceville, Alabama, after forty-three years.

Later that same year, in October, E.B. Walker traveled to Myrtle Beach, South Carolina, to attend a scheduled reunion of the 305th MPEG unit—the unit Chet Eisenhauer had joined on a rainy night in 1943 when he thought he was being transferred to Aliceville to repair military motorcycles. Like many former army units, these guards met somewhere every year or so with their wives and reminisced about their war days. E.B. went to the MPEG gathering in South Carolina with the idea of inviting the veterans to hold their next reunion near Aliceville, where they could renew memories of guarding German POWs early in the war. The guard veterans liked the idea and voted to come to Aliceville the following year.

E.B. then got in touch with Sue Stabler, and plans were set in motion for "Aliceville's Reunion of Friendship" to be held in October 1989. As plans developed, the reunion was added to the official event calendar of a statewide, year-long reunion celebration entitled "Come Home to Alabama," which had been designed to encourage Alabamians everywhere to make return visits to their home state. Aliceville's POW reunion event would mark the first occasion that former American MPEG guards and former Camp Aliceville POWs met with each other officially after the end of World War II.

Citizens of Aliceville began to spruce up for this event, led by Sue Stabler who arranged to have the weed-strangled gate posts from the Post Engineer grounds cleaned up and moved to the area next to the flagstone chimney and fireplace where the Enlisted Men's Club had been. The grounds of the old club were cleaned up, and a new city mini-park, complete with picnic shelter, was created on the site. During cleanup, workers discovered the original concrete sidewalk that had surrounded the outside of the clubhouse and other sidewalks leading off from the building. They'd been hidden for forty-five years under several inches of sod.

To encourage local support, Sue Stabler wrote a special article for the *Pickens County Herald and West Alabamian,* giving background about the camp and describing the events planned for the reunion. She mentioned that the Lions and Rotary Clubs and the VFW Auxiliary, as well as the Mayor and the City Council and the Historical Preservation Commission, were all participating. "So far as we know," she wrote, "this is the first time that any town in the U.S. that contained a POW camp has invited everyone connected with the camp including former prisoners to come for a reunion.... We feel that an event such as this makes for warm personal relations between countries and makes the best public relations for the United States that could have been dreamed of."

The local Rotary Club ordered an Alabama Historical Association historic marker. The Aliceville Historical Preservation Commission set up a museum room on the lower level of the civic center and began soliciting POW camp-related donations and loans of artifacts from Aliceville residents. The Chamber of Commerce launched a campaign to locate former POWs and drafted a letter from the current mayor, C.R. Carroll, inviting them to participate in the reunion.

When this letter arrived at Walter Felholter's home in Friedberg, Germany, he read it carefully two or three times and concluded it was probably some kind of mistake. The German army had been rigidly structured, and Germany society remained that way to a large degree. Walter could not imagine a city mayor wanting to socialize with former rank and file soldiers. "This is not for me," he thought. "It must be for high officers and people like that. I was just a soldier. They wouldn't be inviting me for a reunion there."

Walter set the letter aside, but one Sunday afternoon in August, he received a telephone call from a man named Karl Bayer who spoke to him in an odd mixture of British-accented English and Frankfurt-dialect German. "He said he'd been asked to call to invite me for the reunion in Aliceville. 'You should come,' he said. 'Please come there.'" The man also asked if Walter had the names and addresses of any other former German soldiers who'd been prisoners at Camp Aliceville. "Just one," Walter told him. "He lives quite near to me, and he visited Aliceville after I did in 1982."

Walter had become acquainted with Heinz Most in an odd way. He was working in his office in Friedberg one afternoon when there was a soft knock on the door. Walter opened it, and a man stepped in, smiling and laughing. "I don't know you," Walter said. "Do you know me?"

Instead of answering, the man took out a business card. He handed it to Walter who studied it for a moment and then looked up, puzzled. "This is my card," he said, "but I didn't give it to you."

The man smiled. "Please, turn it over," he said.

Walter turned it over and read on the back the handwritten address of Stanley Pendrak in Aliceville, Alabama. "Have you met Stanley Pendrak?" he asked, still puzzled.

Heinz Most nodded and then told Walter about his own trip to the United States. He'd traveled with his niece and her husband and had asked them to drive him down through Aliceville, where he, too, had been a prisoner of war. He'd gone into several shops on the main street and tried to explain, with his limited English, that he wanted to see the camp. In one shop, two young ladies directed him to the butcher shop next door. The owner was able to understand that Heinz was a former POW looking for the camp. "Just a moment," he said. He went to his office behind the shop and came back with Walter Felholter's business card. Heinz tucked the card in his pocket and looked up Walter when he returned home.

Eventually, both Walter Felholter and Heinz Most decided to return to the United States to attend the 1989 reunion in Aliceville. Heinz had saved his copies of *Der Zaungast* all through the years, and he packed them carefully so he could present them to the new museum that would be dedicated during their visit.

Sallie Alston, executive director of the Aliceville Chamber of Commerce at the time, encouraged a number of local families to host German guests. Chuck and Jane Gwin invited Heinrich Most to stay with them. They have no family connection to German culture or history, but Chuck has always been a history buff, especially when it comes to the Civil War and World War II. "Because of that and because we're very civic minded—we like to do things in the community, and Sallie asked us to," Jane has said.

Sonny and Ann Stirling invited Walter Felholter and his wife, Lieselotte, to stay with them. Walter and Lieselotte arrived at the Stirling home on Thursday, October 5. Ann suggested they might like to view the exhibits in the museum room at the civic center that afternoon, instead of waiting for the official dedication the next day. She was happy to drive them over so they could enjoy them undisturbed.

When Walter entered the museum room, the first display that caught his eye was a newspaper spread out on a table in the middle of the room. The newspaper, a copy of *The South Bend* (Indiana) *Tribune* dated February 26, 1978, was open to an article describing the life journey of another former Aliceville POW who'd emigrated to the United States in 1949. The article began with the narration of a horrible experience in North Africa—a German sergeant being blown out of a foxhole the POW had vacated moments earlier. Then it flashed back to the night the POW lost his belief that combat would be a glorious adventure—when bombs from a German war plane accidentally killed several of his buddies and wounded him.

As Walter scanned the article, he experienced a sense of *Eindruck des Nochmalerlebens*—what the French call *déjà vu*. "The further I read, the more I was fascinated by what I was reading," he explained later. On the fourth page of the article was a photograph of the POW with the sweetheart who became his wife, a young woman named Katie that he'd met while recuperating, before going to North Africa. Walter didn't recognize the man in the photo, but that story, too, rang a far-off bell in his memory. "The content became more and more familiar to me. It was clear that I knew all of this—I already knew the whole story—but I could not connect it to a person I remembered. I read the name again and then read the rest of the report."

When the POW was quoted about holding up his hands to surrender to the British and then realizing that the others around him had not, Walter was certain he'd heard this exact description before. The only part of the article not familiar to him was about this POW at Camp Gordon Johnston in Florida, after he'd left Camp Aliceville.

Although Walter could not pinpoint exactly how and when he'd heard these stories before, he was deeply moved by his discovery of them. He glanced up and noticed an American woman standing nearby and watching him. "The change in my facial expression as I read appeared to interest her, and I was so moved that I had to share my thoughts. I said to her, 'I knew him. He was a friend of mine.'"

Sue Stabler smiled and nodded as if she understood. Then she told Walter that the man in the article would be arriving the next day. Walter had not expected to meet anyone he'd known in the camp. He gave Mrs. Stabler his business card and asked her to tell this man about him.

The early part of the next day was busy for Walter and his wife. They visited with their hosts, explored the town, and then attended the opening of the Aliceville Museum, where they listened to presentations by the Aliceville Historical Preservation Society and spoke with local residents. One of those conversations brought back an amusing memory. When Walter was introduced to Aliceville resident Earline Jones, who'd been a civilian employee at the camp, he asked her what her position had been. Earline explained that she'd worked at Headquarters, ordering food for the POWs. "Oh," Walter said with a laugh, "you're the one who gave us the corn." Earline had not known at the time about the burying of the corn, so Walter told her the funny story of the POWS burying the corn so they wouldn't have to eat it. After that, whenever Walter returned to Aliceville, he told everyone he'd come to see how the big cornfield was doing.

All afternoon, Walter wondered when he would encounter the man from Michigan who had told his story to the Indiana newspaper. A picnic had been scheduled for that evening at the Tom Bevill Visitors Center over near the town of Pickensville. When Walter asked what this place was, Sonny Stirling explained about the Tennessee-Tombigbee Waterway, now at long last the shipping lifeline in this part of the South. As a city engineer, Walter listened with interest to the story of the waterway and its positive effect on Pickens County.

Mr. Bevill represented the 7th Congressional District, including Pickens County, and had been chairman of the committee in the United States House of Representatives that approved funding for this huge waterway project. The lock and dam near Pickensville had been named for him, and so had the visitors' center where the picnic would be held.

Ann Stirling explained that the visitors' center was an authentic replica of a beautiful antebellum home that might have stood on a Southern plantation in the years before the Civil War. It was filled with maps and artifacts. When she suggested Walter and Lieselotte might like to go there a little early so they could view the exhibits, the Felholters agreed.

The sun was beginning to slant its late afternoon rays across the fall landscape and the calm waters of the Tenn-Tom waterway when the Stirlings pulled their car up in front of the visitors' center. As he stepped out of the car, Walter looked up at the graceful white cupola on top of the building and then became aware of a slight man with wavy hair and glasses, who jumped up from a rocking chair on the Greek-style portico and bounded down the steps. Hermann Blumhardt had been waiting eagerly to greet the man Sue Stabler had told him about as soon as he arrived earlier in the afternoon.

It was a happy reunion after forty-six years. Walter Felholter and Hermann Blumhardt laughed and nodded as they reminisced about being assigned together to Company 9, Compound C at Camp Aliceville all those years earlier. Walter explained how his memories had gradually unfolded as he read the newspaper story the day before. The two remembered together how good real coffee had tasted that first night in June 1943, and Walter asked if Hermann remembered the strange peanut butter that stuck to the roofs of their mouths and how good it was to sleep and sleep and sleep that first night in Alabama. "Certainly," Walter wrote later, "we would not have recognized each other if we had met by chance on a street somewhere, but in this case, we were prepared."

The picnic was wonderful. A man from Mississippi played the organ, and Robert Hugh Kirksey, now serving as president of the Aliceville Chamber of Commerce, welcomed the visitors—both American and German. Walter was impressed with the program—an invocation by the minister of the First United Methodist Church of Aliceville, followed by words of welcome from the mayor of Pickensville and the Pickens County Judge of Probate. Walter's long ago friend Hermann Blumhardt gave a response on behalf of the German POWs and Chet Eisenhauer gave one on behalf of the 305th MPEG guards. The group was even greeted by a representative from the United States Department of State who had traveled all the way from Washington, D.C., for the event, which ended with an impressive fireworks display beside the waterway.

Saturday was another blur of activity. It began when townspeople, former guards, and former POWs gathered at the site of the former Frisco railroad depot on Third Avenue Northwest to recreate the arrival of that first trainload of prisoners on June 2, 1943. Sue Stabler and Jake McBride were there. Walter and Lieselotte Felholter and Hermann and Katie Blumhardt were there, and so was Heinrich Most. Günther Peter Ertel had come back again from Ohio with Johanna. Many former guards were there, too, wearing baseball caps that signified their proud 305th heritage—Chet Eisenhauer, Harry Warnack, Joseph Samper, and Joey Futschko.

Traffic was halted for twenty minutes at the railroad crossing so veterans from both sides could relive this moment from their history. Walter Felholter stood next to former MPEG guard Chet Eisenhauer, who was now a psychotherapist in private practice in Wisconsin. Together, they looked off up the railroad tracks, recalling that long ago afternoon and hearing the train whistle in their minds. "I remember there was a white painted house on the left," Walter told Chet. "I had one blanket with me and nothing else."

Hermann Blumhardt joked about how impossible it was for the Germans to learn to pick their own weight in cotton. "You should have a train here today, to add to the memory," he said.

If Walter had been impressed with the program the evening before, he was even more impressed by the proceedings on Saturday afternoon. First came the dedication of the new Aliceville City Park on the site of the former enlisted men's club. Mayor Ray Carroll welcomed everyone, the Washington, D.C. representative spoke again, and then Walter's historian friend from Birmingham, E.B. Walker, spoke.

This was followed by a down-home barbecue lunch in the picnic pavilion Sue Stabler had had built at the new City Park. As former POWs and former guards sampled ribs and slaw and beans, a reporter for Alabama Public Television stood to one side narrating the event for a broadcast video. "At one time," he pronounced as the cameras rolled, "the people partying behind me were…on opposite sides of the fence. Some were guards. Some were prisoners. Today they are together again for the first time since World War II. Together again as one group without the fence."

Former guard Harry Warnack declared it a wonderful experience. "It's really great to find out after all these years, and now we have these ex-German prisoners coming down here, and we're going to meet them. I think it's beautiful." He reached out to shake Hermann Blumhardt's hand and said with a smile, as he held up a small flash camera with his other hand, "It's nice to be shooting with cameras."

At two o'clock, everyone moved to Memorial Field, where the minister of the Aliceville First Baptist Church offered an invocation, and Robert Hugh Kirksey asked the crowd to stand for the playing of the national anthems of the United States of America and the Federal Republic of West Germany.

It was quite an occasion. The 20th Special Forces of the Alabama National Guard performed a free fall parachute jump into the stadium. Rotary Club officers, assisted by members of the late Colonel Karl Shriver's family, unveiled the historical marker, and Chet Eisenhauer and the son of a former American POW made remarks. The POWs presented German flags to their former guards, and the guards presented the POWs with American flags the parachutists had carried during their jump. It was clear in this place how very far towards mutual respect the relationship between these two countries and their citizens had come.

At three o'clock, to Walter Felholter's further amazement, the Honorable Guy Hunt, Governor of the State of Alabama, arrived to a twenty-one-gun salute by a field artillery brigade from the Alabama National Guard. The reunion concluded with the Governor's address and a benediction offered by the pastor of Aliceville's First Presbyterian Church.

As Walter was leaving the stadium with his wife, Hermann Blumhardt came up to him. "Look what I have noticed," he said. He handed Walter a small pocket calendar he'd kept with him in 1943 while he was a prisoner. It was open to the month of December, and there, on the date of December 4, 1943, Hermann had written, "Walter Felholter Hospital." It was the date that Walter had been diagnosed with diphtheria and quarantined in the camp hospital, and it was the last time the two men saw each other until this weekend.

Günther Peter Ertel summed up the feelings of those who attended when he told Alabama Public Television that afternoon, "The thing we have to be thankful for, and which is really the meaning of this reunion, is that all this war and hatred and all these things are behind us, that we are looking at each other as human beings and appreciate each other as human beings, and there is peace between us and friendship between us. And I think that's the real meaning of it."

Reinhold Schulte, the former POW who'd brought the chess set and box he'd carved in Camp Aliceville with him when he emigrated to Chicago in 1954, would have loved this reunion, but he was not able to come. He'd retired from his job as a landscaper in 1986, and he and his wife had moved to Lake Geneva, Wisconsin. Earlier in the year of this first reunion, Reinhold suffered a stroke that left him speechless and partially comatose. He died in a nursing home in May 1993.

Reinhold Schulte left the chess set to his son Reinhold Jr,. who took it with him when he returned to Germany to work as a freelance translator. The hand-carved box went to Reinhold's son, Dieter, who became a teacher and transportation coordinator for schools in the Chicago area. In April 2002, Dieter and his family journeyed down the winding roads to Aliceville to bring the box for a display at the Aliceville Museum. "I wanted to let other people see the community that developed within the camp, the things he learned while he was there," explained the son, who had come to the United States at age fourteen, with war memories still fresh in his mind. "The box is giving back in some way so that people might understand the bond that has developed between the town and the former

POWs. They can understand that people who started out as enemies could treat each other with dignity."

It was 1993 before POWs and guards returned to Aliceville for another reunion, but Walter Felholter and Heinrich Most and some of the other POWs gathered occasionally in Germany to share memories. In 1991, Robert Hugh Kirksey's oldest daughter, Mary Bess, had returned to Aliceville from Birmingham, where she'd worked with the Birmingham Public Library for eighteen years. Her husband, John Paluzzi, set up a law practice in Aliceville, and she became chairman of the Chamber of Commerce's Reunion Committee. In this capacity, she handled the planning of the fiftieth-year reunion and began to develop friendships and contacts that would last a lifetime. The 1993 reunion in Aliceville was special because it marked fifty years since the establishment of the prisoner of war camp in the town.

August Wanders, whose diary entries from the war years are mentioned frequently in this narrative, attended the 1993 reunion with his daughter, Ellen, who sent a telefax letter announcing the reunion to Manfred Rommel, son of the famous Desert Fox leader of German troops in Africa. Manfred Rommel was Mayor of the German city of Stuttgart at the time he responded to Ellen Wanders. She presented the original of the reply she received to the Aliceville Museum. It included these comments:

> I would be beholden to you if you would communicate my best wishes to the organizers at Aliceville. Soldiers of the Afrika Korps were interned at

> Aliceville. The most remarkable thing about these German Italian troops of the Afrika campaign was that, during a time that the name of Germans is associated with terrible atrocities, they were able to achieve a reputation among their enemies as fair fighters.

Rommel went on to praise his father's former enemies as well. "All of this depends on mutual exchange. Without the legendary British fairness and the especial efforts of the leadership and troops of the United Kingdom to achieve humanness, the conditions in North Africa could well have been different." Rommel referred to another POW camp in Nebraska (probably Camp Atlanta) and noted that POWs were "treated fairly and well by the Americans."

After mentioning the escalating problems in Yugoslavia in 1993 and concerns about humane treatment in that conflict, Rommel concluded by saying, "We owe the Americans great respect and recognition, not only for the kind treatment of our POWs, but for much else after the second world war." He conveyed his hopes that the reunion October 1 through 3 would be a success, and he wished Ellen Wanders a good trip to the United States.

Wilhelm Schlegel made his first trip to Aliceville for this reunion. Heinrich Most was not able to return, so Chuck and Jane Gwin invited Wilhelm and Otti Schlegel and their son Klaus to stay with them from Thursday afternoon to Sunday morning. Because Klaus spoke English, the Gwins found it easier to communicate than they had during the 1989 reunion. "They're just such nice people," Jane Gwin has said of the

Schlegel family. "We just kind of clicked. We became very close to them from the start, and we've stayed in contact—Christmas cards and New Year's e-mails. We've done lots of things together, just like family when they visit." She explains that Chuck was a banker, and so was Wilhelm, so they had that in common, as well as their interest in World War II history and its effect on both of their countries.

Jane says they always enjoy Wilhelm's many stories about the camp when he visits—how well they were treated and the funny things the POWs did and the jokes they played. "He's very much into soccer and always has been," she says. "He played soccer when he was in the camp."

Eugene Dakan was one of the guards who attended this reunion. The former 436th MPEG came with his wife from their home in Moundsville, West Virginia, and donated his army pith helmet, two issues of the army's Camp Aliceville newspaper, *The Camptown Crier,* and photos he'd taken while stationed at the prisoner of war camp. During a later visit to Aliceville, Eugene would also donate the army visor he'd purchased in Sam Wise's store in 1943—the one with the lost-and-found card inside that read, "Be Wise and Patronize Sam Wise—Aliceville, Alabama."

In October 1993, the Aliceville community again made an all-out effort to welcome its German visitors. Public buildings flew both American and German flags, and the Piggly Wiggly supermarket offered German delicacies like bratwurst and sauerkraut and pumpernickel bread.

A few residents were not impressed with all the hoopla in honor of former enemies. One of them was Wendell Parrish, who continued to remember the way he and thousands of other

American prisoners had been treated by the Nazis in comparison with how well Americans had treated German prisoners. A newspaper reporter once wrote that Wendell refused to attend any of the reunions, and some residents reported that he left town every time the Germans showed up. "Well, that's stretching it a bit," Wendell has said. "But some of these Germans that come back, not most of them, but some of them, were Nazis, and they separated themselves at this camp [Aliceville]. They didn't have anything to do with the other guys."

American interest in modern Germany was keen in the early 1990s because of positive publicity surrounding the tearing down of the Berlin Wall in 1989 and the subsequent reunification of East and West Germany. In Alabama, interest ran especially high at the time of the 1993 reunion because Mercedes Benz had just announced that it would build its first assembly plant in the United States just north of Tuscaloosa, only an hour from Aliceville.

Local residents and their guests, former German POWs and former camp guards, enjoyed a catfish fry one evening, complete with spectacular sunset, on the banks of the Tombigbee River, and also a southern picnic of hickory smoked ham, fried chicken, and sweet potatoes one afternoon at the picnic pavilion named for Sue Stabler. The University of Alabama jazz band played for dancing, and the Stillman College choir entertained with gospel and soul music. At the end of one evening, the German guests launched an impromptu *heimat abend* sing-along which ended, inevitably, with everyone singing *Lili Marlene,* a German song about a soldier meeting a woman under a street lamp—a song hummed first by *Afrikakorps* soldiers after hearing it on the radio, but a song that later stuck in the minds of British and American soldiers as well.

One event during this reunion caused some discomfort for both Germans and Americans. A battlefield reenactment group had been invited to recreate a skirmish from the Battle of the Bulge—a skirmish won by Americans. The Germans, who viewed their military service as honorable in spite of the way the war turned out, were embarrassed by this and surprised that their American hosts would stage such a painful reminder. Walter Felholter has said of this incident, "People like to play war. The Germans [reenactors] ran out of the building, and the American soldiers [reenactors] shot all the Germans down. The stupid Germans were shot down—the play showed that. We were guests, and we had to look at that." Many of the Americans who watched were embarrassed, too, and apologized to their German guests for what seemed to be unintended bad taste.

Wilhelm Schlegel was particularly touched by the memorial service held during this reunion at the First United Methodist Church in Aliceville. "The pastor said that one should speak of this service as a forgiveness celebration," he said. He still talked about it years later.

In 1994, the Aliceville Chamber of Commerce organized a trip to Germany at the invitation of several former POWs. Approximately forty Americans, including Aliceville Mayor W. R. (Billy) McKinsey, Mary Bess Paluzzi, Sallie Alston, Jean and Bill Martin, former MPEG guards Byron Kauffman, Eugene Dakan, Harold Cover, and Gordon Forbes, and former Aliceville resident Sam Love made this trip. Sam Love, a film maker and public relations consultant in Washington, D.C., recorded more than thirty hours of interview tape during this trip and captured the still vivid memories of both Germans and Americans who had been in Aliceville during the war. Along with the memories, Sam also captured the perspectives that fifty years of postwar living had brought to these people. Many of Sam's interviews have enriched this narrative by providing memories and insights not available anywhere else. Sam also produced a fourteen-minute video, based on his interviews. It was donated to the Aliceville Museum in November 1996 and continues to offer visitors an introduction to the history of the camp.

Former 305th MPEG guard Byron Kauffman told Sam Love he believed many of the German soldiers who were captured and came to Aliceville hadn't wanted to be in the army any more than a lot of drafted American soldiers. "They were drafted in, too" he said. "There was conscription." Byron told Sam people often asked him if he'd felt a lot of animosity for the German prisoners. "No, I didn't," he said. Many of his friends in Kansas City didn't understand why he would want to attend reunions where former German POWs would be present. "You have to experience it in order to find out," he said. "If there was more of this going on, there'd be less trouble in the world because we have affirmed a new bond of friendship—I hope an everlasting one."

Harold Cover told Sam Love during the German trip that he never dreamed, when the war ended, that Germans and Americans would ever come together for a reunion, but he did remember the gradual trust that developed between the POWs and their guards in Aliceville. "They probably made the first advances to be friendly," he said, "and then we got to trusting them."

Those who made the trip to Germany were welcomed by Theo Klein, who hosted a dinner for the group with his son, Michael, at the *Gasthaus zum Goldenes Lamm* near his home in Ramberg. The Aliceville guests were introduced to new German foods, including *Pfälzer Saumagen*, a pig stomach stuffed with meat, potatoes, and spices and then roasted.

A major highlight of the trip, probably arranged by toy manufacturer Theo Klein, was a visit to the city of Stuttgart, where Mayor Manfred Rommel greeted the group warmly and posed for photos in the hallway of the Stuttgart *Rathaus* (city hall). One photo shows Rommel shaking hands with Aliceville's Mayor Billy McKinsey.

Whatever else was going on in the world in the mid-1990s, friendships between many Aliceville residents and former Camp Aliceville prisoners continued to grow. Jim Reed, whose father had worked with German POWs at Northington Hospital in Tuscaloosa near the end of the war, attended the 1995 reunion in Aliceville and wrote about the experience in his book *Dad's Tweed Coat*. Jim described visiting the Aliceville Museum on a warm Friday evening and marveling as he enjoyed refreshments prepared by local residents for an odd collection of guests, including former guards and prisoners as well as their neighbors.

> Aliceville is a miniscule place that nobody goes through unless they're on the way to someplace else, but suddenly, this close and mellow Friday night, Aliceville seems like the biggest small town in the world, a town that disproves all the warmongers and all the former cold-war propagandists and everybody who ever looked

> real hard for a reason to hate some people they'd never even met.

Jim concluded that it would be wonderful if gatherings like the one in which he'd participated at Aliceville could occur "anywhere and everywhere else in the world" on similar Friday nights.

The Aliceville Museum, in its present location at 104 Broad Street, had opened for the first time in February 1995. The Meridian Coca-Cola Bottling Company had donated two brick buildings, and the Harry Wheat family had contributed a strategic piece of land. The Museum opened with exhibits in four small counter display cases, ten display boards, and six or seven framed pieces of artwork from the era of the POW camp. It has grown considerably since then.

During this reunion in October 1995, five former German POWs—Hermann Blumhardt, Walter Felholter, Theo Klein, Wilhelm Schlegel, and Bruno Schneider—donated and planted a gingko tree just outside the entrance to the Aliceville Museum. "This tree now we plant at this place," Wilhelm Schlegel announced solemnly. "Let it be a symbol of hope for a peaceful future." These men, who'd grown so far beyond the horrors of war, wanted to express their profound hopes for a future of world peace by planting the tree that had been the first to sprout green leaves in the ruins of Hiroshima and by planting it in the place where they had formed a lasting bond of friendship with former enemies.

Individual family connections and friendships grew through the years, too. In 1996, Tiny Prisock Anderson came to Aliceville to close her mother's home and discovered the letter Fritz Hagmann had written to her grandfather, T.L. Hester, in 1947 (see Chapter Fourteen). Shortly after that, she and her husband made a trip to Germany to visit friends and took the letter with them. With their friends' help, they located the Hagmann family in Tübingen and spent an afternoon visiting with Fritz' widow, Edith, and his son, Ralf. When they returned to the United States, they brought with them the duffel bag issued to Fritz when he arrived at Camp Aliceville from North Africa in 1943. The Hagmanns sent it as a donation to the Museum.

The Andersons visited the Hagmann family again in 2000. Then in May 2004, the Hagmanns came to the United States and visited the Aliceville Museum. It was an emotional moment when they first viewed the exhibit of their father's artifacts from the camp, along with a photo of their now deceased mother presenting the duffel bag to Tiny Anderson in 1996. During their visit, the Hagmanns were also welcomed at a Hester Family Reunion, where they enjoyed good Southern cooking and an afternoon of storytelling by Hester-Prisock family members. Before leaving Aliceville, the Hagmanns presented the Museum with the German-English dictionary Fritz Hagmann had used to study English during his incarceration at Camp Aliceville.

In August 1997, former POW Alvin Tepelmann visited Aliceville with his family. He'd returned to Germany in March 1946 and was now retired after thirty years as an engineer with Volkswagen. During this visit, Alvin and his family were amazed at the hospitality they experienced, both in Aliceville and during a rainy afternoon on an Alabama highway when a stranger stopped and spent more than an hour helping them rewire the light harness between their car and camping trailer.

In November, Alvin wrote from Germany to express his thanks and to send along the slide rule he'd made for himself to use in his math studies at the POW camp (see Chapter Twelve). Struggling to express his thoughts in English, he wrote, "My being in Aliceville was a very great experience for me, a very special experience....Thank you for your welcome." He went on to explain that his time in the Aliceville POW camp had changed the direction of his life. "After a bad time as a German soldier in a very bad time of National Socialism in Germany, I had good luck to come to the USA as prisoner of war. This circumstance opened my eyes. I saw a real new world of democracy for the first time in my life. I often think of this time in Aliceville where I got the chance to lay the foundation stone for my further life." Alvin commented that he had friends who came back from Russian POW camps after World War II "unfed and in bad health." It was such a contrast to what he had experienced in the United States.

Down through the past decade, there have been additional reunions and visits, as well as cards and letters exchanged at holidays. Friendships have grown. In March 1999, Dr. Arnold Krammer, author of *Nazi Prisoners of War in America,* was a guest in Aliceville, along with former guards Chet Eisenhauer and his wife, and Gene Dakan and his wife. German attendees included Hermann and Katie Blumhardt; Leopold Dolfuss with his son-in-law, Dr. Otto Kasper; August Wanders' daughter, Ellen; and the family of Karl Berning. Little Mary Lu Turner (Keef), who had attended Aliceville Elementary School while her parents worked in civilian jobs at the camp, attended this reunion and brought with her donations of bulletins from the camp chapel, holiday dinner menus, a movie pass, copies of *The Camptown Crier,* and a number of photographs.

During her visit, Mary Lu stayed at Myrtlewood, a Victorian bed and breakfast just three doors down from the Harkins' home her family had rented on Red Hill during the war. Memories flooded back when she drove up this street to check in—the water tower where she'd gone with school friends to cool off on hot summer afternoons, story time in the porch swing with Lulabelle Farmer, and the doll she'd created newspaper curl hairdos for. There were new experiences, too. She was delighted to make the acquaintance of Hermann and Katie Blumhardt, who were also staying at Myrtlewood. "I loved going down to breakfast because Hermann is a wonderful storyteller," she has said. "I could just sit there forever listening to him." Mary Lu smiles at the thought that her parents would have liked Hermann and Katie. "To think that I was living here as a little kid, looking across all this barbed wire, and Hermann was behind that, and now he's such a dear friend."

In December 2000, with the dawn of a new century, Wilhelm Schlegel sent Christmas and New Year's greetings to his friends in Aliceville and again expressed his profound hopes for world peace:

> In 1948, returning from prison of war, I would never have believed to attend this historical New Year. But now it is reality. More and more prisoners of war and those who returned home are passing away. Back at those days we had sworn that there should never be another war and war prisoners. We were happy to have peace with those fighting against us, that they became our friends and allies. Still, there is no peace in this world. We truly hope that there will be peace someday

> in this new century all over the world. We wish you all a peaceful, Merry Christmas, and may God bless you and for the New Year, we wish you all good health and happiness. With best regards to all friends.

In March 2001, the Schlegel family returned to stay with Chuck and Jane Gwin during another Aliceville reunion, this time adding a new generation to the visit with Wilhelm's grandson Philip, who was four years old. Philip was delighted, and his grandfather was totally surprised when the children from a local kindergarten arrived at the museum to help celebrate Wilhelm's eighty-third birthday.

"I think it's a wonderful thing that we've learned from them, and they've learned from us," says Jane Gwin. "It's been such a rewarding relationship." Jane knows there is still animosity about the war and that some people in Aliceville continue to feel bitterness, but she and her family have gone beyond that, as have Sonny and Ann Stirling, who have hosted members of the Felholter family during several reunions. At the time of the 2001 reunion, the Gwins were awaiting the birth of their first grandchild in Atlanta, and the Schlegel family arrived with gifts for the child that had not yet been born. When they came again in 2003 they brought gifts addressed to Baby Drew who was now a part of the family. "We have told them they are welcome whenever they want to be here, that this is their home here, and they know that is true....We feel really lucky to have known them through the years, and I just hope Klaus and Pirko and Philip will continue to come back even if Wilhelm can't."

The March 2001 reunion was held just six months before the infamous September 11 attacks against the United States.

Though no one could have foreseen that day of destruction, there were, as always, concerns about world peace at the time. Wilhelm Schlegel again gave a speech as a representative of the POWs. Referring back to the planting of the gingko tree in 1995, he said:

> Four comrades and I planted a gingko tree at the museum, hoping it would be a symbol of hope for a peaceful future. While this wish seems almost an impossibility, for how many wars and conflicts have happened in Europe and the world since 1945 until now, we would like to have a part in contributing to world peace.
>
> Our children, those who come after us, hopefully may remain shielded from the trials our generation experienced. May they be granted, in peace, to live in freedom and contentment [and] mutual respect, just as I experienced it yesterday through the children in the kindergarten, who surprised me with their birthday wishes.

The next reunion would be held in March 2003, marking the sixtieth anniversary of the establishment of Camp Aliceville and the fourteenth year since the first reunion. The events of September 11, 2001, and America's subsequent decision to invade Iraq would weigh heavily on the minds of those who planned for and attended that event.

Afterword

On Wednesday, March 12, 2003, my husband, Barney, and I drove down to attend the sixtieth reunion of Camp Aliceville. Although I'd visited the museum two or three times and interviewed a number of Aliceville residents, I had not experienced a gathering of the German and American people whose lives are uniquely connected by this place.

Ever since the previous July, when the Senate Foreign Relations Committee had begun hearings on the proposed invasion of Iraq, there'd been concern that this reunion might not take place. I'd been stunned and deeply moved on Monday, August 5, 2002, to receive an e-mail from Aliceville Museum Director Mary Bess Paluzzi. "The world may be troubled, but there are still moments when peace can be found," it read. Attached was a beautiful color photograph of a bright yellow and black butterfly amid the foliage of a small, healthy tree. "I took this photo in front of the museum this morning," Mary Bess explained. "The Monarch butterfly is poised on a leaf of the gingko tree that was donated and planted by former Camp Aliceville POWs. The gingko was the first tree to bud at Hiroshima after the destruction of atomic bomb in August 1945. Peace to you all." Mary Bess had sent this e-mail to more than forty people—Aliceville residents, former German POWs and their families, former guards, and friends with an interest in the Camp Aliceville legacy.

Barney and I checked into a motel in Columbus, Mississippi, late Wednesday afternoon and settled in. I'd considered staying at Myrtlewood in Aliceville, where Mary Lu Turner Keef and the Blumhardts would be staying, but I knew I would need some distance each evening in order to absorb experiences and conversations and keep up with my notes. The drive to and from Aliceville each day would not be long, and dinner was scheduled at a Columbus restaurant for the second evening anyway.

Before going out for a bite to eat, Barney and I watched the national news. War in Iraq was definitely looming, and images of the aviation nightmare wreaked in New York, Washington, and Pennsylvania in September were still fresh. Mary Bess had feared former German POWs might cancel their plans to attend this most significant, and perhaps last, reunion. In late January, the European Parliament had passed a nonbinding resolution opposing United States plans for unilateral action against Iraq. Their resolution expressed the belief that a pre-emptive strike would violate international law and the United Nations charter. Germany, like France and Russia, was publicly opposed to American war plans for Iraq.

Following the lead story that kidnap victim Elizabeth Smart had been found alive in Utah, I felt an eerie chill when the news anchor reported that Serbian Prime Minister Zoran Djindjic had been shot and killed earlier in the day as he walked from his armored car to his headquarters in Belgrade. Hadn't the cause of World War I had something to do with the assassination of a Serbian government official? A quick Internet check corrected my faulty memory from high school world history class: The immediate cause of World War I had been the assassination of

Archduke Francis Ferdinand, heir-presumptive to the Austrian and Hungarian thrones, *by* a Serb nationalist on June 28, 1914 in Sarajevo. Not exactly the same scenario, but similar enough to evoke the specter of world war, which I quickly put out of my mind.

On Thursday morning, gunmetal gray skies signaled an approaching springtime storm. As we drove towards Aliceville, grasses along the roadside glowed almost incandescent green against dark clouds, and the air was thick. Redbud trees were beginning to put forth purple blooms at the edges of gray woods, and clumps of yellow daffodils brightened the borders of pastures just as they had in March 1943, when Margie Archibald returned reluctantly to her father's hometown.

Lightning licked at the road ahead of us, and huge, heavy droplets plopped loudly against the windshield. Within seconds, hail almost the size of proverbial golf balls began to assault our car, and we pulled into an old graveyard to seek a shred of shelter. The bare branches of an old oak tree took some of the brunt, but chunks of hail still battered an odd rhythm on the roof of the car, and the creek next to the wrought iron fence began to run rouge red with clay. Then, as quickly as they had begun, the rain and the hail stopped, and we returned to the highway.

In Aliceville, we parked at a slant on Broad Street in front of the museum, and I wondered as I gathered up my notebooks and tape recorder what new connections this day might bring. Aliceville was now a shadow of its former self. Globalization had taken its toll. As Robert Hugh Kirksey had observed in a newspaper column recently, virtually all of the businesses lured to the area after World War II and up into the 1970s had now closed or moved "offshore." The local economy, like that in most of west Alabama, was struggling, but business owners and city officials still had that "flaming community spirit" Gerald Stabler had touted in 1945 and were seeking ways to reinvent the town once again.

As people began to gather, I took a few minutes to wander through the museum and refresh my memory from earlier visits. Just inside the doorway was a small Formica-topped table once used by American guards who ate at Minnie Merle Brandon's café. After the war, retired Colonel Shriver and his wife had used the table in their kitchen at Steelecrest, and now their daughter, Scarlett, had loaned it to the museum.

In a small frame on a wall above the table was a cardboard disk that had once sealed the neck of a glass milk bottle—a bottle delivered before the dairy farm shut down to make room for Camp Aliceville. "Thomas R. Parker Dairy," it said in red and blue. On another wall was a pencil sketch of Johnny Johnston done by the POW artist Hummel and an oil painting of a waterfall done by another POW. Display cases held *Afrikakorps* uniforms as well as dinner plates and flatware from the camp.

Another frame held the paycheck Bruno Schneider had donated to the museum at Christmas in 2001 with instructions to cash it and use the proceeds for the benefit of the museum. The check, in the amount of $204.40, had been issued by the Military Disbursing Officers of the United States when Bruno returned to Germany in 1946. It represented his total earnings from Camp Aliceville, Camp Van Dorn, and Camp Shelby. After some research, the museum staff had decided to keep the check rather than cash it because of its historic value, but an anonymous benefactor had donated the amount of its face value in honor of Robert Hugh and Millie Kirksey. "Imagine," Mary Bess said at the time, "how few of these checks were not cashed by the POWs after they returned home to Germany."

Several albums rested on top of a bookcase. Some were full of black-and-white photographs detailing life in Camp Aliceville. There were photos of Dot Latham singing with the Stardusters at the Camp Aliceville Officers' Club and photos Jake McBride had taken of the huge drainage ditch the POWs dug at the back of the camp. One album lay open to a page with a photograph of the "four positives" that had faked their diphtheria tests in the spring of 1944. The men, including Walter Felholter who would arrive later that afternoon, were seated on a rustic bench beside a neatly shingled barracks in Camp Aliceville's Compound B.

Other albums contained carefully preserved letters and bio sketches shared by former POWs and their families over the years. A letter I had seen before caught my eye. It had been sent to Mary Bess in September 2001 by Wilhelm Schlegel's daughter-in-law, Pirko, who would also arrive today with her son, Philip; her husband, Klaus; and her father-in-law. "I don't know if you saw on CNN the reactions of the people here in Germany," Pirko wrote of September 11. "Yesterday 200,000 people gathered in Berlin to walk through the city in solidarity with the American people. Chancellor Schroeder was the man leading in this march." Pirko continued her description as follows:

> On Thursday 12:00 noon everything, really, everything stopped for five minutes in honor of the people who died in this horrible attack. The busses stopped, the trains, the factories, just everything, the radio and TV programs stopped. It is amazing how big

> the solidarity is. We have put out our American flags (I have only little ones) to show our solidarity and friendship. Firefighters in Germany are donating to the colleagues in New York and have asked the people to donate, too. I think so far they have already gathered a tremendous amount of money.

Pirko mentioned her young son, Philip, who sensed on that day that something horrible had happened and kept asking questions. "When he played in his room and wanted to build something, he built the World Trade Center. These are the moments when I start to cry." Pirko wrote that it was difficult to find words to describe her reaction to the PowerPoint photos Mary Bess had sent her of what had happened in New York:

> One cannot understand what is going on in those minds of the perpetrators. I guess you need a great deal of hatred, fanaticism, and no feeling for life to do something like this. I still have the feeling to wake up and that someone will tell me that this was just a really bad dream. I know it is not. I hope that normality will return soon and that we will not face a third war.

Pirko's letter gave me another eerie chill as I thought back to the news broadcast I'd watched the evening before. The whole world had empathized with America when the World Trade Center and the Pentagon were attacked, but now the leaders of Germany and many other European countries were not supporting the intention to invade Iraq. They did not view that as the appropriate response. German Chancellor Gerhard Schroeder's stern criticism of an Iraq invasion had led Secretary of Defense

Donald Rumsfeld to label Germany, along with France, "old Europe," yet the Schlegels and the Felholters were still arriving today from Germany to be with their American friends.

I first glimpsed Wilhelm Schlegel and his family at the Aliceville Hat Luncheon held that day in conjunction with the Camp Aliceville reunion. Most of Aliceville turned out at City Hall for this event, wearing hats of every description. It's a rite of spring, apparently, in small Southern towns. Not only were there elegant, stylish hats like the bright red one with netting worn by the Mayor's wife, Johnie McKinzey, but also cowboy hats, giraffe hats, and hats with blooming flowers and seed packets—even a blinking chartreuse and yellow dragon with a long tail down the wearer's back.

Wilhelm wore a pith helmet presented to him by his reunion host, Chuck Gwin, and promptly won first place in the "Hunting" category of the hat parade. He posed happily for a group picture of winners, along with Chuck Gwin who was wearing a wonderful brown felt German hat with a pheasant feather and a dog pin that Wilhelm had brought him from Germany. Then lunch was served—chicken casserole, tossed salad, sweet tea, and banana puddin'.

Back at the museum, I admired a huge map of Aliceville and another of the POW camp with Mary Lu Turner Keef, who'd driven all the way down from New York state for this reunion. "These were all row houses made out of cinder block, and I think this was our community center," she said, pointing to the spot where her family had moved into an army apartment from their rented house on Red Hill when she was eight years old. She pointed out where the octagonal search towers had been—

inside the barbed wire area near the hospital where her mother worked—and the location of the small guard shack where she'd used her family pass to visit her father's office.

Mary Bess's cousin Robbie Davis showed me a photo of her husband's grandmother's house with him sitting on the front porch. "This house was right on Third Avenue, the first one past the railroad tracks," she explained. "Third Avenue was the main street coming out of town, and the depot was right there. The prisoners marched to the camp from there." Robbie remembered the POWs coming into town when she was a little girl to do yard work and help out on people's farms. "I was real blond, and my mother said that when they'd come by our house, I'd be out on the porch waving at them, and they'd call me *Fräulein* because I reminded them of German children."

There were hugs all around at the front door of the museum when Hermann and Katie Blumhardt arrived from their retirement community in Florida. Their faces were familiar to me from a feature program about Camp Aliceville filmed by the History Channel the year before. The Blumhardts had spent Wednesday night in Dothan and stopped for lunch at the Shoney's Inn in Tuscaloosa. When Hermann described the torrential rains they'd driven through between Tuscaloosa and Aliceville, he said, "All hell broke loose." The phrase made me smile because it was the exact same phrase he'd used in his gently accented English on the History Channel video when he described the British attack on his unit's position in North Africa in May 1943.

The Blumhardts were sad that Sue Stabler had passed away the previous July and could not enjoy this sixtieth reunion. Hermann told me about the first time he'd returned to Aliceville to show Katie where he'd been a prisoner during the war. Like Günther Peter Ertel, he'd taken his wife to the library to show her the copies of *Der Zaungast.* Sue Stabler had come into the library, overheard some of the conversation, and introduced herself. She immediately invited the Blumhardts to stay with her that night, but they explained that they already had a room in Tuscaloosa. "I couldn't have stayed with a stranger I'd just met," Katie told me, "but we did spend the entire afternoon talking and talking and talking with Sue, and when we came back for the 1989 reunion, we did stay with her. She was a great lady."

Hermann wanted to be sure I remembered that E.B. Walker should get some of the credit for arranging the first reunion, and Walter Felholter agreed when he arrived with his daughter, Hildegard. They told me E.B. was in poor health and confined to a wheelchair in Birmingham, and they asked me to check on him for them. (E.B. Walker died on August 13, 2004, at the age of seventy-five.)

Walter Felholter displayed his subtle sense of humor when he told me about working one week in the kitchen and then one week cleaning up the mess hall at Camp Aliceville before he got diphtheria. He talked about using some kind of machine that took the eyes out when he used it to peel potatoes. "When we finished peeling potatoes for the American soldiers, they'd have only little bitty potatoes, but when we finished peeling ones for the German POWs, they'd have big potatoes," he said with a twinkle in his eye. He also commented that he never liked the duty of cleaning up the mess halls. "The American soldiers loved chewing gum, and when they would come to meals, they'd take it out of their mouths and stick it on the underside of the tables. It was very hard to clean off."

August Wanders' daughter, Ellen, arrived with her friend, Mattheus. Both had been here before, and Mattheus was looking forward to participating in a 5K run with Aliceville residents the following morning. Ellen is a striking woman with jet-black hair and bright red lipstick. She works for a chemical company in Germany and has helped, long distance, with plans for dinners and other events at previous reunions. As we stood and chatted amid the artifacts from Camp Aliceville, Ellen enjoyed relating what her father had told her about the balloon incident at the camp. "The prisoners enjoyed teasing their American guards," she said with a smile. "One of the balloons they sent up was painted with a mustache so it would look like Hitler. It was all in fun. They never discovered who did it, and no one was punished."

Wilhelm Schlegel was listening, and he nodded in agreement. "They were playing a joke," he said.

Before dinner, which was to be held at the Plantation House Restaurant across the highway, Barney and I left the museum for cocktails at the home of Wendell and Clem Parrish. My husband had spent many hours playing basketball and going to summer camp with the YMCA in Selma, and Wendell had been the director when Barney was a child. In 2002, Wendell had generously spent an entire morning sharing his own POW experiences with Barney, and then he and Clem had taken us and Mary Bess to lunch at the Plantation House.

On this first evening of the reunion weekend, Wendell and Clem had invited Jean and Bill Martin, who'd gone to Germany with the Aliceville group in 1994, and Libba Park, whose mother-in-law had memories from the time of Camp Aliceville. The seven of us enjoyed a pleasant hour getting acquainted and sharing conversation. I soon discovered that Libba Park's mother-in-law was the woman Walter Bryant had written about in *The Birmingham News* at the time of the first reunion in 1989—the woman who'd been criticized for offering a glass of tea to a German POW who was mowing her lawn. Mrs. Park had replied simply that she hoped a German woman might do the same for an American prisoner in her country. Libba added that Mrs. Park had made the gesture even after her own son, Robert Hugh Kirksey's friend Francis Park, had been killed at Normandy. The Parrishes and their friends were not attending the dinner that evening, but Wendell and Clem did plan to come to the museum presentation on Saturday morning where I would give a brief talk about my book research and Wilhelm Schlegel would present a plaque.

Barney and I arrived at The Plantation House, with its tall white columns and high-ceilinged rooms, to find the German guests and a number of others busy with conversation. Someone was telling the story of how the house had been moved to its present location before it became a restaurant. The truck that moved it broke an axle, and the house sat in the middle of Highway 17 for three days while the town and the Alabama Department of Transportation argued about how the truck should be fixed. This house had belonged to the James Murphy Summerville family. Major Paul Dishner and his wife had rented a two-room apartment on the first floor during the war.

As we settled in at long tables in the dining room, Mary Lu nodded towards a door in the corner of the room. "I remember visiting the Dishners here with my parents," she said. "I'd go out that door right there to play on the porch and pick sweet fresh figs from a tree in the yard."

The German guests had brought bottles of white wine to share. Although they found it strange, they knew from previous visits that wine would not be on the menu because Pickens is a dry county. This is hunting and fishing country, and Mary Bess ordered a platter of fried quail for everyone to sample.

The next day, Friday, was Wilhelm Schlegel's eighty-fifth birthday. He'd been born on this date in Asslar, Germany, in 1918. As had happened once before during a Camp Aliceville reunion, a group of local kindergarten children arrived at the museum to play with Philip and to help celebrate the birthday. Cake and ice cream and popcorn were served right there among all the war displays, and Wilhelm beamed as he patted the children and called them by name. Hermann Blumhardt played his accordion in the background and Katie Blumhardt offered a sample of authentic yodeling. The children presented Wilhelm with a book containing crayoned birthday cards.

At lunchtime, the group walked down to El Rodeo and ordered tacos and burritos with refried beans and rice. After all the reading I'd done during the past year, I was truly amazed to be sitting at a table in a Mexican restaurant with Wilhelm Schlegel, Walter Felholter, and Hermann Blumhardt, as well as members of their families.

Except for Hermann, their English was halting, and so was my German, but we managed a good conversation. Pirko, who'd gone to college in Canada and once worked in the United States, speaks excellent English. So does Walter's daughter,

Hildegard. Wilhelm talked about how young he'd been and ready to fight when the war began and how he hadn't believed the POWs who arrived at Camp Aliceville after D-Day and insisted German cities had been destroyed and women and children killed by Allied bombs.

Wilhelm's son, Klaus, an Audi dealership manager in a town north of Frankfurt, told me he's only talked to his father once about the war and that was during another reunion. He seemed surprised when his father began talking about the food in Camp Aliceville, saying how good it was and how much there was in the beginning. "We couldn't eat it all, but we would hide the leftovers so the Americans wouldn't cut back our rations," he said, "but when the war ended, that all changed. We were often hungry then, and even malnourished."

Walter Felholter talked with Katie Blumhardt about the German music CD she and Hermann had recorded for their children and grandchildren. "It was our daughter's idea," Katie explained. "We rented a studio, and it took two hours. I made a couple mistakes, but then when you are eighty, you can do that."

Walter expressed hope that the children and grandchildren would be interested and listen to it. "I've made hundreds of slides of my travels and given lots of talks about them," he said. "I also have a room full of good literature, and I hope the next generation will care about the slides and the books."

The conversation touched at times on the new terrorist threats and the impending war. Klaus, who has a friend in Berlin who works with airport security, said he wished, as I did, that the friendly relationships among individuals in the world could somehow transcend political negotiations.

That evening, the German guests and their Aliceville host families drove over to Columbus, Mississippi, for an elegant dinner at Broussard's. Barbara Heisler, a sociology professor at Gettysburg College who was attending the reunion and doing research, also joined the group. There were many toasts before dinner—to friendship, to peace, to Germany, and to America. Hermann and Walter led the group in the traditional German singing toast, *Ein Prosit, Ein Prosit, der Gemütlichkeit!,* which simply means "a toast to something like camaraderie," or as one website translates it, "to all the good things in life." We talked at our table about the fact that the word *Gemütlichkeit* is uniquely German. You can know what it means—a bit of being comfortable with each other, being at home with each other, and feeling good—but there's no one word to translate it. Still, we all knew that *Gemütlichkeit* was a good description of the atmosphere in the room.

Saturday morning, a crowd of people, including Wendell and Clem Parrish, gathered at the museum for the presentations. Mary Bess announced that Klaus Schlegel had placed third in the 5K run earlier in the morning. Philip Schlegel came in, grinning from ear to ear because his host, "grandfather" Chuck Gwin, had spray painted his hair blue and then painted his own hair in red, white, and blue stripes.

Mary Bess read greetings from Bruno Schneider, who was not able to come. I gave a brief presentation about the research I was doing for my book and encouraged people to share their stories and experiences with me during the rest of the day. Then I read a few paragraphs from Chapter One, the part of *Guests Behind the Barbed Wire* that was already finished. The room grew silent, and there were smiles and nods of recognition as I read the words, "In the summer of 1942, a rumor spread in west Alabama that a military complex was about to be built in Pickens County, probably near Aliceville."

Then Wilhelm Schlegel presented a beautifully framed gray and black certificate to Mary Bess in appreciation for all of her work with the museum. "Ladies and Gentlemen, dear American friends," he began. After the presentation, Robert Hugh Kirksey invited all of the former German POWs to come to the front so he could take pictures while they were all here together. It was not said, but everyone knew this would most likely be the last reunion these men would be able to attend. Like America's Greatest Generation, they were fast approaching the end of active life, yet it was clear among them and their American hosts, and also among other former POW families who had visited in recent years, that the friendships and the visits, along with the memories, would continue into succeeding generations.

For the rest of the day, people streamed in and out of the museum, sharing stories and viewing the many displays. Betty and Hubert Taylor from Reform, Alabama, were among the visitors. They told me that both L.D. Orr and James Scott Browning, who'd been captured and endured horrible hardships in Japanese POW camps, came home after the war. "They both gave presentations about their experiences in the school auditorium," Betty told me. "One of them said a Japanese girl had befriended him and helped him survive. The Japs beat L.D. real bad. He had a place on his back that didn't heal."

Hubert remembers LD. saying later that, if they hadn't dropped the atomic bombs, he doesn't think he'd have ever gotten back home. "The Japanese told them that if the Americans invaded Japan, the prisoners would be the first ones killed. L.D. didn't do much of anything after he came back home," Hubert said. "He was on disability."

Saturday evening, inside the museum, we feasted on pulled pork barbecue, smoked chicken, baked beans, potato salad, slaw, and garlic toast, with yellow cake topped with burnt sugar icing and toasted local pecans for dessert. There were iced tubs of beer and pitchers of fresh lemonade. Hermann told me, as we ate, that he is now learning Polish and Italian music, which he also enjoys playing and singing. I told him how much I'd enjoyed singing with my German family the summer I spent in Ravensburg as an exchange student—the summer the wall went up in the middle of Berlin—and about the piano book of German folksongs they'd given me when I left. Together, Hermann and I hummed a few bars of *Du, du liegst mir im Herzen* and *Ein Jäger aus Kurpfalz*.

Hermann expressed distress about the very real possibility of war, and Ellen Wanders nodded. "I don't understand President Bush," Hermann said. "I don't think he has looked far enough ahead to the consequences of war."

Then it was time to return to Birmingham. Wilhelm Schlegel's son clasped both my hands in friendship and said he hoped for peace. I looked around this small, warm, self-contained space in this small, mostly self-contained Alabama town and marveled at the unlikely camaraderie. I had wondered before this long weekend if I could pull the story of these people together and make it come alive for readers. As I turned to leave, I felt their friendship and their heritage and looked forward to the task.

Endnotes

Abbreviations:

PCH/WA, (*Pickens County Herald and West Alabamian*)

Chapter One

Page

25 *History of Aliceville* Golden Jubilee brochure (p. 42) gives the 1940 census figure as 1,475.

25 …Fourth, Seventh, and Eighth Service Commands…Krammer, *Nazi Prisoners of War in America,* p. 26.

26 …more than 170 miles…Krammer, p. 27.

26 on climate considerations— Kruse, "Custody of Prisoners of War in the United States." *The Military Engineer* 38 (February 1946): 70-74.

26 Alien Program internment sites—Lewis and Mewha, *History of Prisoner of War Utilization by the United States Army 1776-1945,* p. 72. See also E.B. Walker, *A Brief History of Prisoner of War Camp Aliceville*, p. 1 and Robert Hugh Kirksey, "History of Pickens County, part three."

27 …five miles from a railroad…Krammer, p. 28.

27 According to several sources, the town was originally called Alice City. Soon after its founding, the United States Post Office asked that the name be changed to Aliceville so it would not be confused with another small rural Alabama town—Alice. (I found no explanation of why Mr. Cochrane did not spell the name of the town Alyce.) See *History of Aliceville* Golden Jubilee brochure, p. 10 and Kirksey, *History of Pickens County, part two: Reconstruction through the arrival of railroads.*

28 For numbers of prisoners in America in 1942, see Table 1 "Monthly Census of Prisoners of War interned in Continental United States." Pluth's Dissertation, p. 438.

29 boll weevil poisoning demo—*PCH/WA,* July 9, 1942.

30 George Downer and D.B. Love credits—*PCH/WA,* July 16, 1942.

31 "Bomb 'em with Junk" ad—*PCH/WA,* October 1, 1942.

31 Thomas R. Parker Dairy description—*Museum News*, August 1999 (Volume 6, Issue 3), p. 1.

31 Quotations from Tom Parker—telephone conversation with the author in Aliceville on April 4, 2002.

32 *We're just building…* from an interview with Sue Stabler on the Alabama Public Television broadcast.

32 The original owners of the land purchased for the camp were as follows: N.H. Grant, 10.12 acres; Alice Horton Morris, 123.60 acres; S.R. (Doc) Parker, 103.47 acres; Mrs. Nannie S. Parker, 248.00 acres; Bettie M. Archibald, Estate, 66.27 acres; A.B. Crompton, Estate, et al., 139.21 acres; Lula Salmond Carpenter, Estate, 64.80 acres; S.R. (Doc) Parker, 50.57 acres; H.C. and Isabel Horton, an easement of 3.84 acres; and Bessie T. Compton, et al, an easement of 4.90 acres.

32 …shrubs, and tall grasses…Kruse, p. 71.

33 *I wasn't exactly a girl…*Sue Stabler's article in the *PCH/WA,* September 29, 1993.

34 *…alien concentration camp…PCH/WA,* September 24, 1942.

35 *…would be sitting…*Hoole," Alabama's World War II Prisoner of War Camps." *The Alabama Review* 20 (April, 1967): 86.

35 *…The Jap Camp…*Kirksey, "History of Pickens County, part three."

35 *We certainly didn't…*from an interview with Sue Stabler on the Alabama Public Television broadcast.

35 *Every citizen of the county…PCH/WA,* October 22, 1942.

36 information about paying guests—Tom Parker interview with the author.

36 *There is work…PCH/WA,* October 8, 1942.

37 *Laborers and carpenters…*Jack Pratt, *PCH/WA,* October 15, 1942.

37 Dirt daubers are related to what are called mud wasps, mud daubers, and potter wasps in other parts of the country.

37 *If I were a Jap…*Jack Pratt, *PCH/WA,* October 15, 1942.

38 *Reform!* "How Reform Named" in *The Birmingham News,* February 18, 1953.

38 Zentsuji prison camp information is from the Center for Research, Allied POWs Under the Japanese and the author's correspondence with Roger Mansell.

38 *…very good treatment…PCH/WA,* September 10, 1942.

39 James Scott Browning capture—*PCH/WA,* March 5, 1942.

39 *He's big enough…PCH/WA,* July 30, 1942.

39 Rumor of alien numbers—*PCH/WA,* October 1, 1942.

39 British offensive information in North Africa—Atkinson, *An Army at Dawn,* pp. 419-420.

40 Figures on sizes and numbers of POW camps in Alabama—"Prisoners of War," Chapter Eight in *Forth to the Might Conflict* by Cronenberg, pp. 94-97.

40 Rotary Club attendees—*PCH/WA,* October 29, 1942.

41 *...a really beautiful black horse...* Will Peebles interview with the author on August 1, 2003.

41 Information on Colonel Shriver's family background—correspondence from his daughter, Scarlett Shriver Parker, in March 2003.

41 *...people here appealed to me...* Quotation is from an undated and unidentified news clipping headlined "'Southerner By Choice' Typifies Attitude of Col. Karl H. Shriver" in the files of his daughter, Scarlett S.Parker.

42 ...largest and the first of seventy-two—*PCH/WA,* November 4, 1943.

42 *To give up Africa...* Atkinson quotes these words of Hitler on p. 164 in *An Army at Dawn.*

42 *This is not the end....* From a speech given by Winston Churchill at the Lord Mayor's Luncheon at Mansion House in London on November 10, 1942.

43 The photo referred to, donated by Mary Lu Turner Keef, is in the Aliceville Museum collection. It was published in the May 1999 issue of *Museum News.*

43 *I was feeling sorry for myself.* Quotes are from the author's telephone interview with Ward Turner's stepdaughter Joyce Roeding in August 2003.

45 Trudie Love is the grandmother of Sam Love.

45 *...at the concentration camp below...PCH/WA,* December 31, 1942.

45 Janie's McCaa's birthday party description—*PCH/WA,* December 24, 1942.

45 Rationing details—*PCH/WA,* December 15, 1942.

46 Official completion and activation date—See Sue Stabler speech to DAR in October 1988; Hoole, p. 85; and E.B. Walker, p. 5.

46 Description of opening ceremonies—See E.B. Walker, p. 4.

46 Background on Captain Strohecker is from *Camptown Crier,* Volume 1, Issue #4, February 12, 1944.

47 Robert Hugh Kirksey background is from *PCH/WA,* December 10, 1942.

47 *Richard was one of the finest...PCH/WA,* December 17, 1942.

48 For description of public reaction to women in the military, see p. 44 in Aileen Kilgore Henderson's *Stateside Soldier.*

49 *That's the reason...*Will Peebles interview with the author on August 1, 2003.

50 Jack Pratt profile of Frank Chappell—*PCH/WA,* July 23, 1942.

51 *I don't remember...*Elma Henders Emerson interview with Sam Love, 1994.

51 See Krammer, pp. 1-2 for concerns about American and British prisoners in German hands.

53 The battle for Longstop Hill is described in Atkinson's *An Army At Dawn,* pp. 254-255.

Chapter Two

Page

55 Biographical information about Wilhelm Schlegel is from his personal correspondence with the author and with the Aliceville Museum and also from "Wilhelm Schlegel, Asslar, Germany" by Kim Cross on the www.datelinepickens.com website.

57 *Heute wollen wir...* p. 184 in Willy Schneider's *Deutsche Weisen.*

57 *I enjoyed friendships...*letter from Wilhelm Schlegel to the author on February 21, 2004.

59 For references to the rumor about Field Marshal Rommel touring Confederate battle fields, see e-mail to the author from Gregg Morse at The Highland Inn in Monterey, Virginia (June 1, 2003). See also *Ghosts of Virginia, Volume III* by L.B. Taylor Jr.

59 Unless otherwise noted, all references to German, British, and American troop locations in this chapter are based on Rick Atkinson's *An Army at Dawn.*

61 *All of a sudden we had...*Karl Silberreis interview with Sam Love, 1994.

62 Biographical information about Walter Felholter is from his personal correspondence with the author and with the Aliceville Museum, his 1994 interview with Sam Love, and also from David Coombs' article, "Walter Felholter, Osnabrueck, Germany" on the www.datelinepickens.com website.

63 *the only way in which...*Winston Churchill as quoted by Atkinson, p. 13.

66 effects of American raids on supply line from Sicily—"Tunisia," p. 23. www.ibiblio.org.hyperwar/USA/USA-C-Tunisia.

66 *Lie down...Don't make a sound...* Walter Felholter interview with Sam Love, 1994.

67 *Everyone has to dig...* Walter Felholter interview with Sam Love, 1994.

68 *Here is something at least...*Walter Felholter's conversation with the author during the March 2003 reunion.

69 *C'mon, c'mon...Hands up!...* Walter Felholter interview with Sam Love, 1994.

70 Biographical information about Hans Kopera is from Randy Wall's article in *Alabama Heritage* (Winter 1988), Ed Watkins's article in the *Tuscaloosa News* on April 27, 1975, and E.B. Walker, pp. 17 and 20.

71 British and American control of North Africa—see "Tunisia" on HyperWar project site, p. 16.

72 *If the German people...*Adolf Hitler in 1944 as quoted by Atkinson, p. 411.

73 Biographical information about Walter F. Meier is from "Unser Meier" by Wilhelm Stüdl in *Der Zaungast,* August 4, 1944, p. 3.

74 Biographical information about Leopold Dolfuss is from his article for the November 1998 issue of *Museum News,* p. 3, and from "Austrian Family Visits former Aliceville POW Camp" on datelinealabama.com website, May 19, 2002.

74 Biographical information about Hermann Blumhardt is from his personal correspondence with the author and with the Aliceville Museum, and from articles in *The South Bend Tribune* (February 26, 1978 and March 21, 1990) and the *Niles Star* (October 24, 1949). Also from Scott Parrott's article "Former German POW Shares Story" in the *Tuscaloosa News* (March 16, 2003) and David Coombs' article, "Hermann Blumhardt, Stuttgart, Germany" on www.datelinepickens.com, March 21, 2003.

75 *I was an altar boy...*article by Hermann Blumhardt in *The South Bend Tribune,* February 26, 1978, p. 3.

76 *He promised and did unify...*ibid., p. 3.

77 *The few voices of mostly older...*ibid., p. 3.

77 *The radio kept the people...*ibid., p. 4.

79 Quotations from Katie Blumhardt on this page are from her telephone interview with the author in August 2003.

80 *My wounds healed...*article by Hermann Blumhardt in *The South Bend Tribune,* February 26, 1978, p. 4.

85 *Some of the German soldiers...ibid.,* p. 5.

87 *It is indeed an awful moment...ibid.,* p. 6.

87 Biographical information about Erwin Schulz is from Lewis H. Carlson's *We Were Each Other's Prisoners.*

90 One source for this figure is Randy Wall's *Alabama Heritage* article, p. 7.

91 Information on the Hermann Göring Division surrender is from *Uniforms, Organization and History of the Afrikakorps* by Roger James Bender and Richard D. Law, p. 92.

Chapter Three

Page

93 meals for enlisted men—Elma Henders Emerson interview with Sam Love, 1994.

94 *If he's in the service... PCH/WA,* January 14, 1943.

95 *Beverly will give 'em hell... PCH/WA,* April 29, 1943.

95 Biographical background about Mary Lu Turner (Keef) and her sister, Joyce, comes from their telephone interviews with the author.

98 *Lulabelle was so much fun...*Mary Lu Turner Keef telephone interview, November 18, 2002.

99 *I'd gone to get something...*Joyce Roeding telephone interview, August 2003.

99 *This great show has in the background... PCH/WA,* April 29, 1943.

99 *It affected her much more...*Keef telephone interview, November 18, 2002.

100 *Temple Negroes Are...PCH/WA,* April 22, 1943.

100 Background and service record of Alva Temple—*Museum News,* November 2004.

101 Lillian Brandon military training—*PCH/WA,* March 11, 1943.

101 J. M. Davidson missing in action—*PCH/WA,* March 18, 1943.

101 *...distinguished gentlemen and attractive women...just folks...*"Here, There and Everywhere" by Jack Pratt, *PCH/WA,* February 11, 1943.

102 *...the cordial relations which we believe...*letter to Harvey Stapp from Colonel Prince dated February 4, 1943—on file at the Aliceville Museum.

103 *Personally I like to forget...are taking place. Camptown Crier.* Volume I, Issue 1, November 15, 1943.

104 The house in Camden, Alabama, where Margie Archibald Colvin was born is also the house where civil rights supporter Clifton Durr (husband of Virginia Foster Durr) was raised.

105 *That was the first thing*...Margie Archibald Colvin interview with Sam Love in 1994.

106 *We hadn't seen very many Yankees*...ibid.

106 *We'd serve them a beautiful meal.* ibid.

106 *We could go out every night*...*Alabama Heritage,* p. 21.

106 *We'd pile up in one or two*...Margie Archibald Colvin interview with Sam Love.

107 *James Verner Park wasn't*...ibid.

107 *Here Larry would come*...ibid.

108 Arrival of 305th MPEG—*Camptown Crier,* Issue 1 and E.B. Walker, p. 8.

109 305th duty details—Bob Siddall letter to E.B. Walker, Joe Samper interview on Alabama Public Television broadcast, and *Camptown Crier,* Issue 1.

109 *You know, close order*...Joseph Samper interview on History Channel broadcast in January 2002.

110 *We promise to secure*...*PCH/WA,* March 18, 1943.

110 *It was still pretty much a swamp*...Byron Kauffman interview with Sam Love in 1994.

111 *I had never left*...Zurales's article "The Day 1,000 Germans Goosestepped into Town." *Mobile Register,* March 19, 1995.

111 *We've been around this thing*...Stanley Pendrak interview with Sam Love in 1994.

112 *Everyone agrees*... From Kathryn Tucker Windham's "The Face in the Courthouse Window" in *Thirteen Alabama Ghosts and Jeffrey.*

112 Robert Hugh Kirksey's memories of the courthouse window—*Places and People,* p. 2.

113 *So we loaded up*... Stanley Pendrak interview with Sam Love in 1994.

115 *That was the only dancing*...Dorothy Latham Ryan interview with Sam Love, 1994.

115 Background about Stardusters musicians—*Camptown Crier,* Issue 1.

116 *I even had security guards*...Dorothy Latham Ryan interview with Sam Love.

116 *I had two brothers in the military*...Earline Lewis Jones interview with Sam Love.

117 *Most all of those MPs*...J.T. Junkins interview with the author in Aliceville, October 2002.

117 *I don't think it was*...ibid.

118 *Those MPs would drive up*...ibid.

118 *To us, at that age*...ibid.

118 *I knew Samuel Windle*...ibid.

118 The list of war dead J.T. Junkins was looking at was compiled by the Aliceville Tuesday Study Club in 1995 and 1996 as part of the 50th anniversary of the end of World War II. Titled "Remembering Our Veterans: Honoring Those Who Have Served," it lists all those from Pickens County who served in the Armed Forces. The listing indicates that sixty-three Pickens County people died in action in the war. Another fifteen were prisoners of war. This brochure is on file in the Aliceville Museum.

119 *Most everyone in town*...ibid.

119 *It's just a small world*...ibid.

119 Information about the new housing to be built across from the camp comes from "Aliceville to Have Addition Housing Units" in the *PCH/WA,* March 4, 1943 and from Pep Johnston's telephone interview with the author in March 2003.

Chapter Four

Page

123 U-boat successes—See Jeff Scott's interview with an *Afrikakorps* veteran named Hans (November 10, 1998) at www.feldgrau.com.

123 *No tag—no food*...Pluth, p. 81.

124 bitterness of French guards—Carlson, p. 87.

124 use of DDT to delouse soldiers and prisoners—Agricultural Research Service website for the U.S. Department of Agriculture.

125 prisoner processing information—Krammer, pp. 5-14.

125 *Soldbuch* descriptions—Pluth, p. 84 and Krammer, p. 13.

125 final surrender figures in North Africa—Lewis and Mewha, p. 177.

127 *It is an incident*...Hermann Blumhardt letter to the author in June 2002.

128 *Roads to the front lines*...Krammer, p. 3.

128 *...packed like sardines*...Blumhardt article in *The South Bend Tribune.*

129 *He immediately pleaded*...Conversation with the author at 60th reunion.

129 Marrakesh and Casablanca as POW holding sites—Krammer, p. 3.

129 *heia safari*...Bender, p. 84.

130 *All enemy resistance*...General Harold Alexander's message to Winston Churchill at 2:15 p.m. on May 12, 1943. Quoted in *The Reader's Digest Illustrated History of World War II,* p. 237.

130 general information on Liberty ships—USMM.org

131 *We were going zig zag*...Walter Felholter interview on History Channel broadcast.

132 *You are now under the control*...Pluth, p. 88.

132 *If a [German] soldier failed to*...Yvonne Humphrey's article in the *American Journal of Nursing,* p. 821.

133 *The child-size portions*...Hermann Blumhardt's article in *The South Bend Tribune*, p. 6.

133 *I looked cautiously*...ibid.

134 No German POW ships sunk—Pluth, p. 88.

134 *I was scared stiff*...Heino Erichsen interview on the History Channel broadcast.

135 *a horrible ordeal*...Horst Uhse profile, *Museum News*, May 2004.

135 *machen die Amerikaner kaput!*...Carlson, p. 172.

136 *dignity and respect...win this war!* Yvonne Humphrey's article in the *American Journal of Nursing,* p. 822.

137 *From somewhere or other we dug*...ibid.

137 Camp Shanks, New York details—"Camp Shanks" at www.skylighters.org.

138 statistics on number of camps in United States in June 1944—Pluth, p. 111.

140 early POW complaints about train travel—Pluth, p. 95.

141 rumors about inhumane conditions in POW camps—Scott Parrott article in *Tuscaloosa News*, March 16, 2003.

142 The calendar dates and details of Wilhelm Schlegel's captivity in North Africa are from his unnamed war comrade who wrote the poem, "Captivity in Poetry."

142 *...steep as a mountainside...* "Captivity in Poetry," p. 1.

143 *Wenn wir marschieren*...from *Deutsche Weisen,* p. 204.

143 *Der Wirt muss borgen*...from *Deutsche Weisen,* p. 204.

144 *We lay like herrings in a barrel*..."Captivity in Poetry," p. 2.

145 *Oh, what a horror!*...ibid., p. 3.

146 *Des Wirtes Tochter, die trägt*...from *Deutsche Weisen,* p. 204.

147 ...*that which is forbidden*... "Captivity in Poetry," p. 4.

147 *Il Duce has been captured*...ibid., p. 5.

149 *Weg mit den Sorgen*...*Deutsche Weisen*, p. 204.

150 Glenn A. Sytko (www.uboat.net) describes a number of British interrogations of German POWs, during which "NR" might be stamped on a file. As a means of intimidation, when prisoners asked what the initials meant, they would be told "*Nach Russland,*" which suggested a prisoner who did not cooperate would be sent to Russia—something no German prisoner wanted to consider.

150 *Do you know*...*you pig*.... "Captivity in Poetry," p. 6.

151 Background information on the *Pasteur* is from Hal Stoen's website www.stoenworks.com.

153 *like the Mercedes of trains*...Cross, Kim. "Wilhelm Schlegel, Asslar, Germany." www.datelinepickens.com, March 24, 2003.

Chapter Five

Page

155 Aliceville Arts Club brunch meeting description, *PCH/WA,* June 3, 1943.

156 *It's a pity*.... *PCH/WA,* June 3, 1943.

156 Sue Stabler observations on pending camp—her DAR speech quoted in *PCH/WA,* September 29, 1993.

157 *That's the train carrying the Nazis*..."Ex-POWs to Join Reunion." *The Birmingham News,* July 28, 1989.

158 Johnny Johnston's childhood memory of this day—telephone interview with the author on March 20, 2003.

159 *We jumped in Daddy's car*...Robert Hugh Kirksey in *With Me,* p. 119.

159 *People wanted to see for*...Robert Hugh Kirksey interview on the History Channel broadcast.

160 *I don't know who had the idea*...Dottie Latham Ryan interview on the History Channel broadcast.

161 *Every afternoon they'd fill it up*...Mary Lu Turner Keef interview with the author.

161 Background information on Mary Emory Peebles—"Vienna Landmark Dedicated," *PCH/WA,* August 4, 1983.

161 *Four highway patrolmen were...* "At Alabama's War Prison," by Emory Peebles Hildreth in *The Birmingham Age-Herald,* June 10, 1943.

162 *Germans comin' in on the Frisco!...*"3,000 Axis Prisoners from Tunisia Guests of U.S. at Aliceville," by Jack House in *The Birmingham News,* June 10, 1943.

162 *It was unlike any other...*ibid.

163 *We were kind of a ragtag bunch...*Chet Eisenhauer interview on Alabama Public Television broadcast in 1989.

163 *The civilians will be curious...*Hermann Blumhardt interview on the History Channel broadcast.

164 *They are looking for our horns...*Walter Felholter interview on the History Channel broadcast.

164 *We were a mess...*Hermann Blumhardt interview on the History Channel broadcast.

164 *I remember how I felt...*Sue Stabler interview on the Alabama Public Television broadcast.

165 *They lined up in an orderly fashion...*Robert Hugh Kirksey in *With Me,* p. 119.

165 *You would be, too...*Hildreth article in *The Birmingham Age-Herald,* June 10, 1943.

165 *They all came through...*ibid.

166 *handsome, neat, clean-faced...*ibid.

166 *For these men the war is...*Jack House article in *The Birmingham News,* June 10, 1943.

166 *As it is, though...*ibid.

166 *I just remember that they...*Jack Brookes interview on the History Channel broadcast.

167 *They lined up...*Joyce Turner Roeding interview with the author.

167 *A lot of them were right off...*Jake McBride as quoted in Zurales's article, "The Day 1,000 Germans..." in the *Mobile Register,* March 19, 1995.

167 *We looked like soldiers...*Chet Eisenhauer interview on the Alabama Public Television broadcast.

167 *They were soldiers...*Joseph Samper interview on the History Channel broadcast.

167 *They was nothing but...*Byron Kauffman interview with Sam Love.

168 *We were awed by them*...Stanley Pendrak as quoted by Zurales in "The Day 1,000 Germans..." in the *Mobile Register.*

168 *Wenn wir marschieren...Deutsche Weisen,* p. 204.

169 *So this is what we have to fight*...Robert Hugh Kirksey as quoted by Hoole in *The Alabama Review*, p. 86.

169 *They look like mere boys*...Emory Peebles Hildreth article in *The Birmingham Age-Herald* June 10, 1943.

Chapter Six

Page

172 Title III Geneva Convention requirements—Kruse, p. 70.

174 *We didn't know peanut butter*...Walter Felholter interview with Sam Love.

175 *Prisoners Are Arriving Now*...Jack Pratt in the *PCH/WA*, June 3, 1943.

176 *After the date that*...Elma Henders Emerson interview with Sam Love.

176 *The interesting thing about it was*...ibid.

177 information on camp designations—Lewis & Mewha, pp. 91-92.

178 Krammer, p. 14, says there were 4,500 pro-Nazis at Camp Alva and 3,300 anti-Nazis at Fort Devens by 1945.

178 *Germans and Americans soon discovered*...Billinger, p. 48.

178 *At the first trainload, Opelika...The Montgomery Advertiser,* April 13, 1988.

179 *Hitler's secret chamber of horrors... PCH/WA* (advertisement), June 3, 1943.

180 *...as close to...They were playing*...Frances Edwards interview on the History Channel broadcast.

181 *The mess sergeants would bring*...Earline Lewis Jones interview with Sam Love.

181 *We would go up the street*...ibid.

182 *But they were trained for war*..."Prisoners of War," *The Birmingham Age-Herald,* June 11, 1943.

183 Murphy was a 1942 graduate of Aliceville High School, son of F. L. Murphy of Gordo. He'd enlisted in the air corps in July 1942 and was later declared killed in action.

183 The list of 922 was published in the *PCH/WA* on July 1, 1943.

184 Krammer (p. 80) gives a synopsis of these Geneva Convention articles.

184 *There will be home raised*..."3000 German Soldiers Interned at Aliceville to Dig 'Bama Potatoes." *Birmingham Post,* June 10, 1943.

184 *Some of us couldn't live without work*....Coombs article about Felholter at www.datlinepickens.com.

185 ...*many only raised themselves*..."Der Weg zur Ordnung" by Wilhelm Westhoff. *Der Zaungast*, August 4, 1944. pp. 5-6.

185 *We were mixed up everywhere...for the next day*...Walter Felholter interview with Sam Love.

186 *I was devastated*..."1943 train ride put him on new track to a life of freedom." Article by Hermann Blumhardt in the *South Bend Tribune*, March 21, 1990.

187 ...*separating the bad eggs from*...See letter from General George C. Marshall to author Judith Gansberg on May 18, 1975. Gansberg, p. 59.

188 ...*battle-scarred, desert-toughened...in which to live.* "German War Prisoners at Aliceville Obedient, and Happy over Internment." *The Birmingham News Age-Herald*, June 13, 1943.

188 ...*fair treatment, good food*...ibid.

188 E.B. Walker's analysis of *Afrikakorps* troops is on p. 13 of his book.

189 *The Nazis are exactly*...Jack House article on June 13, 1943.

190 Description of POW "uniforms" appears on p. 97 in Cronenerg, among other places.

190 *When we arrived at Camp Aliceville*...Blumhardt's article, "Youth under Hitler" in *The South Bend Tribune.*

190 Description of mess hall cleanliness—See *Inspection Report,* 14-16 July 1943.

191 *Through German character*...See *Alabama Heritage* article, p. 10.

191 *The Germans themselves*...Jack House article on June 13, 1943.

192 *Are we, the American people*...Letter to the editor from Lucile Umbenhauer in "Voice of the People" letters to the editor, *The Birmingham News*, June 18, 1943.

192 In 1943, the term "United Nations" was simply another name for the Allied Powers.

192 *The News is further convinced*...*The Birmingham News,* June 18, 1943.

193 ...*one of the most religious groups*...see William J. Baldwin article in *The Birmingham News*, June 18, 1943.

194 *There is no shortage*...See Henry C. Flynn article in *The Catholic Week.*

194 *Most of the prisoners are*...See John B. McCloskey article in *The Catholic Week.*

196 *You don't have to be cruel...New York Herald Tribune,* December 3, 1944.

196 Bob Siddall's duty description is from his letter to E.B. Walker on July 26, 1993.

196 Description of guard towers is from *Inspection Report, 14-16 July 1943,* pp. 2-3.

197 Biographical information about Harold Cover is from his interview with Sam Love.

199 *Aliceville in Alabama...*This poem, author unknown, was found in the files of Maxwell McKnight. It is on file at the Aliceville Museum and is also quoted in E.B. Walker's appendix.

199 *We heard a gentle drumming...*Robert Mitterwallner as quoted in the August 2000 issue of *Museum News.*

200 *The suction power...*Robert Hugh Kirksey's *With Me,* p. 55.

201 *Where were you...*ibid.

201 *...a colored tenant on the...PCH/WA,* June 17, 1943.

Chapter Seven

Page

204 Arrival of wounded prisoners—*PCH/WA,* July 1, 1943.

204 The three medical officers included a Major Rand, Captain Arthur Klippen, and John Kellam.

205 Biographical information about Captain Stephen Fleck comes from *Alabama Heritage,* pp. 12, 15, and 26 and from *Museum News,* August 2003.

206 Biographical information about Eugene Dakan comes from his letter to the author in November 2004 and from his interview with Sam Love.

206 *No local gentry lined...* Gordon Forbes interview with Sam Love.

207 *Nichts! Nichts! Eise Wasser.,* ibid.

207 *I guess my general feelings...*ibid.

207 *I was pulled away...*Harold Cover interview with Sam Love.

208 *They told him if he practiced...*ibid.

209 *You had to be on the alert...*Eugene Dakan's interview with Sam Love.

209 *The Germans would be in several...*ibid.

210 For POW camp figures at the end of April 1943, see Lewis & Mewha, p. 90.

211 Biographical information about Erwin Schulz comes primarily from his essay in Carlson, p. 172.

212 Literally, *Gestapo* referred to the German internal security police that terrorized German citizens suspected of treason. It came to mean any Nazi group that terrorized citizens or soldiers.

212 *threatened us just to*...Erwin Schulz in Carlson, p. 176.

212 *We were isolated*...ibid.

213 ...*a rich field to plow*...Wilhelm Westhoff, "Der Weg zur Ordnung" in *Der Zaungast*, August 4, 1944.

214 *Politics and religion got you*...Hermann Blumhardt interview on Alabama Public Television broadcast.

214 *The soldiers and all knew who*...Will Peebles interview with the author.

214 *I'd be the only one*...*hard over there*....ibid.

215 *Remember that there were fifty*...Günther Peter Ertel interview on the Alabama Public Television broadcast.

216 The other organizations in the USO included the YWCA, the National Catholic Community Service Organization, the Jewish Welfare Board, the Salvation Army, and the National Travelers Aid Association.

218 ...*the crystallization point of our community*...Wilhelm Stüdl's article "*Unser Meier*" in the August 4, 1944 issue of *Der Zaungast* (translated by the author).

218 This report is *Inspection Report, Internment Branch Inspection of Prisoner of War Camps, Prisoner of War Division, Provost Marshal General's Office* signed by Maxwell S. McKnight, Captain. Dated 14-16 July 1943. #4038001.

218 This biographical information about Major Maxwell McKnight comes from Robin, p. 46.

220 Information about the pulpwood decisions is in Lewis & Mewha, p. 132.

222 *The roads throughout the reservation*...from *Inspection Report,* 14-16 July 1943.

222 *not very well known in Pickens*... *PCH/WA,* August 12, 1943.

223 *Breakfast at 9*... *PCH/WA,* September 23, 1943.

226 *The minister stood waist deep*...Mary Lu Turner Keef telephone interview with the author August 5, 2004.

228 *They give you these enormous bags*...ibid.

228 *I remember going there*...*was a real treat*...Mary Lu Turner Keef telephone interview with the author November 18, 2002.

229 *My mother worked at*...ibid.

229 *Every home in Alabama can become*... *PCH/WA,* July 22, 1943.

230 *...handpicked warriors of the United States Army... PCH/WA,* August 5, 1943.

231 *We Extend Congratulations... PCH/WA,* June 24, 1943.

231 *When this plane lands... PCH/WA,* August 12, 1943.

Chapter Eight

Page

233 *To get that for the men...*Wilhelm Stüdl quoting Walter Meier in "*Unser Meier"* in the August 4, 1944 issue of *Der Zaungast (*translated by the author).

234 *We didn't have chain saws...*P.M. Johnston interview with the author.

235 *Timber!* Incident—See August Wanders' diary notations on file at the Aliceville Museum and quoted in his interview with Sam Love.

235 *One time myself and another guard...*Eugene Dakan interview with Sam Love.

235 *Once we were out there...*Joey Futchko interview on Alabama Public Television broadcast.

236 *The prisoners got across all right...*Byron Kauffman interview with Sam Love.

238 *Just let me go!...*Conversation with Ben Johnston at the 60th Camp Aliceville Reunion.

238 *Dad couldn't imagine...*P.M. Johnston interview with the author.

240 *He was doing what he had to...*comment by a former MPEG guard at Camp Aliceville (anonymity requested).

240 *I could never understand...*Chet Eisenhauer interview on the Alabama Public Television broadcast.

241 *When they were out on work...*Bryon Kauffman interview with Sam Love.

241 *That's when you found out...*Joseph Samper interview on the Alabama Public Television broadcast.

241 *The first one lingered... PCH/WA,* August 19, 1943.

242 *When confronted by a guard...*E.B. Walker, p. 22.

242 *In this part of the state...Alabama Heritage,* p. 16.

242 The Camp Blanding testimony is outlined in Billinger, p. 68.

243 *I think one of our men...* Gordon Forbes' interview with Sam Love. NOTE: Forbes does not identify this specific date and says that, as far as he knew, the prisoner lived.

243 *No prisoner has been shot...The Birmingham Age-Herald,* August 27, 1943.

244 *It was rather impressive*...Harold Cover interview with Sam Love.

244 Lieutenant Vincent's Defense Council plan appears in his letter to Carl Griffin, dated October 18, 1943. (Folder 19, SG19845—Alabama Department of Archives & History, Montgomery, Alabama).

246 ...*give them a little more prestige*...Vincent letter.

247 Moretti comments on escapes—E.B. Walker, p. 24.

247 *The few who tried were headed*...Jake McBride as quoted by Zurales in "The Day 1,000 Germans..."

248 An additional description of Stalag 3B is in the online article "Ex-POW Experience" by Robert Richard at www.shreve.net.

249 *There is nothing quite so good*...James Scott Browning as quoted in the *PCH/WA,* August 26, 1943.

249 ...*well, strong, and working for pay*...L.D. Orr quoted in the *PCH/WA,* August 26, 1943.

250 The experiences of Frank Nichols Jr. appear in an interview conducted by Roger Mansell on February 18, 2000 for the Center for Research, Allied POWs under the Japanese.

251 ...*news of more German planes*...*PCH/WA,* August 26, 1943.

251 Newte Temple's "months of trouble" *PCH/WA,* September 16, 1943.

252 ...*middling quality or better*...*PCH/WA,* August 26, 1943.

252 *With flyers' lives at stake*...*PCH/WA,* August 19, 1943.

253 *clean from the bur*...Elmo Owens as quoted in the *PCH/WA,* August 26, 1943, "Germans Prisoners Now Picking Cotton."

254 The *PCH/WA,* for September 9, 1943, reported that the Germans were not working out as cotton pickers.

255 *an ordinary negro*... *PCH/WA,* September 9, 1943.

255 Cotton figures appear in the November 18, 1943 issue of *PCH/WA.*

256 See the following regarding the Hawaiian and Japanese recruits: Tara Shioya's article in the *San Francisco Chronicle* on Sunday, September 24, 1995; the internet article "The 442nd Regimental Combat Team" by Joe Byrne, Kyle Kiguchi, Jason Opdyke, and Mario Sani.

256 *Americanism is not*...Franklin D. Roosevelt on February 1, 1943 as he activated the 442nd Regimental Combat Team.

257 *You fought not only*...President Harry Truman on July 15, 1946, when he welcomed the 100th/442nd home after World War II.

258 *Their God-man Hitler*...*PCH/WA,* September 9, 1943.

258 August Wanders's diary comments appear in the *Tagebuch* printed at Camp Aliceville in 1944 and 1945.

259 *I didn't know yet how…*Katie Emberger Blumhardt telephone interview with the author.

259 *His letters were always just personal…*ibid.

260 Information about orders to service commanders—Pluth, p. 343.

261 *…as far as to have his men fail…*This quotation and the testimony of other POWs regarding camp behavior are part of corroborating testimony supporting an order for Transfer of Prisoners of War to Camp Alva, Oklahoma, dated 13 August 1943. The order and its supporting comments, which are in the National Archives, are on file at the Aliceville Museum.

261 The nine prisoners authorized for transfer on August 26 included the following: Horst Feurig, Robert Racher, Helmut Schmid, Ernst Schmidt, Egon Schmale, Karl Schneider, Hans Tschege, Karl Wegmann, and Peter Wirtz. (See Aliceville Museum file on correspondence in the National Archives.)

262 Information about non-German speaking POWs—Gansberg, p. 17.

262 *…give everyone air to breathe…*Wilhelm Westhoff in "Der Weg zur Ordnung," *Der Zaungast,* August 4, 1944.

264 *He took the animosities of many…*ibid., p. 6.

266 *How will we be accepted…*Wilhelm Schlegel in remarks at the 2001 Camp Aliceville reunion.

266 *The land of milk and honey…*Wilhelm Schlegel in remarks made at the 1993 Camp Aliceville reunion.

Chapter Nine

Page

269 *German high officials…PCH/WA,* September 9, 1943.

269 *…this was but the beginning…*President Roosevelt as quoted in the *PCH/WA,* September 9, 1943.

270 wedding by proxy photograph—Krammer, p. 69.

270 double wedding by proxy description—Gansberg, pp. 30-31.

270 death of Otto Ulrich—See diary entry of August Wanders and Heinrich Most's memory as described by E.B. Walker, p. 23.

271 *for the benefit of the service*...Memo from Colonel Waite to Headquarters, Fourth Service Command dated 19 October 1943—copy on file in the Aliceville Museum. The list to be transferred includes Bruno Baum, Willi Schaake, Werner Zwetsch, Erwin E.G. Reese, Wilhelm Kronimus, Heinz Wendelken, Otto Usedom, Ferdinand Tillman, Fred Evers, Max Lakner, Gerhard Thiemig, Paul Zimmermann, Horst Lange, Ignaz Michna, Edgar Schmidtt, Theo T. Taupadel, and Josef Vogtel (all from Company 5).

272 The descriptions of abuses leading to recommendation of transfer to an anti-Nazi camp are included in a secret report attached to a list dated 17 October 1943 requesting transfer of nineteen German POWs. A copy of this report and list, which contains the names Paul Deparade, Josef Elsen, Heinrich Genge, Eduard Kalweg, Franz Hanisch, Franz Hermann, Anton Hofmann, Erich Jarrass, Alfred Knoph, and Siegried Wienhold, is on file in the Aliceville Museum. The original is in the National Archives.

273 *Keeping the above men*...Colonel Waite's memo to the Commanding General, Fourth Service Command, 17 October 1943.

274 *I felt like a shop steward*...Erwin Schulz in his essay, Carlson, p. 177.

275 *Nobody would squeal*...Stephen Fleck in *Alabama Heritage,* p. 15.

275 *I do not accept the premise*...Arthur Klippen in a letter to E.B. Walker in 1988. NOTE: Klippen is probably referring to the suicide of Kurt Knopf, who hung himself in the psychiatric ward at Camp Aliceville on May 1, 1945, just before the end of the war.

275 *We heard that the camp's*...Jack Sisty in *Alabama Heritage,* p. 15.

275 *On the one hand, you were*...Hermann Blumhardt interview on the History Channel broadcast.

276 German-Italian cemetery roster at Fort McClellan—E.B. Walker Collection, Appendix.

276 *There were also cases where*...Arnold Krammer interview on the History Channel broadcast.

276 *...the POWs had more to fear*...History Channel broadcast narration.

277 Heino Erichsen (See Chapter Four) crossed the Atlantic on a Liberty ship that withdrew from its convoy and proceeded to Boston to avoid attack by German U-boats.

277 *...a bunch of guys came in*...Heino Erichsen interview on the History Channel broadcast.

277 *And then he died*...ibid. NOTE: The death of Corporal Hugo Krauss is described in detail in *Lone Star Stalag: German Prisoners of War at Camp Hearne* by Waters, pp. 120-134.

279 *...either wounded or troublemakers*...Billinger, p. 67.

279 *...their segregation in a branch camp*...Billinger, p. 68.

279 Information about pulpwood production in the Fourth Service Command is from Lewis and Mewha, p. 132-133.

280 *...1,000 men ordered to pick cotton*...October 3, 1943 entry in *TaschenKalendar 1945*.

280 *...separated themselves from their fellow*...Billinger, pp. 68-69.

282 *I couldn't swallow*....Walter Felholter interview with Sam Love.

283 *I'm going to write you the address*...Katie Emberger Blumhardt interview with the author.

283 *If I had been on the ball*...Hermann Blumhardt interview with the author.

284 *The whole community was involved*...Jimmy Summerville conversation with the author at the 60th Camp Aliceville Reunion.

285 *...the only thing the town did*...George Bristow Birmingham interview with the author.

285 *The Aliceville Yellow Jackets*...Francis Burns' sports column, *Camptown Crier,* Volume I, Issue 1.

287 *...a favorite in social circles*...*PCH/WA,* October 14, 1943.

287 Kirksey-Aicklen wedding description—*PCH/WA,* November 11, 1943.

289 *The prisoners are living*...*PCH/WA,* November 4, 1943.

289 *It has given employment*...ibid.

290 *Living on the west coast*...Kay Fillingham telephone interview with the author.

290 *...the places we lived were*...ibid.

291 *The upstairs bathroom*...ibid.

291 *It was a vast improvement*...ibid.

292 *The floor slanted*...Fillingham, "A Place in Time."

292 *She had everything down there*...ibid.

292 *I was stationed*...Kay Fillingham telephone interview with the author.

293 *A lot of them were blond*...ibid.

293 *Their rhythm was not like*...ibid.

293 The conversation at the Officers Club dinner is from the Fillingham telephone interview and also from the essay "A Place in Time."

294 *I don't know if he just*...Fillingham telephone interview with the author.

294 *Even Aliceville would look good*...ibid.

295 ...*fought the treacherous Moro*...profile of Colonel Waite in *The Camptown Crier,* Volume I, Issue 1.

295 *Good luck, Dottie!*...*The Camptown Crier,* Volume I, Issue 1.

299 Fistball is a game similar to volleyball that has been played since ancient times around the world.

300 *They were really artists*...Sue Stabler interview on the Alabama Public Television broadcast.

301 *They made their uniforms*...ibid.

303 *They contend that German soldiers*...Inspection report filed by Parker W. Buhrman on January 6, 1944.

304 ...*discipline in these camps*...ibid.

305 E.B. Walker describes the visit of the OWI camera crew on p. 21.

306 The Voice of America was a radio broadcasting network operated by the United States Information Agency, formed in 1942 as part of the OWI. It transmitted information about the United States and its policies during WWII and continues today, broadcasting news, music, and other programming in 40 languages around the world. Its first broadcast, on February 24, 1942, was in German, and its stated purpose was to provide a consistently reliable source of news to people in closed and war-torn societies.

306 ...*honourable and decent*...Bender, p. 248.

307 ...*Die Toten Kommen*...Bender, p. 249.

308 ...*from the Führer*...Gansberg, p. 31. See also December 20, 1943 entry in *Taschenkalender 1945.*

309 *You never know what*...Jack Pratt's "Here There and Everywhere" column in the *PCH/WA,* December 30, 1943.

309 ...*the most successful of the entertainments*...Emmie Lou Archibald social column in *The Camptown Crier,* Volume I, Issue 3—January 8, 1944.

310 *I was in no mood*...Hermann Blumhardt article in *The South Bend Tribune,* 1978.

311 *While it is yet a very new institution*...*PCH/WA,* December 30, 1943.

311 The Hans Kopera sketch was published in the February 2004 issue of *Museum News.*

Chapter Ten

Page

313 *Flamme empor...Deutsche Weisen,* p. 275.

315 *...the services of civilian...from their labors...Birmingham Age-Herald,* January 15, 1944.

317 *You could dissect it like a frog...*Horst Uhse in *Museum News,* May 2004.

318 *...prisoner of war camps with...*Lewis and Mewha, p. 116. Their reference is to the report of Colonel Carl L. Restine, et al., on March 9, 1944, titled "Investigation of the situation obtaining on the housing, controlling and utilizing in productive work of prisoners of war in continental United States."

322 *regular little Las Vegas...*John Richey in *Alabama Heritage,* p. 23.

322 Information about John Richey's "initiation" is from Chip Walker's article in *The Alabama Review* in January 1985.

326 *I may be wrong...*William L. Shirer, "German Captives Need Education, Analyst Asserts: Conditions in Prison Camps Shouldn't Be Tolerated, He Thinks." *New York Tribune, Inc.* reprinted in *The Birmingham News,* January 23, 1944.

326 *...vulgar, uneducated, fanatically bigoted...*Shirer's words quoted in his biography at www.traces.org/williamshirer.

327 *...enough in them to get me...*ibid.

327 Figures for German POWs in United States in January 1944—Lewis and Mewha, Table 2, p. 90.

328 *...a weird super-Nazi...*Shirer article in *The Birmingham News,* January 23, 1944.

328 *...if firmness—with strict justice...*ibid.

329 *I cannot find a single word...*ibid.

330 *Any German prisoner...*Gerhard Seger quoted in "Editor Says Nazis Kill Captives Here," *The New York Times,* February 24, 1944.

330 *...as permitted under...*ibid.

330 Information about the Gabriel Heater broadcast is from Pluth, p. 255.

330 Judith Gansberg points out that columnists Raymond Clapper and Dorothy Bromley also began to attack the government and the military for their treatment of prisoners at about this time. (Gansberg, p. 61).

330 *It is clear that we are going...*"Our Nazi Prisoners of War," an editorial by Dorothy Thompson. *The Birmingham Age-Herald,* April 24, 1944.

331 *Men live in symbols*...ibid.

331 ...*coddled prisoners*...Pluth, p. 256.

331 *I'm so glad you're here*...Gansberg, p. 61.

332 *I've got to talk to Franklin*...Gansberg, p. 62.

332 *We anticipated the problem*...ibid.

334 *The Japs insisted*...Roger Mansell's interview with Frank Nichols Jr., February 18, 2000.

335 The new branch camp announcements appeared in *The Birmingham News* on December 13 and 19, 1943.

336 Information about POWs at Camp Rucker and in Dale County, Alabama, is from ALDALE-L@rootsweb.com.

337 *Once they got away from*...Stanley Pendrak interview with the author.

337 For a complete list of branch camps in Alabama during World War II, see E.B. Walker, p. 3.

338 ...*of high intelligence*...Billinger, p. 74.

338 ...*the worst camp in America*...Billinger, p. 21.

340 *We liked to stay in the hospital*...Walter Felholter conversation with the author at the 60th Camp Aliceville Reunion.

340 The other three of the final four diphtheria carriers in Camp Aliceville were Fritz Freund, Erwin Bauer, and Hartmenn (no first name given).

340 *To get that for the men*...Wilhelm Stüdl "*Unser Meier*" article in *Der Zaungast,* August 4, 1944.

341 Dr. Paul G. Reitzer is a former professor at Marion Institute in Marion, Alabama.

341 "The Frogs in Alabama" was written by Bruno Schneider while he was a POW in Camp Aliceville.

344 *nothing in the study plan*...Erwin Schulz essay in Carlson, p. 179.

344 *The war will soon be*...ibid.

345 *Hell-By-the-Sea*...Billinger, p. 29.

346 *Now we could go*...Hermann Blumhardt article in *South Bend Tribune* in 1978.

348 Hunger strike—*TaschenKalendar 1945.*

348 ...*head troublemakers*...*this type of habitual troublemaker*...Memo from Colonel Waite to the office of the Provost Marshal General on 7 April 1944. In this memo, Waite listed the eight prisoners he considered leaders

of the trouble: Alois Anderwald, Heinrich Fehring, Willi Grosse, Theodor Koeler, Werner Poetter, Gerhard Spoerer, August Telle, and Walter C. Widmann. (Memo on file in the Aliceville Museum).

349 *You didn't see anything about working...*Walter Felholter interview with Sam Love.

350 *To Private First Class Walter...*ibid.

351 *The men are generally cooperative...*Report of Camp Aliceville inspection by Rudolf Fischer representing the Legation of Switzerland, accompanied by Parker W. Buhrman, on May 14, 1944 (on file in the Aliceville Museum).

352 *It is important that the leaders...*ibid.

352 Details about the June 5 and 6 inspection for the International Red Cross are from the report filed by Paul Schyder. A copy of this report is on file at the Aliceville Museum.

Chapter Eleven

Page

356 *big capsules...*Announcement that Beverly McLellan is missing over Germany—*PCH/WA,* February 17, 1944.

356 June Kirksey Etheridge wedding announcement—*PCH/WA,* February 17, 1944.

358 *a favorite in the social circles...PCH/WA,* March 2, 1944.

358 Wedding of Lieutenant Colonel Shriver and Crooks Steele—*PCH/WA,* May 11, 1944. Photos described belong to their daughter, Scarlett Shriver Parker, and were shared with the author.

359 *Here in Italy...*from Alva N. Temple's letter to Jack Pratt, dated March 31, 1944, and printed in "News of Interest to and from the Boys in the Service" in *PCH/WA,* April 27, 1944.

361 Background on Wendell Parrish's flight crew and the "hop" to Ireland is from William E. Black's memoirs, p. 39.

362 *Flying that northern route...*Wendell Parrish interview with Barney Cook in Summer 2002.

364 Notice of the death of Francis Park—*PCH/WA,* August 3, 1944.

364 *Oh, how I wished...*Robert Hugh Kirksey in *With Me,* p. 144.

364 *They gave us seasick pills...*John Griffin quoted by John Surratt in *The Mississippi Press* article, June 6, 1944.

365 *The LST we were in...*ibid.

365 *I liked removing Teller mines...*ibid.

366 *Right now, while you are...*Advertisement in the *PCH/WA,* July 6, 1944.

366 Bond drive figures—*PCH/WA,* July 18, 1944.

371 Ernst Schacht's war experiences are described in detail in his letter to the Aliceville Museum on September 7, 2000. This letter was published in *Museum News* in February 2001.

371 *Only the best were sent...*Ertel quoted by Pete Zurales in "A Tale of Two Prisoners," *Mobile Register,* March 19, 1995.

372 *Everyone was called out...*ibid.

372 *We would have been the first...*ibid.

373 *We had to have...*ibid.

373 *It was a formality...*ibid.

374 *When you see the first American...*Ertel quoted from his wife's letter on the Alabama Public Television broadcast in 1990.

375 *I can only think that maybe...*Ertel interview on the Alabama Public Television broadcast in 1990.

375 Most biographical information about Reinhold Wilhelm Schulte is from his letter to the Aliceville Museum dated March 12, 1999. It was published in the May 1999 issue of *Museum News.*

377 Biographical information about Franz August Hinz appears in an essay written by his son Thomas, published in *Museum News,* February 2004.

378 Biographical information about Horst Spieker comes from his letter to the Aliceville Museum dated June 7, 1998, and published in the August 1998 issue of *Museum News* and from an article in the May 1998 issue of *Museum News.*

378 Biographical information about Werner Kaiser comes from an undated essay written by his granddaughter Sarah Schiffling and from subsequent correspondence with Schiffling.

379 *You are lucky...*Schiffling essay about Werner Kaiser.

380 *We were only up four hours...*Black, p. 40.

382 *We didn't know anything about...*Walter Felholter interview with Sam Love.

384 *Let the storm break loose!...*Nazi Propaganda Minister Joseph Goebbels in his *Sportpalast* speech delivered on February 18, 1943.

384 *Maybe they hadn't fought...*Walter Felholter interview with Sam Love.

385 Information about tung nuts comes from "Tung Oil History" at sutherlandwelles.com. In 1969, Hurricane Camille destroyed the tung plantations in the Gulf Coast states and stopped domestic production of the oil. It is now imported.

385 *We were supposed to pick…*Walter Felholter in conversation with the author at the 60th Camp Aliceville reunion.

386 War Department memo directing all non-working NCOs to Camp Aliceville is referred to by Pluth on p. 354.

386 *I stayed busy all day long…*Zurales's article, "A Tale of Two Prisoners."

387 *If not for the concern…*ibid.

Chapter Twelve

Page

391 *long after the laws…*Black, p. 42.

393 *Fuehrer Burned, Bruised…The Birmingham News,* July 20, 1944.

394 *Let Hitler know this much…The Birmingham Age-Herald,* July 22, 1944.

394 *Too bad they didn't…*Hal Boyle Associated Press article published in *The Birmingham Age-Herald,* July 22, 1944.

395 *It will come soon now…*ibid.

395 *What we heard, we could not believe…*Wilhelm Schlegel's "Fifty Years after Arriving in Aliceville" speech at the October 1993 reunion.

396 *We had not yet seen…*ibid.

396 Soccer competition reference—*TaschenKalendar 1945.*

396 *…two printers threw themselves…*Wilhelm Stüdl writing about Werner Meier (*Unser Meier)* in the August 4, 1944 issue of *Der Zaungast (*translated by the author).

397 Walter Felholter once advised the museum in Aliceville that although the correct translation of *Zaungast* is "onlooker," he thought "fence guest" was a better translation in this instance.

398 *All who know your honorable…"Unser Meier"* by Wilhelm Stüdl in *Der Zaungast,* August 4, 1944.

398 *Often, waves of fire…*"Der Weg zur Ordnung" by Wilhelm Westhoff in *Der Zaungast,* August 4, 1944.

398 *Everyone had to fit into…*ibid.

399 *Only organization and order…*ibid.

399 *We wish these comrades…Der Zaungast,* August 13, 1944. NOTE: These proxy marriages were performed for Ofw. Kast, Officer Maramek, *Unteroffizier* Parlow, and Officer Jahnke.

400 The other two were Werner Elflein, who died July 18, 1944 at Lawson General Hospital in Atlanta, and Otto Ulrich, who died September 12, 1944 in the Camp Aliceville hospital of septicemia from a leg injury.

401 *in filthy, stinking boxcars*...Black, p. 60.

402 *I shall never forget*...Robert Hugh Kirksey in *With Me,* p. 157.

403 *Look! They're German prisoners*...*With Me*, p. 158.

404 Summer 1944 description of Camp Aliceville is based on Paul Schyder's inspection report dated 5 and 6 June, 1944.

404 General Marshall's comments appear in Chapter Six.

405 *return the Germans to*...Ron Robin, p. 19. He uses the Morgenthau statement as quoted in *Swords or Ploughshares? The Morgenthau Plan for Defeated Nazi Germany, 1943-1946* by Warren F. Kimball, p. 31.

405 Opinions about why Roosevelt decided to approve the re-education program are expressed by Robin, p. 27, and Krammer, p. 191.

405 *to give the prisoners of war the facts*...Ginsberg, p. 63.

405 perhaps the German prisoners of war—Krammer, p. 197.

406 Seger's demands outlined—Ginsberg, p. 113.

407 *not merely the anticipation of*..."War Prisoners in Ten Camps." *Birmingham Post,* July 14, 1944.

409 *The success of this type*...Krammer, pp. 197-198.

410 *I have just had to tell*...Erwin Rommel as quoted in *The Rommel Papers* edited by B.H. Liddell-Hart. New York: Da Capo Press, 1982.

411 *His name will always remain*...These quotations are taken from a re-translation of several American newspaper articles that were quoted in *Der Zaungast* on October 29, 1944 (re-translated by the author).

412 Description of memorial service for Rommel at Camp Aliceville is from Heinrich Most's article in the *Museum News,* May 2001.

412 Words to *Ich hatt Einen Kameraden* are from *Deutsche Weisen*, p. 244, and translated by the author.

413 ...*if ever there was*...*Der Zaungast*, October 29, 1944.

414 Information on the two escapes appears in *PCH/WA,* October 19, 1944. Physical description of Hoyer was age 26, 5′8″, wt. 138, brown eyes, blond hair, ruddy complexion. Becker was 27, 5′9″, wt. 161, brown eyes, black hair, and dark complexion.

415 *Recaptured prisoners of war*..."Tight FBI Net Foils Flight," *Birmingham Post,* October 20, 1944.

416 *well versed in the intent*...E.B. Walker, p. 5.

416 *a non-working non-com camp*...Werner Tobler inspection report dated November 3 and 4, 1944.

417 *Tragically, everyone fought*...Carl Heintze article in *The Sun.*

418 The story of the *Leopoldville* and the news media blackout about its sinking in December 1944 is a larger story. See other sources, including *The Leopoldville Trilogy* by Ray Roberts.

418 *...where people were planning to kill*...Robert Hugh Kirksey in *With Me,* p. 202.

418 *We would be the attackers*... *With Me,* p. 211.

419 *Less than twelve hours ago*... *With Me,* p. 238.

Chapter Thirteen

Page

421 *It scared me to death*...Margie Archibald Colvin interview with Sam Love.

422 *We didn't have coffee*...ibid.

422 Margie describes the incident with the POW sketch in her interview with Sam Love.

423 George Bristow states in his interview that he arrived at Camp Aliceville in December 1944, but it is more likely that he arrived earlier in the fall.

424 *We'd call in the FBI*...George Bristow interview with the author March 2003.

424 *How did you rebuild*...ibid.

424 *Each compound had some kind of*...Bristow telephone interview with the author April 2004.

424 *It's beautiful*...George Bristow donated this painting to the Aliceville Museum in April 2004.

425 *I'll come right back*...Bristow telephone interview in March 2003.

426 *We have many Stablers at home*...Sue Stabler speech to the DAR in October 1988.

426 A copy of the *Kriegsweihnachten 1944* Christmas program is with the copies of *Der Zaungast* on file at the Aliceville Museum.

427 *Aliceville in Alabama*...from anonymous poem found in the papers of Maxwell McKnight.

427 *Now I knew I have not*...Günther Peter Ertel on the Alabama Public Television broadcast.

428 *I learned a lesson that day*...Mary Lu Turner Keef interview with the author.

428 ...*went over to the Americans*...See Wilhelm Schlegel diary fragments shared with the author and the Aliceville Museum.

429 *They tried to hide a lot of food*...George Bristow telephone interview with the author in March 2003.

430 *That was the punishment for*...Earline Lewis Jones interview with Sam Love.

430 ...*the hungry against the full*...Wilhelm Schlegel diary fragments.

432 *So they started to make balloons*...Ellen Wanders in conversation with the author at the 60th Camp Aliceville reunion.

432 Hermann Göring was a Nazi leader who successfully built up Germany's air forces early in World War II. He founded and headed the *Gestapo* and managed the German economy in the 1940s. In 1943, Hitler stripped him of authority and dismissed him when he tried to claim his right of succession. After the war, he was the main defendant in the Nuremberg trial for war crimes, was convicted and sentenced to death. Two hours before his scheduled hanging, he committed suicide with a point capsule.

433 W. Sell's version of the balloon incident appears on p. 255 in Bender under the title "Klink's Heroes?"

437 *The human mind knows no bounds*...Black, p. 62.

438 *At intervals of about once a week*...ibid.

439 Wendell Parrish describes the Christmas Day incident when he found out about his son in an interview with Barney Cook in 2002.

439 *In the evening we held*...Wilhelm Schlegel diary fragments.

440 ...*well versed in the intent*...William F. Raugast inspection report.

441 ...*general appearance, attitude*...ibid.

443 *There was enough food in there*...Zurales article, "The long walk home to liberty."

443 Details about this death march in Germany are from Wendell Parrish's interview with Barney Cook, Zurales's article "The long walk home to liberty," and from Gary Turbak's article, "Death March Across Germany" in the *VFW Magazine* in April 1999.

443 *There was a shot*...Turbak, p. 32.

443 *The Germans knew by that time*...Zurales article, "The long walk home to liberty."

444 *…to destroy German militarism…*The Yalta Declaration issued by the Yalta Conference on February 11, 1945.

446 *…troublemaking and non-signing NCOs…*Inspection report dated 11 March 1945 and signed by Major Frank L. Brown.

447 *The labor potential of this camp…*ibid.

447 *There was nothing to stop them…*George Bristow interview with the author in April 2004.

448 *I was shocked…*ibid.

448 *Everybody was sitting under the trees…*George Bristow telephone interview in March 2003.

449 *…nothing less than a mudhole…*Jack House article, "Nazi Prisoners of War in Alabama Still bow Before Shrine of Militarism."

449 *Despite good treatment…*ibid.

450 *…that I am not able to be there…*Karl Berning's letter to his wife, Elisabeth.

450 *The terrifying thing was that…*Dieter Schulte correspondence with the Aliceville Museum.

451 *I peeked out to see…*ibid.

453 *Since it is Sunday…*Günther Peter Ertel's letter to his wife, Johanna.

454 *…on a rainy day exactly like…*ibid.

454 *whenever I look for the happiest…*ibid.

454 *Now it has grown towards dusk…*ibid.

Chapter Fourteen

Page

457 *It wasn't that bad…*Wendell Parrish interview with Barney Cook.

457 *We were a pitiful sight…*Zurales article, "The long walk home to liberty."

457 *We woke up the next morning…*ibid.

458 Information about the new, tougher measures—"Aliceville Gets 'Tough' Nazi PW," *The Birmingham Age-Herald,* May 16, 1945.

459 These guidelines appear in the May 27, 1945 issue of *Der Zaungast.*

460 The Marshall Plan was named for George Catlett Marshall, United States Secretary of State.

462 *If they changed our thinking…*Hans Kopera as quoted in *Alabama Heritage,* p. 25.

462 *I studied languages…*Karl Silberreis interview with Sam Love.

462 *I also studied American history…*ibid.

463 *Life was not the same anymore...*Horst Uhse article in *Museum News,* May 2004.

463 *My morale went to...*Hermann Blumhardt article in *The South Bend Tribune* in 1978.

463 *If you cut less than that...*Horst Uhse article in *Museum News,* May 2004.

464 *I had no idea where he was...*Katie Blumhardt interview with the author.

464 *We got a ration card...*ibid.

464 Transfer figures are from Krammer, p. 239.

465 Transfer figures...ibid.

466 *I'm going home...*Katie Blumhardt's interview with the author.

466 *We knew the bus driver...*ibid.

468 The conversation between Hermann and Katie Blumhardt when they were reunited is from an interview with the author.

468 *You go where your husband goes...*Katie Blumhardt interview with the author.

469 *We were in daily contact...*Hermann Blumhardt's correspondence with the author.

471 *...the notorious hunger brigade...*Werner Kaiser as quoted by his granddaughter Sarah Schiffling.

472 *...should take down every statue...*James Bacques in *Other Losses.*

474 Information about Leopold Dolfuss after the war comes from his article in *Museum News,* November 1999.

475 Information about Erwin Schulz after the war comes from his essay in Carlson, p. 180.

476 *Some of us wrote letters...*Carlson, p. 180.

476 *...the cream of the POW population...*Robin, p. 134.

476 For a discussion of Project II at Fort Getty, see Krammer, pp. 219-224.

477 *...a world without end of tears and anguish...*Günther Peter Ertel, *My Story.*

479 *Many of our comrades...*July 1, 1945 issue of *Der Zaungast.*

479 In July 1945, the staff of *Der Zaungast* included Josef Reiner Zinken, Kurt Ronneburger, and Alexander Wolf.

479 *We wish our readers good health...*This translation of an article in the July 1, 1945 issue of *Der Zaungast* was done by Elizabeth Döllerer Smith of Carrollton, Alabama.

479 *This was when the war was over...*Karl Silberreis interview with Sam Love.

480 *We were very much treated like*...ibid.

480 *You go with my sister*...ibid.

482 *They were the al Qaida*...Jim Reed interview with the author.

483 *air lugers and John-Wayne style*...*I Wish I was in Dixie*, p. 185.

483 *They didn't have any particular reason*...Jim Reed interview with the author.

483 *It was beautifully done*...Elma Henders Emerson interview with Sam Love.

484 *I can still remember the day*...Mary Lu Turner Keef interview with the author.

484 *In Antwerp, the American officer*...Horst Spieker letter dated June 7, 1998, and published in *Museum News*, August 1998.

488 *Everyone had to work then*...Wilhelm Schlegel in correspondence with the author.

489 ...*stretching my feet*...Wilhelm Schlegel correspondence with the author, February 21, 2004.

490 Figures about repatriation in 1946 and 1947 are from Billinger, p. 168.

492 Statistics on POWs still in American custody in 1946 are from Krammer, pp. 245 and 255.

492 *I was always listening*...Hermann Blumhardt interview with the author.

493 *Oh my goodness*....Katie Blumhardt interview with the author.

493 *All the fruit, and all the vegetables*...ibid.

494 *During his confinement*...article in *Niles Daily Star,* October 24, 1949.

494 *I felt like I'd gone to heaven*...Katie Blumhardt interview with the author.

495 *At one time in my life*...Günther Peter Ertel in *My Story.*

495 *It's kind of hard to deny*...Dieter Schulte letter to the Aliceville Museum.

496 Scrap details are from E.B. Walker, p. 12.

497 Advertisement in *The Birmingham Age-Herald,* February 20, 1947.

497 Information about the reburial of German POWs comes from Sue Stabler's 1988 speech to the DAR and from the website of Aaron and Johanna Beck.

498 *I was busy then*...Margie Archibald Colvin interview with Sam Love.

498 *They were just sick*...ibid.

498 Margie Archibald Colvin's comments about selling the shrubbery are from her interview with Sam Love and also from *Alabama Heritage,* p. 21.

499 *Grass and weeds quickly*...Sue Stabler speech to the DAR in October 1988.

Chapter Fifteen

Page

504 Information about Karl Shriver's postwar efforts to promote Alabama comes from an undated and unidentified news clipping in the files of his daughter, Scarlett Shriver Parker.

505 *Yes, you were right*...Gerhard Stroh letter to Gerald Stabler, dated April 27, 1947.

505 *In this time, I was never*...Gerhard Stroh letter to Gerald Stabler, dated June 8, 1947.

506 *We are very hopeful*...Gerhard Stroh letter to Gerald Stabler, dated June 22, 1948.

506 *I received your gift parcel*...Gerhard Stroh letter to Gerald Stabler, July 2, 1948.

507 For eleven months in 1948 and 1949, in response to a Soviet land and water blockade of Berlin, cargo planes sponsored by the United States delivered goods to the city of West Berlin, which the Soviets hoped the Allies would abandon. More than 277,000 flights were made, delivering more than two million tons of goods. In 1949, West Germany was formed from the British and American sectors, and the Soviet Union formed what became East Germany.

507 *For a long time, I was PW*...letter from Johannes Peters, dated September 15, 1947, and shared by Sue Stabler, *Alabama Heritage,* p. 29.

507 *To let you know that*...letter from Werner Stein to Johnny Johnston, dated June 4, 1947.

508 *...the youngest of whom*...ibid.

509 *When we left, you promised*...ibid.

509 *I am not yet back*...ibid.

509 *It was just like they weren't*...P.M. (Pep) Johnston interview with the author.

510 *I was happy to have once again*...Georg Trzakas letter to Claude Earl Martin, dated July 30, 1947.

510 *In Germany we have much work*...ibid.

511 *I have finally arrived back*...letter from Heinz Dorn to T.L. Hester, undated.

512 *Mr. Downer flew back*...Will Peebles' June 18, 2003 letter to the author.

513 *We try not to make it a*..."Pickens Cares." *The Birmingham News,* January 27, 1968.

513 Hans Kopera's visit to Aliceville and the letter he wrote to the city are detailed in the Ed Watkins article "Ex-POW Pays Aliceville a Visit." *Tuscaloosa News,* April 27, 1975.

515 Information about Harvey Stapp's visit from a Catholic priest who was a former German POW comes from Ed Watkins's article.

518 *There was a phone call...*Walter Felholter's conversation with the author at the 60th Camp Aliceville Reunion.

519 *Do you want me to...*Walter Felholter interview with Sam Love.

520 *Don't go in there...*Stanley Pendrak quoted by Walter Felholter in interview with Sam Love.

520 The golden eagle and the other monuments are described in Chip Walker's "German Creative Activities" article in *The Alabama Review.*

520 *He sent me books...*Walter Felholter interview with Sam Love.

521 The incident in the library when Ertel discovered the letter in the issue of *Der Zaungast* is recounted in E.B. Walker, p. 20. Chip Walker also mentions the letter on p. 31 in his article about "German Creative Activities."

521 *...the sole possessors of this beautiful..."Ein Brief"* (A Letter) by Ertel.

521 *...the written page of this warm stream...*ibid.

523 *So far as we know...PCH/WA,* September 14, 1989.

524 *This is not for me...*Walter Felholter interview with Sam Love.

524 The encounter in Germany between Walter Felholter and Heinrich Most is described by Walter in his interview with Sam Love.

525 *Because of that and because...*Jan Gwin interview with the author.

526 *The further I read, the more...*Walter Felholter's essay, *Es War Ein Wunder.*

527 *The change in my facial expression...*ibid.

529 *Certainly we would not have recognized...*ibid.

529 The schedule of events for the 1989 reunion is on file at the Aliceville Museum.

530 *I remember there was a white...*Walter Felholter quoted by Walter Bryant in October 8, 1989 article.

531 *You should have a train here today...*Hermann Blumhardt quoted by Walter Bryant in October 8, 1989 article.

531 *At one time the people partying...*Tom Haliday narrating the Alabama Public Television broadcast in 1990.

531 *It's really great to find out...*Harry Warnack interview on the Alabama Public Television broadcast in 1990.

532 Karl H. Shriver passed away in August 1970.

532 *Walter Felholter Hospital*...Walter Felholter's essay, *Es War Ein Wunder.*

533 *The thing we have to be thankful for*...Ertel interview on the Alabama Public Television broadcast in 1990.

533 *I wanted to let other people see*...Dieter Schulte letter to the museum.

534 *I would be beholden to you*...letter from Manfred Rommel to Ellen Wanders on May 14, 1993.

535 *All of this depends on mutual*...ibid.

535 *We owe the Americans great respect*...ibid.

535 *They're just nice people*...Jan Gwin interview with the author.

536 *He's very much into soccer*...ibid.

537 Pete Zurales reported in "The long walk home to liberty" that Wendell Parrish refused to attend reunions.

537 *Well, that's stretching it a bit*...Wendell Parrish interview with Barney Cook.

538 *People like to play war*...Walter Felholter conversation with the author at the 60th Camp Aliceville Reunion.

539 *They was drafted in, too*...Bryon Kauffman interview with Sam Love.

539 *They probably made the advances*...Harold Cover interview with Sam Love.

540 *Aliceville is a miniscule place*...Jim Reed in "Pow Wow," *Dad's Tweed Coat,* p. 144.

541 ...*anywhere and everywhere else in the world*...ibid.

542 The Hagmann family visits to Aliceville are recounted in *Museum News* issues in August 1996 and August 2004.

543 *My being in Aliceville was a very great*...Alvin Tepelmann letter to the museum.

543 *unfed and in bad health*...ibid.

544 *I loved going down to breakfast*...Mary Lu Turner Keef interview with the author in November 2002.

544 *In 1948, returning from prison of war*...Wilhelm Schlegel, *Museum News,* February 2001.

545 *I think it's a wonderful thing*...Jan Gwin interview with the author.

545 *We have told them*...ibid.

546 *Four comrades and I*...Wilhelm Schlegel's speech at the March 2001 reunion.

Sources

ALDALE-L@rootsweb.com. Information on POWs at Camp Rucker and in Dale County, Alabama.

"The Aliceville Camp," University of Alabama Television Services production recorded on December 11, 1989, and broadcast first on January 18, 1990. Narrator: Tom Halladay. Producer: Bill Connell. Editors: Kevin Clay and Tony Holt. Research Consultant: Earnest B. Walker. Used with permission.

"Aliceville Gets 'Tough' Nazi PW." *The Birmingham Age-Herald,* May 16, 1945.

Ambrose, Stephen E. "Ike and the Disappearing Atrocities." *The New York Times Book Review,* February 24, 1991.

Atkinson, Rick. *An Army at Dawn: The War in North Africa, 1942-1943.* New York: Henry Holt and Company, 2002.

Bacque, James. *Other Losses.* Prima Publishing: 1989.

Baldwin, William J. "German Prisoners at Opelika Camp Seem Glad to be Out of War." *The Birmingham News,* June 18, 1943.

Bender, Roger James and Richard D. Law. *Uniforms, Organization, and History of the Afrikakorps.* Mountain View, CA: R. James Bender Publishing, 1973.

Berning, Karl. Letter to his wife, Elisabeth, dated April 8, 1945. Aliceville Museum, Aliceville, AL.

Billinger, Robert D. *Hitler's Soldiers in the Sunshine State: German POWs in Florida.* Gainesville: University Press of Florida, 2000.

The Birmingham News. "How Reform Named," February 18, 1953.

Black, William E. *My First Seventy Years.* Mount Ida, AZ, 1990.

Blumhardt, Hermann. "Youth under Hitler Lives Nightmares in German Army." *South Bend Tribune,* February 26, 1978.

—"1943 Train Ride Put Him on New Track to a Life of Freedom." *South Bend Tribune,* March 21, 1990.

—Correspondence with the author, 2002.

—Conversations with the author in Aliceville, March 2003.

Blumhardt, Katie Emberger, telephone interview with the author, August 2003.

Boyle, Hal. "German Prisoners Rejoice at News of Attempt on Hitler." *The Birmingham Age-Herald,* July 22, 1944.

Bristow, George, telephone interview with the author, April 2003.

—discussion with author, April 4, 2004.

Bryant, Walter. "Ex-POWs to Join Reunion." *The Birmingham News,* July 28, 1989.

—"WWII Moment Recreated: Ex-POWs, Guards Meet in Aliceville," *The Birmingham News,* October 8, 1989.

Byrne, Joe and Kyle Kiguchi, Jason Opdyke and Mario Sani. "The 442nd Regimental Combat Team" at www.homeofheroes.com.

"Camp Shanks" at www.skylighters.org, the website of the 225th AAA Searchlight Battalion.

Camptown Crier, Issues 1 through 4, published between November 15, 1943 and February 12, 1944 at Camp Aliceville.

Captivity in Poetry. Author unknown. A verse diary of captivity in North Africa written between May 11, 1943 and August 2, 1943 by an unnamed war comrade of Wilhelm Schlegel and shared by Schlegel with the author.

Carlson, Lewis H. *We Were Each Other's Prisoners: An Oral History of World War II American and German Prisoners of War.* N.p.: Basic Books, 1997.

Center for Research, Allied POWs Under the Japanese. Roger Mansell, Director. Los Altos, CA. www.mansell.com.

—Mansell, Roger. Interview with Frank Nichols Jr. on February 18, 2000. www.mansell.com.

Clancey, Patrick and M. P. W. Stone, Secretary of the Army. "Tunisia: US Army Campaigns in World War II. www.ibiblio.org/hyperwar/USA/USA-C-Tunisia.

Connell, Luke. "Austrian Family Visits Former Aliceville POW Camp." www.datelinealabama.com May 19, 2002.

Cook, Barney, interview with Wendell Parrish, Summer 2002.

Coombs, David. "Walter Felholter, Osnabrueck, Germany." www.datelinepickens.com, March 24, 2003.

Cronenberg, Allen. *Forth to the Mighty Conflict: Alabama and World War II.* Tuscaloosa and London: The University of Alabama Press, 1995.

Cross, Kim. "Wilhelm Schlegel, Asslar, Germany." www.datelinepickens.com, March 24, 2003.

Dolfuss, Leopold. "My Experience during World War Two." *Museum News,* November 1998.

Dorn, Heinz, undated letter to T.L. Hester, translated for the Aliceville Museum by Gary Miller.

"Editor Says Nazis Kill Captives Here." *The New York Times,* February 24, 1944.

Ertel, Günther Peter. "*Ein Brief.*" *Der Zaungast,* May 13, 1945.

—*My Story*, his autobiography, a copy of which is on file at the Aliceville Museum.

"Everything Began in the Catholic Bookstore." *Wetterauer Zeitung.* Friedburg, Germany, May 25, 2000.

Felholter, Walter. *"Es War Ein Wunder: Zwei Freunde treffen sich nach 46 Jahren in Aliceville wieder,"* (It Was a Wonder: Two Friends Meet Each Other Again in Aliceville After 46 Years) an unpublished and undated essay shared with the author on March 15, 2004 (translated by the author).

—"Walter Felholter." *Museum News*, February 1999.

—correspondence with the author, March 2004.

—conversations with the author in Aliceville in March 2003.

Fillingham, Kay. "A Place in Time: Aliceville," undated personal essay.

—"Walking in My Footsteps," personal memoir, September 8, 2002.

—telephone interview with the author, August 22, 2003.

Flynn, Henry C. "Aliceville, Ala., War Prisoners Work to Make a Homelike Camp." *The Catholic Week,* August 20, 1943.

"Fuehrer Burned, Bruised In Try At Assassination." *The Birmingham News,* July 20, 1944.

Gansberg, Judith M. *Stalag, U.S.A.* New York: Thomas Y. Crowell Company, 1977.

Gwin, Jan and Chuck, interview with the author, 2003.

Heintze, Carl. "Huertgen Forest Just a Footnote." *The Sun* (Sunnyvale, CA), August 9, 2000.

Henderson, Aileen Kilgore. *Stateside Soldier.* Columbia: University of South Carolina Press, 2001.

Hildreth, Emory Peebles. "At Alabama's War Prison." *The Birmingham Age-Herald,* June 10, 1943.

History of Aliceville (Golden Jubilee brochure). October 1952

Hinz, Thomas. "Franz August Hinz." *Museum News,* February 2004.

"History Undercover: Nazi POWs in America." Broadcast in Alabama on The History Channel, January 27, 2002. Narrator: Arthur Kent. Producer: Youngtales Productions. Executive Producer: Margaret G. Kim. Writer/Producer: Sharon Young. Editor: Dina Potocki. (A&E Television Networks).

Hoole, W. Stanley. "Alabama's World War II Prisoner of War Camps." *The Alabama Review* 20 (April 1967): 83-114.

House, Jack. "3,000 Axis Prisoners From Tunisia Guests of U. S. at Aliceville." *The Birmingham News,* June 10, 1943.

—"German War Prisoners at Aliceville Obedient, and Happy over Internment." *The Birmingham News Age-Herald,* June 13, 1943.

—"Nazi Prisoners of War in Alabama Still Bow Before Shrine of Militarism: Indoctrinated with Prussian Superman Theory, They Cling to Hope They May Yet Win the War." *The Birmingham News*, March 25, 1945.

Humphrey, Yvonne E. "On Shipboard with German Prisoners." *American Journal of Nursing* 47 (September 1943): 821-822.

Inspection Report, Internment Branch Inspection of Prisoner of War Camps, Prisoner of War Division, Provost Marshal General's Office signed by Maxwell S. McKnight, Captain. Dated 14-16 July 1943. #4038001

Inspection Report filed by Alfred Cardinaux as a representative of the International Red Cross Committee after his visit to Camp Aliceville on August 29, 1943. (A copy, in translation, is on file at the Aliceville Museum.)

Inspection Report filed by Parker W. Buhrman, United States Department of State, detailing a visit by V. Tobler representing the Legation of Switzerland on November 26, 1943. Report is signed January 6, 1944. A copy is on file at the Aliceville Museum.

Inspection Report filed by Parker W. Buhrman, United States Department of State, detailing a visit by Rudolf Fischer representing the Legation of Switzerland on May 14, 1944. Report is signed June 12, 1944. A copy is on file at the Aliceville Museum.

Inspection Report filed by Paul Schyder for the International Red Cross Committee in Geneva. Dated June 5 and 6, 1944. A copy is on file at the Aliceville Museum.

Inspection Report filed by Werner Tobler representing the Legation of Switzerland and accompanied by Eldon F. Nelson, United States Department of State on November 3 and 4, 1944. A copy is on file at the Aliceville Museum.

Inspection report on William F. Raugast's visit to Camp Aliceville on 21-22 January 1945 is part of a memorandum issued 1 February 1945 by Major Paul A. Neuland, Chief, Field Service Branch. A copy is on file at the Aliceville Museum.

Inspection report of visit to Camp Aliceville on 8-9 March 1945. This report is dated 11 March 1945 and is signed by Major Frank L. Brown. A copy is on file at the Aliceville Museum.

Johnston, Ben, conversation with the author in Aliceville, March 2003.

Johnston, P. M., telephone interview with the author, March 20, 2003.

Junkins, J. T., interview with the author, October 2002.

Keef, Mary Lu Turner, telephone interviews with the author, November 18, 2002 and August 5, 2004.

— personal correspondence with the author, December 10, 2002, June 12, 2003, and October 30, 2005.

— conversation with the author in Aliceville, March 13, 2003.

Kirksey, Robert Hugh. "History of Pickens County, part two: Reconstruction through the arrival of railroads." *Dateline Pickens County,* February 14, 2003. www.datelinepickens.com.

—"History of Pickens County, part three: Manufacturing in the 20th Century and into the 21st." *Dateline Pickens County*, February 21, 2003. www.datelinepickens.com.

—*Places and People.* Tuscaloosa, AL: Word Way Press, Inc, 2004.

—*With Me: Growing Up in the Faith.* Self-published, 1996.

Koop, Allen V. *Stark Decency: German Prisoners of War in a New England Village.* Hannover and London: University Press of New England, 1988.

Krammer, Arnold. *Nazi Prisoners of War in America.* New York: Stein & Day, 1979.

Kruse, Arthur M. "Custody of Prisoners of War in the United States." *The Military Engineer* 38 (February 1946): 70-74.

Lewis, George G. and John Mewha. *History of Prisoner of War Utilization by the United States Army 1776-1945.* Washington, DC: Center for Military History, 1988.

Liddell-Hart, B. H., ed. *The Rommel Papers.* New York: Da Capo Press, 1982.

Love, Sam, interview with Margie Archibald Colvin (local resident and camp employee), 1994.

—interview with Harold Cover (436th MPEG), 1994.

—interview with Eugene Dakan (436th MPEG), 1994.

—interview with Elma Henders Emerson (camp dietician), 1994.
—interview with Walter Felholter (Camp Aliceville POW), 1994.
—interview with Gordon Forbes (436th MPEG), 1994.
—interview with Earline Lewis Jones (local resident and camp employee), 1994.
—interview with Byron Kauffman (305th MPEG), 1994.
—interview with Stanley Pendrak (389th MPEG), 1994.
—interview with Dorothy Latham Ryan (local resident and singer at the Camp Aliceville NCO club), 1994.
—interview with Karl Silberreis (Camp Aliceville POW), 1994.
McCloskey, John B. "German Prisoners at Fort McClellan are Deeply Religious." *The Catholic Week,* October 22, 1943.
The Montgomery Advertiser, April 13, 1988
Morse, Gregg, correspondence with the author from The Highland Inn in Monterey, Virginia, June 1, 2003.
Most, Heinrich. "Tragic Death of Field Marshal Erwin Rommel: Commemoration Service in Camp Aliceville, 25 October 1944." *Museum News,* May 2001.
Museum News (Volumes 1 through 12), Aliceville Museum, Inc., Aliceville, Alabama (1990 to 2005).
Nelson, Charles. "Dot Ryan: The Alabama Songbird." *By the Brook.* Birmingham: Mountain Brook Independent Church.
New York Herald Tribune, December 3, 1944.
Parker, Scarlett S., correspondence with the author, March 2003.
Parker, Thomas R., telephone interview with the author, April 4, 2002.
Parrot, Scott. "Former German POW Shares Story. " *Tuscaloosa News,* March 16, 2003.
Peebles, Will, letter to the author, June 18, 2003.
—telephone interview with the author, August 1, 2003.
Pendrak, Stanley, telephone interview with the author, October 3, 2002.
"Pickens Cares." *Birmingham News,* January 27, 1968.
Pickens County Herald and West Alabamian (1941-1945), Carrollton, Alabama.
Pluth, Edward John. *The Administration and Operation of German Prisoner of War Camps in the United States During World War II.* Ph.D. diss., Ball State University, 1970.

"POW Lament," also called "Aliceville in Alabama." Anonymous poem found in the papers of Maxwell McKnight. Copy on file at the Aliceville Museum.

"Prisoner Returns with His Family: German is Sold on U. S. During War Prison Stay," *Niles Daily Star,* October 24, 1949.

"Prisoners of War." *The Birmingham Age-Herald,* June 11, 1943.

Real Estate, Aliceville Alien Internment Camp, Aliceville, Alabama, Military Reservation. A map approved June 3, 1944 by the War Department, O.C.E., Construction Division.

Reed, Jim, interview with the author, September 6, 2004.

—*Dad's Tweed Coat: Small Wisdoms, Hidden Comforts, Unexpected Joys.* Nashville, TN: Premium Press America, 1998.

Reed, Jim and Marie Stokes Jemison. *I Wish I Was in Dixie: Two Dozen True Tales about Growing Up in Dixie.* Northport, Alabama: Sevgo Press Publishers, 1992.

"Remembering Our Veterans: Honoring Those Who Have Served." Brochure compiled by the Aliceville Tuesday Study Club in 1995 and 1996 as part of the 50th anniversary of World War II. Copy on file at the Aliceville Museum.

"Revolt Is Declared Still On," *The Birmingham Age-Herald,* July 22, 1944.

Richard, Robert. "Ex-POW Experience," www.shreve.net.

Robin, Ron. *The Barbed-Wire College.* Princeton, NJ: Princeton University Press, 1995.

Roeding, Joyce, telephone interview with the author, August 2003.

Rommel, Manfred, letter to Ellen Wanders, May 14, 1993.

Schacht, Ernst, correspondence with the Aliceville Museum, September 7, 2000.

Schiffling, Sarah. "Life in and After the Second World War: The Story of a German Army Soldier and His Fiancée, 1944-1950." (unpublished personal essay about Schiffling's grandfather Werner Kaiser—shared with and translated by the author).

—correspondence with the author in summer 2004.

Schlegel, Wilhelm, correspondence with the author, February 2004.

—Diary fragments from December 12, 1944 to February 6, 1945 (translated by the author.

—"Fifty Years After Arriving in Aliceville." Speech given at the 50 Year Reunion of Camp Aliceville on October 2, 1993.

—Speech given at the Camp Aliceville Reunion in March 2001. Translated for the May 2001 issue of *Museum News* by Wilhelm's daughter-in-law, Pirko Wedhorn.

Schneider, Bruno. "The Frogs of Alabama."

Schneider, Willy. *Deutsche Weisen*. Stuttgart, Germany: Lausch & Zweigle, 1958.

Schulte, Dieter, correspondence with the Aliceville Museum, March 12, 1999.

Scott, Jeff. Interview with former *Afrikakorps* veteran named Hans on November 10, 1998, www.feldgrau.com.

Shioya, Tara. "The Conflict Behind the Battle Lines," *San Francisco Chronicle*, September 24, 1995.

Shirer, William L. "German Captives Need Education, Analyst Asserts: Conditions in Prison Camps Shouldn't Be Tolerated, He Thinks." *The Birmingham News,* January 23, 1944.

"William Shirer 1904-1993." www.traces.org/williamshirer.

Spieker, Horst, correspondence with the Aliceville Museum, June 7, 1998.

Stabler, Sue Ray. "Speech to Pickens County DAR in October 1988," *Pickens County Herald and West Alabamian,* September 29, 1993.

—"POW Camp Reunion slated for October 7." *Pickens County Herald and West Alabamian,* September 14, 1989.

Stein, Werner, letter to Johnny Johnston from the Russian zone, June 4, 1947.

Stoen, Hal. "Pasteur" at www.stoenworks.com.

Stroh, Gerhard, letters to Gerald Stabler: April 27, 1947; June 8, 1947; June 22, 1948; July 2, 1948.

Stüdl, Wilhelm. "Unser Meier." *Der Zaungast,* August 4, 1944.

Summerville, Jimmy. Conversation with the author in Aliceville in March 2003.

Surratt, John. "Band of Brothers: Veterans of the D-Day invasion reunite on 60th anniversary." *Mississippi Press,* June 6, 2004.

Sytko, Glenn A. at www.uboat.net.

TaschenKalendar 1945, printed at the *Kriegsgefangenenlager* (Prisoner of War Camp) in Aliceville, Alabama.

Taylor, L.B. Jr., *Ghosts of Virginia, Volume III.*

Tepelmann, Alvin. "Letter to Mary Bess Paluzzi from Toronto, September 10, 1997," *Museum News,* November 1997.

Thompson, Dorothy. "Our Nazi Prisoners of War." *The Birmingham Age-Herald,* April 24, 1944.

"Tight FBI Net Foils Flight of Prisoners." *The Birmingham Post,* October 20, 1944.

Trzakas, Georg. "Letter to Claude Earl Martin, July 30, 1947." *Museum News,* February 2004.

"Tung Nuts" at sutherlandwelles.com.

Turbak, Gary. "Death March Across Germany." *VFW* 86, No. 8 (April 1999): 30-34.

Uhse, Horst. "Life Behind Barbed Wire: History is A Reminder of Human Behavior and the Story!" *Museum News,* May 2004.

Umbenhauer, Lucile, letter to the editor, *The Birmingham News,* June 18, 1943.

United States Department of Agriculture: Agricultural Research Service at www.usda.gov.

United States Maritime Service website at www.USMM.org.

Vincent, Lieutenant Joseph E., letter to Carl Griffin, October 18, 1943 (Folder 19, SG19845-Alabama Department of Archives & History, Montgomery, Alabama).

Walker, Chip. "German Creative Activities in Camp Aliceville, 1943-1946." *The Alabama Review,* January 1985.

Walker, E.B. *A Brief History of Prisoner of War Camp Aliceville.* Birmingham, Alabama: 1993.

Wall, Randy. "Inside the Wire: Aliceville and the Afrikakorps." *Alabama Heritage* 7 (Winter 1988): 3-29.

Wanders, Ellen, conversations with the author in Aliceville, March 2003.

"War Prisoners in Ten Camps." *Birmingham Post,* July 15, 1944.

Waters, Michael R. *Lone Star Stalag: German Prisoners of War at Camp Hearne.* College Station: Texas A&M University Press, 2004.

Watkins, Ed. "Ex-POW pays Aliceville a visit." *Tuscaloosa News,* April 27, 1975.

Westhoff, Wilhelm. "Der Weg zur Ordnung" *Der Zaungast,* August 4, 1944 (translated by the author).

Windham, Kathryn Tucker. "The Face in the Courthouse Window." *Thirteen Alabama Ghosts and Jeffrey.* Huntsville, Alabama: Strode Publishers, 1964.

The World at Arms: The Reader's Digest Illustrated History of World War II. Edited by Michael Wright. The Reader's Digest Association Limited, London, New York, Sydney, Montreal, Capetown: 1989.

Der Zaungast: Wochenzeitschrift des Kriegsgefangenenlagers. Approved Periodical published for the German Prisoner of War at Prisoner of War Camp Aliceville-Alabama, 1944-1945. English translations of specific statements are translations by the author.

Zurales, Pete. "The Day 1,000 Germans Goose-stepped into Town." *Mobile Register,* March 19, 1995.

—"A Tale of Two Prisoners: Aliceville 'heaven' for German soldier; The Long Walk Home to Liberty." *Mobile Register,* March 19, 1995.

PLATE 1 – Aliceville Museum collection.

PLATE 2 – Sketch #5 by POW Hermann Kalbe in "Aliceville 1944," a collection of drawings by prisoners of war Unteroffizier Hermann Kalbe and Unteroffizier Hans Fanselow. Collection reproduced by Tenn-Tom Publishing, Inc. and available through the Aliceville Museum.

PLATE 3 – Sketch #39 by POW Hans Fanselow in "Aliceville 1944."

PLATE 4 – Train Ride photograph. Aliceville Internment Camp Scrapbook, Aliceville Museum and the Alabama Department of Archives and History, Montgomery, Alabama.

PLATE 5 – Arrival photograph, #39 in the Aliceville Internment Camp Scrapbook, Aliceville Museum and the Alabama Department of Archives and History, Montgomery, Alabama.

PLATE 6 – Horst Uhse photograph, Aliceville Museum collection.

PLATE 7 – Marching through Aliceville, Aliceville Museum collection.

PLATE 8 – Roll call photograph, #137 in the Aliceville Internment Camp Scrapbook, Aliceville Museum and the Alabama Department of Archives and History, Montgomery, Alabama.

PLATE 9 – Mess Hall photograph, # 124 in the Aliceville Internment Camp Scrapbook, Aliceville Museum and the Alabama Department of Archives and History, Montgomery, Alabama.

PLATE 10 – Greenhouse photograph, #143 in the Aliceville Internment Camp Scrapbook, Aliceville Museum and the Alabama Department of Archives and History, Montgomery, Alabama.

PLATE 11 – Censor stamps, correspondence shared with the author by Werner Meier descendant Gunther Wening.

PLATE 12 – Graves photograph, #110 in the Aliceville Internment Camp Scrapbook, Aliceville Museum and the Alabama Department of Archives and History, Montgomery, Alabama.

PLATE 14 – School photograph, #036 (far right) in the Aliceville Internment Camp Scrapbook, Aliceville Museum and the Alabama Department of Archives and History, Montgomery, Alabama.

PLATE #15 – Track photograph, #040 (bottom left) in the Aliceville Internment Camp Scrapbook, Aliceville Museum and the Alabama Department of Archives and History, Montgomery, Alabama.

PLATE #16 – *Der Zerbrochene Krug* photograph, #042 (bottom right) in the Aliceville Internment Camp Scrapbook, Aliceville Museum and the Alabama Department of Archives and History, Montgomery, Alabama.

PLATE #17 – POW orchestra photograph, Aliceville Museum collection.

PLATE #18 – Print shop photograph, #034 in the Aliceville Internment Camp Scrapbook, Aliceville Museum and the Alabama Department of Archives and History, Montgomery, Alabama.

PLATE #19 – December 3, 1944 front page of *Der Zaungast*, from the Wilhelm Schlegel issues donated to the Aliceville Museum.

PLATE #20 – Mary Turner ID card, Aliceville Museum collection.

PLATE #21 – Shriver photograph, Aliceville Museum collection.

PLATE #22 – Dot Latham Ryan photograph, Aliceville Museum collection.

PLATE #23 – Margie Archibald photograph, March 19, 1995, courtesy of the Mobile Register 1995. All rights reserved. Reprinted with permission.

PLATE #24 – Sue and Gerald Stabler photograph, Aliceville Museum collection.

PLATE #25 – Pendrak photograph, Aliceville Museum collection.

PLATE #26 – Reunion photograph, unpublished staff photo by Jerry Ayres, *The Birmingham News*, shared with the author by Walter Felholter. Copyright, *The Birmingham News,* 2007. All rights reserved. Reprinted with permission.

PLATE #27 – Mary Bess Paluzzi photograph by Robert Hugh Kirksey.

PLATE #28 – Katie and Hermann Blumhardt photograph by Robert Hugh Kirksey.

PLATE #29 – Mary Lu Turner Keef photograph shared with the author by Mary Lu Keef.

PLATE #30 – Wendell Parrish photograph by Barney Cook.

PLATE #31 – Gingko tree photograph by Mary Bess Paluzzi.

Index

H

I

J

K

L

M

N

O

P

Q

R

S

T

U

V

W

X

Y

Z